Education beyond Crisis

ISATT Conference Series

Series Editors

Juanjo Mena (*University of Salamanca, Spain*)
Ruth Kane (*University of Ottawa, Canada*)
Cheryl J. Craig (*Texas A&M University, USA*)

VOLUME 1

The titles published in this series are listed at *brill.com/isac*

Education beyond Crisis

Challenges and Directions in a Multicultural World

Edited by

Daniela Roxana Andron and Gabriela Gruber

BRILL

SENSE

LEIDEN | BOSTON

Cover illustration: *Walking in the Light*, photograph by Rares Helici

All chapters in this book have undergone peer review.

Library of Congress Cataloging-in-Publication Data

Names: Andron, Daniela Roxana, editor. | Gruber, Gabriela, editor.
Title: Education beyond crisis : challenges and directions in a
  multicultural world / edited by Daniela Roxana Andron and Gabriela
  Gruber.
Description: Leiden ; Boston : Brill Sense, [2020] | Series: ISATT
  conference series, 26667819 ; volume 1 | Includes bibliographical
  references and index.
Identifiers: LCCN 2020017448 (print) | LCCN 2020017449 (ebook) | ISBN
  9789004432024 (paperback) | ISBN 9789004432031 (hardback) | ISBN
  9789004432048 (ebook)
Subjects: LCSH: Multicultural education--Cross-cultural studies. |
  Culturally relevant pedagogy--Cross-cultural studies. |
  Teachers--Training of--Cross-cultural studies.
Classification: LCC LC1099 .E3445 2020 (print) | LCC LC1099 (ebook) | DDC
  370.117--dc23
LC record available at https://lccn.loc.gov/2020017448
LC ebook record available at https://lccn.loc.gov/2020017449

Typeface for the Latin, Greek, and Cyrillic scripts: "Brill". See and download: brill.com/brill-typeface.

ISSN 2666-7819
ISBN 978-90-04-43202-4 (paperback)
ISBN 978-90-04-43203-1 (hardback)
ISBN 978-90-04-43204-8 (e-book)

Contents

PART 3
Teaching in a Multicultural World

Preface

Dear Reader,

Please think for a minute about Benjamin Franklin's quote *"Either write something worth reading or do something worth writing"*. Then, have a glimpse into this book, and you will find ideas worth reading that are the result of mature and thorough research, worth writing about. This book is born of passion, optimism and shared vision of a bright future. We are proud to share with you, the readers, valuable insights of hard and dedicated work for a better tomorrow. The authors are prominent educators and researchers looking into the tempestuous present to plant the seeds of the time to come.

The world is getting smaller, the challenges are new and sometimes hard to deal with and education seems to be the most powerful instrument in shaping this new world for a bright future. This is something we all know and how we express the idea might be different but the direction is somehow the same for all those dedicated teachers that confidently scrutinize the future. Sharing ideas and experience has always been the best path found by those driven by a common purpose in their attempt to clarify objectives and routes.

This is what this book intends to find – a common path for diverse approaches meant to reach a better vision on the future of education – a better education, a better way of adapting to the most spectacular and rapid changes that modern human evolution has ever faced. Remarkable education specialists are bringing their research into this volume – the chapters of this book offer the ideas or solutions presented in the 19th Biennial Conference of the International Study Association on Teachers and Teaching (Sibiu, Romania, July 2019). The best papers of the conference have been selected and these have furtherly been developed into the chapters of this book – a hopeful vision on the future of education as the main theme proclaims it: education beyond the crisis.

The themes have been grouped as these evolve following three major courses – defining directions for the future of teaching, challenges of the contemporary teaching context and teaching in a multicultural world. The volume itself stands for the multicultural approach of education – you will find here not only the vision of a multicultural world, but the valuable ideas and research of 43 authors representing 16 countries, aiming to offer a unitary picture out of the puzzle pieces of their different background, professional horizon and concerns.

Part 1: Directions for the Future of Teaching

Without pretending to cover all the directions for the future of teaching, the volume focuses on major ideas such as educational policies, curriculum design and the actors involved in the process: students and teachers. Student voice and teacher training are thus the key concepts around which this first part of the book will evolve.

A generous theme considered by this book, as this is the main concern of most of the researchers nowadays, directions for the future of teaching can be unified by working together – the opening chapter reveals a unified vision of authors of different national background and using different research methodology on the same challenging idea – "The Impact of Reform Policies on Teachers and Their Practices". Based on case studies conducted in Brazil, Canada, USA and Portugal, the chapter reveals the reform's possible negative effects on teacher's behavior, the narrative conceptual model based on "dialogical knowledge" building process and the analysis of two different educational projects applied to a large number of subjects. The reader will find in this chapter consistent qualitative research of four outstanding researchers – Cheryl Craig, Maria Flores, Maria Ines Marcondes and Darlene Ciuffetelli-Parker – based on semi-structured interviews, focus groups, document analysis and implementation of a professional development program for teacher training.

A different challenge is considered in the second chapter – student voice in teaching writing. The scientific novelty of the chapter is an objective of the current research, as the authors specify from the beginning how they want to contribute to the development of the knowledge in teaching the writing process. The novelty of the research proposed by Vassiliki Tzika, Stavroula Kaldi, Evgenia Vassilaki and Christos Govaris is underlined by the research questions, as well as by the selection and application of the research methods and tools. The structure of the interview guide, as well as the answers given by the subjects, clearly shows the originality of the research. The questions and answers are adapted to the specific learning environment in Greece. The ideas obtained during interpreting the answers and, also, the observations based on defined criteria allow a visible effort of deepening the conclusions. Although related to previous international research, the authors' conclusions contain original elements tailored to the specific learning environment in Greece.

The interest in curriculum design has led to Chapter 3 of the volume, providing insight into valuable and innovative techniques for curriculum design in a provocative area – citizenship education. The chapter proposes rather wide research on a new approach to curriculum design. Scientific research and literature referred to bring value to the ideas and techniques proposed while the domain is indeed a most discussed one, civic education being subject of dramatic influences nowadays. Italian teachers all over the country have been directly involved in the project conducted and presented by Loredana Perla, Laura Sara Agrati and Viviana Vinci and contributed to the research results, being not only beneficiaries of the research but also part of it, thus bringing teacher training to a different level.

Teacher training is and will remain the most important for education and adapting to change means being creative. Chapter 4 analyses the teacher training from a theatre pedagogy perspective. The author's reflection on the theatrical simulation effectiveness in the teachers' education is original. The research conducted at the University of Vienna by Julia Kohler aims to find the students' interest in the method of simulation in theatrical education and in teachers' education. The qualitative research organizes the students' answers into four categories, each of them being characterized and exemplified with these answers. The conclusions and their implications for the practical training of teachers are based on the analyzed data and these are highly relevant for the theatrical education practice.

The creative approach of teacher training is getting deeper into creativity with Chapter 5 – learning to teach for creativity is the main concern of the three authors at Radboud University, the Netherlands – Ida Oosterheert, Paulien Meijer and Ingeborg van der Neut. The scientific novelty consists of applying a previously constructed framework as a starting point for designing contexts that facilitate the cultivation of the learners' creativity. Another aspect of the scientific novelty is represented by the current research problem of analyzing the efficiency of the university course on "teaching for creativity", using a research instrument that is also original. The chapter also presents the identified categories of creative aspects in student teachers' learning reports, bringing to innovative conclusions. Thus, the student teachers that achieved the course on teaching for creativity reported a grown sense of agency as young professionals and they developed new traits of their professional identity.

Part 2: Challenges of the Contemporary Teaching Context

This part of the volume looks into some of the most important challenges of the contemporary teaching context, such as inclusive education, use and misuse of technology, the need for adapting teaching to the innovative course of the social evolution.

Inclusion and integration are key-terms in defining modern education. The difficult path from defining directions to implementing them has brought the Italian education system on a well-deserved leading position in integrating disabled students. In Chapter 6, Antonella Galanti and Tamara Zappaterra are sharing valuable insights into the vision of education seen as a life project, defining the model of this performing inclusive/integrative education system. They do it through historical analysis focused on the support teacher's role and on the specific teacher training required for this extremely important role.

Remaining in the same area and in the same Italian educational system, Chapter 7 considers special needs education from a different perspective. Loredana Perla and Virginia Magoga are looking into using art as a valuable educational tool. Maybe the main idea is not an innovative one, nor is innovative the use of the theory in new special education but the idea of facing the new challenge of social isolation is actual. Also, the practical approach of the idea is valuable and the results of the study perfectly fit into the main theme of challenges that education is successfully facing nowadays.

The dynamic progress that accompanies the socio-economical evolution has also brought major influences in teaching by introducing technology in the classroom. Chapter 8 provides valuable information on using new tools to improve teaching practice, bringing into attention the results of consistent research expecting to connect teaching practice to the digital era. The authors – an international team of researchers from Spain (Paula Martín-Gómez, María Luisa García Rodríguez, Juanjo Mena) and China (Gang Zhu) have brought for this volume well-established methodology and clear results for their work aiming to design a valuable instructional tool – a mobile application to digitalize teacher's professional journals in the practicum.

The same technical progress that education benefits may also bring challenges of the side-effects specific for the digital era – fake news, manipulation and propaganda carried out by political and economic actors (and not only). Thus, Chapter 9 is looking into media education, digital literacy – the required competencies for the digital natives. According to Minodora Salcudean and Raluca Muresan media teachers should guide the students in their conscious access into the online content, teaching about media being a desirable direction for the present and future of a complete education.

Concluding the part dedicated to the challenges education needs to face, Paulien Meijer is shaping the main idea somehow contained by all the previous contributions in this volume: the need for innovative practices in teaching. Chapter 10 is a thoroughly documented reflection on bringing innovation and creativity into teaching, considering not only the need for creativity but also translating the definition of creativity into practice tools that teacher education could and should use for innovative teaching.

Part 3: Teaching in a Multicultural World

Educational progress is the result of bringing to life every valuable idea generated by the melting pot of cultures that defines contemporary society. This final part of the volume is trying to highlight the multicultural image of education today. Sound research, innovation, bright and colorful vision upon the future of education is brought here from Canada, Turkey, Namibia, USA, Romania, Singapore, The Netherlands, India, Greece, and the Amazonian Forrest.

Building a bridge between two major themes of this volume – challenges of contemporary society and the multicultural approach of education – Chapter 11 opens the third part by bringing into attention an important challenge, the refugees' migration. The chapter is the result of a collaborative (multicultural, of course) research, a consistent, very dense and well-documented study concerning the global issue of the refugee children's education provided by an impressive research team – Snežana Obradović-Ratković, Vera Woloshyn, Kari-Lynn Winters, Neelofar Ahmed, Christos Govaris, Stavroula Kaldi, Christiana Deliewen Afrikaner, and Feyza Doyran. Important concepts, such as refugee student, trauma, teacher's cultural and reflective competence are defined based on a rich and updated literature, that is critically approached. The authors identify countries that best answer to the educational needs of the children, exemplifying with educational or intercultural programs developed in these countries, providing not only description of the educational programs and examples of good practices, but also consistent statistical data and information from extended literature. The study also includes recommendations on the most effective pedagogical strategies or the necessary changes in teacher training to better answer to the current needs of migrants and refugee children, while the conclusions of the study are dense and relevant.

In Chapter 12, two American researchers – Estela Ene and Sydney Sparks – are looking into the issues of EFL teachers' education in Romania. The study continues older research, of 2013, of the main author, extending the research to almost the whole surface of Romania, and diversifies the research subjects, which come from all the Romanian universities that are training English teachers. The authors' interest in the beliefs and attitudes of English teachers towards the English speakers' language and cultures is also a new research concern. Connecting the English teachers' beliefs and attitudes to the efficiency of EFL teaching is innovative, at least in Romania. The research findings could determine changes in the process of English teachers' training in universities, but also in their practices during their classes.

Chapter 13 describes the Singaporean educational space, an outstanding educational system, offering rigor of research, with start from a synthesis of a very well-selected and updated literature. Specific concepts, such as "matching paradigm", "adaptation paradigm" and "practical reasoning" are attentively defined, characterized and compared, leading to a critical presentation of the Singaporean educational background. The scientific novelty of the research is also proved by the descriptive and numerical data included in the tables and by the image meant to visualize the practical way of organizing data. The proposed analysis model, as well as the research laddering method proposed by Heng Jiang and co-authors could be successfully used to analyze other educational spaces and determine the causes that block the reforms of the educational systems.

Teacher education professional learning is considered in Chapter 14. Although the theme is not innovative, and the search for professional development is not younger than the profession itself, the approach is interesting. The authors provide a coherent and thorough approach of literature, good structuring of information, clear presenting results on a wide sample of Dutch educators, within a study conducted in the Netherlands by Cui Ping, Gonny Schellings and Douwe Beijaard.

The same concern for teacher professional development is considered in Chapter 15, from a different perspective. Manpreet Kaur, of India, is approaching the role of emotions in defining teacher educators' professional identity. The chapter deals with the delicate issue of teachers' becoming, bringing into discussion the construction of the professional identity seen by the teachers themselves. The study highlights four key signs of professional identity development: identity beliefs, emotional events and identity negotiation, teachers' attributes and adjustment.

Teachers' becoming in the heart of the Amazon rainforest is the focus of Chapter 16. Ana Flávia Souza Aguiar shares a self-analysis on her teaching style and of her ethical judgments over the teaching and assessing decisions she made during the course on the philosophy of education, with student-teachers in the deep Amazon area in Brazil. The scientific quality of the paper is ensured by the reflective process, based on Freire's and Brookfield's pedagogical concepts.

Concluding the volume, we cannot consider shaping a better future without looking into history. The final chapter considers the inquiry-based learning for a better historical thinking. Alexandra Stavrianoudaki and Antonis Smyrnaios are teaching in Greece – a cradle of history – and Chapter 17 intends to contribute to the development of the current pedagogical knowledge, but also to the main characteristics of the historical thinking concept. History domain exploration is based on a rich and updated literature, which is well synthesized, organized and quoted. The research methodology is based on case-study research design and on semi-structured interviews that facilitate qualitative research.

Illustrations

The following illustrations have been provided, exclusively for the present volume, by courtesy of Rares Helici@crispus-art, official photographer for the ISATT 2019 Conference in Sibiu:

- Cover illustration: *Walking in the Light*, photograph by Rares Helici, for *Education beyond the Crisis* (Sibiu, 2020).
- Part 1: *Choose the Way,* photograph by Rares Helici, for *Directions for the Future of Teaching* (Sibiu, 2020).
- Part 2: *Puzzle Mirror,* photograph by Rares Helici, for *Challenges of the Contemporary Teaching Context.*
- Part 3: *Layers of Light,* photograph by Rares Helici, for *Teaching in a Multicultural World.*

Acknowledgements

We are here addressing our thanks to the anonymous reviewers who have not only selected and proposed the contributions for this volume, but also provided valuable help in guiding the authors to bringing their ideas into the pages of this volume. Our special thanks to Evelien van der Veer and Jolanda Karada (Brill | Sense) for professionally and carefully guiding our book through the production process and for bringing it to your hands.

Figures and Tables

Figures

Tables

Notes on Contributors

Christiana Deliewen Afrikaner
of Walvis Bay, Namibia has received a PhD (Arts Education) from the University of Porto, Portugal. She is a Senior Education Officer with the Ministry of Education, Arts and Culture, a Teacher by profession, a World Councilor for International Society for Education through Arts, and a country representative of the International Study Association on Teachers and Teaching. She is also a Chairperson of Society for Arts Education in Namibia and Sub-Saharan Africa Society for Education through Arts, a founding member of Africa Arts Association, a board member of Walvis Bay School of Arts and Omaruru School of Arts, and a past Vice Chairperson of Namibia Craft Centre. She served on the National Arts Curriculum Panel for three consecutive terms.

Laura Sara Agrati
is an Associate Professor at the 'Giustino Fortunato' University of Benevento in Didactics and Educational Technologies, Special Education and Inclusion. Her main research interests are didactic mediation/mediatization of learning content; professional development of teachers. She published monographs on teacher training and teaching mediation and scientific articles in national and international reviews. She is a member of international – AERA, ISATT, AAPT (American Association of Philosophy Teachers Studies in Pedagogy) – and national – SIPED, SIRD, SIPES research associations. She's the winner of the Italian Society of Pedagogy Award for *Il sapere appreso dei bambini* (2015).

Ana Flávia Souza Aguiar
is working for the Amazonas Ministry of Education in Brazil. She is specialized in Humanities – Philosophy of Education.

Neelofar Ahmed
is a doctoral student at OISE, the University of Toronto, Canada. She examines the interaction between global dynamics and international and domestic policies for refugees. Ahmed has presented at various international conferences, participated in three videos, and assisted in developing a webinar. She was interviewed by the *Voice of America*, Washington DC, to discuss refugee students' education in North America and Pakistan. Ahmed serves as an advisory committee member to an international organization that provides education to students in conflict affected zones. Her scholarly contributions include a major research paper, book chapters, journal articles, and research reports.

Daniela Roxana Andron

is an Associate Professor at Teachers' Training Department of Lucian Blaga University of Sibiu, Romania, since 2007. She has studied engineering, economics and teachers' training, with her PhD in Management (2009). Her publishing record covers her interest both in Management and Education; she has published or co-authored 13 volumes and book chapters, edited three volumes of students' educational research, and published over 30 articles in international and national journals. She joined ISATT in 2017.

Douwe Beijaard

is a Professor of Professional Learning at the Eindhoven School of Education (ESoE), Eindhoven University of Technology, Eindhoven, The Netherlands. He has been both dean and research director at ESoE. He was and still is (executive) editor of several scientific journals in the domain of teaching and teacher education. His research focuses on the professional identity, quality, and development of (beginning) teachers.

Terence Titus Chia

is a research assistant with the National Institute of Education, Nanyang Technological University, Singapore; graduated and received his Bachelors of Psychology Degree from James Cook University Singapore in 2016. He is currently pursuing a Master of Education in Developmental Psychology.

Cheryl J. Craig

is a Professor, Chair of Technology and Teacher Education and an Endowed Chair at Texas A&M University (USA). Her empirical research is situated at the intersection where teaching/teacher education and curriculum meet. She is an American Educational Research Association (AERA) Fellow, a recipient of AERA's Division B (Curriculum) Outstanding Lifetime Career Award and has been honored with AERA's Michael Huberman Award for Outstanding Contributions to Understanding the Lives of Teacher in addition to ISATT's ST2AR Award for Significant and Exemplary Contributions through Research, Teaching and Professional Service in the International Field of Teaching and Teacher Education.

Feyza Doyran

is an Associate Professor in the Department of English Language Teaching at Hasan Kalyoncu University, Gaziantep, Turkey. She received her MA in English Language Teaching and PhD in Curriculum and Instruction from Middle East Technical University. Doyran conducted her post-doctoral studies in the Department of Educational Psychology at the University of Texas in Austin. She has published books and articles on teacher education and training, effects of verbal and non-verbal teacher behaviors, professional morality, cooperative syllabus design, and reflective journal writing. Since 1999, Doyran has offered seminars and in-service/pre-service teacher training sessions on curriculum and instruction, effective teaching, interpersonal relations, effective communication skills, neuro-linguistic programming, non-verbal communication skills, emotional intelligence, and learning to learn. She trains IB PYP teachers. Doyran has been the National Representative of the International Study Association on Teachers and Teaching for two years.

Estela Ene

is Associate Professor, Director of the EAP Program, Director of the TESOL MA Program, at Indiana University-Purdue University Indianapolis. Her work about EFL/ESL/translingual writing, including research about EFL writing in Romania, China, Mexico, and Poland, has appeared in book chapters and articles in the *Journal of Second Language Writing, Assessing Writing* and many others.

Maria Assunção Flores

is an Associate Professor with a qualification at the University of Minho, Portugal. Her research interests include teacher professionalism and identity, teacher education and professional development, teacher appraisal, curriculum, assessment, leadership and higher education. She has published extensively on these topics both nationally and internationally. She is Editor of the *European Journal of Teacher Education* and Executive Editor of *Teachers and Teaching: Theory and Practice* in addition to being the past-Chair of the International Association on Teachers and Teaching (ISATT) (2013–2019). She recently was the first in Portuguese history to receive the Research Award from the International Council on Education for Teachers (ICET), one of the most distinguished global honors in the field of education.

Maria Antonella Galanti

is Full Professor of Teaching and Special Education at University of Pisa (IT). She is member of the Italian Society of Special Pedagogy. She is director of "Corso di Ateneo di specializzazione per insegnanti di sostegno" and "Centro Musicale di Ateneo". Her research topics are focused on normal and pathological identity, conflict elaboration and Special Education. Among her publications, two worth to be mentioned are *Sofferenza psichica e pedagogia. Educare all'ansia, alla fragilità e alla solitudine* (Carocci, 2007); *Disturbi del neurosviluppo e reti di cura. Neuropsichiatria e Pedagogia in dialogo* (in collaboration with B. Sales, ETS, 2017).

Paula Martín-Gómez

is a primary school teacher in the community of Madrid. She obtained her degree in Early Childhood and Primary Education with mention in English

Foreign Language as well as a master's degree in Language, Communication and its Pathologies at the University of Salamanca. She is currently studying in the PhD program at the University of Salamanca. Her research is focused on the practicum, professional development and the improvement of teaching practice.

Christos Govaris

is a Professor in Pedagogy and Intercultural Education in the Department of Primary Education at the University of Thessaly, Greece. He holds a PhD in Sciences of Education from the University of Tubingen. He instructs the following academic courses: (a) Introduction to Education Sciences, (b) Intercultural Education: Theory and Practice and (c) School Teaching Practice, Level I. He has published a great number of books and articles in various international journals, edited volumes, and international conferences. He participates in national and European research programs for the education of immigrants, refugees, and Roma pupils.

Gabriela Gruber

is an Associate Professor, Ph.D. (2006), in the Teachers' Training Department, Lucian Blaga University of Sibiu, She has published books and articles on History teacher education, teachers' professional ethics, and pedagogical practice. Thus, her researches interconnect her interests in History, History teaching, and Social Sciences Didactics, but she is also writing about the process of moral development and students' ethical education. Some of her latest publications are Etica academică și elemente de didactică a acesteia (Academic Ethics and its Teaching Aspects) (2019) and Becoming a Preschool or Primary-School Teacher: Initial Teachers' Beliefs and Professional Training (2018).

Heng Jiang

is an Assistant Professor at the Policy, Curriculum, and Leadership Academic Group at the National Institute of Education, Nanyang Technological University, Singapore. She has published two scholarly books on teacher learning and classroom assessment practices with Springer and articles in academic journals, such as Journal of Teacher Education, Intercultural Education, and Professional Development in Education. Her first book won the Outstanding Book Award of the International Study Association of Teachers and Teaching. She has led two competitive grants on teacher professional learning in Singapore, and her third book (forthcoming) is based on what she has learned from these projects.

Stavroula Kaldi

is a Professor in Pedagogy and Instruction in the Department of Primary Education at the University of Thessaly, Greece. She is a PhD graduate from the Sussex

University, UK. She instructs the following academic courses: (a) School Teaching Practice, Level IV, (b) Teaching Methodology: Structural Elements of Teaching and (c) Group work teaching and co-operative learning. She is co-author of a book on project-based learning: Theory and Practice. Her research is published in various refereed international journals, conferences, and edited volumes.

Ria George Kallumkal

is currently a research assistant in the Curriculum, Teaching and Learning group at the National Institute of Education, Singapore. She holds a Master of Education in Curriculum and Teaching from National Institute of Education, Singapore and Bachelor of Technology in Electrical Engineering from National Institute of Technology, India. She moved into education research as a research assistant in the project "Teacher Learning with Classroom Assessment" after working for more than 6 years as a teacher in both Singapore and India. Her research interests include teacher education, teacher emotions, and curriculum implementation.

Manpreet Kaur

is Full Professor and designated as Principal at Partap College of Education Ludhiana, Punjab, India for over 15 years. She loves teaching, leading, challenging and supporting colleagues and students to be the best they can be. She awarded a PhD in Education from Punjabi University Patiala. She has 15 years of teaching experience to teach graduate and postgraduate classes and providing research guidance. She has chaired sessions, presented papers and keynote addresses in 15 international and 20 national conferences. She has published two books and various research papers in reputed international and national journals and articles on education in newspapers. She is Honorary Secretary of the International Professional Development Association (IDPA) India, Executive Committee member IPDA UK, Member International Study Association of Teachers and Teaching (ISATT), Global Educational Research Association (GERA) and Review Editor of *Frontier in Education, International Journal of English Literature and Culture* and *Journal of Information Technology Research*. She is working as a resource person for Career Long Professional Learning of school teachers and teacher educators. Her areas of interest are well-being, professional development, and leadership.

Julia Köhler

of the University of Vienna, is Senior Lecturer at the Centre of Teacher Education. After obtaining her university diploma in acting at the University for Music and Performing Arts, Vienna, she was trained in theatre pedagogy and received her master's degree in Educational Sciences at the University of Vienna. Her research focuses on theatre pedagogy, teacher professionalism, and cultural education. She has published among others about theatrical ways in teacher education. Currently, she is Co-Chair of the Austrian Drama Education Teacher Network, cooperating with International Drama in Education Association (IDEA).

Malathy Krishnasamy

is a research associate with the Curriculum Teaching and Learning Department, NIE. She holds a PhD (Education) from NIE, NTU. Her doctoral research was on transition outcomes for youth with intellectual disabilities. She obtained the Dean's Commendation Award for Research (2015) for her published paper on a quality of life framework to assess transition outcomes. Malathy also holds an MA in English Studies from NUS. Her research interests include teacher learning, differentiated instruction, and inclusive classrooms. Prior to taking up research work, Malathy was a school teacher, a journalist, and a special needs educator.

Virginia Grazia Iris Magoga

holds a master's degree in Art History from the University of Bari "Aldo Moro". She is currently in the third year of her PhD at the Department of Education, Psychology and Communication Sciences at the same University, her research interests focus on the relationships between citizenship education, the languages of contemporary art and museum education, with attention to the role of the museum and creative laboratories as educational devices for development of social skills. She has published many articles on the educational value of the museum as an institution and on the teaching of art.

Maria Ines Marcondes

is Associate Professor of the Master and Doctorate Program in Education of the Pontifical Catholic University of Rio de Janeiro (PUC/Rio). She is currently professor and researcher, having published several articles in specialized journals and presenting papers in national and international events. Researcher and member of research associations such as American Educational Research Association (AERA) and is National Representative of the International Study Association on Teachers and Teaching (ISATT). She is member of the Editorial Committee of Teachers and Teaching (UK-Taylor and Francis Group). Visiting scholar at the Faculty of Education/University of Cambridge in January and February (2014) and February (2015).

Paulien C. Meijer

is PhD Professor, Teacher Learning and Development, at Radboud University, Nijmegen, the Netherlands. In her research, she focuses on teacher identity development and on innovative and creative practices in teaching and teacher education.

Juanjo Mena

is Associate Professor, PhD, at the Department of Education at the University of Salamanca (Spain). He obtained his PhD in Educational Psychology in 2007 with honors. He received a scholarship to culminate his tertiary studies at the University of Leiden (the Netherlands) in 2005. He is currently an affiliate professor at the Center for the Study of Teacher Education at the University of British Columbia (Canada) and research collaborator at Kazan Federal University. His research interests are focused on the analysis of the teaching practice, mentoring and the practicum, Teacher Education and ICT.

Raluca Muresan

is PhD Associate Professor at Faculty of Social and Human Sciences, "Lucian Blaga" University of Sibiu, Romania. She conducts lectures and seminars on Mass Media Ethics, Mass Media Law, Crisis Communication and CSR. Her research interests are ethics, communication, journalism, and media education. More specifically, her work examines traditional and new media ethics, ethics of social movements and the culture of protest, freedom of speech and manifestations of hate speech, academic integrity, media literacy, and critical thinking. She has co-written original studies and articles, published in well-known journals from the area of her research interest, such as *Comunicar* and *Journal of Mass Media Ethics*.

Snežana Obradović-Ratković

is a Research Officer and an Instructor in the Faculty of Education, Brock University, Ontario, Canada. Her master's research explored the influence of media on immigrant children's values, self-concepts, and aspirations while her doctoral research investigated professional identities of refugee women teachers from Yugoslavia who immigrated to Canada between 1993 and 1998. Dr. Obradović-Ratković led a Social Sciences and Humanities Research Council of Canada funded study entitled "Supporting Refugee Students in Canada: Building on What We Have Learned in the Past 20 Years." Her scholarship focuses on migration and indigeneity, transnational and trans-disciplinary teacher education, decolonizing arts-based research methodologies, research education, and knowledge mobilization.

Ida Oosterheert

is Associate Professor PhD at Radboud University, the Netherlands – "Teacher Learning & Development". Her expertise is on learning to teach. Her current research is on how student teachers can learn to teach for creativity.

Darlene Ciuffetelli Parker

is a Professor in the Faculty of Education at Brock University. Her research intricately fosters a deeper understanding of various topics relating to systemic discrimination in schools (i.e. poverty, mental health, gender, identity, racism). Ciuffetelli Parker advances partnerships in communities and readily is an invited keynote/speaker, providing impactful talks to various organizations. She was a prior school administrator, literacy consultant, and teacher in Toronto and has received the Early Career Award of the Narrative Research Special Interest Group in the American Education Research Association, the Award for Excellence in Teaching at Faculty of Education at Brock University, and the Brock University Award for Distinguished Teaching.

Loredana Perla

is Full Professor in Methodologies of teaching and special education, at the University of Bari Aldo Moro. She is Coordinator of Education and Learning Sciences Degree Course (L19), Rectors's delegate for the Teachers Training in Bari, ISATT and Ideki (Information, Didactique, Documentation, Enseignement, Knowkedge Kultur, Ingénierie) and National Representative and peer reviewer for AERA. She has published national and international works about the professional teacher training, the school curriculum, the evaluation research. She's winner of the Italian Society of Pedagogy Award for "L'eccellenza in cattedra" (2012) on grounds of proposing a referential of competences for the evaluation of the quality of teaching.

Cui Ping

currently is a PhD student at the Eindhoven School of Education (ESoE), Eindhoven University of Technology, Eindhoven, the Netherlands. She majored in comparative education at the Northeast Normal University, Changchun, China. Her master thesis focused on understanding the construction of a knowledge base for teacher educators by the Dutch Association of Teacher Educators. Her PhD project is about teacher educators' professional learning, and mainly focuses on what teacher educators have learned for doing their work, the learning activities they undertake for that, and their reasons for learning.

María Luisa García Rodriguez

is a tenured professor in the Department of Education at the University of Salamanca (USAL, Spain). She obtained her PhD in Education. Her specialty is early childhood education and her research interests include teacher development, mentoring and written language. She is an active member of the editorial board of several journals. She was a school teacher in Madrid and Salamanca.

Minodora Salcudean

is PhD Associate Professor at Faculty of Social and Human Sciences, "Lucian Blaga" University of Sibiu, Romania. Among her courses are Online Journalism, Journalism through Social Media, Public Discourse, History and Mentality.

During the last decade, the research areas she explores are interdisciplinary and oriented towards the confluence of traditional mass-media and new media. Her recent studies and articles address topics such as: digital natives, production and consumption of digital content, social media and protests, digital misinformation, hate-speech in online medium. As co-author she published scientific works in prestigious journals (e.g. *Comunicar*). She is the author of the book *New Media, Social Media and Current Journalism* (Tritonic, 2015).

Gonny Schellings

is an Assistant Professor at the Eindhoven School of Education (ESoE), Eindhoven University of Technology, Eindhoven, the Netherlands. She completed her PhD project about learning strategies applied to instructional texts. She published about meta-cognition and meaningful learning. She was a regional project leader of a national founded government project to support beginning teachers. Her current research focuses on professional identity development of (beginning) teachers, learning environments, and learning strategies.

Antonis Smyrnaios

is an Associate Professor of Modern Greek History at the University of Thessaly, Greece. He is a PhD graduate from the School of Philosophy of Athens, Greece (2002). He instructs the following academic courses: (a) History of Modern Greek Education and (b) History Didactics. He has published monographs and articles, including *History's Learning: Issues on Philosophy and Didactics of History* (Athens, 2013). He has participated in international conferences and has co-authored articles in scientific journals.

Sydney Sparks

is a MA in TESOL student at Indiana University-Purdue University, Indianapolis. She is interested in multilingual writers and social justice.

Alexandra Stavrianoudaki

is a PhD candidate researcher in the Pedagogical Department of Primary Education at the University of Thessaly and a primary school teacher. She has participated in international conferences and has co-authored articles in educational journals. Her main research interest lies in the field of history education and in particular the use of inquiry-based learning (IBL) in class. Topics of interest include participants' beliefs about inquiry, doing history techniques, learning environment, and controversial issues in history. Next to IBL, she has also participated on other researches, such as: cross-curricular skills, peer tutoring, school effectiveness, gifted children and professional development. She works also as a primary education teacher.

Vassiliki Tzika

is a PhD Candidate researcher in the Pedagogical Department of Primary Education at the University of Thessaly and a primary school teacher. Her research interests focus upon contemporary teaching methods and processes, cross-curricular skills, project-based learning, students' voice, life-long learning, students' collaboration, differentiated instruction, teaching writing texts' process and also projects about cultivation and promotion of emotions, empathy and diversity. She has participated in international conferences and has co-authored articles in educational journals.

Ingeborg van der Neut

is a biology teacher, Msc, and a school-based teacher educator at Ludger College in Doetinchem, the Netherlands, a school for secondary education that works together with Nijmegen University to educate future teachers.

Evgenia Vassilaki

is an Assistant Professor in Greek Language and Language Teaching in the Department of Primary Education at the University of Thessaly, Greece. She holds a PhD in Linguistics from the University of Athens. She instructs the following academic courses: (a) Linguistics and Greek Language I, (b) Greek Language Teaching Methodology, (c) School Teaching Practice, Level II: Language Teaching, (d) Multilingualism in primary education: implications for language teaching and (e) Research in Language Teaching and Learning. She has participated in research projects on language teaching and language teachers' training and she has published papers in conference proceedings, edited volumes and journals on pragmatics and on language teaching

Viviana Vinci

is Assistant Professor at the Mediterranea University of Reggio Calabria, Italy, in "Didactics and Special Inclusion". She has achieved the National Scientific Qualification as Associate Professor in the Italian Universities. She is Delegate of Department's Director for "Transversal Skills and Orientation Programs" and Referent for eTwinning Teacher Training Institutions Initiative. Her main research interests are teacher education, evaluation, higher education, inclusion. She is a member of international – AERA, ISATT – and national – SIPED, SIRD, SIPES, SIREM – research associations. She's the winner of the Italian Society of Pedagogy Award for *Le routine per l'insegnamento scientifico* (2011).

Kari-Lynn Winters

is an Associate Professor at Brock University, where she teaches drama-in-education, dance-in-education, and language arts to teacher candidates. She holds a PhD from UBC in literacy education and the arts, a teaching degree from the University of Toronto, and a BA and a certificate in drama/theater from Brock University and the National Theatre School of Canada. Her research interests include: body image, embodied pedagogies, children's literature, equity, drama, and multimodal literacy. Kari-Lynn is also an award-winning Canadian children's author, scholar, playwright, and performer.

Vera Woloshyn

is a Professor in the Faculty of Education at Brock University. She holds advanced degrees in education, counseling, and psychology. Vera is a second-generation Canadian and only child of immigrant parents who were trauma survivors. Vera holds a strengths-based, holistic approach to learning, mental health, and wellness that recognizes the interconnectedness of individuals' cognitive, emotional, social, cultural, familial, physical, and spiritual experiences. Her scholarship explores ways to support the academic success and wellbeing of learners and educators within higher education and school-based settings. Related interests include exploring the experiences of those who serve in the helping professions.

Tamara Zappaterra

is Associate Professor, PhD, in Teaching and Special Pedagogy at the University of Ferrara, previously at University of Florence. She has been a member of the Board of the Italian Society of Special Pedagogy. She collaborates with the Ministry of Education, as a member of the scientific committee to train teachers and educators on the issues of inclusion. Her research concerns pedagogical topics on the subject of disability and inclusion. Among her last publications are *Users' Needs Report on Play for Children with Disabilities* (De Gruyter, 2019, co-edited with M. Allodi Westling,); *Perspectives on Autistic Spectrum Disorders* (ETS, 2019, co-edited with L. Al Ghazi).

Gang Zhu

is an Associate Professor at the Institute of International and Comparative Education, East China Normal University. Gang Zhu's scholarship mainly focuses on teacher education, urban education, and comparative education. Gang Zhu is an editorial board member of *International Journal of Contemporary Educational Research* and a former assistant editor of *Asia-Pacific Journal of Teacher Education* (SSCI). His publications appear regularly in *Urban Education, Compare, Journal of Language, Identity, Education, Journal of Education for Teaching, The Asia-Pacific Educational Researcher*. Gang Zhu has presented his research in US, UK, Canada, Spain, Romania, South Korea, and China.

PART 1

Directions for the Future of Teaching

..

CHAPTER 1

The Impact of Reform Policies on Teachers and Their Practices: Case Studies from Four Countries

Cheryl J. Craig, Maria Assunção Flores, Maria Ines Marcondes and Darlene Ciuffetelli Parker

Abstract

Educational reform tops the world agenda. Since the introduction of international testing programs (i.e., PISA), nations have competed with one another to gain international prominence. Educational improvement has become a $2-trillion business annually. Policymakers are seeking to find the next-best thing to lift local and national scores. Their mandates, however, can only be realized by teachers who, by law, must implement them. For their part, teachers want to be curriculum makers, not curriculum implementers, enacting others' demands. They know that policies cannot be implemented cleanly due to human and contextual complexities. In this chapter, researchers from four countries (Brazil, Canada, Portugal, United States) each introduce one or more recent reform policies that were adopted and illuminate how it/they affected local teachers and their practices in unanticipated ways.

Keywords

educational policy – teacher impact – teachers' practices – case studies – Brazil – Canada – Portugal – USA

1 Introduction

According to McKinsey et al. (2007), "educational reform is top of the agenda of almost every country in the world" (p. 16). Nearly every country participates in the more than $2-trillion industry that has been created. Every nation wishes to improve its standing from the previous year. Thus, policymakers search for educational changes that they can mandate teachers to implement. Policymakers are right-headed in focusing their efforts on teachers. Evidence from around the world (i.e., Barber & Moushed, 2007; Darling Hammond, 2000; OECD, 2010; Fullan, 2010) suggests that "the single most significant means of improving education ... is through teaching" (Pollard, 2010, p. 1). In the words of the United Kingdom Department for Education, "the first, and most important, lesson [of school reform] is that no education system can do better than the quality of its teachers" (DfE, 2010, p. 3). Unfortunately, policymakers are also wrong-headed in thinking that teachers can implement their policies exactly as they dictate. Even if teachers were inclined to do exactly as they were told, it would not be possible. Reform policies are meant for ideal situations; teachers' classrooms are practical places filled with exigencies (Schwab, 1969, 1971, 1973). Unfortunately, change never happens in input-output ways due to the unpredictable nature of human beings and the contexts within which they live and learn.

To further complicate matters, teachers are not simply curriculum implementers, dutifully putting policymakers' demands into action. They want to be curriculum makers (Connelly & Clandinin, 1992; Craig & Ross, 2008). They long to use their own intellectual resources. They strive to interpret the complexities of their teaching-learning situations. They seek to mingle their unique knowing with what is expected of them as agents of the state. Policymakers and teachers worldwide are wrestling with the paradoxical situation of what happens to supposedly well-meaning policy mandates when they meet the real world of schools filled with diverse, flesh-and-blood teachers and children. This is especially important at the present time, given globalization, immigration of refugees across nations, sudden world issues pertaining to climate, poverty, war, and the ever-fast, non-stop digital world confronting classroom walls world-wide.

It is imperative that policy-curriculum-reform solutions to education be problematized on a world-scale. While there is some research about various programs in Canada (Falkenberg, Goodnough, & MacDonald, 2014), as well as contextual literature on Canadian policy trends (Young & Boyd, 2010), for example, there needs to be more research in the field that is international and which specifically attends to the teaching profession, student and teacher identity, teacher education programming, engagement of public confidence, and current world knowledge experiences during such large-scale shifts on the planet.

In this chapter, cases from four countries (Portugal, Brazil, Canada, United States) are presented. Each is the product of an individual research program. Each case deals with a different dimension of educational policy and depicts the challenges inherent in it when those in schools attempted to live it.

By way of preview, the Brazilian case, which forms part of Maria Ines Marcondes' research agenda, focuses on the benchmarking of curriculum, which detracts from teaching-learning relationships between teachers and students.

The Brazil case is followed by a Canadian example from the province of Ontario that is part-and-parcel of Darlene Ciuffetelli Parker's scholarly work. The case revolves around teacher educators situated at the interstices of policy prescriptions, poverty and professional identity.

The third study we spotlight comes from Portugal. Shared by Maria Assunção Flores, the case centers on austerity measures and the performativity agenda that is increasingly becoming a European phenomenon.

We conclude with the American case based on two decades of research in one urban school milieu in the state of Texas, which is part of Cheryl Craig's research program. The work shows what happened in one school site and to the teachers as accountability policies (American word for performativity) took hold. We begin now with the Brazilian case introduced earlier.

2   Case 1: Educational Policies in The Public School System in Brazil: New Challenges to Teachers and Pedagogical Coordinators (Maria Ines Marcondes)

Since the 1990s, educational proposals in Brazil have given priority to setting minimum national standards for the basic school curriculum and application of external evaluations aimed to improve quality. This quality has been comprehensively measured through the performance of students, teachers and institutions. These reforms have assigned new roles to teachers, often disregarding their acquired knowledge and experiences as professionals. Coordinators and teachers have new benchmarks for their work (Marcondes, 2017; Marcondes, Freund, & Leite, 2017). In addition to their own concepts and theories, they must attend to numbers and figures, performance indicators, comparisons and competition. Teachers must achieve specific externally imposed goals, even though it frequently means ceasing to establish relationships with the children with whom they work. As for the pedagogical coordinators, they now primarily regulate teachers' work.

This case analyzes the consequences for the process of education in Brazilian classrooms and how teachers and pedagogical coordinators have forcibly had to restructure their practices. In the team of management professionals of basic schools and high schools, the pedagogical coordinator has been the agent responsible for keeping teachers involved and committed to the fulfillment of performance goals established by external indicators. This gives rise to the main research question, which is: How have teachers responded to

6

CRAIG ET AL.

changes in curriculum and assessment conducted by the authorities who are now in power at the Brazilian educational context? The theoretical perspective is based on the scholarship of Ball, Maguire, and Braun (2012). For Ball et al., policies are not merely implemented, they are re-created in accordance with professional cultures and with the material context, the external context and the situated context. Zeichner's work (2008) on teacher education is also used, particularly his concept of teachers as reflective practitioners.

It is true that teachers are influenced by the discursive context in which the policy is produced, however, they do not have such unambiguous meanings and in the different fields of their performance the interpretation of the political text has clear links with the cultural marks and the social relations of these spaces. Ball, Maguire, and Braun (2012) also point out that in the dynamics of interaction between the different contexts of curricular reforms emerge, in the space of school life, in the place of classrooms, a plurality of movements that manifest resistance, accommodation, subterfuges or conformism. Therefore, there is a reinterpretation of reform by teachers and even managers when it comes to schools.

The context of public-school education in Brazil currently has new characteristics. The permanent search for desired qualities in elementary education has become linked to the widespread contracting and use by public networks of prescriptive guidelines for teachers' work – so-called apostilled (Brazil) – accountability (US)/performativity (UK) – system. This system is directly linked to the improvement of student achievement scores on standardized tests. Material is subsequently prepared by the Municipal or State Secretariats with input from external experts either from the universities or services contracted from private groups.

In many of the networks across Brazil, increases in the indices have been translated into salary bonuses for teachers. The produced material is based on 'minimum common curriculum' and activities presented are very close to the items on the tests. Thus, teachers sought better and presumably quicker results, often through relying on multiple-choice tests.

2.1 Changing Routines, Reorganization in Relation to Curriculum and Evaluation

This Brazil case was carried out in the municipal network of the city of Rio de Janeiro. It directly investigated new curricular policies implemented in the municipal education system based on the curricular materials prepared to support teachers' practices. The seven teachers in the study taught Grades 1–5. The analysis of the data (observations, interviews, document analysis) revealed the responses of two coordinators and seven teachers facing the curricular, didactical and assessment demands inherent in Brazil's new educational policy.

The materials formed the basis for the tests and the apostille system (the accountability or performativity agenda) in turn determined working hours and teaching strategies. Also, there was implicit monitoring of the implementation of the material that resulted in greater control of teachers' work because the students' results revealed whether the teachers had employed the required material or not. These results were also used to reward teachers and schools through the achievement of the index measures, thus increasing control over the teachers' work.

The reorganization of the curriculum in the school that was studied was also observed. Additionally, the coordinator tried to continue to develop the curriculum based on the interests of the children as well as the activities in the Pedagogical Support Notebook that was preparing them for the exams. A tension existed between what had been previously planned which seemed to better account for the interests of children, and the new demands of the tests. The Political Pedagogical Project at the school was then re-contextualized by incorporating new levels to be reached according to the indices set by the Secretariat.

The process of mediation work of the coordinators effectively re-contextualizes the new policies. It is a constantly moving cyclic process. The mediation work is aimed at receiving the guidelines issued by the higher administrative bodies. The coordinator and the entire management team, in general, aims for reception in which there is acceptance of the policies are being re-contextualized based on the personal history of those who will work in the field. The negotiation process involves fully accepted, partially accepted and even denied aspects. Another important point to remember is that the new policies are often incorporated into aspects of previous policies.

The new requirements changed the work routines of the teacher and students in the investigated school. The classroom routines underwent a complete restructuring, not only where teaching material and strategies were concerned, but also through the introduction of additional testing measures and external evaluations. Teachers began to focus exclusively on Language and Mathematics because of impending evaluations. There was a clear loss of curricular attention to Science, Geography, History and the Arts. These subject areas were abandoned in the time period leading up to the testing. Although this was not the wish of the teachers, many creative activities were sidelined, and greater emphasis was placed on filling-in-the-blank exercises to 'train' behaviors needed for the multiple-choice tests. But there also was an invention by the teachers related to their use of the Pedagogical Support

Notebooks. They were sometimes used as anchoring or complementary activities.

Although the tests took center stage in the teaching process, the teachers at the research site continued to concurrently evaluate the students paying attention to the evidence required by the Secretariat and other activities that the teachers themselves developed. Additionally, the coordinators tried to discourage any formal 'practice testing' for the standardized tests, since from their perspective, the students needed to learn content, procedures and attitudes and use them in different situations. They felt that the Secretariat's assessment was "not enough" because it did not cover all aspects of learning. Learning was deemed to be larger and more complex than what was presented in the material, which seemed restrictive in its content and cursory in its explanations of concepts and associated ideas.

2.2   *How Teachers and Coordinators Re-Contextualize*

Teachers were critical of the improvement of the quality of teaching provided by the strategies in the learning environment but acknowledged the need for minimum standards to be taught and evaluated in all schools. Thus, teachers incorporated the materials and preparation for assessments into their routines, but they did not fail to carry out the activities and assessments in which they believed. The coordinators supported this practice because they too agreed that the external evaluations, being of the multiple-choice variety, failed to evaluate students' basic skills, such as text production, for example. In this context of re-contextualization of an educational proposal, we perceive an acceptance and commitment to the strategy because the teachers felt evaluated by the instruments and their students' results.

Re-contextualization has taken place in a different way in each school and each teacher has used the handouts differently, transforming the overarching goal. According to Maguire (2010), teachers may sometimes have to 'teach for the test' and set aside any other pedagogical concerns, such as moral, social, or other cognitive goals, because they are expected to comply with policy makers' demands. This creates inevitable tensions with teachers focusing more on testing than on understanding. They unfortunately, end up offering what they believe to be a 'limited and diluted' curriculum.

2.3   *Case 1: Interim Summary*

The analysis of the data gathered through observation, interviews and document analysis reveals the responses of the coordinators and teachers facing the curricular, didactical and assessment demands of the new educational policies in Brazil. This case's findings show that the identity of teachers and the culture of schools should be accounted for when considering policies that will end up changing aspects of a teacher's daily practices.

External evaluation is being partially accepted by the coordinators and the teachers of the schools that are being surveyed. This has happened because the change is regarded as provisional, temporary transformations and, as long as they do not compromise the political pedagogical projects of the schools, they can be accepted. External evaluations are also seen primarily as new ways of regulating the teaching profession not as factors that can contribute directly to improving the quality of teaching in schools.

The remaining issue is that teachers should be seen as intellectual (Giroux, 1988) and students as producers of knowledge. Despite providing opportunities to monitor pedagogical practices, the accountability tests have not produced many benefits because they affect the day-to-day activities that need to be evaluated in order for the indices to improve. The question arises: Would the improvement of the index related to test questions ever improve student learning?

From the perspective of the research carried out in the Rio de Janeiro network, the proposed changes in terms of descriptors, curricular guidelines and pedagogical support books are incorporated into teachers' practices but are seen as 'temporary measures'. The new demands of the Secretariat in terms of curricular determinations and application of tests to monitor student performance are incorporated into school routines. On the other hand, few believe that this will bring about improvement in the quality of teaching in the short or long term. The coordinators and teachers accept that they need to fulfill these new orientations because they feel pressured to maintain the index relating to their own performances.

Considering that the curricular content is low and basic, schools must reconcile what they had programmed in their political pedagogical proposals with the new demands in terms of curriculum. The fact that the proposal seeks to homogenize the network is of little interest to the local community. If furthermore does not account for the students' experiences and their family and cultural environments. Therefore, many planned activities remain in the lived curricula.

Regarding the way in which the present assessments are made, the pedagogical coordinators and the teachers consider that the external evaluations, being of multiple choice, failed to evaluate students' basic skills. The teachers emphatically revealed that they were poorly heard in the processes of change and that their claims were seldom considered.

In sum, this Brazil reform should not have prioritized the improvement of statistical indices. Teachers are more convinced to change by matters of social justice that form part of their professional identities, their mission to teach and their commitment to student learning (Goodson, 2007, 2008) than by external rewards and incentives that lead to competition between schools, regions, nations and children.

3   Case 2: Policy, Curriculum Reform, and Public Confidence: Dialogic Knowledge Building to Re-shape Lives on the Boundaries of Prescriptions, Poverty, and Professional Identity in Ontario, Canada (Darlene Ciuffetelli Parker)

In Canada, the second case in our chapter, education is primarily a provincial responsibility. However, over the years there has been a national policy shift in governance across Canada that is characterized by both professionalization and deregulation issues (Grimmett, 2009; Grimmett, Young, & Lessard, 2012).

Many teacher education institutions in Canada are restructuring their programs (i.e. extended 2-year teacher education programs in Ontario) while coping with the oversupply, underemployment and attrition rates of teachers.

Canadian literature on teacher education underscores current issues relating to theory-practice integration (Falkenberg, Goodnough, & MacDonald, 2014; Goodnough, Falkenberg, & MacDonald, 2016), teacher education policy (Grimmett, 2009; Walker & von Bergmann, 2013), teacher certification and governance (Grimmett, Young, & Lessard, 2012; Young & Boyd, 2010) and innovations in teacher education (Beck & Kosnik, 2006).

This case incorporates a narrative conceptual framework modeled from a research project (Ciuffetelli Parker, Orr, Mitton, Griffin, & Pushor, 2017) which explored the lived experiences of five tenured teacher educators, across three provinces in Canada, whose teacher education programs differ from province to province but whose experiences resonate with recent movements towards nationalism, prescribed business-model implementations, and what that implies for teacher education in Canada.

Bringing together the conceptualizations of narrative inquiry, curriculum making, and teacher education, the educators were mindful in attending to narrative accounts of experience (Clandinin & Connelly, 2000) in their respective programs and research during a problematic time in the existing national teacher education landscape. The resulting dialogue, which the group termed *dialogic knowledge building* (Ciuffetelli Parker et al., 2017), became a pivotal structure to problematizing the issues of teacher education on a national scale.

This case borrows the pedagogical inquiry approach of *dialogic knowledge building*, to burrow deeply into one narrative account which focuses on a recent poverty research program in Ontario secondary schools conducted by Ciuffetelli Parker. By examining poverty in terms of "small stories that educators and students live and tell, often on edges ... the overall intent is to illuminate in more nuanced ways the complex factors that shape [educators'] lives outside the boundaries of policy prescriptions" (Ciuffetelli Parker & Craig, 2017).

The case features Grade 11 teacher Tomaso teaching in a mixed socio-economic high school, and his efforts to challenge mindset of students as he works toward policy implementation of inclusive design, safe schools, and cultural competency. Using *dialogic knowledge building*, Tomaso recognizes the need for deeper insight and discussion of policy, curriculum reform, and public confidence within his own teaching identity, curriculum making, and personal professional inquiry. Stories of poverty and poverty stories in his own lived experiences become the backdrop of his teaching, along with narratively constructed data results that garner considerations for teaching and teacher education.

3.1   *Dialogic Knowledge*

Dialogic knowledge building is the mode of inquiry for this case and presented through a narrative inquiry lens using a 3R framework of how educators *reveal, have revelations*, and *reform* their storied experiences into new practices (Ciuffetelli Parker, 2013, 2014).

Dialogue is critical to community building and knowledge building. Listening is a key factor in the school community and, as Bohm, Factor, and Garrett (1991) suggest, it is an opportunity for a group of people to participate in a critical process that allows for thought, reflection, deeper meaning, and communication where there is no hierarchy and no place for the control of any member or a particular right solution. Following Bohm et al.'s (1991) notion of dialogue, German researcher Weigand's (2008, 2010) body of scholarship on dialogue in action is especially valuable as it relates to dialogue 'in action' and exchanging back and forth, new thought and insights. Like Weigand's work, the seminal works of Craig's authentic knowledge communities (1995, 2009) and Olson's (1995) notion of narrative authority, give testament to narrative as negotiated. The pedagogical approach to *dialogic knowledge* building lies at the center of three interconnected concepts of teacher education, curriculum making, and narrative inquiry (Ciuffetelli Parker &Pushor, 2014).

3.2   *Reveal, Revelation, Reformation: 3R Narrative Elements*

Narratives explored Tomaso's core values to more deeply understand the story of the school community, youth, and Tomaso as teacher. The method that underpinned the research case is narrative inquiry, represented in stories of systemic barriers as lived and told through Tomaso's own life and school experiences (Ciuffetelli Parker, 2014; Clandinin & Connelly, 2000; Connelly & Clandinin, 1990; Connelly & Clandinin, 2006; Dewey, 1938; People for Education, 2013). Using a 3R narrative framework first developed by Ciuffetelli Parker (2013) to analyze storied school experiences, the case informs a dialogic knowledge building that re-shapes lives (of teachers, youth, and the school community) on the boundaries of prescriptions, poverty, and professional identity.

The 3R narrative framework was developed from an earlier research program on poverty and education to apply narrative ways of excavating storied experiences and unconscious assumptions from the stories shared by research participants.

The terms *narrative reveal, revelation* and *reformation* are useful to help burrow deeply into issues of bias and systemic barriers in educational landscapes. Observing, from a wider perspective using the elements of reveal, revelation, and reformation, helps untangle how teaching and learning get enacted when assumptions also get enacted in classrooms, schools, and the larger community. Stories that *narratively reveal* help excavate unconscious assumptions that surface in the living and telling of experiences of teaching or learning; as stories are lived and retold, *narrative revelation*s show enlightened insight and allow further interrogation of our own experiences to gain perspective of unconscious biases, or hardened stories (Conle, 1999) that make us stuck in ways that may be discriminatory, regardless of intention; and *narrative reformation* is a storied path toward reforming a new understanding through an awakened belief or mindset.

3.2.1   A Teacher Reveals

Tomaso is a Grade 11 teacher, teaching in a mixed demographic school in southern Ontario, Canada.

Tomaso grew up in Ontario, to immigrant parents who were self-employed in an extended family auto-body repair company. He lived on a farm with all his extended family where the family "grew the crops and then we used them for consumption".

The family income was well below the poverty line, and bills were paid with nothing else left except for food. Tomaso felt guilty growing up in a family business that relied on the misfortune of others (car accidents or car misfunctions) to sustain their own living. "Hand me downs were a necessity. I remember wearing clothes with patches on the knees and was always told that I had to wear them".

For this and other storied experiences, Tomaso shared that he never takes any student for granted, especially in the new curriculum guidelines on the topic of Indigenous Studies and Canada's discriminatory history of the country's Indigenous people:

> My perspective is very different. Teaching about poverty in the Indigenous sector allows me the opportunity to make more viable connections. Students see what poverty is like when I show videos. I always tell my students that every child has a story and to never make assumptions. [I tell them] never to let any obstacle come in the way of success, as much as things are daunting, have faith that things will work out. Thankfully going to school, I was able to access [grants] because my parents were not making much money. I always share my story with students and let them know that we all have a story ... When I teach Indigenous studies, students have an awakening and I know teachers need to be involved in meaningful dialogue and professional development to understand the dynamics. I think there are some insignificant professional development sessions that could be better structured for teachers to engage in equity and inclusivity workshops, Indigenous Studies, and cultural sensitivity training and more understanding of poverty, [rather than accountability measures and online systems].

Tomaso relies on his lived experiences and shares his stories with his high school senior students. He prepares lessons that with an awareness of equity and inclusivity, while also realizing that his understanding and knowledge may be at another level than other teachers in his school or district. He is a teacher lead and represents committees of inclusivity and safe schools at the district level, and Tomaso has an excellent rapport with students who often seek him out on a daily basis for academic as well as socio-emotional school issues. He values inquiry-based learning and often sets his lessons with dialogue circles (akin to Indigenous ways of knowing), and discussion formats.

3.2.2   A Teacher's Revelation

During a lesson in Tomaso's Grade 11 Civics class, he had the students in small groups. Tomaso created scenarios based on the research and had students engage in a financial literacy activity based on different family situations, with the basis of understanding budget and funds for families to survive. Each group was given a salary to work with and dependents to take care of. From there the discussion then began about how they would spend their money. Tomaso assumed that students would consider social activities as necessities, but many groups did not and one group, in particular, was argumentative amongst themselves on what constitutes 'needs' and 'wants' and who gets what and who does not, and why.

The activity led to very heated whole classroom discussions that were then taken beyond the class lesson and into how school cliques and friendships were formed or discounted based on class, color, gender, and so on. For Tomaso, this activity, as heated as it was in the beginning, led to a larger inquiry-based learning project for himself and his students. He was awakened to the unconscious biases and assumptions that students themselves had of others who were not like themselves, even in this mixed socio-economic class.

One student, living in a low socio-economic household, remained silent, while another student also struggling financially, had no sympathy for those less fortunate than she was, and articulated her point of view. It was a watershed moment in the complexity of how issues having to do with vulnerable populations get taken up. This classroom lesson was happening prior to the unit on Indigenous Studies, and the realization of how discriminated, racialized and marginalized such populations continue to be, as witnessed by Tomaso from one of his own students.

The critical lesson shifted Tomaso's way of understanding his students, the teaching landscape, and the work ahead of him as it pertained to equity issues. He was left to plan his curriculum in a manner that reflected his students' own way of discovering truth and the realities of social injustices. He did this through an inquiry-based model, beyond the stated curriculum guidelines. He researched and read and took up a secondary stance on how to have students understand issues of injustice at a more critical level. The inquiry-based discussion led to a final independent project by each student to take up a social justice issue from their course studies and present a multi-modal digital piece of their personal learning of a topic. The curriculum piece became a watershed moment for students and teacher alike.

Tomaso said of this experiential revelation, "In terms of shift, I need to be very aware of every child and their individual needs. You must never take for granted anything as you teach".

3.2.3   A Teacher's Reformed Mindset and Practice

One of the prescribed policies of the school district was that finance matters from each school be dealt with on a financial online system. Many parents of students struggled to pay online for school trips, sport uniforms, and other curricular activities because many households relied on bi-weekly or monthly paychecks and the online system did not allow for these sorts of parameters. Many students were marginalized even further by this policy issue.

Tomaso complained about this to the principal and the principal took it up with the school board with no avail to provide parents with an alternative but with a caveat to protect students as much as possible from issues of finances and inability to afford curricular activities. For Tomaso, this was rectified by his own doing in the school as he worked tirelessly to protect his students from shame, ridicule, or inequities because of the way the administrative system had been set up by the central district. Despite his best efforts, there arose a situation where Tomaso felt disheartened. He tells the story:

> I had a rough week. I did something I am not proud of and it was an oversight on my part.
>
> I [wrote] the list of the cross-country runners and a student who made the team (the one I gave my shoes to and discreetly bought shirts for) was also on the list. [Teachers] have to activate the cash on the online system with the finance secretary and on the sheet I put brackets beside his name with the words "financial support needed" so the secretary knows we will cover his cost to participate. I posted the team list [as a routine I always do for sports related matters] outside of my room and two other lists at about 12:35 pm. The day ends at 2:15 pm and, as I was walking by the class I saw the list again and noticed what I had done (left the information for financial aid for that student in public for all to see). I ran so fast to first blackout the name with a sharpie and then I ripped it down I confided in my colleague and she too was upset because she said in this day and age with social media for sure someone took a picture of it. I spoke to the administration about it. I have never been so upset with myself. Fortunately, nobody saw the list nor said anything to me. I saw the boy yesterday and he was all smiles with me.
>
> But in terms of shifts, [I learned] you need to be very cognizant of all the things you do because it could cause and could be devastating.

Tomaso's reformed way of teaching is evidenced in this story that was not an ignorant error, but one that has struck him as very serious in the context of how he teaches with an open mindset. Tomaso goes above and beyond because his reformed mindset is part and parcel of his teaching identity and his attention to issues of equity.

3.3   *Case 2: Interim Summary*

This Canadian case illustrates how an equity-based curriculum is advancing in school systems, yet the issues of systemic barriers and discrimination, albeit unconscious by many stakeholders, including students as seen in one narrative account, still exist.

Tomaso tries to reconcile these tensions with a profound moral ethic of care that goes beyond the prescribed policies of administration and his curriculum lessons. He reworks and makes his curriculum empathetic to students' needs; and, he maneuvers the administrative financial online system to allow for equity for students in need. When both backfired, Tomaso is left to reawaken his mindset in a rapidly changing world of technology, social justice knowledge of Indigenous People by his students, and his own habits of nature. These experiences show a narrative reformation of policy, curriculum reform and Tomaso's own public confidence. The dialogue he has with students, colleagues, and his own reflection of his teaching experiences, reshapes his life and his students' lives.

4   Case 3: Uncertainty, Resilience and Hope: How Policy Reforms Affect Teachers' Lives and Work (Maria Assunção Flores)

Concerns about student achievement in national and international assessments and the need to raise the standards of teaching and learning have led to the introduction of different kinds of policies in many countries. Portugal is no exception as this third case will show. This case looks at teachers' perceptions and experiences of mandated reforms in Portugal aimed at enhancing student outcomes.

Literature on teacher professionalism has highlighted its complex and dynamic nature which relates not only to the policy environment but also to the ways in which teachers see themselves as professionals and the conditions needed for them to exercise their professionalism. Generally, issues such as intensification and bureaucratization, increased forms of managerialism, and greater accountability and public scrutiny are but a few examples of the changes in the teaching profession identified in the literature (Day, 1999; Helsby, 2000; Osborn, 2006; Day, Flores, & Viana, 2007; Kelchtermans, 2009; Flores, 2012). In many countries, teachers' work has been characterized by "ruptures rather than continuities" (Carlgren, 1999, p. 44). Issues such as the existence of greater control over teachers' work and performance of schools (Ball, 2003) through accountability mechanisms has led to more pressure upon schools and teachers to increase standards of teaching, learning and achievement (Osborn, 2006; Day & Smethem, 2009), a culture of managerialism and performativity (Ozga, 2000) and standardization and overregulation (Hargreaves, 2003) of teaching and teachers' work.

This case draws on two recent research projects. The first one is a 3-year research project (2011–2014) which included three phases of data collection, including a national survey in which 2702 teachers participated (Phase I); semi-structured interviews with principals in 11 schools located in different regions of mainland Portugal and focus group involving 99 teachers and focus groups involving 108 students in the same 11 schools (Phase II) and the design, implementation and evaluation of a 1-year professional development program in which 66 teachers participated (Phase III) (Flores, 2014).

The second research project (2016–2017) included a survey in which 1307 teachers participated. It aimed to shed additional light into the ways in which teachers have been dealing with recent policies and their effects on their work and professional development.

The lowering of the budget for education, salary cuts and lack of career progression, the increase of poverty among children and families, the growing emphasis of an outcome-led orientation perspective to teaching and policies of accountability, intensification, and bureaucratization of teachers' work have been identified especially during the financial and economic crisis (2011–2014) during which austerity measures were intensified as a result of the implementation of the Memorandum of Understanding with the International Monetary Fund, the European Central Bank and the European Commission known as the Troika. Among the policy changes are new mechanisms for teacher evaluation, new protocols for school governance, and the introduction of national exams, and more recent initiatives related to school curriculum, student assessment and inclusion. In general, more pressure has been placed on schools and teachers to increase teaching standards and student achievement. Teacher surplus and the aging of the teaching workforce are also two features that characterize the teaching profession in the Portuguese context. According to the latest TALIS report (OECD, 2019), the average teacher is 44 years old, but in Portugal the average teacher is 49 years of age. The same report states that 47% of Portuguese teachers are aged 50 or above and that there has been a "dramatic change" in this regard since TALIS 2013. In other words, there was a significant increase of teachers aged 50 or above in Portugal from 28% in TALIS 2013 to 47% in TALIS 2018.

4.1 Managing Policy Initiatives: Tensions and Dilemmas in Teachers' Work

Dealing with ongoing and sometimes contradictory policy initiatives and managing tensions and dilemmas in context are at the forefront of teachers' accounts. They reiterated issues of professional instability and insecurity, precarious jobs, intensification and bureaucratization of their work. When asked about the changes that took place in teaching, teachers participating in the national survey (n = 2702) claim that their working conditions deteriorated over the last few years. They state that their workload has increased (96.7%), bureaucracy has increased (95.4%), there was an accentuation of criticism of teachers (92.2%), there was greater control over teachers' work (75.6%), and there was an increase of teachers' public accountability (74.6%). They also reported that the negative image of teaching and teachers in the media (90.0%) has led to the deterioration of the teaching profession. The following quotes are illustrative of this:

> There are lots of documents that you need to fill in. I mean you could do important work at the department meetings. But because of changes you always need to adapt documents. So, every year there is always something new to be done. Changes in government mean ongoing changes. (...) But pressure is too high, you need to do meetings, you need to adapt things that sometimes in practice are meaningless. (Primary school teacher, 26 years of teaching)

> Bureaucracy is all over your work ... you need to report on everything, bureaucratic tasks have increased over the last few years (...) Every year there is something new. Your work is more and more demanding in terms of bureaucratic tasks. (Secondary school teacher, 23 years of teaching)

> The lack of motivation is leading many people to leave teaching. They have asked to be retired ahead of time. As a teacher, you are confronted with a novelty almost every day and this is hard especially for the oldest teachers. (Secondary school teacher, 23 years of teaching)

Teachers clearly identified the ways in which their lives have been affected by the deterioration of their working conditions and policy initiatives. The lack of career prospects, the lack of valorisation of the teaching profession, the lack of motivation and feelings of tiredness and disappointment were emphasized in their accounts.

Amongst the more critical aspects are the massive legislation impacting upon schools and teachers' work (a legislative "tsunami" that invades schools (as one of the teachers described it) and bureaucracy: "Bureaucratic procedures (...) administrative and bureaucratic records have been increasing in recent years"; "I see my work a bit of in a schizophrenic way. It is really how I feel. You have to comply with curricula and programs and all the paperwork that is required ... it is difficult to manage it". Added to this are feelings of uncertainty related to the deterioration of the working conditions and to endless changes at a policy level "The most problematic factor is the news, the lack of safety and instability (...) you never know what tomorrow will bring".

4.2   *External Pressures and Teachers' Responses: The Capacity for Resilience*

In the face of ongoing changes and dilemmas in teaching, some teachers seem to adopt a survival perspective, but others tend to become more resilient. The survival perspective was marked by external pressures linked to greater control, an increase in workload and in bureaucracy, greater public accountability, greater emphasis on an outcome-oriented perspective of teaching along with endless changes in education through top-down policy initiatives.

However, teachers' professional values, their sense of professionalism and their capacity for being resilient (despite the negative policy environment and the challenging social and economic context) as well as their sense of identity as teachers explain why some teachers seem to become more resilient and resistant than others (Flores, in press). Along with this are issues of self-image as a teacher, professional values sense of professionalism, as well as the influence of school culture and leadership (Flores, 2018). As Gu and Day (2007, p. 1314) assert, resilience is determined by "the *interaction* between the internal assets of the individual and the external environments in which the individual lives and grows (or does not grow)" (emphasis in original). The following passages illustrate this:

> As a teacher you may be de-motivated with regard to salary cuts, and to the lack of career progression, but in regard to your work with your pupils, your classes, the families, etc. you do the best you can. (Elementary school teacher, 17 years of teaching)

> There is heavy workload ... Nowadays you need to do more in schools with fewer resources. This means extra work for you as a teacher ... and you need to do your best against the odds. (Elementary school teacher, 27 years of experience)

> The impression that I have in regard to my colleagues is that they are tired, exhausted, de-motivated but willing to be with their pupils. You can influence your pupils and this has to do with your action as a professional, your ability to mobilize knowledge and to enhance their motivation (...) Each day you take all your energy and you go to the classroom to get your work done. (Primary school teacher, 25 years of teaching)

Looking at resilience as "a construct that is relative, developmental, dynamic, connoting the positive adaptation and development of individuals in the presence of challenging circumstances" (Gu & Day, 2007, p. 1305) enables the analysis of teachers' work and lives in contexts that are more and more characterized by increasing contradictory demands and expectations as a result of intense school reform.

4.3 Core Issues of Teaching, Professionalism and Hope

The teachers participating in the two research projects highlighted the changing nature of their work and the complexities and tensions in their daily lives. Amongst other features they spoke of the need to focus on teaching, on teacher collaboration and on pupils' learning needs and well-being but they stressed at the same time the pressure for immediate results within a context marked by greater accountability and control (see also Ben-Peretz & Flores, 2018). As Lipman (2009, p. 71) argues, accountability regimes "created and exacerbated contradictions between substantive long-term projects to improve teaching and learning, and short-term accountability-driven goals".

When asked about the key dimensions of their work, teachers (n = 1307) highlighted the pedagogical and collaborative elements of their work such as motivating pupils (66.1%), devising new strategies for them to learn better (62.1%) and reflection on their work in the classroom (53.7%) as the most important ones. Following their work in the classroom, the Portuguese teachers also stressed the collaborative work with colleagues (49.2%) and professional learning (46.1%) as two key dimensions of their profession. Not surprisingly, doing administrative work was the least important dimension identified by the teachers (1.3%). However, sharing materials with colleagues (16.8%), using ICT (11.5%) and assessing pupils' learning (16.2%) were also less valued dimensions of their work although these are considered to be relevant to improve teaching and learning in schools and classrooms. This is even more interesting at a time when the use of ICT and the classroom of the future have been widely discussed. The over emphasis on summative (and external) assessment that has been highlighted may explain why Portuguese teachers do now attach importance to assessing pupils' work even if it is important to redefine pedagogical strategies in the classroom.

As such it is possible to identify in teachers' accounts sources of motivation and resilience but also reasons for hope in teaching. Their professional attitudes and motivational responses are related to the core issues of teaching, particularly to its moral, social and relational dimensions. Thus, despite the external negative factors impacting on their work and lives, their professional attitude and ethical and emotional commitment were associated with their ability to make decisions and choices between what their considered to be the essential and non-essential elements in teaching. Their professional responses were influenced by their values and sense of professionalism but also by contextual factors such as school culture and leadership.

Although most of them spoke of the lack of social recognition, low morale and feelings of tiredness, issues such as the joy of teaching and commitment to pupils were also identified. Elements such as inclusion, meaningful learning, and the affective-relational dimension in the teaching and learning process, the promotion of pupil involvement at school were reiterated in their accounts. This is in line with earlier research in the context of changes in educational policies marked by bureaucratization in Portugal which showed that negative emotions were related to policy reform whereas positive ones were related to classroom interactions (Bahia, Freire, Amaral, & Estrela, 2013).

> There is no single teacher who does not have a concern in regard to an ethical and social attitude ... at the end of the day it is about pupils ... the concern of not segregating anyone, of including everyone ... (Pre-school teacher, 28 years of experience)

> And now you can ask where I am going to look for strength, willingness, and energy to change? I believe this is an inner thing ... the desire to make a difference ... (Pre-school teacher, 28 years of experience)

> It is professionalism that makes you do what you do ... nobody is able to deal with so much work ... it is because teachers are professionals that they do what they do. (Elementary school teacher, 33 years of teaching)

Teachers emphasized their commitment to pupils, to their learning and well-being as well as their hope in teaching. This view resonates with Cribb's discussion (2009, p. 40) of the "ethical reasons for resisting work-role pressures". As he argues, "we might simultaneously accept an obligation to conform while using our individual and collective efforts to redefine and redraw these same role commitments" (p. 40).

4.4   Case 3: Interim Summary

Findings suggest that recent Portuguese policy initiatives associated with austerity measures and the economic crisis have led to a decrease in teachers' motivation, to greater control of their work, to an increase of their workload and bureaucracy and to the deterioration of their working conditions, including their social economic status. Data also indicate that teachers have been subject to greater public scrutiny and that the image of teaching and teachers in the media has contributed to the weakening of the teaching profession. However, the conclusions also showed that teachers' strong professional values, their sense of professionalism and their capacity for resisting and for being resilient (despite the negative policy environment and the challenging socio-economic context) as well as their sense of identity as teachers emerged from the data to explain the ways in which some teachers became more resilient than others.

This finding concurs with Day and Gu's (2014, p. xvii) idea of "persistence of hope and endeavor among teachers to do their best" and their notion of "everyday resilience". In sum, factors and sources of teacher motivation and job satisfaction were analyzed in challenging contexts and findings ranged from feelings of frustration and low morale to resilience and professionalism.

5   Case 4: The Unanticipated Influence of Policy Reform on Teachers and a Department in an Urban Middle School in the U.S (Cheryl J. Craig)

This US case, the fourth of our 4-country series, centers on how policy-related reforms unfurled in an urban middle school in the fourth largest urban center in the US T. P. Yaeger, which is located on the longest street in Texas, is one of the oldest and most distinguished campuses in the mid-southern region of the country. It serves some of the richest and poorest teens in America. Because the middle school has been a research site for 20 years (1997–2017), a policy sweep is presented, which shows changes and casualties of changes that were instituted over time.

The main study participants from the literacy department included Daryl Wilson, department head(Craig, 2010, 2013); Laura Curtis, experienced literacy teacher (Craig, 2012); and Anna Dean, a beginning literacy teacher who taught therefore six years before quitting the profession (Craig, 2013, 2014).Policies these three teachers implemented over time involved:(1) standardized teaching methods (Models of Teaching) (1997–2000); (2)standardized teacher communities (Professional Learning Communities) (2002–2006); (3) standardized teaching practices (Readers' and Writers' Workshop) (2007–2009); (4) standardized teacher evaluation (School District Digitized Format) (2009–2012); (5) standardized workbooks (Testing Company-Produced) (2013–2015) and (6) standardized pay-for-performance (Value-Added Measures) (2015–2017). Each of these reforms will be elucidated to show the influence of these various reform policies on teachers and their practices.

5.1   *Standardized Teaching Methods (Models of Teaching) (1997–2000)*
The models of teaching standardized reform effort emanated from a division of the state department of education. Six teaching models were introduced to the Yaeger teachers which they were required to implement "cleanly, not creatively". This meant that the teachers were not allowed to deviate from the

mandated models in their teaching practices. Soon, the teachers resented the models because they did not allow them to "use their own smarts". The teachers' increasing knowledge, forged through their flesh-and-blood in-school experiences, led Daryl Wilson and three of his fellow teachers to concur that "... [school reform] is 'the monkey's paw'. It appears as if it is a gift, but it really is not a gift. It holds many ironies for teachers" (Craig, 2001, p. 301). Hence, when the models of teaching reform – the "monkey's paw" approach to teacher change – ended, 25 of Yaeger's 85 teachers lost their positions because their campus was an in-district charter school. Shortly after that, T. P. Yaeger's long-term principal, Brianna Larson, retired as well, declaring she had "spent too many years on the short end of the stick" (personal communication). She did not like the way the state consultant treated her nor what had happened after-the-fact to Yaeger's faculty. She intimately learned the irony of school reform that Daryl Wilson and his colleagues in the literacy department had foreshadowed in deep and personal ways. In "monkey's paw" fashion, what came to T. P. Yaeger Middle School in the guise of a gift was not a gift because an unprecedented number of teachers lost their jobs, and everyone's autonomy was jeopardized, Brianna Larson's included.

5.2   *Standardized Teacher Communities (Professional Learning Communities (2002–2006)*

The requirement that all schools create professional learning communities (PLC) was a policy mandate of the local school district. As a result, T. P. Yaeger's new principal required that all departments in the middle school form learning communities, which caused significant uneasiness among Yaeger's faculty because no consultation with the teachers had taken place. Laura Curtis storied her cumulative experience of the PLC reform this way:

> Laura: We gained a lot, but we have lost a lot, too. I became unhappy when I realized it [the particular reform] was being forced on us and I began to feel like a butterfly under a pin. A lot of us were feeling that way ...
>
> Cheryl: A butterfly under a pin???
>
> Laura: Yes, I was very uncomfortable with the demeanors of our staff developer and our principal. It was making me feel not in charge of my own teaching when throughout my career I have felt in charge. (Craig, 2012, p. 90)

In the end result, four of the fourteen literacy teachers left Yaeger (some forced; others conscientious objectors), five teachers left the mathematics department (the next department in which the PLC reform would be implemented) and the literacy assistant principal, who was Latina, quit education altogether because she felt "used" in the plan the principal and staff developer had devised. Another unexpected person to exit the school was the principal, who was promoted to a superintendent position in the school district.

5.3   *Standardized Teaching Practices (Readers' and Writers' Workshop 2007–2009)*

After the professional learning community policy-related reform was initially introduced to T. P. Yaeger Middle School, its impact deepened as the demand to teach readers' and writers' workshop morphed into the expectation that all of the Yaeger literacy teachers would teach workshop in the same way.

A major controversy erupted when a new teacher, a male who came to Yaeger a year after the old principal left, a teacher whose terminal degree made him more qualified in literacy, gifted education, teacher development and leadership than the staff developer or any of the administrators, refused to comply with the request. According to Daryl, Laura, Anna and others, the roots of the "head-on collision" (Craig, 2012b, p. 14) between the workshop consultant and the new teacher traced to the basic tenets of workshop as they understood them. The new teacher was vexed by how the consultant had "handcuffed" (Daryl's, word) the Yaeger teachers to her version of workshop (Craig, 2012b, p. 14) at the exclusion of their own or others' versions. When this teacher riled against the standardization the consultant had imposed on the department, she went ballistic. She declared that he was not doing workshop, and that he had been hired to do workshop. He retorted that "what he was hired to do, and who he was hired by, was not the staff developer's business" (Craig, 2012b, p. 15). In the midst of this "crisis", Daryl Wilson and some other literacy colleagues appealed to their new female principal for support. On this occasion, the principal sided with the teachers. Yaeger's neophyte principal knew that "paying a [consultant] to contribute to a group's dysfunction was too much" (Craig, 2014, p. 16). Unfortunately, though, her support came too late. Hence, Yaeger's third policy-related reform ended with three literacy teachers exiting the department and the staff developer not returning because her contract had ended. Also, Yaeger's new principal was appointed to a superintendent position a few months into the following year and the long-term literacy assistant principal retired. As for the new teacher, he was named director of literacy at a nearby school district.

5.4   *Standardized Teacher Evaluation (School District Digitized Format)* (*2009–2012*)

The old literacy assistant principal was replaced by a new assistant principal who had no background in reading and writing and had never taught middle school. Although he had no experience in the area, he was charged by the school district to standardize the literacy teachers' evaluations. He proceeded to judge the quality of the teachers' performances using the Professional Development Assessment System (PDAS), which has 8 domains ranging from successful student participation to compliance with policies and operating procedures to the improvement of all students' academic performances. In the end result, none of Yaeger's literacy teachers retained their 'exceeds expectations' (5/5) ratings on any of the domains of their evaluations. In their individual feedback, a teacher who expressed concerns about teachers not being treated like professionals received a score of 27 points lower than her previous one, Daryl Wilson received a rating 20 points less than his past evaluation, and Anna Dean's score was 32 points lower than what she had been awarded the previous year by Yaeger's past assistant principal. In fact, Anna – the literature department's beginning teacher--had dropped from 5s (exceeds expectations) to 3s (average) in all categories. Domain VII (Compliance with Policies, Operating Procedures and Requirements) was the section where all the teachers received the most problematic feedback. What Anna Dean found most reprehensible about her evaluation was that she "was docked for not setting the discipline policy for the school" – "as if that is my responsibility" (Craig, 2014, p. 107). The year Anna quit teaching in the school district, one ESL teacher, two special education teachers and the assistant principal left T. P. Yaeger Middle School as well.

5.5   *Standardized Workbooks (Testing Company-Produced)* (*2013–2015*)

The next policy-related reform introduced to the literacy department by the school district was the use of workbooks produced by testing companies.

On this occasion, the teachers were given a choice of two commercialized workbooks. Yaeger's teachers dutifully selected the school's preferred workbook. However, the school district subsequently mandated that Yaeger use the workbook the teachers did not choose. The teachers were told that $75,000 (1500 students x $50 per expendable workbook) per year for a purported six years ($450,000) would be committed to purchasing the expendable workbook despite Yaeger being steeped in workshop teaching and historically purchasing novel sets and non-fiction books for instructional purposes. Hence, the teachers found creative ways to hide the workbooks while keeping them in open sight, should a school district inspection occur. Consequently, the standardized workbook reform, which may still be continuing due to contract extensions, was innocuous – with central leadership's wastage of the public purse being the only significant casualty.

5.6   Standardized Pay-For-Performance (Value-Added Measures) (2015–2017)

Before the new school year began, yet another new principal at Yaeger reviewed the pay-for-performance allocations associated with a district-related policy on her campus. She found that some teacher bonuses – while still substantial – had fluctuated. Based on this questionable evidence (i.e., different years = different students = different text scores = different dollar value of bonuses), she proceeded to remove Daryl Wilson from his position as literacy department chair. She took a similar action with at least one other literacy teacher who was a grade-level leader and a supporting research participant in this research. When this decision was made, Yaeger's faculty was dumbfounded. Excellence in teaching, which for nearly a century had successfully scaffolded the learning of thousands of T. P. Yaeger students, no longer felt empowering to them. Instead, their lived experiences had been translated into behavioral data that was being used to diminish their efforts and identities (Zuboff, 2019, p. 53). The logic behind publicly shaming highly reputable teachers by demoting them from their leadership positions raises many questions for which answers may never be known. But what is known is that 80% of the teachers in the large, urban, diverse school district had five or less years of experience and that 50% of the administrators also had five or less years of experience (Craig, 2014).

In short, the level of teacher and principal expertise in the school district – and increasingly at T. P. Yaeger – was extremely "thin" where both teacher and administrator experience was concerned. Further to this, the policy-related reforms introduced to the school over two decades diluted teachers' positives impacts on students through placing ongoing restraints on teachers' practices.

5.7   Case 4: Interim Summary

The American policy sweep shows that most of the six Houston-area policy-driven reforms aimed at improving the quality of literacy instruction for urban youth resulted in unintended consequences that intensified teachers' work and accelerated teacher attrition and/or their early retirement. Only the fifth policy reform had no effect other than creative resistance. Hence, the American case makes vividly apparent that what seems to be the next-best step to policymakers outside of schools can be disastrous to those inside of schools because it does not fit with how teachers work together, alone and with students.

6   Common Themes: Four Countries

Our international inquiry into reform policies indicates that all four countries (Brazil, Canada, Portugal, US) in our sample of convenience are grappling with enormous changes in the global marketplace that are, in turn, affecting education and schooling. Each nation in its own way faces global challenges and keeps a close watch on its international rankings.

Brazil seems to be mirroring the US's policy footsteps and Portugal, for its part, has been affected by the European Union's austerity measures. Canada, which has historically scored higher than the US, seems to be in the introductory stages of putting an accountability policy in place while the US is in an advanced stage of accountability policy development. However, Canada has no national body like the US Department of Education to make its provinces and teachers comply. Also, Canada is known for being more like the Nordic countries and New Zealand where matters of social responsibility and social justice are concerned.

To varying degrees, teachers in all four countries have dealt with outside policy interventions, some burdening teachers' work and others having higher social purposes in mind. On the whole, the countries have not included the professional judgment of their teachers in their policy making. Hence, teacher attrition is a resonant theme echoing across all four cases. Also, there have been negative ramifications on teachers' work with teachers in Brazil and the US being treated aggressively by policy makers (probably due to dropping test scores) and those in Portugal struggling to professionally make up for its nation's shortfall.

Lastly, the mindset of international policy makers needs to be discussed. Repeatedly, those in the policy domain favor top-down approaches to school reform in order to achieve positive results. Fear for the future and narrow views of teachers/teacher professionalism tend to underpin their reform agendas. Unfortunately, the policies they favor are articulated as ready-made solutions not as processes needing teachers' input, which would ensure more productive enactment. Finally, trying to control teachers as a way to improve learning and test scores almost certainly gives way to compliance and resistance. While those in charge know what they want at face value, how they may receive it may be quite a different manner because both compliance and resistance have concomitantly occurred.

References

Antonio, A., Astin, H., & Cress, C. (2000). Community service in higher education: A look at the nation's faculty. *Review of Higher Education, 23*(4), 373–398.

Baldwin, R. G. (1996). Faculty career stages and implications for professional development. In D. Finnegan, D. Webster, & Z. F. Gamson (Eds.), *Faculty and faculty issues in colleges and universities* (2nd ed., pp. 1–11). Boston, MA: Pearson Custom Publishing.

Ball, S., Maguire, M., & Braun, A. (2012) *How schools do policy – Policy enactments in secondary schools.* London: Routledge.

Barber, M., &Mourshed, M. (2007). *How the world's best performing systems came out on top.* London: McKinsey & Company.

Ben-Peretz, M., & Flores, M. A. (2018). Tensions and paradoxes in teaching: implications for teacher education. *European Journal of Teacher Education, 41*(2), 202–213.

Carlgren, I. (1999). Professionalism and teachers as designers. *Journal of Curriculum Studies, 31*(1), 43–56.

Ciuffetelli Parker, D. (2013). Narrative understandings of poverty and schooling: Reveal, revelation, reformation of mindsets. *International Journal for Cross-Disciplinary Subjects in Education (IJCDSE), 3*(2) (Special Issue).

Ciuffetelli Parker, D. (2014). Literacy narratives for 21st century curriculum making: The 3Rs to excavate diverse issues in education. In C. J. Craig & L. Orland-Barak (Eds.), *International teacher education: Promising pedagogies (Part A)* (pp. 233–253). Bingley: Emerald Publishing.

Ciuffetelli Parker, D., & Craig, C. (2017). An international inquiry: Stories of poverty – poverty stories. *Urban Education, 52*(1), 120–151.

Ciuffetelli Parker, D., Murray Orr, A., Mitton-Kukner, J., Griffin, S., & Pushor, D. (2017). Problematizing complexities and pedagogy in teacher education programs: Enacting knowledge in a narrative inquiry teacher education discourse community. *Canadian Journal of Education, 40*(2).

Ciuffetelli Parker, D., & Pushor, D. (2014). How to make teacher education better: The making of an international narrative inquiry teacher education discourse community. In S. Feller & I. Yengin (Eds.), *21st century education: Constructing meaning and building knowledge in technology supported learning environments* (pp. 181–202). Dialogue Series. Amsterdam, the Netherlands: John Benjamins.

Clandinin, D. J., & Connelly, F. M. (1992). Teacher as curriculum maker. In P. Jackson (Ed.), *Handbook of curriculum* (pp. 363–461). New York, NY: Macmillan.

Clandinin, D. J., & Connelly, F. M. (2000). *Narrative inquiry: Experience and story in qualitative research.* San Francisco, CA: Jossey-Bass.

Connelly, F. M., & Clandinin, D. J. (1990). Stories of experience and narrative inquiry. *Educational Researcher, 19*(5), 2–14.

Craig, C. (2001). The relationships between and among teachers' narrative knowledge, communities of knowing, and school reform: A case of "The Monkey's Paw". *Curriculum Inquiry, 31*(3), 303–331.

Craig, C. (2009). Research in the midst of organized school reform: Tensions in teacher community. *American Educational Research Journal, 46*(2), 598–619.

Craig, C. (2010). Coming full circle: From teacher reflection to classroom action and back again. *Teachers &Teaching: Theory & Practice, 16*(4), 423–435.

Craig, C. (2012). "Butterfly under a pin": An emergent image of teaching amid mandated curriculum reform. *Journal of Educational Research, 105*(2), 1–12.

Craig, C. (2013). Coming to know in the 'eye of a storm': A beginning teacher's introduction to different versions of teacher community. *Teaching and Teacher Education, 29*, 25–38.

Craig, C. (2013). Teacher education and the best-loved self. *Asia-Pacific Journal of Education, 33*(3), 261–272.

Craig, C. (2014). From stories of staying to stories of leaving: A US beginning teacher's experience. *Journal of Curriculum Studies, 41*(1), 81–115.

Craig, C., & Ross, V. (2008). Cultivating the image of teachers as curriculum makers. In F. M. Connelly, M. F. He, & J. Phillion (Eds.), *The Sage handbook of curriculum and instruction* (pp. 282-305). Thousand Oaks, CA: Sage.

Cribb, A. (2009). Professional ethics: Whose responsibility? In S. Gewirtz, P. Mahony, I. Hextall, & A. Cribb (Eds.), *Changing teacher professionalism. International trends, challenges and ways forward* (pp. 31–42). London: Routledge.

Darling-Hammond, L. (2000). Teacher quality and student achievement. *Education Policy Analysis Archives, 8*, 1.

Day, C., Flores, M., & Viana, I. (2007). Effects of national policies on teachers' sense of professionalism: Findings from an empirical study in Portugal and in England. *European Journal of Teacher Education, 30*(3), 249–266.

Day, C., & Gu, Q. (2014). *Resilient teachers, resilient schools*. London: Routledge.

Day, C. (1999). *Developing teachers. The challenges of lifelong learning*. London: Falmer Press.

Day, C., & Smethem, L. (2009). The effects of reform: Have teachers really lost their sense of professionalism? *Journal of Educational Change, 10*, 141–157.

DfE. (2010). *The case for change* (DFE-00564-2010). London: Department for Education.

Falkenberg, T., Goodnough, K., & MacDonald, R. (2014). Views on and practices of integrating theory and practice in teacher education programs in Atlantic Canada. *Alberta Journal of Educational Research, 60*(2), 339–360.

Flores, M. A. (2012). Teachers' work and lives: A European perspective. In C. Day (Ed.), *The Routledge international handbook of teacher and school development*. London: Routledge.

Flores, M. A. (2014). *Profissionalismo e Liderança dos Professores*. Santo Tirso, PT: De Facto Editores.

Flores, M. A. (2018). Teacher resilience in adverse contexts: Issues of professionalism and professional identity. In M. Wosnitza, F. Peixoto, S. Beltman, & C. F. Mansfield (Eds.), *Resilience in education. concepts, contexts and connections* (pp. 167–184). Cham: Springer.

Flores, M. A. (in press). Surviving, being resilient and resisting: Teachers' experiences in adverse times. *Cambridge Journal of Education.* doi:10.1080/0305764X.2019.1664399

Fullan, M. (Ed.). (2010). *All systems go: The change imperative for whole system reform.* Thousand Oaks, CA: Corwin Press.

Giroux, H. (1988). *Teachers as intellectuals: Toward a critical pedagogy for learning.* Westport, CT: Bergen & Garvey.

Goodnough, K., Falkenberg, T., & MacDonald, R. (2016). Examining the nature of theory-practice relationships in initial teacher education: A Canadian case study. *Canadian Journal of Education, 39*(1), 1–28.

Goodson, I. (2007). All the lonely people: The struggle for private meaning and public purpose in education. *Critical Studies in Education, 48*(1), 131–148.

Goodson, I. (2008). *As políticas de currículo e a escolarização: abordagens históricas.* Petrópolis, RJ: Vozes.

Grimmet, P. P. (2009). The governance of Canadian teacher education: A macro-political perspective. In F. Benson & C. Riches (Eds.), *Engaging in conversation about ideas in teacher education* (pp. 22–32). New York, NY: Peter Lang.

Grimmett, P. P., Young, J., & Lessard, C. (2012). *Teacher certification and the professional status of teaching in North America: The new battleground for public education.* Charlotte, NC: Information Age Publishing.

Gu, Q., & Day, C. (2007). Teachers resilience: A necessary condition for effectiveness. *Teaching and Teacher Education, 23,* 1302–1316.

Hargreaves, A. (2003) *Teaching in the knowledge society: Education in the age of insecurity.* Maidenhead: Open University Press.

Helsby, G. (2000). Multiple truths and contested realities. The changing faces of teacher professionalism in England. In C. Day, A. Fernandez, T. E. Hauge, & J. Moller (Eds.), *The life and work of teachers. International perspectives in changing times.* London: Falmer Press.

Kelchtermans, G. (2009). O comprometimento profissional para além do contrato: Auto-comprensão, vulnerabilidade e reflexão dos professores. In M. A. Flores & A. M. Veiga Simão (Eds.), *Aprendizagem e desenvolvimento profissional de professores: contextos e perspectivas.* Mangualde, PT: EdiçõesPedago.

King, M. L. (1963). *Letter from the Birmingham jail.* University of Alabama.

Lipman, P. (2009). Paradoxes in teaching in neo-liberal times: Education 'reform' in Chicago. In S. Gewirtz, P. Mahony, I. Hextall, & A. Cribb (Eds.), *Changing teacher professionalism. International trends, challenges and ways forward* (pp. 67–80). London: Routledge.

Maguire, M. (2010). Toward a sociology of the global teacher. In M. Apple, S. Ball, & L. A. Gand (Eds.), *The Routledge handbook of the sociology of education* (pp. 58–68). Milton Park: Routledge.

Marcondes, M. I. (2017). Desenvolvimento Curricular e Materiais Padronizados no Contexto Brasileiro. In M. A. Flores (Ed.), *Práticas e Discursos sobre Currículo e Avaliação: contributos para aprofundar um debate* (1st ed., pp. 55–80). Santo Tirso, Portugal: De Facto Editore.

Marcondes, M. I., Freund, C., & Leite, V. F. (2017). Uma nova abordagem ao estudo das políticas educacionais. *Práxis Educativa* (UEPG, Online), *12*, 1–7.

Morison, S. E. (1936). *Harvard College in the seventeenth century*. Cambridge, MA: Harvard University Press.

OECD. (2010). *Education at a glance 2010: OECD indicators*. Paris: OECD.

OECD. (2019). *TALIS 2018 results: Teachers and school leaders as lifelong learners* (Vol. I). Paris: TALIS, OECD Publishing. https://doi.org/10.1787/1d0bc92a-en

Olson, M., & Craig, C. (2009). Small stories and mega-stories: Accountability in balance. *Teachers College Record, 111*(2), 547–572.

Osborn, M. (2006). Changing the context of teachers' work and professional development: A European perspective. *International Journal of Educational Research, 45*, 242–253.

Ozga, J. (2000). Education: New labour, new teachers. In J. Clark, S. Gewirtz, & E. McLaughlin (Eds.), *New managerialism, new welfare?* London: Sage.

Pollard, A. (2010). *Professionalism and pedagogy: A contemporary opportunity.* A commentary by the Teaching and Learning Research Programme and the General Teaching Council for England.

Schwab, J. J. (1969). The practical: A language for curriculum. *School Review, 78*(1), 1–2.

Schwab, J. J. (1971). The practical: Arts of eclectic. *School Review, 79*, 493–542.

Schwab, J. J. (1983). The practical 4: Something for curriculum professors to do. *Curriculum Inquiry, 13*(3), 239–265.

Walker, J., & von Bergmann, H. (2013). Teacher education policy in Canada: Beyond professionalism and deregulation. *Canadian Journal of Education, 36*(4), 65–92.

Young, J., & Boyd, K. (2010). More than servants of the state: The governance of initial teacher preparation in Canada in an era of school reform. *Alberta Journal of Educational Research, 56*(1), 1–18.

Zeichner, K. (2008, October). *Neo-liberal ideas and the transformation of teacher education in the U.S.* Keynote address, International Conference – "Justice, Equality, and Efficiency: Educational policy under the situation of Multiple Societies, East China Normal University, Shangai.

Zuboff, S. (2019). *The age of surveillance capitalism: The fight for a human future at the new frontier of power.* New York, NY: Public Affairs.

CHAPTER 2

Student Voice in Teaching Writing

Vassiliki Tzika, Stavroula Kaldi, Evgenia Vassilaki and Christos Govaris

Abstract

This chapter aims to explore student voice about literacy instruction and more specifically writing. Student voice is considered as a fundamental right that includes not only students' views but also their feelings, motives or ideas, their participation and collaboration in the teaching and learning process. A significant facet of this process is writing instruction through which students learn how to express their voice in a variety of everyday life situations integrated into the school curriculum. Writing involves synthetic, divergent and critical thinking, and provides the opportunity for students to develop their meta-cognitive skills. The study is theoretically based on student voice and the process approach of teaching writing, incorporating aspects of community learning, constructivism, collaborative learning and multicultural education.

The research method was qualitative and the research tools used were structured interviews and classroom observation field notes. Participants were 20 Year-5 and Year-6 native and non-native students in Greek primary schools. Thematic analysis was applied in order to identify categories, subcategories and modes within them concerning student voice in literacy instruction and teaching writing.

The outcomes showed that students hold a positive stance towards literacy instruction and writing, although they face various difficulties in each writing stage. Some differences appeared between native and non-native students' voices concerning the understanding of textual genres, the teacher's support, the instructional strategies applied and students' suggestions for improving the learning process. The findings are discussed within the theoretical framework of equal opportunities in school education.

Keywords

student voice – teaching writing – multicultural education – collaborative learning – process approach – elementary classroom – student-centred approach – interviews – thematic analysis – qualitative research

1 Introduction

This chapter aims to explore student voice during the teaching and the learning process and more specifically during writing instruction in Year-5 and Year-6 Greek classes.

Student voice is strongly related to fundamental child's right to education according to the United Nations Convention on the Rights of Child (UNCRC, 1989). During the last decades, the inclusion of students from diverse cultural backgrounds is an indispensable part and duty of the teacher's role (Bragg, 2007; Kumar & Lauermann, 2017). Student voice can lead to multifaceted development of personality and skills of every student through a variety of educational experiences. Active student participation during class has been also claimed to be an urgent quest but teachers are not often very willing to make it happen or do not have the appropriate instructional skills (Appleton et al., 2008).

Therefore, there is a constant need for the student voice to be heard in the learning process as well as for the design of appropriate pedagogical techniques in writing instruction in order to become a more student-friendly, participative and essential process for students who are about to adopt a more active role (Jeffery & Wilcox, 2013; Jesson & Rosedale, 2016).

2 Theoretical Framework

The term "student voice" first appeared the 1970's in Meighan's research (1978a) "The learners' viewpoint: Exploitation of the pupil perspectives on schooling". This research field was extremely neglected but an emerged need for a fuller understanding of students' school life triggered the research interest.

Meighan (1978b) also reported that the biggest obstacle he faced was teachers. They often disapproved his attempt suggesting that "students are not neither able nor mature enough so as to consider or discuss about such teaching issues"; this is still happening to an extent until nowadays (Rudduck, 2006). Hopefully, despite such kind of difficulties, some organizations appeared with aim the promotion and the enactment of student voice.[1] The first official definition attempt was made by the United Nations Convention on the Rights of Child (UNCRC) in 1989. They define student voice like a child's right to express his/her perspective (Article 12) and since then student voice makes an impact as an attempt or a need of transforming schools into places more friendly to knowledge and learning where students have different perspectives for learning, teaching and school (Cook-Sather, 2006, p. 1; Rogers, 2005).

As Cook-Sather (2006) points out, student voice could be seen as "opinion", "ability", "participation", "active listening and response" which unsettle the traditional student role as a passive receiver giving the opportunity of a new, more active role. In the relevant literature, there are many definitions for student voice that mutually complete and reinforce each other. Student voice is not only about students' words but also includes the expression of their emotions or ideas on a variety of issues that are important for them referring to their active opportunities in order to make decisions about planning, implementing and assessing their learning experiences (Robinson & Taylor, 2007; Rogers, 2005).

Moreover, it refers to a variety of activities both inside and outside the classroom as a form of creative expression, motivation for active participation, collaboration in the teaching and learning process and a better understanding of it (Toshalis & Nakkula, 2012). This kind of expression affects not only their learning but also the relationships with their classmates and their life outside school (Harper, 2000, as cited in Britton et al., 2014, p. 4). It is regarded as an effort to make schools better and student-friendly places in order for students to learn and to live in a democratic environment within the spirit of community-based learning incorporating principles of intercultural education through constructive approaches and project-based learning (Bahou, 2011; Fielding, 2010; Robinson & Taylor, 2007; Rogers, 2005; Toshalis & Nakkula, 2012).

According to Flutter and Rudduck (2004, p. 135) "education is for students and that's why they must have a say for it". This quote makes us better understand the fundamental aim of student voice which searches for a cultural transformation of the educational system and educational mentality (Baker et al., 2005; Cook-Sather, 2006, p. 5) based on four values: (a) communication, (b) participation and democratic spirit, (c) ability to transform, and (d) dynamic relationships (NASUWT, 2012, pp. 6–10; Robinson & Taylor, 2007).

Student voice reforms, as mentioned above, the student role in the teaching and learning process. More specifically, the student is regarded as a data source (Cook-Sather, 2006; Fielding, 2004). He/she expresses himself/herself through activities and the teacher is able to elicit and collect the needed information according to learning goals. Moreover, the student is able to be an active respondent who talks in groups about their learning experiences, shares or evaluates learning goals and formats small groups as student councils in order to solve minor or major problems (Cook-Sather, 2006; Fielding, 2004).

Another important role that a student can adopt, in the student voice context, is the role of a researcher or a co-researcher. Students in small groups, either with or without teacher's guidance, decide about an issue for investigation, discuss, divide roles, make a research, collect data, draw outcomes and discuss and reflect about their findings, shaping actively their learning according to their interests, needs, abilities and skills (Baker et al., 2005; Cook-Sather, 2006; Fielding, 2004, 2010).

Last but not least, the student is able to be a co-creator of the course design, teaching approaches and even curricula (Bovill et al., 2011; Jagersma & Parsons, 2011; Joseph, 2006). These roles differ in extent according to the degree of students' participation. So, the impact of student voice can range successively from sole expression and recommendation to participation, collaboration and ultimately, mutual management of the teaching and learning process (*Student Voice: Transforming Relationships*, 2013).

Previous research has tracked down some domains which are enhanced when student voice is actually heard and taken into consideration. More specifically, students' active participation and engagement in the task is increased when they have more opportunities and choices to reinforce their self-esteem and responsibility (Manefield et al., 2007, pp. 13–14; *Student Voice: Transforming Relationships*, 2013; Shanker, 2013).

Moreover, teachers adopt a different perspective for teaching and learning because they regard their students as more energetic, more powerful in knowledge construction by creative ways and consequently students' behavior improves because they feel welcome and useful (Peacock, 2011; Wien, 2008, as cited in *Student Voice: Transforming Relationships*, 2013, p. 4). This has an undeniably great impact on interpersonal students' relationships between each other and between students and their teachers as they share common learning experiences, interests and difficulties. What's more, under such a school context students with an immigrant background feel safer, more familiar and acceptable to express themselves and to participate (Mitra, 2009; *Student Voice: Transforming Relationships*, 2013). The whole school community is developing, finding resourceful, innovative and more student-friendly solutions to a variety of problems that affect students' everyday life (Bahou, 2011, p. 4; Bovill et al., 2011, p. 8; Ngussa & Makewa, 2014, p. 26; *Student Voice: Transforming Relationships*, 2013).

As a result, students feel a stronger commitment to the teaching and learning process and school (Crawford et al., 1999, as cited in Jagersma & Parsons, 2011, p. 117; Manefield et al., 2007, p. 9). They respect and trust each other and phenomena of behavioral problems or bulling are fading (Bovill et al., 2011, p. 9; Manefield et al., 2007, pp. 9, 14; *Student Voice: Transforming Relationships*, 2013).

Except for students, teachers are also highly benefited by the adoption and implementation of student voice. They are fellow-travelers with their students in the journey of knowledge construction and they re-define their role discovering their potentials and abilities through a different perspective (Bahou, 2011, pp. 3–4; Toshalis & Nakkula, 2012, pp. 25–26).

However, the incorporation of student voice in the teaching and learning process may be challenged by the part of the teachers and the school routine. As a result, further research is needed to provide insights into the ways that student voice could be incorporated and the challenges faced within this process (Bahou, 2011).

Student voice can also be integrated during teaching writing. Internationally, the mainstream teaching approach of writing is process-based combining elements of the genre-based approach (Behrman, 2006). This approach emphasizes on the process, the content and the communicative context. It is structured in three stages (a) pre-writing/planning, (b) drafting/translating and (c) post-writing/revising stage, each one with its own meaning and validity (Bereiter & Scardamalia, 1987; Ferguson-Patrick, 2007; Flower & Hayes, 1981; Matsagouras, 2009, pp. 174, 215, 240; Spantidakis, 2011, pp. 28–32).

Specifically, the first stage (pre-writing/planning) has consisted of three successive phases: (a) "contextualization", i.e. embedding of the text in authentic contexts of students' everyday life according to their interests, motives, problems in order to decide as a team about the goals, the role, the genre, the style and the audience of their text, (b) generation of ideas via more structured or less structured techniques and (c)organization of ideas using field notes, keywords or concept maps in order to gather together what students need for the production of their text.

The second stage (drafting) consists of only one phase, the phase of initial textualization. During this stage, the ideas and the thoughts of the previous one are recorded on paper and the student is called to combine them in a coherent text using the appropriate grammar and vocabulary (Matsagouras, 2009, pp. 243–246; Michalis, 2011; Spantidakis, 2011, pp. 32–33).

The third and last stage is called post-writing or revising and it has also consisted of three successive phases. In the first phase of improving the initial text, students should reconsider their initial text adding or extracting structural parts, reviewing vocabulary and expressions, checking for clarity and other editing developments, as a process for students' self-regulation. The second phase concerns the final editing of the written text. The third phase is about the evaluation of the final product in terms of the goals set at the first stage and the procedures followed. This phase is difficult, cognitively demanding but very essential for students and teachers (Matsagouras, 2009; Michalis, 2011; Spantidakis, 2011, pp. 32–33).

The process-based approach in teaching writing has its strong and weak points.

It is structured in stages, which helps students to be focused on the demands of each one, therefore it seems to be a beneficial process for students. Cognitive and meta-cognitive skills, divergent and synthetic thought are promoted (Graham & Sandmel, 2011; Graham, et. al., 2013). Moreover, the approach provides teaching tools to accommodate the instructional needs of individual students, because each stage is constructed and guided if necessary (Graham & Sandmel, 2011, p. 397; Matsagouras, 2009). Last but not least, it enhances collaboration among students and peer problem-solving activities which further empower students; motivation and engagement (Graham & Sandmel, 2011).

On the other hand, this process-based approach can be time-consuming, especially in the first times of implementation until all participants feel more familiar with this process (Michalis, 2011).

However, research has shown that these three stages of teaching writing are not fully followed by primary school teachers. They mainly claim that there is a lack of time in timetable schedule; they also claim that its implementation is hindered by the presence of bilingual students in the classroom, which is also the case for the Greek context (Garcia-Sanchez & de Caso-Fuertes, 2004; Skourtou, 2007).

Hopefully, the above-mentioned obstacles could be surpassed. Teachers need to organize beforehand school time and program very well. Besides, students' first languages should be turned to an advantage for all if they are wisely integrated into the learning process (Kourti-Kazouli, 2000, as cited in Skourtou, 2007, p. 155; Vassilaki, 2013).

Moreover, recent research has indicated many factors that affect writing. Motives, interests, perspectives, and feelings of students, which constitute student voice, play an important role in their writing. Eventually, if the school climate is positive and triggers students, they become more confident and safe to create and cultivate their self-respect and self-esteem on what they can achieve or on what they need to improve (Garcia-Sanchez & de Caso-Fuertes, 2004, p. 142; Hashemian & Heidari, 2013, p. 477; Pajares & Valiante, 2001, p. 367).

However, more research is needed internationally due to the lack of information about the native and the immigrant student voices during teaching writing in primary schools.

Therefore, this study aims to address student voice about their school reality and more specifically their views about teaching writing in the primary school classroom. The contribution of the present study lies in the attempt to create a new school climate where teaching and learning are based on students' active participation and engagement.

Subsequently, our research questions are framed as follows: (1) What does student voice tell us about writing?, (2) To what extent is student voice taken

into account in the process of teaching writing? and (3) Are there any differences between the voices of Greek native students and students with an immigrant background in the process of writing instruction?

3   Research Method

The present study follows the qualitative paradigm of research. Qualitative
research methods are commonly used to capture student's deeper beliefs and
perceptions and the quality assurance pylons, such as credibility, transferability, dependability and confirmability were under consideration (Braun &
Clarke, 2006). The data were processed via qualitative thematic analysis
(Charalampous & Kokkinos, 2017).

Participants were twenty (20) students of four (4) Year-5 and four (4) Year-6
classes. They were selected via conveniently sampling strategies from public
elementary schools in urban and semi-urban areas of central Greece. Fifteen
(15) of them were Greek native students and five (5) were students with an
immigrant background. More specifically, there were eight (8) native girls,
seven (7) native boys, and three (3) girls and two (2) boys with an immigrant
background respectively.

The conduct of the research lasted about one month. Two research tools
were employed: (a) formal structured interviews and (b) non-systematic
non-participant observation of the teaching and learning process and more
specifically of teaching writing.

Formal structured interviews were undertaken individually for each student.
The interview's context was pre-defined but if needed, there was question flexibility so as to elicit as much information as possible. It is worth-mentioned
that the school director, teachers, parents, and students were informed of the
research aim before their volunteer participation. They were also reassured
about the anonymous and confidential character of the research (Isari &
Pourkos, 2015, pp. 88–93).

The interview guide was constructed by the authors of the chapter based on
previous research studies with the necessary adjustments to the requirements
of the study and was divided into three sections. In the first section, there were
general questions for ice-breaking and making students feel more comfortable. For example, "How are you?", "What's your name?", "How was your day?",
"Have you ever been interviewed?", etc. The questions of the second section
referred to the teaching and learning process. Some characteristic examples
follow: "Do you like school? What do you like more or less about it?", "Do you
give your advice to your classmates or your teacher?", "Do you participate in

problem-solving discussions among your classmates and teacher? If not, would you like to?", "Do you feel free to choose your exercises or all of them are compulsory for everybody?", "Do you cooperate in order to find solutions in daily problems? Are your opinions taken into consideration of teacher?", "Why do you study?", etc. The third section focused on teaching writing. For instance, "Do you like writing? What do you like more or less?", "When, where and how would you like to write?", "What do you think that writing offers to you?", "How do you feel when teacher asks you to write about a topic?", "Do you think that it is important to learn how to write a good text according to communicative circumstances?", "If you were a teacher and one of your students asked you what is good writing, what would you reply?", "Do you face writing difficulties? Which? How do you manage to surpass them?", "Before you begin writing, what are your steps?", "During writing about what do you care? Do you need help? From whom?", "When you finish writing, what is your next step?", "How does your teacher correct your writing?", "Do you have the opportunity to revise your writing? If not, would you like to?", etc. The interview ended with questions about how he/she felt during the interview, if he/she would like to add something more and a thankful certification of participation.

We would like to mention that the results of the second section of the interview guide are not a part of this chapter because it focuses on teaching writing.

The research tool of non-systematic and non-participant observation was also used in the research field (Braun & Clarke, 2006; Papanastasiou & Papanastasiou, 2005). There were some indicative axes according to which field notes were taken such as teaching writing, student participation, pedagogical climate and classroom's material environment decoration. All interviews and observations were transcribed and coded. The analysis of the qualitative data was constructed on three successive levels. The first one was the formation of thematic categories and subcategories. The second one was the cross-tabulation of the units of discourse analysis to the thematic categories and the last one was the identification of motives and several greater themes of the analysis.

4 Results

The main outcomes of this study indicate that student voice is an authentic source of information and is connected to the current research literature pointing out its emergent role in the learning process. Student participants express positive attitudes towards the literacy class and the writing process, which are claimed to be a pleasant learning experience for both native and nonnative students with future benefits for them: "I like it (literacy class) very much because you learn how to express correctly, how to talk to others" (INT13-SM/N-Y5),[2] "I like to write down my adventures" (INT3-SM/N-Y5), "I like it because we will create something on our own" (INT5-SM/N-Y5), "It is beneficial because when we will grow, we should know and check what a text tells us to do and what it means" (INT16-SM/NN-Y6).

However, writing texts seems difficult to them. This difficulty is often strongly linked with their spelling skills: "I don't like doing spelling mistakes" (INT19-SF/NN-Y5) or with class noise: "When there is noise I cannot concentrate to write" (INT7-SM/N-Y5). Also, writing difficulties are attributed to the lack of understanding, knowledge or imagination to write: "If a child doesn't understand ... for example, I must know something about what I am going to write" (INT15-SF/N-Y6), "I don't know what to write sometimes ..." (INT13-SM/N-Y5), "If we do not write often, we do not practice and we cannot write well" (INT8-SM/N-Y5).

Moreover, students' voice doesn't seem to be taken into account during writing instruction because the process is strictly guided by the teacher who does not give students opportunities to express their opinions or take initiatives: "He tells us how to start and we continue ... then he gives us more instructions" (INT9-SF/NN-Y5), "I would like to write something ... with my friends, ... as a team, but the teacher doesn't let us ..." (INT11-SM/N-Y6). According to their views, the whole learning process during writing instruction is mainly focused on grades and a monolithic type of assessment whereas constructive feedback and metacognitive skills are not included in the learning process: "I want to get a good grade" (INT16-SM/NN-Y6), "The teacher doesn't give it back to us to make any corrections. He only puts a grade on it and that's all" (INT18-SF/NN-Y5).

Concerning the differences between native Greek and immigrant students' reports about using writing strategies or asking for teacher's help, immigrant students appeared to face more difficulties because they lacked knowledge about the genre types and they did not receive or even asked for any support during this process: "Yes, I know ... We don't write the same things ... The context differs when we describe something or when the teacher gives instructions but I need help" (INT8-SM/N-Y5). They do not refer to their families as a source for help: "I write it alone" (INT17-SF/NN-Y6). They do not know and do not have any favorite genre types, they only restrict to texts they prefer without analyzing it more: "I write different things ... hmmm ... what the teacher tells us" (INT11-SM/N-Y6), "I like when we wrote about that thing that we made today" (INT16-SM/NN-Y6) and they refer to their home countries: "I liked it a lot when I wrote about my village ... hmmm ... It isn't here ... It is in another country" (INT17-SF/NN-Y6). Moreover, no immigrant student proposed an alternative writing or review strategy: "I hmmm I don't know ... I write whatever I think" (INT17-SF/NN-Y6), "No, no, only the teacher corrects our texts" (INT12-SF/N-Y6).

Student participants seem to have developed an awareness of the importance of the pre-writing/planning stage during the writing process: "I want to reflect about the text, I don't want to write it without any planning ..." (INT1-SF/N-Y5) and of the post-writing/revising stage: "Only the teacher puts a grade and I look after not to make the same mistakes again" (INT8-SM/N-Y5), "I don't write it correctly again ... no ... the teacher doesn't want to" (INT9-SF/NN-Y5) but they report that they need more support concerning the organization of their ideas: "I'm thinking about it ..., sometimes I write down some ideas quickly so as not to forget them" (INT14-SF/N-Y5), "The teacher tells us what to write and I write" (INT3-SF/N-Y5). Moreover, they provide suggestions with respect to different aspects of the writing process such as a more detailed step by step writing process incorporating their voices, interests and needs: "I would like him to help us by giving more guidance gradually, not to write it all but to see other examples, or characters or ideas and to give us the space to write" (INT7-SM/N-Y5); a different assessment system: "I would like us, as students to assess each other's writing texts" (INT20-SF/N-Y5); freedom of choice regarding the topics they work on: "I would like the teacher to let us write what we want ..." (INT4-SF/N-Y5); extra-curricular activities which could support writing: "I would like to read more books or write more" (INT14-SF/N-Y5).

5 Discussion

Although students in the present study are positive towards writing because they feel they can create and use their imagination, this condition is not taken under consideration by teachers. This finding is corroborated by Mellaville et al. (2006) and Toshalis and Nakkula (2012) referring to the existence of internal and external motivation of students which seem to affect their whole learning progress (Larsen, 2003, as cited in Silva & Kapper, 2004, p. 92) if teachers take them into consideration, and they further reinforce students' autonomy (Kormos, 2012; Ryan & Collen, 1989). It is worth mentioning that Geer and Sweeney's (2012) research detects comparable findings of the expression of student voice in the learning process. As a result, in our study, students usually work individually, not in pairs or small groups, as they wish, and follow the teacher's guidelines without expressing their own needs, opinions or interests; thus the whole process becomes just another routinized school activity. The proposed three stages for teaching writing are not fully followed leading to a variety of mentioned difficulties (Elliot, 1999). What seems to be surprising is the students' claimed need to experience the processes of the third stage, i.e. of revising which sometimes, they try to manage on their own without the teacher even knowing about that, a finding that is also confirmed by Love and Sandiford (2016) and Jesson et al. (2016). So, inappropriately, the teaching writing process focuses on the final product not on the gradual progress (Hashemian & Heidari, 2013, p. 477) and that is in need to change. Although it hopefully seems that all students are encountered equally, immigrant students hesitate to a greater extent to express and participate actively (Skourtou, 2007). This brings forward the discussion about providing students with an immigrant background with further equal opportunities in the teaching processes. In sum, students' voice as reflected in the data of the study claims for more space, collaboration and active participation in the writing process, which does not follow the officially proposed method as Ambati (2011) mentions.

Student voice should be further integrated into the Greek educational system so as to offer its benefits for students and teachers. The integration of student voice could possibly help teachers to rethink and revise their practices towards more learner-centered, community-based and collaborative approaches. There are many ideas and ways to this direction and it depends on teachers' awareness of how they will make use of student voice to the fullest in the learning process.

For instance, the teacher should investigate students' needs, interests, strong and weak points, and concerns through a conversation in class or via other activities. Afterwards he/she could adjust writing instruction accordingly so as to give students the opportunity to be active creators of teaching materials or tools, as is also suggested by Turley (1994) and Bovill et al. (2011). Moreover, the writing process should take place in the classroom, not at home, as it usually happens. Students in the classroom have multiple stimuli and when they are reinforced socially and emotionally could lead to great results, as evidenced by similar good practices implemented in Australia (Commonwealth of Australia, 2013). It is important for students to know which of their actions and behaviors are helpful, which are not, and how they could change them. Some examples of such kind of awareness could be achieved by the development of empathy via relevant projects (Tzika, 2014), fairytales, movies and also the implementation of cooperative learning (Kaldi & Konsolas, 2016), differentiated instruction (Filippatou & Panteliadou, 2013) through the lens of multicultural education (Govaris, 2013).

A good idea for improving the teaching of writing should be the creation of a "book of writing tips". In this book, students – individually or in teams

– in collaboration with their teacher could add whatever they think is helpful and have it as a guide for their future writings. They could also use it as a portfolio for their personal progress check and assessment. The assessment of writing is an integral part of the post-writing/reviewing stage. Assessment should be accomplished via multiple ways, not only by teacher but first as a self-assessment process by students themselves. They must raise their voice in the assessment process either by reviewing their own writings or the ones of their classmates (peer-review). Only when they do have an active role in this process, they can substantially improve their writing, they can check if the learning objectives have been accomplished and they can develop their meta-cognitive skills (NASUWT, 2012).

Concluding, student voice has the potential to improve learning, students, teachers and even the whole school community. It should be heard and take to advantage in order to change the traditional school roles and to make schools open to every voice with respect to society and to democracy.

Notes

1 See e.g. www.soundout.org
2 Abbreviations of interview excerpts: INT = Interview, numbers 1–20, SM = Student Male, SF = Student Female, N = Native, NN = Non Native, Y5 = Year-5 and Y6 = Year-6.

References

Ampati, A. (2011). Education of students of another language in an intercultural school. *Studies for Greek Language, 31*, 53–65. [in Greek]

Appleton, J., Christenson, S., & Furlong, M. (2008). Student engagement with school: Critical conceptual and methodological issues of the construct. *Psychology in the Schools, 45*(5), 369–386.

Bahou, L. (2011). Rethinking the challenges and possibilities of student voice and agency. *Educate~, 1*(1), 2–14. Retrieved from http://www.educatejournal.org/index.php/educate/article/view/286

Baker, W., Connolly, M., Hemming, P., Power, S., & Taylor C. (2005). Thematic review: Pupil voice: Purpose, power and the possibilities for democratic schooling. *British Educational Research Journal, 31*(4), 553–540.

Behrman, E. (2006). Teaching about language, power, and text: A review of classroom practices that support critical literacy. *Journal of Adolescent and Adult Literacy, 49*(6), 490–498.

Bereiter, C., & Scardamalia, M. (1987). *The psychology of written composition.* Hillsdale, NJ: Laurence.

Bovill, C., Cook-Sather, A., & Felten, P. (2011). Students as co-creators of teaching approaches, course design and curricula: Implications for academic developers. *International Journal for Academic Development, 16*(2), 133–145.

Bragg, S. (2007). 'But I listen to children anyway!' – Teacher perspectives on pupil voice. *Educational Action Research, 15*(4), 505–518.

Braun, V., & Clarke, V. (2006). Using thematic analysis. *Qualitative Research in Psychology, 3*(2), 77–101.

Britton, M., Flynn, J., Baker-Wright, T., &Toshalis, E. (2014). *Motivation, engagement and student voice: Professional development series* (Students at the center series) Retrieved from http://studentsatthecenterhub.org/wp-content/uploads/2015/10/I.c-Student-Voice-Professional-Development-Module.pdf

Charalampous, K., & Kokkinos, C. (2017). The "what is happening in this class" questionnaire: A qualitative examination in elementary classrooms. *Journal of Research in Childhood Education, 31*(3). Retrieved from https://www.researchgate.net/publication/296159962

Cook-Sather, A. (2006). Sound, presence and power: 'Student voice' in educational research and reform. *Curriculum Inquiry, 36*(4), 359–390.

Commonwealth of Australia. (2013). *"I think it's important we get a say": Kids Matter and student voice.* Retrieved from http://www.kidsmatter.edu.au

Elliot, J. (1999). Motivating students to write. In *40 encontro sobre o ensino das linguas vivas no ensino superior em Portugal* (pp. 51–64). Universidade do Porto, Faculdade de Letras, Instituto de Estudos Franceses. Retrieved from http://ler.letras.up.pt/uploads/ficheiros/6021.pdf

Ferguson-Patrick, K. (2007). Writers develop skills through collaboration: An action research approach. *Educational Action Research, 15*(2), 159–180.

Fielding, M. (2004). 'New wave' student voice and the renewal of civic society. *London Review of Education, 2*(3), 197–217.

Fielding, M. (2010). The radical potential of student voice: Creating spaces for restless encounters. *The International Journal of Emotional Education, 2*(1), 61–73.

Filippatou, D., & Panteliadou, S. (2013). *Differentiated instruction: Theoretical approaches & educational practices.* Athens: Pedio. [in Greek]

Flower, L., & Hayes, T. (1981). A cognitive process theory of writing. *College Composition and Communication, 32*(4).

Flutter, J., & Rudduck, J. (2004). *Consulting pupils: What's in it for schools.* London: Routledge.

Garcia-Sanchez, J. N., & de Caso-Fuertes, A. M. (2004). Effects of a motivational intervention for improving the writing of children with learning disabilities. *Learning Disability Quarterly, 27*(3), 141–159.

Geer, R., & Sweeney, T. A. (2012). Students' voices about learning with technology. *Journal of Social Sciences, 8*(2), 294–303.

Govaris, C. (2013). *Teaching and learning in multicultural school.* Athens: Gutenberg. [in Greek]

Graham, S., Gillespie, A., & McKeown, D. (2013). Writing: Importance, development, and instruction. *Reading and Writing, 26*(1), 1–15.

Graham, S., & Sandmel, K. (2011). The process writing approach: A meta-analysis. *The Journal of Educational Research, 104*(6), 396–407.

Hashemian, M., & Heidari, A. (2013). The relationship between L2 learner's motivation/attitude and success in L2 writing. *Procedia-Social and Behavioral Sciences, 70*, 476–489.

Isari, F., & Pourkos, M. (2015). *Qualitative research method: Implementations in psychology & education.* Retrieved from http://www.kallipos.gr [in Greek]

Jagersma, J., & Parsons, J. (2011). Empowering students as active participants in curriculum design and implementation. *New Zealand Journal of Teachers' Work, 8*(2), 114–121.

Jeffery, J., & Wilcox, K. C. (2013). 'How do I do it if I don't like writing?' Adolescents' stances toward writing across disciplines. *Reading and Writing: An Interdisciplinary Journal.* Retrieved from http://www.researchgate.net/publication/259635588

Jesson, R., & Rosedale, N. (2016). How teachers might open dialogic spaces in writing instruction. *International Journal of Educational Research, 80*, 164–176.

Joseph, R. (2006). The excluded stakeholder: In search of student voice in the systemic change process. *Educational Technology, 46*(2), 34–38.

Kaldi, S., & Konsolas, M. (2016). *Project-based learning and cross-curricularity: Theory, research and practice.* Athens: Grigoris. [in Greek]

Kormos, J. (2012). The role of individual differences in L2 writing. *Journal of Second Language Writing, 21*, 390–403.

Love, K., & Sandiford, C. (2016). Teachers' and students' meta-reflections on writing choices: An Australian case study. *International Journal of Educational, 80*, 204–216.

Manefield, J., Collins, R., Moore, J., Mahar, S., & Warne, C. (2007). *Student Voice: A historical perspective and new directions.* Department of Education, East Melbourne. Retrieved from https://www.eduweb.vic.gov.au/edulibrary/public/publ/research/publ/student_voice_report.pdf

Matsagouras, I. (2009). *Genre-based approach in written discourse or as long as they think, why don't they write?* Athens: Grigoris. [in Greek]

Meighan, R. (1978a). Editorial. *Educational Review, 30*(2), 125–137.

Meighan, R. (1978b). A pupils' eye view of teaching performance. *Educational Review, 30*(2), 125–138.

Melaville, A., Berg, A. C., & Blank, M. J. (2006). *Community-based learning: Engaging students for success and citizenship.* Washington, DC: Coalition for Community Schools. Retrieved from http://www.communityschools.org

Michalis, A. (2011). *Teaching writing: Modern creative approaches*. Retrieved from: http://filologoi.pblogs.gr/2011/03/a-mihalhs-paragwgh-graptoy-keimenoy-syghrones-dhmioyrgikes-prose.html [in Greek]

Mitra, D. L. (2009). Student voice and student roles in education policy and policy reform. In D. N. Plank, G. Sykes, & B. Schneider (Eds.), *AERA handbook on education policy research* (pp. 819–830). London: Routledge. Retrieved from http://samples.sainsburysebooks.co.uk/9781135856472_sample_529469.pdf

NASUWT. (2012). *Student voice: A guide to promoting and supporting good practice in schools*. Retrieved from http://www.teachersunion.org.uk

Ngussa, B. M., & Makewa, L. N. (2014). Student voice in curriculum change: A theoretical reasoning. *International Journal of Academic Research in Progressive Education and Development, 3*(3), 23–37.

Pajares, F., & Valiante, G. (2001). Gender differences in writing motivation and achievement in middle school students: A function of gender orientation? *Contemporary Educational Psychology, 26*(3), 366–381.

Papanastasiou, E., & Papanastasiou, K. (2005). *Methodology of educational research*. Nicosia: Kailas. [in Greek]

Robinson, C., & Taylor, C. (2007). Theorizing student voice: Values and perspectives. *Improving Schools, 10*(1), 5–17.

Rogers, L. A. (2005). *Student voice: Bridge to learning*. Retrieved from http://depts.washington.edu/k12admin/l4l/capstone/docs/AndyExecSummry.DOC

Rudduck, J. (2006). The past, the papers and the project. *Educational Review, 58*(2), 131–143.

Ryan, R. M., & Connell, J. P. (1989). *Self-regulation questionnaire-academic*. Retrieved from http://selfdeterminationtheory.org/self-regulation-questionnaires/

Shanker, S. (2013). *Calm, alert and learning: Classroom strategies for self-regulation*. Toronto: Pearson Canada. Retrieved from http://www.cea-ace.ca/education-canada/article/self-regulation-calm-alert-and-learning

Silva, T., & Kapper, J. (2004). Selected bibliography of recent scholarship in second language writing. *Journal of Second Language Writing, 13*, 87–96.

Skourtou, E. (2007). The "other" languages of our students: Help or hinder in learning? In N. Mitsis & D. Karadimos (Eds.), *Teaching language: Markings, notes, perspectives* (pp. 149–160). Athens: Gutenberg. [in Greek]

Spantidakis, I. (2011). *Issues in teaching writing in elementary school. Diagnosis-assessment-confrontation*. Athens: Pedio. [in Greek]

Student Voice: Transforming Relationships. (2013). Retrieved from http://www.edu.gov.on.ca/eng/literacynumeracy/inspire/research/CBS_StudentVoice.pdf

Toshalis, E., & Nakkula, M. J. (2012). *Motivation, engagement and student voice: Students at the center series*. Retrieved from https://studentsatthecenterhub.org/wp-content/uploads/2012/04/Motivation-Engagement-Student-Voice-Students-at-the-Center-1.pdf

Turley, S. (1994). 'The way teachers teach is, like, totally whacked': The student voice on classroom practice. *American Educational Research Association, 3*, 1–26.

Tzika, V. (2014). *The implementation of differentiated instruction within project-based learning* (Final year undergraduate dissertation). University of Thessaly, Volos. [in Greek]

United Nations Convention on the Rights of the Child (UNCRC). (1989). Retrieved from http://www.uncrcletsgetitright.co.uk/

Vassilaki, E. (2013). Reading comprehension in the mainstream classroom: Differentiation of instruction. In S. Panteliadou & D. Filippatou (Eds.), *Differentiated instruction: Theoretical approaches & teaching practices* (pp. 283–313). Athens: Pedio. [in Greek]

CHAPTER 3

Vertical Curriculum Design and Evaluation of Citizenship Skills

Loredana Perla, Laura Sara Agrati and Viviana Vinci

Abstract

Promoting equity and active citizenship through school education represents one of the main objectives of the current European Policy Cooperation. In Italy the 'National Plan of Teachers Training' (2016–2019) and the document "Indicazioni Nazionali Nuovi Scenari" (MIUR, 2018) have highlighted inclusion and citizenship competences among the priorities of school education. Moreover, the Ministry Decree 62/2017 has stated the obligation for teachers to evaluate and certify students' citizenship skills. We present the research project 'At citizenship school. Vertical curriculum design and evaluation of citizenship skills', carried out by the University of Bari (Italy), in cooperation with the CREMIT research group (University of Milan), UCIIM teachers' professional association and a national network of schools (N = 10; target: 72 teachers, 10 headmasters).

Keywords

citizenship – evaluation – curriculum design

1 Citizenship Education as a Priority of Global Education Policies

Citizenship education is a priority of international educational *policies* (Kerr, Keating, & Ireland, 2009; Eurydice, 2012, 2017; UNESCO, 2015; CE, 2016; ICCS/ IEA, 2016; Center for Universal Education at Brookings, 2017). People educated to commit themselves to community, to an open-minded society, to solidarity, and social equity is what democracy needs (Dewey, 1916/2004). For this reason, the construct of 'citizenship' refers to a corpus of *interdisciplinary* meanings and to a dynamic set of knowledge, attitudes, and ethical choices – that are, among others, reflexivity, autonomy of judgment, critical thinking, cognitive decentralization (Ten Dam et al., 2011; Santerini, 2010; Eurydice, 2012) – already formalized in a frame of reference in Europe (Eurydice, 2017).

As Kerr, Keating and Ireland (2009) say, the citizenship concepts, components and contexts are interrelated in that the citizenship concepts are expressed through the citizenship components and both are then delivered, learnt and experienced by pupils through the citizenship contexts.

In the same perspective stands the UNESCO that in 2015, with *Global Citizenship Education: Topics and Learning Objectives,* provides pedagogical guidance to UN member states on global citizenship education. This document outlines

TABLE 3.1   Global citizenship

Global citizenship competencies identified by the GCED-WG

1. Empathy
2. Critical thinking/problem solving
3. Ability to communicate and collaborate with others
4. Conflict resolution
5. Sense and security of identity
6. Shared universal values (human rights, peace, justice, etc.)
7. Respect for diversity/intercultural understanding
8. Recognition of global issues – interconnectedness (environmental, social, economic, etc.)

Global citizenship domains and learning objectives from the UNESCO framework

Cognitive domain	Socio-emotional domain	Behavioral domain
Valuing human dignity and human rights	Openness to cultural otherness and to other beliefs, world views and practices	Autonomous learning skills
		Analytical and critical thinking skills
Valuing cultural diversity	Respect	Skills of listening and observing
		Empathy
Valuing democracy, justice, fairness, equality and the rule of law	Civic-mindedness	Flexibility and adaptability
	Responsibility	Linguistic, communicative and pluri-lingual skills
	Self-efficacy	Co-operation skills
	Tolerance of ambiguity	Conflict-resolution skills

SOURCE: CENTER FOR UNIVERSAL EDUCATION AT BROOKINGS (2017, PP. 5–6)

an extensive list of *Global Citizenship Education* (GCED) topics, learning objectives, and themes organized under three GCED domains – the socio-emotional, cognitive, and behavioral.

The Council of Europe (2016) has also proposed a conceptual model of citizenship competences – *Competences for Democratic Culture* – closely linked to the concept of *participation* in a democratic and intercultural culture and based on four broad categories of competence – values, attitudes, skills, knowledge and critical understanding – as shown in Table 3.2.

TABLE 3.2   A conceptual model of citizenship competences

Value	Attitudes	Skills	Knowledge and critical understanding
Valuing human dignity and human rights Valuing cultural diversity Valuing democracy, justice, fairness, equality and the rule of law	Openness to cultural otherness and to other beliefs, world views and practices Respect Civic-mindedness Responsibility Self-efficacy Tolerance of ambiguity	Autonomous learning skills Analytical and critical thinking skills Skills of listening and observing Empathy Flexibility and adaptability Linguistic, communicative and pluri-lingual skills Co-opera on skills Conflict-resolution skills	Knowledge and critical understanding of the self Knowledge and critical understanding of language and communication Knowledge and critical understanding of the world: politics, law, human rights, culture, cultures, religions, history, media, economics, environment, sustainability

SOURCE: COUNCIL OF EUROPE (2016, P. 1)

2   Educate and Evaluate Citizenship in Italy

Citizenship education also has a long tradition in Italy. Although it started in 1958, with the decree no. 585, it never attained at a school curricular integration, despite the regulatory statements over the last few years. For this reason, it is possible to define citizenship education as 'ambiguous teaching'.

TABLE 3.3   Citizenship competence areas and specific citizenship competences

Interacting effectively and constructively with others	Thinking critically	Acting in a socially responsible manner	Acting democratically
Self-confidence Responsibility Autonomy (personal initiative) Respect for different opinions or beliefs Cooperation Conflict resolution EmpathySelf-awareness Communicating and listening Emotional awareness Flexibility or adaptability Inter-cultural skills	Multi-perspective Reasoning and analysis skills Data interpretation Knowledge discovery and use of sources Media literacy Creativity Exercising judgement Understanding the present world Questioning	Respect for justice Solidarity Respect for other human beings Respect for human rights Sense of belonging Sustainable development Environmental protection Cultural heritage protection Knowing about or respecting other cultures Knowing about or respecting religions Non-discrimination	Respect for democracy Knowledge of political institutions Knowledge of political processes (e.g. elections) Knowledge of international organizations, treaties and declarations Interacting with political authorities Knowledge of fundamental political and social concepts Respect for rules Participating Knowledge of or participation in civil society

SOURCE: COUNCIL OF EUROPE (2016) AND EURYDICE (2017, P. 48)

What are the reasons for this 'ambiguity'? First, citizenship education would be a weaving of knowledge, values and attitudes. Second, the concepts of civic-political literacy and the terminology that expresses them have ideological implications that must be framed in their philosophical, religious and political perspectives (Sarsini, 2003). Third, teaching ambiguities are a reflection of external social conditions.

The face of citizenship in Western countries is rapidly changing due to a series of causes: the weakening of the social bond within the nations due to the neo-liberal turn; the intense migratory currents from the north to the south of the world and from east to west in Europe, which favor tensions in and between States; the phenomenon of globalization that changes the appearance of the world and establishes new relationships between national states.

Globalization determines a two-sided situation: on one hand, disorientation and disintegration that favor neo-tribalism and fundamentalist phenomena, in the West as well as in the East of the world; on the other, an increased network of communications that has made the world infinitely smaller (Santerini, 2018).

It is urgent then to work on a new idea of citizenship: detached from ideologies and far from all forms of political-religious radicalization; inspired by the human dignity and the inclusion for all, that, for this reason, inspires civic engagement, solidarity and social link from school. It is equally urgent to work on the teaching *devices* of this peculiar education through an 'integrated' curriculum that harmonizes the citizenship educational requirements and the disciplinary learning objectives.

The last Italian curricular document 'New Directions National Scenarios' (MIUR, 2018) underlines, not surprisingly, the 'transversal' aspect of the teaching of 'Citizenship and Constitution' so that 'everyday behaviors in the school (...) promote an ethics of responsibility, as well as a sense of legality', also in response to the Recommendations (CE/18.12.2006; CE/23.4.2008 – QCEQ) and European solicitations (*Competence for democratic culture*, 2016).

Also, the last normative document on the school leaving Exam for the secondary education courses (DM no. 37 of 18/1/2019 and OM no. 205 of 11/3/2019, art. 19) states that 'part of the interview is dedicated to the activities, the paths, the projects carried out in the context of Citizenship and Constitution included in the educational path'. The emerging orientation, also in Italy, is to assess citizenship skills. The importance to evaluate students in the area of citizenship education has, in fact, for a long time been reaffirmed at international level, both in literature (see Turnbull, 2002; Breslin, 2006; Halstead & Pike, 2006; Jerome, 2008; Kerr, Keating, & Ireland, 2009), that in international comparative surveys, such as those promoted by the International Association for the Evaluation of Educational Achievement (IEA) (Ainley, Schulz, & Friedman, 2013). Evaluating the different components of citizenship education, such as attitudes and values, is a complex task: while the cognitive dimension of learning is always assessable, attitudes are more difficult to evaluate systematically. This difficulty is deepened in the technical report of the ICCS 2016 (Schulz et al., 2018) and has inspired the research-training project, aimed at the construction of a vertical curriculum of 'Constitution and Citizenship' for the Italian schools.

3   A Curriculum Framework for Citizenship Skills at Schools: The Research-Training Project

We discuss some outcomes of the research project Grant Miur 444/2018 '*At citizenship school. Vertical curriculum design and evaluation of citizenship skills*' with the scientific coordination of L. Perla with the DIDASCO research group, supported by the *Dipartimento di Scienze della Formazione, Psicologia, Comunicazione* (Department of Education Sciences, Psychology, Communication Science) of University of Bari (Italy), in cooperation with the CREMIT research group (Pier Cesare Rivoltella, Catholic University of Milan, Italy), UCIIM teachers' professional association and a national network of schools (N = 10; three regions: North, Central, Southern Italy; target population: 72 teachers, 10 headmasters) to design a vertical citizenship curriculum and new tools for the evaluation of students' citizenship skills.

The project falls within the framework of professional teaching through the 'analysis of practice' devices (Altet, 2003; Vinatier & Altet, 2008; Laneve, 2005; Perla, 2005, 2010; Maubant & Martineau, 2011) and the collaborative research (RC), already effectively used in previous research projects (Perla, 2010, 2011, 2012, 2014). The aim is to define the curriculum and the goals of development of social and civic citizenship competences for different degrees of school, to be evaluated using specific devices (i.e., scoring rubrics, accompanied by indicators and level descriptors; performance tasks; systematic observations, autobiographies cognitive).

The project has three types of objectives:

1.   *institutional* – knowing the long historical-regulatory path that has redesigned education for the Constitution and Citizenship in Italy;
2.   *ideational* – co-building together (researchers and teachers) the vertical curriculum of Constitution and Citizenship. This design is oriented by specific criteria:

   a   *verticality*: adopt a vertical school curriculum that embodies the educational proposal, unitary and organic, for students from 3 to 14 years old and that integrates key competences, development goals and disciplinary skills/knowledge;

   b   *consistency*: connecting the didactic proposals and the methods of assessing, consistently with the designed curriculum, not fragmentary or impromptu;

   c   *documentation*: formalize the didactic proposals in useful models for documentation, evaluation, reporting, rationalization and transferability of the initiatives and experiences gained.

3. *professional development* – enhancing the evaluation ability of teachers
    involved in research. Starting from the Audigier's framework (2000), that
    reports the main categories of the democratic education curriculum to
    citizenship (Audigier, 2000; Birzea, 2000; Circle & Carnegie Corporation,
    2003; Cox, Jaramillo & Reimers, 2005; Duerr, Spajic-Vrakas, & Martins,
    2000; Engle & Ochoa, 1988; Johnson & Morris, 2010; Parker & Jarolimek,
    1984; Veldhuis, 1997), and from Mattei's curriculum matrix (2007).

TABLE 3.4   The main categories of democratic citizenship education curriculum

Active democratic citizen		
Knowledge	**Value, attitudes, dispositions**	**Skills**
Forms of participation	Value	General skills
Economic	Attitudes	Participation
Cultural	Dispositions	skills
Social		
Political		

SOURCE: AUDIGIER (2000)

The teachers involved in the project were asked to declare the aims, values,
attitudes and dispositions of education to the Constitution and Citizenship
by grading objectives, contents, activities and unitary learning tasks according
to school grades, from kindergarten (3–6 years old students) to the two-year
upper secondary school (14–16 years old students).

The project has completed the pilot phase of theoretical-laboratory training, involving 17 school classes – totaling 60 teachers – at national level and
focused on specific objects: knowledge and critical-deconstructive analysis
of the Italian Constitutional Charter as a possible democratic instrument of
social cohesion and guide for active and responsible citizenship; hypothesis of
differentiation of citizenship paths in the school, linked to the school subjects
with respect to four 'guiding concepts' (politics, identity, economy, relationships); knowledge of historical-philosophical-pedagogical sources that substantiate the concept of citizenship (MacIntyre, 1988; Habermas, 1992; Sandel,
1994; Cogan & Derricot, 1998; Gagnon & Pagé, 1999; Ong, 1999; Benhabib, 2002,
2005; Mortari, 2004, 2008; Romano Tassone & Manganaro, 2005; Benhabib,
2008; Cambi, 2009; Fiorucci, 2014; UNESCO, 2015; Rivoltella, 2017).

The second phase of the Project involves the implementation of curricular
hypotheses and the construction of scoring rubrics of citizenship competences
that will be subject to validation starting from the 2019–2020 years.

4   State-of-the-Art of the Collaborative Research-Training

At the moment the results of the first 84 post-training works have been returned. These are professional writings (Perla, 2013), the outcome of the training work, assumed as relevant 'topos' by the professional didactic research (Pastré, Mayen, & Vergnaud, 2006), as 'spaces' overcoming the traditional difference between the promotion of the personal competences and the promotion of the 'skills for work' in the synthesis of the answers offered to the individual, as well as, to the training organizations needs – in case, the school. The professional writings, requested to the involved teachers, are of three different typologies: reflexive type and two of the programming work.

The post-training phase involved a number of 75 teachers in 10 schools of all grades in three Italian regions (Lombardia, Toscana, Puglia) in order to have a guaranteed representation of the Italian territorial areas: north, central and south. In this phase, each teacher was assigned three deliveries to be developed, by choice, either individually or in groups, and to be uploaded, after accreditation, in a web platform within three months.

a) Identify a topic within the Constitution and Citizenship/Civic Education area that you feel is useful to develop vertically – from the preschool up to the two-year secondary school degree – and give a brief reason for the choice (max 2500 characters).

b) Depending on the school grade in which you work, decline the theme chosen in one or more learning units, following the format.

c) Upload, in the folder relating to the geographical area in which you work, a project of Citizenship Education and/or Civic Education that you have already carried out in your school.

The analysis of the answers and of the didactic documentation produced by the schools involved in the study had the purpose of making inferences about two research questions: is it possible to promote a curriculum design and evaluation model of citizenship education and Constitution? In planning citizenship education and teaching the Constitution, what are the main themes? The aim was to bring out one or more common 'cultural objects', capable of overcoming the inhomogeneity of proposals that usually characterize this type of education, not only in the Italian schools.

The analysis of the answers has been made through the QDA (Qualitative Data Analysis) procedure in the less objectivistic version of Strauss and Corbin (1990) (see also Cipriani, 2008; Tarozzi, 2008), alongside the exploratory use of the NVivo software. QDA is a GT (Grounded Theory) analysis procedure based on a mainly *bottom-up* system, built on a recursive cycle of three phases: *data collection*, *data encoding*, and *data analysis*. As known, the GT process of analyzing, according to Strauss and Corbin, is based on three operations of reading and coding[1] textual corpus – in this case, interviews and

TABLE 3.5   Total writings (N = 84)

School name	Request no. 1	Request no. 2	Request no. 3
1. Istituto Alberotanza	1	1	1
2. Capozzi Galilei	6	6	6
3. Don Milani	1	5	1
4. Michelangelo	1	1	1
5. Panetti-Pitagora	5	5	5
6. Re David	2	1	1
7. Tosi Busto Arsizio	2	2	3
8. Ungaretti di Melzo	1	1	1
9. Pacinotti Bagnone	6	6	6
10. Volterra	2	2	2
Total	27	30	27

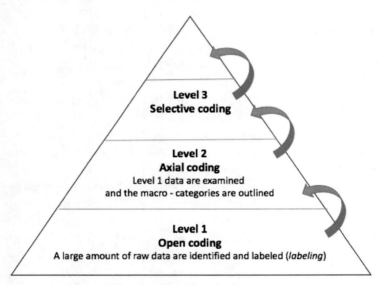

FIGURE 3.1   Phases of the GT analysis procedure

micro-narratives – according to a scale of increasing conceptualization (*open*, *axial* and *selective* coding), represented in Figure 3.1.

The procedure was scanned as follows.

Before the first analysis, all the answers texts were subjected to a first sep-arate reading by the researchers to grasp the overall meaning that was not intentionally shared in the research group to avoid inducing conditioning of the subsequent interpretation. This reading was accompanied by the one with *NVivo*.

The first phase of corpus analysis (*initial* or *open* coding), therefore, was started in parallel by three researchers. This is the first level of exploration of a text, aimed at bringing out all the possible meanings that can also be linked indirectly to the unit of analysis chosen – that is, the theme(s) (intended as 'cultural objects') considered more consistent with a vertical adaptation in the different school grades, from pre-school to secondary school, in the field of civic education.

The open coding was intended to *discover* and *name* the phenomenon expressed by the unit of analysis with conceptual labels that characterized it as much as possible (*labeling*). We proceeded as follows. After subdividing the corpus of answers into 'text units'[2] (pieces of text, more or less short), 'conceptual labels'[3] have been applied in order to essentialize their meaning as much as possible. Each label summarized the contents of the text unit in a very brief note. This reading-coding, however, is only apparently synthetic: it has the effect of expanding the meanings of the initial research questions even further: at the end of the labeling work there are dozens of labels and the feeling of not having the 'thread' of an argument (but it is an absolutely 'physiological' feeling) (Tarozzi, 2008).

In addition, the reading of the corpus has been accompanied by the writing of some *memos* or *field notes*, namely brief notes which, as a kind of micro-diary in the logbook, can be used to integrate the labeling operation with additional descriptions or some reflective estimation

Memos help to remember what the analysis is producing; they are short-term mini-reflections that bring order to the experiences and help to intensify the ability to 'detail' the reflection as the analysis focuses on the macro-categories. In short, they are a precious exercise of reflective thinking (Mortari, 2003) but also, obviously, of an integrative detail of the analysis of the corpus. The second level of analysis is the *axial coding*.

The real *emerging process* of the macro-categories starts at this level, thanks to the types of relationships between the labels: logical (of similarity), ontological and concrete relations that link a given concept to the parts of which it is made up, based on contiguity in space-and-time and on cause-effect); equivalence (of synonymy) and function (related the placement of a conceptual label within a broader conceptual system that contains it).

At this level, the *properties* of the object of study are becoming clearer: the themes that can be developed vertically in the field of civic education and citizenship. The purpose of focused coding is to initiate a first and effective process of synthesis: from labels to macro-categories, from macro-categories to themes that are gradually becoming more 'conceptual' and 'far from the data'. The last level of selective coding identifies *core categories/y*[4] (Strauss & Corbin, 1990, p. 116), around which all the others are placed as the constellation of a system of planets around a star.[5] A *core category* is the 'solid core' that unifies all the threads – the different macro-categories – in order to provide a cogent representation about dimensions and properties of the studied object (Goulding, 1999).

A small integration, experimented in a previous study (Perla 2009), has been adopted in the QDA procedure. At the end of the axial coding phase, questions were asked to teachers as 'explanatory suggestions', aiming at focusing reflection on interesting e emerged elements. The strategy helps to clarify some issues of the analysis and to bring out further categories, integrating those already identified. This co-reflective deepening, in tandem, between researcher-teacher, reduces the risk of a distorted reading of the corpus, more probable if this is carried out only by the researcher; moreover, it allows the real involvement of the teacher in the analytical procedure, which otherwise might appear to be excluded. This aspect should not be neglected in working with teachers and is central to collaborative research. Follow the themes emerged from the analysis, grouped of the function of schools belonging to the three regions involved.

This first analysis raises two main aspects. First of all, there is a certain confusion about the difference between 'themes' and 'educations' due perhaps to the misunderstanding of the request: the first question asked to identify one or more themes, that is 'cultural objects', potentially declinable in the three grades of school in the teaching field of civic education, not specific *areas of learning*. Furthermore, it is possible to note a poor familiarity with the principle of curricular continuity in the choice of themes that can be effectively interpreted vertically.

These aspects ask the question of whether a curriculum, which has these contents as a theme, can be effectively declined vertically or if it should not be tackled in a 'horizontal' mode, i.e. in search of nodes of connection with the territory and its institutions. This question will be addressed in the third part of the research when the elements of a possible curriculum of civic education will be outlined and the final design will be formalized.

Another aspect that emerged concerns the almost total absence of themes that are now considered central to the policy of citizenship education: 'digital citizenship', *soft skills*, 'participation', the responsible use of ICT, 'protection' of cultural heritage' (a central theme in a rich country in cultural heritage such as Italy), the 'correct lifestyles', affective education. There have also been few references to methodologies or to the evaluation of civic competences.

TABLE 3.6   Emerged themes

Countries	Emerged themes
Lombardia	Market
	Addiction prevention
	Motor and sports activity
Toscana	Work
	Territory
	Motor and sports activity
	Education for differences
	Rights education
Puglia	Knowledge of the Constitution
	Human rights education
	Education to the rights of the child
	Creative writing
	Environmental sustainability
	International relations

The analysis shows, instead, that the teachers have well understood the difference between the Constitution (as cultural content) and Citizenship (as a juridical condition, the bond of belonging to the State) as well as the multiple values of the concept of Citizenship, variable in all European countries who are interested in this teaching at the curriculum level.

Request no. 2 concerned the elaboration of the theme chosen in one or more learning units, based on a format, made available by the research group in the web platform. The large number of the collected learning units has been analyzed, according to the themes (see request no. 1), the titles and the requested citizenship competences. The main difference regards the choice of outgoing skills between the schools of the north-central and the south: the choice fell, on the one hand, on the development of European skills, such as entrepreneurship, spirit of initiative and responsibility, autonomy, social and civic competences; on the other hand, on disciplinary cultural competences, in response to functional alphabetic emergencies, even before civic issues.

This aspect is confirmed by the analysis of professional writings in response to the third question, related to the citizenship education and/or civic education projects already completed. Despite the loaded products presenting characteristics of undoubted interest for the purpose of formalizing the curriculum – to deal with in the third and final part of the research – the comparison between the number of these (no. 24) and that of the involved teachers (no. 75) allows to infer a limited project activity in the area of citizenship education.

TABLE 3.7   Curricular projects for citizenship education: titles

Geographical areas	Titles
North	The citizen's participation in the life of the State
	False? No thanks. We protect the made in Italy!
	Curriculum of key competences of European citizenship
Center	The curriculum vitae of the European citizen
	We were not born to hate
	AmbientiAMOci. First title: the water[a]
	Educating to legality – Active citizenship. Educate to respect the law and develop the competence of active citizenship
	A blue knot against bullying
South	All people smile in the same language
	Let's take the measures to cyber-bullying
	CHILDREN SPEAK (on) RIGHTS [O][b]
	Write CREA-ACTIVE-MIND[c]
	We are world
	Continuous growth
	Bullying and cyber-bullying STOP
	Who loves you makes the difference
	Citizenship and Constitution Projects
	Affectivity and sexuality: the new educational challenges
	Legality and sport
	We represent legality
	Like threads, tied to legality

a   The word 'ambientiamoci' in the Italian language allows a play-on-words between 'ambiente' (= environment) and 'amare' (= love). It means that people are taking care of themselves respecting the environment.

b   The title is based on another play-on-words. It takes on two meanings: children speak directly and children speak of law (Italian 'diritto' means 'low').

c   The 'creatively' adverb is transformed with another play-on-word trough the combination of 'creare' (creating), 'attivare' (activating) and 'mente' (mind).

The reading of the practices – 'declared' as much as 'implemented' by the group of teachers – offered the undoubted opportunity to develop a curricular project with some characteristics: to be in dialectic with the territory, to be in continuity between the school grades, to be the guarantor of national unity – that has a not very long history in Italy (1861) and that sometimes seems to be questioned by an overly territorial attitude regarding what should be understood as citizenship and civic sense.

5   Conclusions

This project aims to design and realize *a vertical curriculum* of citizenship education and, alongside, to train teachers for its development, as it is a complex but useful device, in order to make visible the citizenship skills of students that often remain implicit.

This is not a simple but urgent challenge given that in Italy the behavior vote has recently been replaced by the assessment of citizenship competences.

On the strictly didactic level, there is also the urgency to integrate the 'citizenship' education to the disciplinary curriculum, welcoming the ideas offered by the most recent *curriculum studies* (see He et al., 2015; Kridel, 2010; Scurati, 1997, 2008; Perla, 2014) that offer guidance to teachers in orchestrate learning content within organized routes and inclusive educational environments. The second step of the research has provided some interesting evidence in view of the first curriculum prototype that will be "put in shape" by June 2020. Some answers to the research questions have already emerged at the end of this phase. The schools involved in the study have expressed the need to deepen, on the one hand, the normative evolution on the teaching of civic education and, on the other hand, the curricular connections – today necessary after the issuing of the L. no. 92/2019. This law recommends dedicating a well-defined curricular space of 33 hours per year to the civic education and assumes the theme of citizenship as an integrating background for all disciplines in each grade of school.

Citizenship education in Italy today is an objective of ordinal intervention, no longer experimental; pertains to the assessment of the outcomes for students at the end of middle and high school; it is part of the certification of social and civic competences at the end of middle school and the compulsory two-year high school.

The analysis of the writings confirms the hypothesis that citizenship education and the teaching of civic education take place in the interweaving of cognitive, affective and motivational aspects, between values and attitudes. The research-training project *'At citizenship school. Vertical curriculum design and evaluation of citizenship skills'* aims to meet the challenge of designing a curriculum capable of supporting the complexity of this educational area.

Acknowledgements

The authors are thankful for the support of the National Project "A scuola di Cittadinanza. Curricolo Verticale e Valutazione delle Citizenship Skills", *Legalità* Monitor 440 Grant No. 444/2018.

This chapter is the result of a shared project. However, Loredana Perla is the author of Sections 3–4, Laura Sara Agrati is the author of Section 2 and Viviana Vinci is the author of Section 1.

Notes

1 Coding is the analytical process of conceptualizing data that is identified in the corpus as the analytical reading progresses.
2 The text unit is a portion of text, more or less short (the selection criterion is to make the text unit coincide with a unit of meaning), coinciding with the analyzed data, to which the conceptual label is applied.
3 The label is a faithful but synthetic statement of the content of the text unit.
4 A *core category*, or central category, is 'the central phenomenon around which all the other categories are related' (Strauss & Corbin, 1990, p. 116).
5 Strauss and Corbin (1990) also describe a series of specific techniques (conditional matrix, memos, diagrams) aimed at the practical management of data and which are easy to access after a certain familiarity with the operations connected to the various levels.

References

Ainley, J., Schulz, W., & Friedman, T. (Eds.). (2013). *ICCS 2009 encyclopedia. Approaches to civic and citizenship education around the world.* Amsterdam: IEA.
Altet, M. (2003). *La ricerca sulle pratiche di insegnamento in Francia.* Brescia, Italy: La Scuola.
Antonio, A., Astin, H., & Cress, C. (2000). Community service in higher education: A look at the nation's faculty. *Review of Higher Education, 23*(4), 373–398.

Audigier, F. (2000). *Project "education for democratic citizenship": Basic concepts and core competencies for education for democratic citizenship.* Strasbourg: Council for Cultural Co-operation.

Baldwin, R. G. (1996). Faculty career stages and implications for professional development. In D. Finnegan, D. Webster, & Z. F. Gamson (Eds.), *Faculty and faculty issues in colleges and universities* (2nd ed., pp. 1–11). Boston, MA: Pearson Custom Publishing.

Benhabib, S. (2002). *The claims of culture: Equality and diversity in the global era.* Princeton, NJ: Princeton University Press.

Benhabib, S. (2005). *La rivendicazione dell'identità culturale, eguaglianza e diversità dell'era globale.* Bologna, Italy: il Mulino.

Benhabib, S. (2008). *Cittadini globali. Cosmopolitismo e democrazia.* Bologna, Italy: il Mulino.

Bîrzéa, C. (2000). *Education for democratic citizenship: A lifelong learning perspective. Project on "education for democratic citizenship".* Strasbourg: Council for Cultural Co-Operation.

Breslin, T. (2006). Calling citizenship to account: Issues of assessment and progression. In T. Breslin & B. DuFour (Eds.), *Developing citizens.* London: Hodder Murray.

Cambi, F. (2009). *Cittadinanza e intercultura oggi.* In M. Galiero (Ed.), *Educare per una cittadinanza globale. Costruire un mondo giusto a partire dalla scuola* (pp. 20–28). Bologna, Italy: Emi.

Center for Universal Education at Brookings. (2017). *Measuring global citizenship education. A collection of practices and tools.* Washington, DC: The Brookings Institution. Retrieved from https://www.brookings.edu/wp-content/uploads/2017/04/global_20170411_measuring-global-citizenship.pdf

Circle & Carnegie Corporation of New York (2003). *The civic mission of schools.* New York, NY: Carnegie Corporation of New York.

Cogan, J. J., & Derricott, R. (Ed.). (1998). *Citizenship for the 21st century. An international perspective on education.* London: Kogan Page.

Council of Europe. (2016). *Competences for democratic culture. Living together as equals in culturally diverse democratic societies.* Strasbourg: Council of Europe Publishing.

Cox, C., Jaramillo, R., & Reimers, F. (2005). *Education for citizenship and democracy in the Americas: An agenda for action.* Washington, DC: Inter-American Development Bank.

Dewey, J. (2004). *Democracy and education.* Mineola, NY: Dover Publication. (Original work published 1916)

Duerr, K., Spajic-Vrakas, V., & Martins, I. F. (2000). *Strategies for learning democratic citizenship.* Strasbourg: Council of Europe.

Engle, S. H., & Ochoa, A. S. (1988). *Education for democratic citizenship: Decision making in the social studies.* New York, NY: Teachers College Press.

Euridyce. (2012). *Citizenship education in Europe.* Brussels, Belgium: Education, Audiovisual and Culture Executive Agency.

Eurydice. (2017). *Citizenship education at school in Europe – 2017. Eurydice report.* Luxembourg: Publications Office of the European Union.

Fiorucci, M., Catarci, M., & Trulli, M. (2014). *L'ABC della cittadinanza. Indagine sulle Scuole di italiano per stranieri promosse dall'associazionismo a Roma e provincia.* Milano, Italy: FrancoAngeli.

Gagnon, F., & Pagé, M. (1999). *Conceptual framework for an analysis of citizenship in the liberal democracies: conceptual framework and analysis* (Vol. I). Department of Canadian Heritage.

Habermas, J. (1992). *Morale diritto politica.* Torino, Italy: Einaudi.

Halstead, M., & Pike, M. (2006). *Citizenship and moral education: Values in action.* London: Routledge.

He, M. F., Schultz, B. D., & Schubert, W. H. (Eds.). (2015). *The Sage guide to curriculum in education.* Thousand Oaks, CA: Sage Publications.

Jerome, L. (2008). Assessing citizenship education. In J. Arthur, I. Davies, & C. Hahn (Eds.), *Sage handbook of education for citizenship and democracy* (pp. 545–558). London: Sage.

Johnson, L., & Morris, P. (2010). Towards a framework for critical citizenship education. *The Curriculum Journal, 21*(1), 77–96.

Kerr, D., Keating, A., & Ireland, E. (2009). *Pupil assessment in citizenship education: Purposes, practices and possibilities.* Report of a CIDREE Collaborative Project. Slough: NFER/CIDREE.

Kridel, C. (Ed.). (2010). *Encyclopedia of curriculum studies.* London: Sage.

Laneve, C. (Ed.). *Analisi della pratica educativa. Metodologia e risultanze della ricerca* (pp. 80–100). Brescia, Italy: La Scuola.

MacIntyre, A. (1988). *Dopo la virtù. Saggio di teoria morale.* Milano, Italy: Feltrinelli.

Mattei, M. (2007). *Insegnare con i concetti educazione alla cittadinanza.* Milano, Italy: FrancoAngeli.

Maubant, P., & Martineau, S. (Eds.). (2011). *Fondements des pratiques professionnelles des enseignants.* Ottawa, Canada: Presses de l'Université d'Ottawa.

MIUR. (2018). *Indicazioni Nazionali Nuovi Scenari.* Retrieved from http://www.indicazioninazionali.it

Morison, S. E. (1936). *Harvard College in the seventeenth century.* Cambridge, MA: Harvard University Press.

Mortari, L. (2004). *Educare alla cittadinanza partecipata.* Mantova, Italy: Sometti.

Mortari, L. (2008). *A scuola di libertà. Formazione e pensiero autonomo.* Milano, Italy: Raffaello Cortina.

Ong, A. (1999). *Flexible citizenship. E cultural logics of transnationality.* Durham, NC: Duke University Press.

Parker, W. C., & Jarolimek, J. (1984). Citizenship and the critical role of social studies. *NCSS Bulletin, 72.*

Perla, L. (2005). *L'intervista per dire della pratica.* In C. Laneve (Ed.), *Analisi della pratica educativa. Metodologia e risultanze della ricerca* (pp. 80–100). Brescia, Italy: La Scuola.

Perla, L. (2010). *Didattica dell'implicito. Ciò che l'insegnante non sa.* Brescia, Italy: La Scuola.

Perla, L. (2011). *L'eccellenza in cattedra. Dal saper insegnare alla conoscenza dell'insegnamento.* Milano, Italy: FrancoAngeli.

Perla, L. (2012). *Scritture professionali. Metodi per la formazione.* Bari, Italy: Progedit.

Perla, L. (Ed.). (2014). *I Nuovi Licei alla prova delle competenze. Per una progettazione nel biennio.* Lecce, Italy: Pensa MultiMedia.

Rivoltella, P. C. (2017). *Media education. Idea, metodo, ricerca.* Brescia, Italy: Morcelliana-La Scuola.

Romano Tassone, A., & Manganaro, F. (Eds.). (2005). *Dalla cittadinanza amministrativa alla cittadinanza globale.* Atti del Convegno. Reggio Calabria, 30–31 ottobre 2003. Milano, Italy: Giuffrè.

Sandel, M. J. (1994). *Il liberalismo e i limiti nella giustizia* (tr. it.). Milano, Italy: Feltrinelli.

Santerini, M. (2010). *Educare alla cittadinanza. La pedagogia e le sfide della globalizzazione.* Roma, Italy: Carocci.

Santerini, M. (2019). *Da stranieri a cittadini. Educazione interculturale e mondo globale.* Milano, Italy: Mondadori Università.

Sarsini, D. (2003). *Il corpo in Occidente. Pratiche pedagogiche.* Roma, Italy: Carocci.

Schulz, W., et al. (2016). *IEA international civic and citizenship education study 2016 assessment framework.* Cham: Springer.

Schulz, W., Carstens, R., Losito, B., & Fraillon, J. (2018). *ICCS 2016 technical report.* Amsterdam: IEA.

Scurati, C. (1997). *Pedagogia della scuola.* Brescia, Italy: La Scuola.

Scurati, C. (2008). *Nuove didattiche. Linee di ricerca e proposte formative.* Brescia, Italy: La Scuola.

Ten Dam, G., et al. (2011). Measuring young people's citizenship competences. *European Journal of Education, 46*(3), 354–372.

Turnbull, J. (2002). Values in educating for citizenship: Sources, influences and assessment. *Pedagogy, Culture and Society, 10*(1), 123–134.

UNESCO. (2015). *Global citizenship education: Topics and learning objectives.* Paris: UNESCO.

Veldhuis, R. (1997). *Education for democratic citizenship: Dimensions of citizenship, core competencies, variables, and international activities.* Strasbourg: Council for Cultural Cooperation.

Vinatier, I., & Altet, M. (2008). *Analyser et comprendre la pratique enseignante.* Rennes, France: PUR.

CHAPTER 4

The Role of Reflective Simulation in the Context of Theatre Pedagogical Paths in Teacher Education

Julia Köhler

Abstract

Based on the hypothesis that simulation of classroom reality in teacher train-ing is an important contribution to the development of self- and social compe-tences, theatre pedagogical interventions offer a special way of expression. As a conscious embodiment of 'as if' situations in a simulated framework, theatrical interventions can test possible and expected processes and serve the reflection of the actions and situations experienced in everyday practice (Köhler, 2017). The simulative, imaginary character of theatre pedagogy is that it plays with possibilities of reality, with proposals that have no structural effect on social interactions or the status or affiliation of a person outside the theatrical frame-work. Based on the reflection model (1983) of Donald Schön and the under-standing of the EPIK concept's (Schratz, Paseka, & Schrittesser, 2011) ability to reflect, professional teachers have the ability to view themselves critically and distantly in their teaching, to question themselves and to draw constructive conclusions about future practice. The experiences made theatrically can give rise to rethinking perspectives and testing alternative approaches to action.

Keywords

teacher training – teacher professionalism – theatre pedagogy – theatrical simulation

1 Introduction

The ability to reflect in the teaching profession can be seen as a fundamental area of competences in order to satisfy the complexity of the pedagogical pro-fession and the demands of everyday practice. This competence consists of "independently assessing pedagogical knowledge and relating it both flexibly and creatively to specific and constantly changing situations" (Koller, 2006, p. 13).

The ability to critically question oneself without succumbing to various temptations, ranging from existential self-doubt to the permanent trivialization of one's incompetence, is an art that appears to be of particular importance above all in professions with specific pedagogical tasks (Oevermann, 1996).

The theatre pedagogy, according to my thesis, offers manifold possibilities in learning the ability to reflect. This includes the cognitive as well as the sensual-physical perception and cognitive faculty. "By playing theatre, we distance ourselves from our world in such a way that we can dedicate ourselves to it all the more intensively at a distance" (Liebau, 2009, p. 157). This means that the affective parts of experiential situations are made conscious and thus enable us to "comprehend" them in the literal sense and to process them into experiences or to view them from a critical distance and, if necessary, to facilitate alternative options for action. "Thus, theatrical learning is always learning in and at human conditions – learning entangled in them and at the same time learning emancipated from them" (Wiese, Günther, & Ruping, 2006, p. 18).

The chapter contains three thematic areas. First, I will give a brief overview of the theoretical framework in the context of the work on reflectiveness in teacher training. In a second step, I will discuss possibilities of theatrical methods in the context of reflection and finally, I would like to give a short insight into empirical approaches of a special teacher training course at the Centre of Teacher Education at University of Vienna.

2 Theoretical Framework

The discussion surrounding the several discourses on professionalization within teacher training has been booming for several years.

An attempt to present the characteristics of pedagogical professionalism coherently is the EPIK concept, which can be considered a contribution to an action-oriented approach in the professional debate (Schratz, Paseka, & Schrittesser, 2011). The EPIK concept (Entwicklung von Professionalität im internationalen Kontext/Development of professionalism in an international context) is based on five key competences, which are not only reduced to the action aspect but likewise, consider the context of structures.

The objectives of the development group were, among other things, to put into practice domains of teacher professionalism as new patterns of thought. Through self-reflexive processes of the teachers, teacher educator and other persons involved in the system, both the structural and institutional framework conditions and the didactic approaches were critically reflected. This resulted in a new professional awareness and diverse development perspectives.

The EPIK model is based on the consideration that actions and structures are to be thought of as dialectically related aspects. The notions of professional action and the organizational or structural constitution of the teacher's profession are interdependent and can, therefore, be perceived in their reciprocal entanglement. In order to capture this interweaving of the two perspectives linguistically, fields of competence, so-called "domains" were defined:

- On the one hand, domains describe individual competences, demand corresponding knowledge and skills from the teachers, but at the same time they require structures in which these competences can develop, grow and develop further.
- Domains are an expression of a "professional habitus" of teachers, regardless of the field of education in which they work. They thus represent a kind of "binding bracket" that constitutes the professionalism of teachers across all types of schools.
- Although the domains must be worked out and developed by the subjects, they can only fully unfold if, in addition to individual learning processes, higher-level processes and developmental thrusts in the sense of 'next practice' of the entire system take place.
- The domains open up manifold starting points for considerations on school development, on the further development of teacher education and training, and on pedagogical concepts that focus on the diversity of children and young people. (Schratz, Paseka, & Schrittesser, 2011)

The interwoven domains are as follows: (1) ability to reflect and discuss, (2) professional awareness, (3) cooperation and collegiality, (4) ability to differentiate and (5) personal mastery. They can be understood as building blocks of a professional practice (Schratz, Paseka, & Schrittesser, 2011, p. 24).

The domains are not stand-alone, verifiable areas, but relate to each other or overlap within their thematic fields, which constitutes their multi-perceptivity (Schratz, Paseka, & Schrittesser 2011, p. 26). They also do not follow fixed rules and regulations that apply forever, but they are repeatedly renegotiated and further developed depending on the structural framework conditions. The domain concept primarily serves the interdisciplinary acquisition of professional-pedagogical competences.

According to the domain concept, the ability to reflect constitutes one of the fundamental areas of competences in the teaching profession. It should help to respond to the complexities of the pedagogical profession and meet the demands of everyday practice. Hans-Christoph Koller (2006) describes reflection competence as the epicenter of pedagogical action competence.

Reflection competence consists of the ability to independently assess pedagogical knowledge, and in acting both flexibly and creatively in specific and constantly changing situations (Koller, 2006, p. 13). Reflective thinking and action, according to the OECD Framework of Reference (2005), is a fundamental component of the framework of competences. Reflexivity, for instance, allows people who have acquired certain ways of reflection, to relate those approaches to other aspects of their experience and modify or adapt them accordingly. Reflective teachers put such thought processes into practice or action. Reflexivity requires demanding thought and action processes and involves the subject's ability to transform, and to objectify one's thinking and action, which means perceiving one's own as something foreign or different, and drawing conclusions for future behavior from this process of reflection. The ability to verbalize and substantiate one's pedagogical actions, and thus to gain insights into one's past courses of action, the capacity to formulate and to draw conclusions from them for future actions, is a main characteristic of professional thinking and acting. In this context, Ilse Schrittesser (2011) speaks of the ability to reflect as the core of pedagogical professionalism.

Werner Helsper (2001) states that practice is often threatened by risks and the irritation of routine, in short, by crises. Further, he emphasizes that the necessary practical skills to cope with dealing with such kinds of crises in a professional manner 'cannot be learned through science or theoretical reflection', but exclusively "through practical experience and [...] the acquisition of a practical pedagogical habitus" (p. 11). Helsper accentuates that only a composed posture toward the crisis can create a comprehensive opportunity for teachers to reflect on it. Accordingly, prospective teachers need scientifically grounded opportunities for reflection. This reflective habitus can only be developed in teacher training spaces and not under the pressure of acting in the classroom.

Based on the reflection model of Donald Schön (1983), the understanding of the EPIK concept's ability to reflect, and the assumptions of Helsper, that teacher has to go through practical experiences, professional teachers possess the ability to view themselves critically and distantly in their teaching, to question themselves and to draw constructive conclusions for future practice. But how can student teachers gain practical experience, and reflected on action within university teacher training programs?

3   Reflecting by Theatrical Simulation

The word 'simulation' originates from the Latin word simulation 'simulatio' (= make similar, imitate, imitate) as follows: Facts, processes [with technical, scientific means] model-like for exercise, knowledge purposes imitate, realistically imitate.

Based on the hypothesis that the simulation of classroom reality in teacher training constitutes an important contribution to the development of self- and social competences, theatre pedagogical interventions offer a special way of expression and of addressing the execution of classroom actions and their consequences for the self and consequently for others, i.e. the pupils (Köhler, 2015, 2017, 2018).

Theatre is 'the' art form within which the actors simultaneously become subjects and objects of an aesthetic transformation (Kotte, 2005, pp. 272f.). The subjective reality becomes a particular kind of reflected practice through the process of stepping into the representation of another figure and back into reality. Hence, theatre can be regarded as a creative social process, which is only possible because of the social constellation of human beings (Hentschel 2010, p. 106). The different levels of opportunity of experience and experiencing are fundamental to this process. Helmuth Plessner describes in his remarks on the eccentric positionality of human beings' eccentricity. Plessner explains human's eccentricity with the awareness that, in contrast to the animal, a person can behave freely in her/his existence despite instinct and affect (Plessner, 1965). The doubling in the conscious embodiment of others illustrates the individuality, but also the disappearance of the human being. "The transformation is carried by the personality" states Plessner. Through the representation of another person with one's body as "material of one's own existence" (Plessner, 1982, p. 407), the change between inside and outside, the feedback of one's own existence, the eccentric position in the world becomes particularly clear. Thus, when

> we talk about the aesthetic and learning, we talk about three quite different, though possibly interrelating, things: learning about the aesthetic, learning through aesthetic experience, and a kind of learning that is not predominantly intellectual but that is located in the body: that is visceral, emotional and intuitive. (Greenwood, 2011, p. 49)

Theatrical learning is experiential, since it ties in with both one's own experiential spaces and those of the imagined figures, thus incorporating the foreign into one's own knowledge. Theatrical learning is inherent in the confrontation with one's physicality.

Playing theatre, as a conscious embodiment of 'as if' situations in a simulated framework, can test possible and (non-)expected processes and serve the reflection of actions and situations experienced in everyday practice (Köhler,

2017). The subjective reality becomes a particular kind of reflected practice by stepping into the representation of another figure and the back into reality. The simulative, imaginary character of theatre pedagogy plays with possibilities of reality, with proposals that have no structural effect on social interactions or on the status or affiliation of a person outside the theatrical framework. (Liebau, 2009, p. 37) Theatre pedagogy pursues the goal of opening up spaces of experience in a playful way for the acting persons, in which they can move consistently reduced, in order to draw reflexive conclusions from the theatrical experience after the play. Options regarding possible consequences or future strategies are simulated in a space deprived of action – within the theatrical experience.

The theatrically made experiences can lead to a rethinking and testing of alternative action approaches and create a "playful" security in dealing with a multitude of affects and reactions without fear measures. In this context, Michael Wrentschur (2005) speaks of attitudes and actions that can be experienced effectively and coherently in scenic play and that are put to the test in everyday life, in social practice fields in the sense of a "pragmatic validation" (Wrentschur, 2005, p. 201). With the help of theatre pedagogical working methods, spaces for simulated practice can be created within the course of study, which opens up possibilities of identification on 'other' levels of reality and thus prepares for practice.

In teacher training, the ability to reflect school actions should be trained. Through theatrical approaches, this competence can be supported and promoted to build a pedagogically professional self and to question it creatively and fruitfully. Theatrical methods can, therefore, be understood as theatrical educational components that help student teachers better understand and reflect on their role. Thus, with the help of theatrical approaches, not only action competences but to a large extent also reflection competences concerning the professional role of the teacher are promoted. Ilse Schrittesser and Monika Hofer (2012) assume that teacher training must be perceived as an area whose 'practice' is not limited to the completion of school internships, but requires a practice of joint structured reflection (Schrittesser & Hofer, 2012, p. 152).

With the help of theatre pedagogical working methods, places for simulated practice can be created within the course of study, which opens up possibilities of identification on 'other' levels of reality and thus prepares for practice. Last but not least they can also contribute to the development of pedagogically professional habits.

Theatre pedagogy is more action- and application-oriented field in German-speaking countries. In this respect, it is more to be understood as an action science, which means that theory is directly related to practice. The work on a theoretical basis will also be necessary in the future to legitimize theatre pedagogy as an independent scientific discipline and to integrate theatrical methods into teacher training.

4   An Empirical Perspective on the Reflection Capacity of Teacher Training Students

In a course offered in the master's degree teacher education program at the University of Vienna, students have the opportunity to further develop their personal and social competencies. The students get acquainted with concepts of teacher personality and pedagogical professionalism and can critically examine their own subjective theories and biographical experiences.

The Qualitative Content Analysis should fulfill methodical quality criteria and the following aspects appear to be central to the development of qualitative content analysis. Using a rule-based and systematic procedure, the material is broken down into analysis units following a content analytical process model and processed step by step. In content analysis, in contrast to free interpretative procedures, every step of the analysis, every decision in the evaluation process, can be traced back to a well-founded and tested rule (Mayring 2008, p.43). The analytical aspects are grouped into categories, which are revised in the course of the evaluation.

The students are given the task of preparing a case in a group of approximately four people, in which personal or social skills of a teacher are required. The situation should last about 15 minutes and afterwards the discussion is led by another group of colleagues. It is very important to know, that the reflection should not thematize the performance of the case bringer respectively the acting quality of the presentation. Otherwise, there would be the risk, that the students attach too much importance to the performance itself. But the elaboration of the question or problem should be the subject of discussion. Afterwards the students are asked to present their experiences in a short reflection paper.

In the following study, the research interest lies in the feedback of the students concerning the method of simulation. The texts of 31 students were subjected to a Qualitative Content Analysis to investigate the following basic question:

> *To what extent does simulative access to questions of personal and social competences help you in your future profession?*

4.1 *Methodology*

The Qualitative Content Analysis, states Philipp Mayring, is to be understood as a data analysis technique within a rule guided research process. (Mayring, 2008) Qualitative Content Analysis aims to reduce the breadth and complexity of data material to a minimum while still maintaining a measure of the quality of the source data (Mayring, 2008).

The Qualitative Content Analysis fulfills methodical quality criteria and the following aspect appears to be central for the development of this particular approach: Using a rule-based and systematic procedure, the material is broken down into analysis units following a content analytical process model and processed step by step.

In Qualitative Content Analysis, in contrast to free interpretative procedures, every step of the analysis, every decision in the evaluation process, can be traced back to a well-founded and tested rule (Mayring, 2008, p.43). It is the only method of qualitative text analysis that separates itself early and consistently from the original text and attempts to systematically reduce the wealth of information and structure it by the research objective (Mayring, 2008). The core of this procedure is the extraction, i.e. the extraction of the required information from the text.

The category system is the central point in Qualitative Content Analysis. The analytical aspects are grouped into categories, which are revised in the course of the evaluation. The inductive category formation develops categories directly out of the material in a generalization process (extraction) without referring to previously formulated theoretical concepts. Here the categories are extracted step by step from the data material and checked in several loops and, if necessary, will be reviewed and revised. The data material will be generalized through paraphrases and be connected with theoretical preconceptions. After the final material pass, the final evaluation takes place with the help of theoretical justifications.

4.2 *Data Collection and Analysis*

Thirty-one reflective papers were analyzed and interpreted. The students submitted their statements in written form and anonymously. The inductive categories resulting from the analysis steps are as follows:
1. positive effects of the course
2. advantages of simulation
    2.1. personal competences
    2.2. social competences
3. drawbacks
4. suggestions for improvement

(1) *Positive effects of the course*: The students explain the positive learning atmosphere as a prerequisite for experiential learning. Warm-up exercises are described as a precondition for creating a trusting environment. "In this course, the warm-up exercise certainly contributed very positively to generating a setting in which nobody felt ashamed or had to hold back" (B/M3/358–360). Also, Adrian Haack (2018) speaks in this context of the positive effect of playful experimental forms of learning and the associated reduction of blockages.

The students also notice that this type of training creates a closer and more binding contact with their colleagues. In addition, the joy of active participation is described. "This course was the first of my studies in which the necessary framework conditions were created in such a way that the exchange between the participants could take place so closely and directly" (A/F1/10–12).

(2) *Advantages of simulation*: The principal advantages of the simulation are a strong reference to reality and an absolutely action-oriented tool. Furthermore, the students state that their theoretical, as well as their practical knowledge, will be broadened by this approach. Here, too, the exchange of experiences between future colleagues is emphasized. A realistic insight into practical problems helps to deepen the perception and the possibility of trying out different options for action.

The subsequent joint reflection of the individual simulations is regarded by the students as extremely important. "In my opinion, the simulations have enabled a new form of reflection and well-connected theory and practice" (A/ F2/61–63). Having the time and space to make mistakes and discuss them afterwards is also a positive effect of this course for the students. "What I personally appreciate about it are these 'aha-moments' which one gets when "getting involved" with another role" (A/F5/113–114).

(2.1) *Personal competences*: Haack (2018) describes self-competence as key qualifications in dealing with oneself, as self-reflexive and productive action in relation to one's talents and motivations as well as personality traits, self-concepts and the understanding of social roles. (Haack 2018, p.11) Apart from reflecting on their strengths and weaknesses, the students see the advantage of simulation in various solution-finding processes at the personal and professional level. The students also see the advantage of being able to gain experience in a protected environment and discuss it on a practical level.

(2.2) *Social competences*: By slipping into foreign roles, the comprehensibility of actions, especially of pupils, becomes more conscious. Some students also speak of an increase in empathy by allowing insight into other roles. "The simulations made the situations described easy to understand and it was possible to really empathize with those teachers who were confronted with more or less major difficulties" (B/F6/608–611). As a result of the different points of view during the simulation, a change of perspective could take place that would not have taken place on a purely cognitive level.

Social competences were also acquired at the level of preparation and implementation of the tasks required in the course.

(3) *Drawbacks*: Some students claim to have no enthusiasm for special access. As for disadvantages of this special access, one student stated that "my enthusiasm for role-playing is limited" (A/F6/136). There have also been reports of difficulties with the imagination. Christoph Wulf (2014) speaks in this context of the human ability to represent inner images, imaginations, and events and also to arrange them scenically. In the course of socialization and education, however, this ability is increasingly replaced by purely cognitive processes and must first be awakened in part and we cannot assume that all students will accept this kind of explorative learning.

(4) Suggestions for improvement: One student proposes to accompany the scenes by video, in order to deepen the reflection, because this result, among other things, can be used – in a pool of experiences – in similar situations in the future (B/M4/387 and 392–393). Some students also expressed their wish to work with given situations. Significantly, the wish was expressed to integrate this kind of work even more into the teaching profession studies.

4.3 The Implication for Research and Practice

In summary, theatre pedagogical work within the framework of teacher training opens up possibilities to playfully – far away from everyday reality – put oneself in 'as if' situations and thus explore other realities. The resulting experiences of difference set reflexive processes in motion. Theatrical space – as 'rehearsal space' – enables simulated practice. The integration of theatre pedagogical elements in teacher training can help to constructively deal with the emotional and insecure experiences inherent in the teacher's profession and, consequently, to develop creative strategies that help to remain capable of action in the long term and full of enjoyment. Theatre pedagogy can be an important contribution within the development of pedagogical competences and the ability to reflect.

On the one hand, there is a need for university lecturers who deal explicitly and theoretically with theatrical working methods. Educational, theatrical, social and psychological knowledge is required. Another important criterion for being able to teach theatrically is to have a basic understanding of social structures and group-dynamic processes. This competence is of particular importance in order to teach theatrically, since in the theatrical process the learner is to a large extent given the responsibility for shaping his or her own experiential spaces in the context of the entire group. In addition, a critical view of the history of the subject is essential as well as a systematized practical knowledge, which contains a wide spectrum of methodical approaches and working methods within theatre pedagogy.

On the other hand, questions about the effects and their presumed effects will have to be empirically tested. In order to answer these questions, challenging and wide-ranging studies are required. This is happening to an increasing extent, which can be seen not least from the significant increase in the number of publications in this field in recent years, but there is still a lot of work to do.

References

Greenwood, J. (2011). Aesthetic learning, and learning through the aesthetic. In E. D. Schonmann (Eds.), *Key concepts in theatre/drama education*. Rotterdam, The Netherlands: Sense Publishers.

Haack, A. (2018). *Dramapädagogik, Selbstkompetenz und Professionalisierung. Performative Identitätsarbeit im Lehramtsstudium Englisch*. Wiesbaden, Germany: Metzler.

Helsper, W. (2001). Praxis und Reflexion. Die Notwendigkeit einer „doppelten Professionalisierung" des Lehrers. *Journal für LehrerInnenbildung, 3*, 7–15.

Hentschel, U. (2010). *Theaterspielen als ästhetische Bildung. Über einen Beitrag produktiven künstlerischen Gestaltens zur Selbstbildung*. Strasbourg, Germany: Schibri.

Köhler, J. (2015). Theatrale Wege in der Lehre. In E. Sattler & S. Tschida (Eds.), *Pädagogisches Lehren? Einsätze und Einsprüche universitärer Lehre* (pp. 149–169). Wien, Austria: Löcker.

Köhler, J. (2017). *Theatrale Wege in der Lehrer/innenbildung. Theaterpädagogische Theorie und Praxis in der Ausbildung von Lehramtsstudierenden*. München, Germany: kopaed.

Köhler, J. (2018). Reflexion als theatrale Erfahrung. In E. Christof, J. Köhler, K. Rosenberger, & C. Wyss (Eds.), *Mündliche, schriftliche und theatrale Wege der Praxisreflexion. Beiträge zur Professionalisierung pädagogischen Handelns* (pp. 135–160). Bern, Switzerland: hep.

Koller, H.-C. (2006). *Grundbegriffe, Theorien und Methoden der Erziehungswissenschaft*. Stuttgart: Kohlhammer.

Kotte, A. (2013). *Theatergeschichte. Eine Einführung*. Köln, Germany: Böhlau.

Liebau, E. (2009). Schulkünste. In E. Liebau & J. Zirfas (Eds.), *Die Kunst der Schule. Über die Kultivierung der Schule durch die Künste* (pp. 47–65). Bielefeld, Germany: transcript.

Mayring, P. (2014). *Qualitative content analysis: Theoretical foundation, basic procedures and software solution*. Retrieved November 1, 2019, from November 11, 2019, https://www.ssoar.info/ssoar/handle/document/39517

OECD. (2005). *Teachers matter. Attracting, developing and retaining effective teachers*. Retrieved September 30, 2019, From https://www.oecd.org/education/school/34990905.pdf

Oevermann, U. (1996). Theoretische Skizze einer revidierten Theorie professionalisierten Handelns. In A. Combe & W. Helsper (Eds.), *Pädagogische Professionalität. Untersuchungen zum Typus pädagogischen Handelns* (pp. 70–182). Frankfurt am Main, Germany: Suhrkamp.

Plessner, H. (1965). *Die Stufen des Organischen und der Mensch*. Berlin, Germany: Walter de Gruyter.

Plessner, H. (1982). *Gesammelte Schriften. VII. Ausdruck und menschliche Natur*. Frankfurt am Main, Germany: Suhrkamp.

Schön, D. (1983). *The reflective practitioner. How professionals think in action*. New York, NY: Basic Books.

Schratz, M., Paseka, A., & Schrittesser, I. (Eds.). (2011). *Pädagogische Professionalität: quer denken – umdenken – neu denken*. Wien, Austria: Facultas.

Schrittesser, I. (2011). Professionelle Kompetenzen: Systematische und empirische Annäherungen. In M. Schratz, A. Paseka, & I. Schrittesser (Eds.), *Pädagogische Professionalität: quer denken – umdenken – neu denken* (pp. 95–122). Wien, Austria: Facultas.

Schrittesser, I., & Hofer, M. (2012). Wie Pierre Bourdieus Habitusbegriff die Kulturen der Lehrerbildung und der Schulpraxis einander näher bringen könnte In C. Kraler, H. Schnabel-Schüle, M. Schratz, & B. Weyand (Eds.), *Kulturen der Lehrerbildung. Professionalisierung eines Berufsstands im Wandel* (pp. 143–156). Münster, Germany: Waxmann.

Wiese, H.-J., Günther, M., & Ruping, B. (2006). *Theatrales Lernen als philosophische Praxis in Schule und Freizeit*. Berlin, Milow, Strasburg: Schibri.

Wrentschur, M. (2005). Szenisches Forschen – Zwischen Erfahrungs-, Wahrnehmungs- und Handlungsbezug. In H. Stigler & H. Reicher (Eds.), *Praxisbuch empirische Sozialforschung in den Erziehungs- und Bildungswissenschaften* (pp. 196–206). Innsbruck, Austria: Studienverlag.

Wulf, C. (2014). Mimesis. In C. Wulf & J. Zirfas (Eds.), *Handbuch Pädagogische Anthropologie* (pp. 247–257). Wiesbaden, Germany: Springer.

CHAPTER 5

Towards Broader Views on Learning to Teach: The Case of a Pedagogy for Learning to Teach for Creativity

Ida Oosterheert, Paulien C. Meijer and Ingeborg van der Neut

Abstract

Teacher education programs increasingly tend to include a variety of views on learning-to-teach. These not only focus on knowledge acquisition and development of skills, but also include attention to the formation of professional identity and to social and societal aspects of becoming a teacher. Little is known, however, about pedagogies that have such broad development as their goal. Building on research indicating the dynamic, interactive and often transformative nature of becoming a teacher in the broad sense, a course was designed for Dutch university student teachers that focused on 'teaching for creativity' and the creation of 'creativity cultivating contexts'. Data were gathered in four subsequent courses (N = 67) that were designed according to the characteristics of such a context. The findings indicate that student teachers reported outcomes that refer to all aspects of their learning and, more than anything else, outcomes indicated extensions or (re)considerations of various aspects of their emerging identity as teachers. This leads to the conclusion that learning to teach for creativity goes hand in hand with a reconsideration of one's identity as a teacher.

Keywords

creativity – teaching for creativity – teacher identity – pedagogy – teacher development – teacher education

1   Becoming a Teacher

For decades, attention has been paid to what Linda Darling-Hammond and John Bransford (2007) phrased as "What teachers should know and be able to do". In their edited book, which assumes that teachers should be prepared to teach in "a changing world", the complexity and sheer magnitude of skills and knowledge that teachers need become ever-so evident. Needless to say, since publication of their book, the world has continued to change, particularly with regard to information technology and social media that has great influence on society and teaching in it. The need to pay attention to the building of democratic societies, care for the environment, and other worldwide needs, has pointed at the central roles that education at large, and teachers in particular, should play in addressing these needs. In this chapter, instead of piling more tasks on the shoulders of schools and teachers, we explore how the education of future teachers might be reconsidered in such a way, that it addresses how societies call-out to teachers. A way of doing so is to experiment in teacher education, with courses that explicitly address the complex task of being a teacher nowadays, and that are built on a comprehensive and holistic view of learning that underlies the process of becoming a teacher.

One of the reasons that people want to become teachers is that they aim for goals with their pupils that encompass much more than going through the standard curricula, such as development of all kinds of personal talents, the development of a purpose in life, and related to subject matter, the development of a sense of history, enjoy reading, et cetera. All of these goals ask for much more than the development of knowledge and skills that are also (important) parts of the school curriculum and all ask for an authentic, creative stance towards most current practices. At the same time, research shows that teachers experience difficulties with putting such encompassing goals into practice in, for them, satisfying ways. This has all kinds of reasons which refer to the whole scope of being a teacher as described above: they feel that they do not have the necessary knowledge and skills, they have not found the right materials, their colleagues or administration hinder any deviation from the core curriculum that does not seem to value such goals, the pupils become uncertain when doing things they are not used to, and they themselves join their pupils in feelings of uncertainty (see, e.g., Mansfield, Beltman, Broadley, & Weatherby-Fell, 2016). In addition, they feel that they have not been properly prepared to address such advanced goals. Based on the literature that appeals to a broader view on learning to teach (e.g., Darling-Hammond & Bransford, 2007), one might also say, that teacher education not automatically addresses what it means for a teacher's identity, or a teacher's relationship to others (pupils, colleagues) when a teacher pays attention to such goals. Considering the fact that many of these advanced and far-reaching goals relate to creativity, we choose to focus on this concept in studying student teachers' learning in the broad sense.

2   Teaching for Creativity

Several studies point out that developments in society are calling for educational approaches in which students acquire not only knowledge and skills, but also learn to creatively apply these to discover, devise, and realize new possibilities (e.g., Redecker, 2008; Pédro, 2006; Ferrari, Cachia, Ala-Mutka, & Punie, 2009; Voogd & Pareja Roblin, 2010; cf. Oosterheert & Meijer, 2017). As a result, teachers as well teacher educators are facing the challenge to achieve this goal. But despite policy attention and newly developed educational materials (e.g., Beghetto & Kaufman, 2010; Kaufman & Sternberg, 2010), Sternberg (2015) and Blamires and Peterson (2014) observed that the cultivation of creativity has not penetrated the average classroom in the USA and the UK. Likewise, Dutch teachers, although motivated to get started on the cultivation of creativity, indicate that they lack the knowledge and support to do this in a systematic and responsible manner (SLO, 2015). Several explanations have been put forward for teachers' hesitation to take up creativity cultivation in their teaching. Among these are teachers' attachment to existing convictions and routines, traditional practices in schools and teacher education and the culture of testing in schools, which Sternberg (2015) labeled as incompatible with creativity cultivation.

Although these are plausible explanations, we think that there might also be a more fundamental cause, which we will explore in more depth in the present study. We depart from two interrelated ideas (cf. Meijer & Oosterheert, 2018). The first is that teaching for creativity demands teachers to take up a role that is fundamentally different from their role in more traditional ways of teaching. This implies the second idea, that is, that *learning* to teach for creativity is unavoidably a process of becoming a teacher in every sense of the word, and should be approached as such. For aspirant and novice teachers this means that they should engage in 'learning to cultivate creativity' not just as the individual development of a set of skills or the acquisition of knowledge, but as part of their identity formation as professional teachers and as a way to (re)consider their relation to subject matter and to others, among which are their fellow-student teachers, their pupils, colleagues, administrators and the school system.

3   A Creativity-Cultivating Context

Building on research about creativity in education and what it takes to cultivate creativity in the school context, we constructed a framework (cf. Oosterheert

& Meijer, 2017), which formed a starting point for designing contexts that are supposed to cultivate learners' creativity. In designing such contexts, one needs to consider (a) the goals of the cultivation of creativity, (b) the nature of the creative challenges, (c) the role of the teacher in the cultivation of creativity, (d) the role of the students, and (e) the embedding of the cultivation of creativity in the curriculum. These elements are not dissimilar when designing other educational contexts, but their contents need to have a particular focus when creativity is supposed to be cultivated. We elaborate on such a focus below.

a. *The goals of the cultivation of creativity*: Goals in a creativity-cultivating context focus on the increase of confidence and ability of learners to tackle creative challenges and contribute to ideas that can be considered new and useful within a given group/school and on learners discovering the domain(s) in which they want to further develop their creativity.

b. *The nature of the creative challenges*: Creative challenges in a creativity-cultivating context include divergent and convergent activities to form a meaningful whole, within or across disciplines. They offer space for the generation of a wide variety of ideas and stimulate students to deal with context boundaries and limitations. They cover a combination of original, usable, and at times elegant products and ideas. The outcomes of challenges are often unknown prior to the completion of the process, also to the teacher. This might initially lead to resistance and feelings of uncertainty, as people struggle with the task. Still, this is an inherent feature of a creative challenge.

c. *The role of the teachers in the cultivation of creativity*: Teachers create learners' space to tackle the creative challenges, individually and with peers. They openly value unconventional thinking and at the same time set (safety) boundaries if necessary. They emphasize the pleasure and benefit, and sometimes the frustration of creative functioning and discuss what constitutes creative quality within a particular challenge or domain. Learners know ahead of time just how, by whom, and for what purpose(s) their creative ideas will be looked at. Teachers curiously watch, from a broad developmental perspective, how learners' creativity gets cultivated. Teachers are appreciative of and offer support and feedback on learners' efforts, and on their (growing) creative qualities, ideas and products.

d. *The role of the learners*: In a creativity-cultivating context, learners notice that teachers have high expectations for them and appreciate their creative qualities. They also notice that their ideas are given sufficient space and respect, even when they are not particularly creative. Learners fearlessly put all of their imaginative powers, thinking, practical skills, and courage to work. They discover their own qualities, those of others and how these qualities complement and strengthen each other. Learners gradually think up their own (collective) creative challenges.

e. *The embedding of the cultivation of creativity in the curriculum*: In full-fletched creativity cultivating contexts, learners are stimulated from the start – sometimes spontaneously, sometimes intentionally – to take on both little and bigger creative challenges across subject domains and with each other. These creative challenges are elements or reconstructed parts of the larger curriculum (long-term as well as across subjects). Specific talents and interests of learners are given room within elective and extracurricular components. Assessment, then, largely has the character of "evaluating to learn" or of "becoming creative (together)". Summative assessment of creativity occurs on an incidental and collaborative basis for components of the curriculum for which all involved have shown to have some substantive affinity, such as through peer review.

4   This Study

4.1   *Objective and Research Question*

In this study, the objective was to examine whether and how a course on 'teaching for creativity' contributes to student teachers' learning, and how this learning might be conceptualized. The research question was exploratory in nature and phrased as:

> *In what sense does the course 'Teaching for Creativity' contribute to the process of becoming a teacher?*

5   The Course

5.1   *Participants and Course Structure*

We designed a course 'Teaching for Creativity'. The participants were university student teachers following a one-year postmaster teacher education program, aiming to prepare for teaching in (upper) secondary schools. The program is dual, in the sense that student teachers follow courses at university two days a week, and spend three days a week at their practice school in order to observe and provide lessons. In the second semester of the program, they enrolled in an elective course 'Teaching for Creativity'. The course consisted of four meetings of 90 minutes with intervals of one or two weeks. In this course, groups of 15–25 student teachers with various backgrounds regarding subject matter discipline (biology, math, English, etc.) were challenged to experiment with the concept of creativity in their secondary classrooms.

5.2   *Goals and Pedagogy*

The framework described above served as a starting point for the course. Learning to teach for creativity was the main goal (for student teachers) and exemplification and enactment were the main pedagogical approaches of the course. During the course-meetings at the university, we intended that the student teachers would have experiences that inspired them for what they could establish in their own classrooms. Besides developing student teachers knowledge about creativity and addressing their own creativity, we challenged student teachers' emerging professional identities, throughout the course, in order to reframe common notions of education, and to learn to deal with uncertainty, open-end learning and out-of-the-box thinking (Oosterheert & Meijer, 2017; Sternberg, 2006). Throughout the course, student teachers were invited to develop their answers on the following three questions: What do creativity and the cultivation of creativity mean for (1) my pupils, and for my subject area; (2) me as a person and as a teacher and (3) my professional context? We purposefully aimed to evoke dynamic, interactive and transformative processes, associated with identity formation, to take place. At the final meeting, student teachers presented their learning outcomes as a result of an open assignment. "Be creative" was the only guideline given for this assignment and student teachers developed their own evaluation criteria, including criteria for evaluating their learning when designing and working on their assignment.

The broader approach we tried to establish, and in particular the roles of student teachers and educators therein, can be outlined according to the following five elements that were at the core of the course design:

a.   Do the unusual, create discomfort: Student teachers were involved in unusual exercises, meant to lure them out of their comfort zones. The first question was 'what are we going to do?'. A variety of spaces was used, such as classrooms, corridors, and gardens. A miscellany of seating unfolded, ranging from pub-like to auditory-like seating. The final assignment was entirely open. Conditional for such potentially unsafe learning to take place is the establishment of a safe environment, which we paid much attention to.

b.   Stimulate (collaborative) enactment in practice: Student teachers were stimulated to use and provide room for uncommon teaching practices in their secondary classrooms, with the explicit risk of 'failure'. The actual (collaborative) design of these teaching practices, including student teachers' expectations, fears, and surprises before and afterwards were exchanged and discussed in various groupings during the university meetings.

c. Relate the micro-level, school level and macro-level of teaching: In the exchange of experiences, student teachers were stimulated to relate micro situations of teaching to the school level and macro-level of teaching and teaching policy, and vice versa. As such, we discussed the purposes of education as well as teacher's and pupils' role in it. Close attention was paid to teachers' collective responsibilities for pupils' growth and development and to positively value and utilize differences between pupils in order to appeal to the collaborative responsibility to shape (future) society.

d. Pay explicit attention to affective processes: Affective reactions to experiences, literature, and discussions, positive and negative were approached explicitly. Students were invited to explore the origin of their reaction, whether it be affirmation or surprise, confrontation or else and to listen to other reactions. We attempted to flexibly adapt the program to attune to students' reactions as much as possible, evoking resistance if necessary to challenge each other's routines and assumptions, and explicitly accommodating the sometimes emotional outbursts that were associated with breakthrough moments.

e. Pioneer with your students: As educators, we were not experts at all times. Often we were pioneers with the students, searching for new possibilities, having fun with them, and then being serious and sharing on the spot our own discomfort, questions and struggles. In explicitly modeling the course's principles as much as possible, one would see us, educators, in a central position in the group, sometimes observing from the side, or mingling in, in many ways. Theories and contents were presented interactively in various forms and 'just in time'.

5.3   *Methods and Analysis*

Data were gathered from four groups of student teachers attending the course for two consecutive years (N_{total} = 67). The data sources were student teachers' learner reports, field notes by the educators and student teachers' creative products. After the course, student teachers wrote a learner report (e.g. De Groot, 1980). They completed sentences such as: "For me as … a teacher, a person, a colleague in a school, cultivating creativity means …". "What surprised me (most) in this course is …". "For me, the most valuable learning (experience) in/as a result of this course is …". See Appendix A for the full outline of the learner report. We analyzed their answers cross case in light of literature on identity formation. This meant that the search for meaningful categories representing the data was inductive but restricted to teacher identity aspects. For example, data referring to feeling uncertain as an impetus to develop the courage to do something new were considered relevant in light of the work of Illeris (2013). Likewise, student teachers' reconsiderations regarding 'being a teacher' could often be related to the work of Verhaeghe (2012), describing identity as a result of negotiating the personal needs and aspirations and those of significant others (in this case: the teaching practices and teachers in their school).

The teacher educators made field notes during and after the meetings of the four courses. Notes regarded as noteworthy were student teachers' insights or questions and their signs indicating emotional involvement (surprise, joy, frustration, etc.). The field notes were exchanged after each meeting and selected in light of the study's research question. The creative products presented in the final meeting served as complementary sources of information.

The analysis process started with reading through all data, and categorizing student teachers' learner reports. During this step, we developed categories and found that the way student teachers reported on their learning, could best be labeled as "aspects of identification", as their reports mostly seem to reflect what they identify as important for their teaching and for themselves as teachers. We found seven identification aspects in the learner reports.

As a second step, we looked at the number of student teachers that reported each identification aspects, to find out what they seem to agree most on and what the differences are.

Thirdly, we went through our field notes, in which we had written down the most striking moments during the meetings. Along with students' creative products, these were used as complementary sources of information, in order to better understand their replies in the learner reports.

5.4 *Results*

Table 5.1 shows the seven categories identified in the 67 learner reports and the relative frequencies of occurrence. The right-hand column shows example quotes from the learner reports.

Table 5.1 shows that student teachers' identification with routines in their schools became less self-evident during the time span of the course. They started to see the value of space for playful learning, using imagination (teachers and students) and various forms of interaction. The need for a teacher to (learn to) be flexible and open to experience was often reported as well as to provide sufficient safety and boundaries. In addition, the course appeared to provide opportunities to employ other perspectives on teaching; one in which

TABLE 5.1   Identification aspects (percentages of occurrence) and examples from student
              teachers' learner reports

Identification aspect	Examples
Identification with aspects of good teaching (for creativity) All (100%) student teachers report on new (emerging) views on learning and teaching.	'Teaching for creativity is not about collecting new didactic tools; it is rather about the establishment of a new learning environment where students can develop themselves'. 'I know now that my subject involves so much more that the book or the study planner'. 'Producing your own language, being an artist with language; I want to see what's inside them'.
Identification with pupil roles in particular. About 48% of the student teachers articulate their changing view on the role pupils can and should play in education in particular.	'I want to let pupils search and find out more by themselves and be open to what they find'. 'I need to build up my lessons in interaction with the pupils'. 'I have confidence in my pupils! They can sometimes produce amazing products in open settings without 'grades'. 'I feel I (will) learn a lot from my pupils when TfC'. 'Most surprising for me is that pupils are so open to new things, to new challenges!' 'I want to initiate dialogue with pupils, let go control, give choices, trust that pupils can, and that they have to unlearn the thinking in right and wrong'. 'Students can handle fewer instructions and also they can think along with teachers about new challenges'.
Identification with the current educational practice in their school. About 32% of the student teachers express their stronger awareness of and willingness to reconsider existing structures and habits in their school and/or the educational system as a whole.	'I may let go more of what seems evident'. 'I have become aware that I can actually question the assessment practices in my school'. 'I probably have to stick to the rules and structures in my school, what I do not want'. 'I have obtained more distance to 'evident' features of the school system. From this, I am critically searching for improvements'. 'I can be critical about the assessment & testing system'.

(cont.)

TABLE 5.1   Identification aspects (percentages of occurrence) and examples from student
teachers' learner reports (*cont.*)

Identification aspect	Examples
Identification with other (student) teachers. About 39% of the student teachers express their positive surprise about unexpected qualities and ideas of their fellow students, particularly of students from other disciplines.	'You educate together, with your colleagues' 'Surprising for me is that so many of my fellow students feel restricted in the current practices in their schools'. 'Other students are so creative as well'! 'Creativity can be nurtured in all disciplines' 'I want to search for collaboration with colleagues of other disciplines
Sense of professional space and agency in their own practice and in the school. About 88% of the student teachers express their discovery of the possibility of taking up a (more) proactive role in their classrooms and in their school.	'I can just show my colleagues what I have tried out in my classroom, instead of waiting for some kind of permission'. 'I need to let go of all kinds of control, to develop stamina instead of compliance'. 'I can do something; communicate, take up multidisciplinary initiatives'. 'I have to keep thinking for myself' 'I want to share materials with my colleagues. And have fruitful discussions with them on pupils' creative thought processes'.
Identification with a need for certainty and predictability. About 43% of the student teachers report their changing stance towards certainty and predictability.	'I want to learn to accept uncertainty and trust that it will be all right in one way or another'. 'I need to let go of my desire for control and regularity. Although that leads to resistance and uncertainty at first, I want to develop the courage to do something deviating, and to let go of restrictive norms'. 'I have to step out of my comfort zone, take risks, and be willing to make exceptions to the rule'.

(*cont.*)

TABLE 5.1   Identification aspects (percentages of occurrence) and examples from student
             teachers' learner reports (*cont.*)

Identification aspect	Examples
Identification with personal or teacher characteristics. About 43% of the student teachers express (emerging) personal or teacher characteristics they identify with.	'To my surprise, in this course with much freedom, I experienced joy instead of anxiousness. Trying things out is good and fun!' 'I am surprised by my own ideas!' 'In my teaching I show characteristics of an artist'. 'I want to have fun when I teach'. 'I have been confronted with my prejudices and unconscious well-rooted boundaries'. 'The open assignment was so hard for me ... Being a perfectionist, I am more proud of having done it (with so many open options!) than of the final result. So educative'.

the discovery of creativity of both pupils and oneself as teacher, is central. It seems that the course not only leads to "learning more", but also to how a different approach to learning (more open and creative) enables a range of other types of learning outcomes. What strikes is that student teachers as well their pupils highly value these outcomes. It might be that this is affected by the experience of some student teachers of a "personal victory" to get there.

Mostly because of pupils' reactions to their new ways of teaching, about half of the student teachers reported their surprise and increased trust in pupils' abilities, motivation, and learning intentions. They started to identify more with a teacher being receptive to pupils' ideas and willing to work together. New ways of *being educated* (in the course) had a similar effect; many students reported their positive surprise about –prior to this course - unknown qualities, ideas and experiences of their fellow students, particularly of other disciplines. They started to see teaching as a collaborative endeavor and came to realize that there is more space than they initially thought, to just start doing things in a (slightly) different fashion.

Quite a few student teachers (re)discovered personal qualities and aspirations as teachers, just by being confronted with and overcoming anxieties and uncertainties during the course. Some student teachers rediscovered why they wanted to become a teacher in the first place. A decreasing identification with their need for certainty and predictability was also often reported. The desire is to 'let go control more often', 'overcome uncertainty' and to 'develop courage', in their own classrooms as well as in their schools.

From the field notes it is noteworthy to mention that during the meetings there were at times emotional expressions or even outbursts of student teachers; positive, negative or sad. These gave rise to rich discussions and insights. Two examples:

− Some student teachers realized how little their creative potential has been valued during their entire educational career. One student teacher (Physics) in particular, shared how much he felt 'trapped' by the ways he had been taught thus far and how he had been labeled 'non-creative' by a former teacher. He firmly stated '… I NEVER want to feel it again!'

− The open character of the final assignment was an exciting challenge for most student teachers and educators. Several students initially showed strong frustration and resistance. Later they acknowledged that it was just this lack of structure that made them surprise themselves and have new aspirations for their pupils.

In sum, the results indicate that the course 'Teaching for Creativity' evoked a broad array of learning processes and outcomes; student teachers not only acquired new knowledge and skills regarding teaching for creativity and creative teaching, but many also engaged in fundamental professional and personal identity formation processes. Consequently, they reconsidered the social and societal aspects of being and becoming a teacher and often started to explore new lines of thinking about schooling as a phenomenon and pupils' and teachers' roles therein.

6   Conclusions and Discussion

This study departed from the assumption that learning to teach for creativity can be a way to prepare student teachers for the important task they face as teachers: guiding their pupils to be able to co-contribute to a society-in-flux and an uncertain future. The findings indicate that the framework we used as the fundament of this course evokes a process in most student teachers, in which they acquire new knowledge and skills but also reconsider various aspects of their emerging identities as teachers and as learners. Most remarkably, the confrontation with often unexpected, positive pupil behavior as a result of trying out new approaches to teaching had an almost immediate (decreasing) effect on student teachers' identification with current school practices and pupils' and teachers' roles therein (aspect B in Table 5.1). In addition, student teachers reported a grown 'sense of agency' as young professionals in a school context, which is not self-evident for Dutch (student) teachers (e.g. Oolbekkink-March-and, Hadar, Smith, Helleve, & Ulvik, 2017). We found that they developed a much stronger sense of identification with other aspects of being a teacher (see Table 5.1): Identification with aspects of good teaching (for creativity), identification with pupil roles in particular, identification with other (student) teachers, a sense of professional space and agency in their own practice and in the school, identification with a need for certainty and predictability, and identification with personal or teacher characteristics. Together, these reflect a view on learning that encompasses the development of teaching skills as well as new insights into how one relates to others in schools (pupils, colleagues) and into one's personal characteristics.

7   Significance

Considering the relatively short duration of this course, the findings are promising in light of the aforementioned goals. At the same time, just because of this short duration, we estimate that the observed learning outcomes, for the most part, indicate an influence on how student teachers further develop. It is uncertain how their development evolves over time in everyday school life. Longer interventions are perhaps needed to ensure sustaining effects (Meijer & Oosterheert, 2018) and further research is needed to see whether they indeed become teachers who provide time and space for creativity in their classes and address the characteristics of a creativity-cultivating context.

This study provides initial evidence that a pedagogy that builds on broad views of learning and is laid out as teaching for creativity, as operationalized here, evokes (emerging) professional identity changes in student teachers who prepare to become a subject matter teacher in secondary education. The changes were induced in the interplay of cognition, emotion and social learning and as such add to Illeris' model of identity learning (Illeris, 2013). Additional research should shed more light on the sustainability of the findings.

References

Alsup, J. (2006). *Teacher identity discourses. Negotiating personal and professional spaces*. New York, NY: Routledge.

Beghetto, R. A., & Kaufman, J. C. (Eds.). (2010). *Nurturing creativity in the classroom*. New York, NY: Cambridge University Press.

Blamires, M., & Peterson, A. (2014). Can creativity be assessed? Towards an evidence-informed framework for assessing and planning progress in creativity. *Cambridge Journal of Education, 44*(2), 147–162.

Darling-Hammond, L., & Bransford, J. (2007). *Preparing teachers for a changing world: What teachers should learn and be able to do.* New York, NY: John Wiley & Sons.

De Groot, A. D. (1980). The learner report as a tool in the evaluation of psychotherapy. In W. de Moor & H. R. Wijngaarden (Eds.), Psychotherapy, research and training (pp. 177–182). Amsterdam, the Netherlands: Elsevier/North Holland Biomedical Press.

Ferrari, A., Cachia, R., Ala-Mutka, K., & Punie, Y. (2010). *Creative learning and innovative teaching: Final report on the study on creativity and innovation in education in EU member states.* Institute for Prospective and Technological Studies, Joint Research Centre.

Illeris, K. (2013). *Transformative learning and identity.* London: Routledge.

Kaufman J. C., & Sternberg, R. J. (2010). *Cambridge handbook of creativity.* New York, NY: Cambridge University.

Meijer, P. C. (2011). The role of crisis in the development of student teachers' professional identity. In A. Lauriala, R. Rajala, H. Ruokamo, & o. Ylitapio-Miintyla (Eds.), *Navigating in educational contexts: Identities and cultures in dialogue* (pp. 41–54). Rotterdam, The Netherlands: Sense Publishers.

Mansfield, C. F., Beltman, S., Broadley, T., & Weatherby-Fell, N. (2016). Building resilience in teacher education: An evidenced informed framework. *Teaching and Teacher Education, 54*, 77–87.

Meijer, P. C., Oolbekkink, H. W., Pillen, M., & Aardema, A. (2014). Pedagogies of developing teacher identity. In C. Craig & L. Orland-Barak (Eds.), *International teacher education: Promising pedagogies (Part A)* (pp. 293–309). Bingley: Emerald Publishing Limited.

Meijer, P. C., & Oosterheert, I. E. (2018). Student teachers' identity development in relation to 'teaching for creativity'. In P. Schutz & Y. Hong (Eds.), *Research on teacher identity and motivation: Mapping challenges and innovations.* New York, NY: Springer.

Oolbekkink-Marchand, H. W., Hadar, L. L., Smith, K., Helleve, I., & Ulvik, M. (2017). Teachers' perceived professional space and their agency. *Teaching and Teacher Education, 62*(2), 37–46. doi:10.1016/j.tate.2016.11.005

Oosterheert, I. E., & Meijer, P. C. (2017). Wat creativiteitsontwikkeling in het onderwijs behoeft. [What it takes to cultivate creativity in education]. *Pedagogische Studiën, 94*, 196–210.

Pedró, F. (2006). *The new millennium learners: Challenging our views on ict and learning.* OECD-CERI.

Redecker, C. (2008). *Review of learning 2.0 practices: JRC-IPTS.*

Scardamelia, M., & Bereiter, C. (2014). Knowledge building and knowledge creation: Theory, pedagogy, and technology. In R. Keith Sawyer (Ed.), *The Cambridge handbook of the learning sciences* (pp. 397–417). Cambridge: Cambridge University Press.

SLO. (2015). *21e eeuwse vaardigheden in het curriculum van het funderend onderwijs* [*21st century skills in the curriculum of primary and secondary education*]. Enschede, The Netherlands: SLO.

Sternberg, R. J. (2006). The nature of creativity. *Creativity Research Journal, 18*(1), 87–98.

Sternberg, R. J. (2015). Teaching for creativity: The sounds of silence. *Psychology of Aesthetics, Creativity, and the Arts, 9*(2), 115–117.

Toompalu, A., Leijen, Ä., & Kullasepp, K. (2017). Professional role expectations and related feelings when solving pedagogical dilemmas: A comparison of pre- and in-service teachers. *Teacher Development, 21*(2), 307–323.

Verhaeghe, P. (2012). *Identiteit* [*Identity*]. Amsterdam, The Netherlands: de Bezige Bij.

Voogd, J., & Pareja Roblin, N. (2010). *21st century skills.* Enschede: Universiteit Twente.

Appendix A: Outline of the Learning Report

1. When I think about addressing the development of creativity/creative thinking with my pupils (in my subject area), the insights and ideas that pop up are …

2. (Learning to) work with pupils on the development of creativity implies for me, *as a person,* that I …

3. (Learning to) work with pupils on the development of creativity implies for me, *as a colleague in my school*, that I …

4. I think that, in my subject area, teaching for creativity is characterized by …

5. In my forthcoming lessons, I really want to get to work with …

6. The most valuable that I learned or experienced in this course is …

7. This teacher educator [name] has …

8. My biggest surprise was …

9. What I missed most was …

PART 2

Challenges of the Contemporary Teaching Context

∴

CHAPTER 6

From Integration to Inclusion: Some Critical Issues about Teacher Training in the Italian Experience

Maria Antonella Galanti and Tamara Zappaterra

Abstract

Starting from the 70s of the last century, Italy has represented a particular reference point, in Europe, with regard to the integration of persons with disabilities into public training courses, first at school and then at University level. In the last fifteen years we have moved on to consider the possibility of making the training path not only able to integrate but also to include persons with disabilities and more generally anyone with a significant difference in terms of behavior models and ability and skills learning compared to typical development. What practices have become necessary for training effective inclusive teachers, specialized in the various Neurodevelopmental Disorders as well as in curricular teaching? The chapter aims to critically discuss the path from integration to inclusion especially with regard to Italy, through a double glance: the theoretical one and the experiential one, analyzed through data collection. From the theoretical point of view, we believe that the inclusive principle should not only look at people and their relationships, but also the point of view of the different subjects and their possibility to dialogue, and tolerate the conflict of interpretation. This view should turn itself into a resource for understanding in a critical way the socio-psycho-pedagogical dynamics that regulate the relationship with diversity. From the surveys significant progress is shown in inclusive teaching practices, but much work still needs to be done especially in relation to training students with disabilities to achieving adult life, autonomy and, where possible, work-life integration.

Keywords

teacher training – disability – special needs education

© KONINKLIJKE BRILL NV, LEIDEN, 2020 | DOI: 10.1163/9789004432048_006

1   **Introduction**

In Italy, the path to integration began with a law issued 42 years ago in 1977: Law 517, which quietly opened the door to an epochal change. It decreed the end of the so-called special classes in which children with disabilities were segregated, and placed them in regular school, with the support of a new figure, the support teacher. This teacher was not meant to be a caretaker, but rather served as a communicative filter and a mediator of conflict, reinforcing the entire class to which they were entrusted with the task of integrating pupils with disabilities and relative learning disadvantages. Law 517 (MIUR, 517) concerned only compulsory education, but over the years, through new legislative provisions integration has expanded to all levels of public education, from nurseries for children aged 0–3 years to university.

2   **The Cultural Climate at the Start of the Integration Process**

In order to fully comprehend the direction of the path from integration to inclusion, it is important to consider the cultural climate during the years when the law was enacted, as well as the historical evolution of our understanding of integration. As with many other groups of people subjected to prejudice or injustice and discrimination due to being different, new collective subjectivities emerged in the 1970s. For example, this was the case with the women's and student movements, with what is known as "anti-psychiatry", or again, with the movement addressing the rights of the sick and the elderly. This is reflected in many writings published in the late 1960s and the 1970s that proved to be milestones along the path of inclusion with respect to differences (Basaglia, 1968; Bettelheim, 1974; Goffman, 1961, 1970). The common idea in these various expressions of desire for change is a sort of aspiration to happiness understood not in an individualistic sense, but as something shared that is capable of creating greater harmony between the aspirations of the individual and the collective.

In the 1970s, the tendency of many teachers to embrace a profoundly innovative idea of school, in conflict with others eager to maintain traditional certainties, was also pervasive on a social level. Moreover, such a combination of opposing points of view is typical of moments of great social ferment and historical transformation. On one hand, the idea of integration appeared as a sign of openness that would have improved the quality of life not only of students with disabilities, but also of those without particular problems because it would have encouraged them to measure themselves against diversity and

develop relational and social skills linked to solidarity, to the elaboration of
the desire for self-realization in itself more negatively self-centered, and also
to the de-dramatization of each individual's imperfections, including one's
own. It would also have reinforced their ability to adapt to shared social rules
by learning to postpone their immediate needs in favor of harmonious and
united community life among peers. However, on the other hand, this same
integration gave rise to insecurities and new anxieties.

The passing of time can make the emotional aspect of complex historical
events such as the innovative school legislation of those years seem less dramatic. Not a few teachers were disoriented and affected by an intense sense of
inadequacy, powerlessness and even fear. However, despite the upheaval, most
of them managed to accept the idea of a school that was open to the territory
and to transform themselves in relation to it, even changing their didactic style.
In fact, the gradual move from integration to inclusion was due to a bottom-up
process carried out by many teachers willing to rethink their role and their
educational and didactic habits in order to transform the school, making it
able to accommodate every difference. Thus, from the point of view of integration, Italy has been able to offer a model that is also appreciated in other countries, both for the inclusive process carried out from below by many teachers,
and for its advanced legislative network.

3   Propulsive and Conservative Thrusts with Respect to the
         Welcoming and Inclusive School Model

In an exhilarating climate of aspiration to greater social equality, freedom
from prejudice and mental stereotypes, and openness to diversity experienced
as an enrichment of one's relational skills and no longer as an obstacle for
one's own realization, Law 517 not only started off the introduction of subjects with disabilities in regular school classrooms, but implicitly contained
a new idea of the school, generally inclusive: a school for all understood as a
valuable common good. It was precisely after this law was passed that a real
change in school practices began to be seen in Italy; that is, the possibility of
eradicating obsolete traditions by opening up the insurmountable walls of
scholastic and university knowledge to the whole territory and to the widespread need for knowledge. In this process premises were also created for the
subsequent creation of Special Pedagogy as a specific sector of study of the
condition of disability, as well as of the path of integration and scholastic
inclusion (Canevaro, 2007; d'Alonzo & Caldin 2012; Goussot, 2007; Pavone,
2010, Crispiani, 2016).

The contrast still exists between propulsive and other more conservative if not regressive, with respect to the school model that is considered in harmony with one's point of view, places the figure of the support teacher in a difficult balance between science and affectivity, between technique and care. This is the unresolved element of all figures with a caring function; that the figure of the support teacher has always had to maintain a difficult balance between science and emotion, technique and concern, an unresolved element for all figures with a function of care. Even today defining the role of the support teacher is the most complex problem among the many issues surrounding integration.

A great deal has been said and written about Law 517 (MIUR, 1977), precisely because it is considered one of the most advanced at the international level and is still highly relevant today. The legal landscape of the 1970s was full of innovative elements that moved in parallel to it and in a certain sense served as a background, starting with the Delegated Decrees (Italian Ministry of Education, 1974) that made possible forms of social participation in school management, seen as a community space that was no longer self-referential and circumscribed by its own boundaries, but sustained an interactive dialogue with the surrounding territory. However, since then there have been discrepancies and resistance in school practices, due to backward thinking or stereotypes and persistent prejudices. In short, there has been a conflict between legislative innovation and operative school procedures, and profound differences (not only in points of view, but operational ones as well) from school to school. At the time, this contrast also reverberated in the collective imagination.

As previously mentioned the 1970s were characterized by great social upheaval and by the emergence of many different utopias related to accepting diversity in all its aspects, supporting the inalienable right of every person to be acknowledged in his own subjectivity. In those years a movement had already exploded that was given the name (in many ways inappropriate) of "anti-psychiatry", but there were also the student movements of 1968, seeking a different sort of education, and the women's movement, arguing for the first time that gender discrimination crossed all political and social contexts. These are only the best-known examples among many that characterized a historical era linked to the desire to break down boundaries and barriers, and offer new forms of solidarity between people.

The conflict between utopian social tensions and others linked to conservative desires that characterizes the era when Law 517 was issued, has remained over time and has meant that the practices aimed at integration could be reduced to empty formal rituals. For this reason, today's problems relating to inclusion are linked to the ability of schools and families, in communication with health services, to plan a program that goes beyond the scholastic, both diachronically and synchronically. A "life project" should in fact cover all aspects of existence, starting from the extracurricular ones of entertainment and social commitment, and continue over time into adulthood, with a work outlet when the disability allows it. The difficulty of creating a dialogue between what occurs at school and in the classroom and the life project of a student with disability can be linked to many variables, including traces of old prejudices that remain in our imagination, determining behavior that can be (sometimes unintentionally) discriminatory. For example, there is a tendency to overprotect pupils with disabilities, considering them to be like eternal children and assuaging our anxiety and guilt with purely caretaking practices. In fact, faced with appreciable developments in the field of socialization of people with disabilities, at least at school, we cannot say the same with respect to the places for free time. Furthermore, the question of learning is still very critical, as it is often too much tied to that of the class and is proposed in a simplified way, yet it is still inadequate with respect to the real potential of a student with medium or severe intellectual disability (Galanti, 2019).

In closing this premise, we must recall the contribution to the inclusion process made by the associations of families of people with disabilities. In addition to acting as a mediator filter between school and society, they have often made up for institutional deficiencies and especially since the last two decades of the 20th century, have contributed to calling not only the rights of people with disabilities to public attention, but also their desires and aspirations, going well beyond the point of view of mere welfarism.

Law 517 was the beginning of a great transformation in Italy, so retracing its history, including the applicative aspects, arouses gratifying and even moving feelings. It is a story about the profound transformation of the collective imagination with respect to diversity, which nevertheless has never completely overcome all dark fears, resistance and prejudice. However, after more than 40 years, we need to know how to identify any critical issues that today can translate into the danger of regression. Many new fears are connected with the loss of certainties about identity as well as with widespread egoism.

To be able to introduce subjects with disabilities into schools, Law 517 presupposed two variables: the creation of the new figure of the support teacher explicitly indicated as a support to the class and not just to the single student with disabilities, and the transformation of teaching and the educational relationship.

However, sustaining the path to integration often ended up falling on the shoulders of the support teacher, with delegation by colleagues, school directors and institutions, and sometimes the need to deal with hostility from parents worried that the including persons with learning difficulties in regular class could hinder their children's normal educational course. This gave rise to the many differences among contexts in terms of willingness and openness to integration, both in school and in society (Canevaro, d'Alonzo, & Ianes 2009).

Even today, meetings between teachers, doctors and other professional figures involved in the process of inclusion can sometimes turn into mere ritual encounters that produce documents filled with empty formulas or abstract educational and didactic prescriptions, elaborated in a climate of delegation and mutual reproach aimed at each other and family members. This conflict also results from the fact that the various professional figures adhere to different disciplinary epistemological approaches, which they should learn to compare.

Sometimes students with disabilities in the age of development seem to be divided up between a plethora of professional figures, each of whom creates a plan for what they consider a priority, but without any certainty that someone will create a synthesis of the various programs in order to build a real shared project (Galanti & Sales, 2017). Furthermore, it must be emphasized that our understanding of the idea of health has changed over the years. Regarding conditions of disability from which it is not possible to recover, even when there are feasible programs for treatment and improving scholastic learning and general quality of life, this can translate into less attention to the subjectivity of the person in favor of the objectivity of a nosographic category.

Producing a diagnosis based on the indispensable Diagnostic Manuals (APA, 2013; WHO, 2007), often becomes a merely descriptive course, to the detriment of an interpretation that might run the risk of error, forcing one to acknowledge it and correct it. Schools do not escape this tendency, entrusting evaluation to tests and giving quantitative aspects supremacy over qualitative aspects of learning. This way of evaluating learning processes can become an almost compulsive search for measurable signs and numerical data in the firm belief that one is achieving greater objectivity by considering segments of reality as separate, rather than part of a network of relationships. Even the internal world is dissected, in order to trace back every single deviation from the norm to pathology, perhaps biologically determined.

All of this can seem very reassuring because it is free from subjective responsibilities regarding behaviors that arouse fear or that we cannot accept, such as destructiveness, violent tensions, mental illness, self-injury or relational closure. Such reductionist visions of psychic pathology or disability mainly lead to reliance on pharmacological, surgical and generally technical remedies. Attention must be paid to the risks of technicality, without however being contrary to technique. In fact, the error of technicality does not reside in assigning the correct value to a technique as a tool to improve the quality of life, but in considering it nearly as an end in itself, transforming it from a means into an end, without accompanying it with adequate relationships including those of an educational nature. In the field of research and treatment, it is an increasingly frequent error to consider as scientific only that which presents itself as aseptic, that is, completely removed from the dimension of subjectivity. This can also occur in the school when complacent, uncritical and excessively adaptive attitudes to adult expectations are encouraged in students. In a school that operates this way, also the space for inclusion risks shrinking day after day.

4   The Current Specialization Course for Support Teacher in Italy

The widening of the cultural horizon that marked the passage from the ortho-pedagogy to the genesis of Special Pedagogy is the same broadening of the horizon that has characterized the transition from the professional profile of the special teacher of orthophrenic schools to that of today support teacher who aims to include the student with disabilities in a mainstream class (Trisci-uzzi, 2005; d'Alonzo, 2017; Cottini, 2018).

The Specialization Course for support teacher in Italy is now governed by the Decree of Ministry of Education, 30 September 2011. This is for the first time an annual Specialization Course, independent of other university courses (in the past it was an optional additional course to the teacher training courses), with a programmed number reserved for teachers with a teaching qualification. The Course is the same for all school orders (kindergarten, primary, secondary level, secondary level II) and provides for differentiated divisions by level of education through internships and laboratories. The course, lasting one academic year, equal to 60 University Formative Credits (CFU), is structured in: *Subjects* (36 CFU): Teaching and special education, 20 CFU; Pedagogy of help relationship, 1 CFU; Developmental psychology and educational psychology, 8 CFU; Childhood neuropsychiatry, 4 CFU; Public law institutions, 3 CFU; *Laboratories*, 9 CFU; *Internship*, 12 CFU; *Final Exam*, 3 CFU.

The internship is 300 hours and consists of a direct internship and an indirect internship. The direct training in schools lasts at least 5 months. The indirect one consists of professional re-elaboration activities, also from a personal and psycho-motivational point of view, with the coordinating tutor.

As regards the outgoing profile, the decree outlines the skills of the support teacher in an extremely detailed manner: theoretical and practical skills in the field of special education; psycho-educational knowledge on the types of disabilities; skills in the field of the pedagogy of the helping relationship; knowledge and skills on the interaction and educational relationship with pupils in the class by promoting pro-social relations between them and between them and the school community; educational skills in family dynamics and ways of involvement and cooperation with families; theoretical and operational

knowledge for the interdisciplinary approach to the study of body-mind interaction, psychomotor development, behavior and learning of the human being;
theoretical and operational knowledge in relation to communication processes; familiarity and competence with simulative, observational and experimental practices and methods in the field of special education and teaching;
skills to co-design, co-monitor and co-lead innovative projects aimed at promoting the integration process within the classroom context; teaching skills
in meta-cognitive and cooperative approaches; pedagogical-didactic skills
in the integrated management of the class group; skills to monitor and evaluate educational and training interventions; pedagogical competence in the
development of the IEP (Individualized Educational Plan) for the Life Project;
teaching skills aimed at developing communication and language skills; skills
in observation and evaluation of various aspects of human functioning according to the International Classification of Functioning approach of the World
Health Organization (MIUR, 30.09.2011).

First of all it is taken for granted that the support teacher since its establishment is a teacher assigned to the whole class and not to the individual student
with disabilities. In the new path, we note that a profile of a teacher emerges
that must embody in itself the widening of the pedagogical horizon that the
disability sector has seen in the last thirty years. This figure derives from that
change in the culture of disability. The knowledge of the techniques and of the
methodologies is emphasized in the laboratories that are numerous, diversified by scholastic level and which are dedicated to disciplinary teaching, to the
knowledge of specific languages and non-verbal languages.

The centrality of the relational dimension of the support teacher is recognized, in the collegiality of the class, in the dialogue with the family and
working groups with health services. The attention is placed on the integrated
management of the student with disabilities and on the role of the teacher
as the bearer of a new culture on disability. In fact, the pedagogical-didactic
field related to disabilities is a sector in which the fundamental aspects, the
constructs, the paradigms are constantly in progress, they move on the basis
of recent theories whose efficacy tests are not yet fully consolidated or are not
have been systematized in a metanalytic framework that can openly indicate to
teachers which methodologies and intervention strategies are to be preferred
in specific cases (Zappaterra, 2017).

5   Some Data of a Research on the Support Teachers Training

In previous contributions the results of a research conducted at the University of Florence in the first two cycles of the Specialization Course for Support

Teacher (DM 30.09.2011) were pres e nted, with the aim of evaluating the learning process from a quality perspective (Calvani, Menichetti, Pellegrini, & Zappaterra, 2017; Zappaterra, 2018). During the first two cycles, tools for monitoring, evaluation and self-assessment of learning by students were created and used. Based on the results of these investigations, corrections have been made within the third cycle of the course, which has just ended, which intend to start a process of continuous evaluation of this training in order to build a quality support training model, from which can clearly emerge the basic elements of the training profile of the specialized support teacher that is going to be profiled by the DM 66 of Law 107/2015.

We have also put into action interventions to respond to the need to deal with the organization of disciplinary contents. Not only to solve the questions relating to the epistemological aspects of the disciplinary domain, to which are added those relating to the thematic overlaps between one discipline and another and the lack of curricular connection between disciplines and laboratories, but also, beyond contingencies and the need to carry out the Course pursuant to the Ministerial Decree 30/09/2011, we considered it important to identify some strong foundations of this field of training which, while they have the merit of linking objectives and contents, can be identified as blocks of activities that significantly characterize a specialization path for support teacher, hopefully beyond the current one. Below the founding core knowledge are identified:

– basic theoretical knowledge of disability
– ability to observe pupils with disabilities and individualized planning
– ability to manage interpersonal relationships with other professional figures involved
– ability to use open resources at the school
– professional awareness
– ability to act in the school setting
– ability to act in the class setting
– ability to use multimodal and multimedia communication.

A further step was carried out by the coordination of the course in identifying an intersection between the core knowledge and the learning objectives. We have linked the aspects in which the founding core knowledge are declined to a strong thematic nucleus, to the point of identifying 6 major thematic nuclei that underpin the professionalism of the support teacher: the Historical-legislative, the Neuropsychological, the Pedagogical-didactic, the Technological-communicative, the Management-relational, the Docimological-evaluative-self reflexive, as shown in Table 6.1 (Calvani, Menichetti, Pellegrini, & Zappaterra, 2017).

The data of Self-assessment of Learning and Customer Satisfaction are given below.

TABLE 6.1   Thematic nuclei and training objectives of the specialization course for support
             teacher

Thematic nuclei	Learning objectives
Historical-legislative	Knowing the historical-cultural references
	Knowing the legislation
Neuropsychological	Knowing the International Classification of Functioning (WHO)
	Knowing the main neurological aspects
	Knowing the psychological aspects
Pedagogical-didactic	Knowing the effective didactic models
	Knowing how to identify features based on the ICF
	Knowing how to formulate an Individualized Educational Plan (IEP)
	Knowing how to make use of scientific evidence at an international level
	Knowing how to make use of relevant international models of effective teaching for inclusion
	Knowing how to use open educational resources for inclusion
	Knowing how to adapt curriculum (simplification, individualization)
	Knowing how to plan educational interaction (tasks, feedback, reinforcement)
	Knowing how to use specific strategies (Learning Disorders, intellectual, sensorial, motor disorders, autism)
Technological-communicative	Knowing the effective technologies for disability
	Knowing how to adapt settings (school rules, logistics, spaces, furnishings)
	Knowing how to use content simplification techniques
	Knowing how to make use of visual communication (images, languages and graphic symbols)
	Knowing how to use editing software (text, graphics, audio, video)
	Knowing how to use specific software for disability

(cont.)

TABLE 6.1   Thematic nuclei and training objectives of the specialization course for support
teacher (*cont.*)

Thematic nuclei	Learning objectives
Management-relational	Knowing the quality of relational modalities
	Knowing how to manage relationships with the class teacher
	Knowing how to manage relationships within the school team
	Knowing how to manage relationships with the family
	Knowing how to manage relationships with local health authorities and associations
	Knowing how to use centers, services, associations in Italy
	Knowing how to promote attitudes and a climate of school favorable to inclusion
	Knowing how to encourage attitudes and a climate of class conducive to inclusion
Docimological-evaluative-self reflexive	Knowing the professional ethics for support teaching

5.1   *Results Related to Self-Assessment of Learning*

At the beginning and the end of the Specialization Course each participant
was asked to self-assess their knowledge, skills, and competences in relation to
the objectives indicated and areas in which the Support Teacher is deemed to
be an expert. These are the aspects analyzed:
– historical-cultural references
– legislation
– International Classification of Functioning (WHO)
– Neurology
– Psychology
– Effective teaching models
– Effective technologies for disability
– Quality of relationships
– Interventions according to the ICF
– Formulate an Individualized Educational Plan (IEP)
– Relationship between Support Teacher and Class Teacher

- School Team
- Family
- Healthcare company and associations
- Disability centers and associations
- International knowledge based on evidence
- Effective teaching models for inclusion
- Educational open resources for inclusion
- Professional ethics for support
- Techniques for professional improvement
- Adapt setting
- Adapt curriculum
- School climate conductive to inclusion
- Class climate favorable to inclusion
- Didactic interaction (feedback, tasks, etc.)
- Strategies for individual types of disabilities
- Simplification of contents
- Visual communication
- Editing software (audio, video, text, images)
- Specific software for disability

For each aspect, each participant was asked to score themselves according to a rating scale from 1 to 10, where 1 = "at the moment I know almost nothing, I would not know what to do about it", 6 = "I believe I have a sufficient knowledge in this regard", 10 = "I can consider myself a true expert in this regard".

The text submitted to the students was identical in entry and exit. 158 incoming and 155 outgoing participants responded (out of a total of 163). An average value of 4.96 is recorded, with 83% of entries deemed insufficient; in output the average value is 7.60 and no item is estimated insufficient (minimum value 6.55). At entry there are perceived voices as more critical knowledge of scientific evidence at international level, models of effective teaching for inclusion, elements of neurology, ICF and identification of functionality according to ICF, access to centers and associations in Italy, specific software for disabilities, educational resources open for inclusion.

Outgoing many of these items remain among those with the lowest rating, as was to be expected. The voices, instead, according to which the outgoing students declare to be more competent are didactic interaction (tasks, feedback, etc.), visual communication, professional ethics for support teaching, the ability to create a favorable climate for inclusion in the school and in the classroom, the ability to relate with the family and with the class teacher, to create a solid school team, with evaluations 7.88–8.21 (Calvani, Menichetti, Pellegrini, & Zappaterra, 2017).

The pedagogical reflection on teacher training in an inclusive perspective has followed the approaches generated by a series of cultural, institutional and categorical changes concerning the theme of disability. Many open knots remain, such as: the allocation of the conceptualization of disability in a framework of multiple differences that solicit, on an egalitarian basis, a radical change in the educational policies that inspire it; the culture of disability that becomes a 'system' also at the level of teacher training: professional knowledge and skills that have traditionally characterized the professionalism of the support teacher today must become part of the curriculum, in basic form, also of curricular teachers, requesting to the whole teaching staff to be able to use training methodologies in view of the didactic differentiation and the participation of all the students (d'Alonzo, 2017); the dialogue between support teacher and curricular teachers, supported by training courses aimed at this, must become the space where the inclusion is actually played, placing the sharing and adoption of effective and inclusive methodologies at the center of reflection, not the mere choice of compensatory instruments or exempt from certain tasks.

5.2   *Results Related to Customer Satisfaction*

Among the tools used for the evaluation of the Course, a Customer Satisfaction questionnaire was carried out for all students, whose results are briefly described here (Zappaterra, 2018). The aim was to know from the participants' point of view the strengths and weaknesses of the whole, for further improvement. The students ($n = 147$) were invited to give a score on a scale of 1–5 with 10 questions, where: 1 = negative; 2 = modest; 3 = acceptable; 4 = discreet; 5 = good.

The first question "How do you assess the quality of the course as a whole?" replied 99% of the participants, as follows:
- 46% discreet,
- 30% good,
- 23% acceptable,
- 1% modest.

To the question no. 2 "How do you assess the overall quality of the methodological-didactic approach?" 99% of the participants responded equally, providing answers in line with those of the previous question:
- 41% discreet,
- 28% good,
- 26% acceptable,
- 5% modest.

The answers to question no. 3 "How do you assess the overall quality of the delivered content?" equally show similar answers in percentage terms to those of the previous questions: 98% of participants provided a judgment:

- 42% discreet,
- 34% good,
- 23% acceptable,
- 1% modest.

In all the first three questions, none of the participants gave a negative opinion.

The following questions were intended to investigate the quality of teaching in its various articulations, of lessons related to the disciplines, laboratory activities and ICT training (Information and Communication Technologies). To the question no. 5 "How do you assess the overall quality of the lessons?" the students, who replied for 97%, expressed a judgment:

- 41% discreet,
- 31% acceptable,
- 25% good,
- 3% modest.

To the question "How do you assess the overall quality of the laboratories?" to which they provided answers for 99% of the cases, they declared a judgment:

- 39% discreet,
- 34% good,
- 20% acceptable,
- 6% modest,
- 1% negative.

To the question no. 6 "How do you assess the overall quality of ICT?", to which they replied in 98%, the judgment was:

- 47% good,
- 33% discreet,
- 16% acceptable,
- 3% modest,
- 1% negative.

The responses related to the quality of teaching therefore showed differentiation in judgments, indicating a higher quality of lessons and ICT training than in laboratories.

The two questions below were intended to highlight the degree of satisfaction of the direct and indirect internship experience. 99% of the students responded to both. To the question no. 8 "How do you assess the overall quality of the direct internship?" answered

- 53% good,
- 34% discreet,
- 10% acceptable,
- 1% modest,
- 1% negative.

To the question no. 9 "How do you assess the overall quality of the indirect training?" expressed opinion:
- 39% good,
- 32% discreet,
- 20% acceptable,
- 6% modest,
- 2% negative.

The students, therefore, showed differentiated judgments between the direct training experience, i.e. in the school context, and the indirect one, at the university institution.

6   Conclusions

In summary, the students showed good satisfaction with the Specialization Course, although with a criticality which was not high: both the last two blocks of questions show that the connection between theoretical area and empirical experience remains one of the elements still lacking, on which to continue to work.

The elements on which the corrective measures, taken from the first two cycles of the course, had gone mostly to intervene are the following: inconsistencies related to the epistemological aspects of the disciplinary domain, to which are added those related to the thematic overlaps between one discipline and another; the lack of a curricular connection between disciplines and laboratories, but also, beyond the contingency of the course according to the DM 30/09/2011, the need to identify core knowledge strong in the field of support teacher training, which can significantly characterize a path of Specialization, in continuity with the training plan outlined by the most recent Ministerial Decree 66 of Law 107/2015.

Note

The chapter is the result of a comparison and scientific collaboration between the two authors. However, the attribution of scientific responsibility is as follows: Sections 1, 2, 3 (pp. 101–107) are by Maria Antonella Galanti; Sections 4, 5, 6 (pp. 107–115) are by Tamara Zappaterra. Abstract, conclusions and references were collaborated on equally by both.

References

APA American Psychiatric Association. (2013). *Diagnostic and statistical manual of mental disorders*. Arlington, TX: APA Publishing.

Basaglia, F. (1968). *L'istituzione negate*. Torino, Italy: Einaudi.

Bettelheim, B. (1974). *A home for the heart*. New York, NY: Alfred A. Knopf.

Calvani, A., Menichetti, L., Pellegrini, M., & Zappaterra, T. (2017). La formazione per il sostegno. Valutare l'innovazione didattica in un'ottica di qualità. *FORM@RE, 1*, 18–48.

Canevaro, A. (Ed.). (2007). *L'integrazione scolastica degli alunni con disabilità. Trent'anni di inclusione nella scuola italiana*. Trento, Italy: Erickson.

Canevaro, A., d'Alonzo, L., & Ianes, D. (Eds.). (2009). *L'integrazione scolastica di alunni con disabilità dal 1977 al 2007*. Trento, Italy: Erickson.

Cottini, L. (2018). *Didattica speciale e inclusione scolastica*. Roma, Italy: Carocci.

Crispiani, P. (Ed.). (2016). *Storia della Pedagogia speciale*. Pisa, Italy: ETS.

d'Alonzo, L. (2017). *La differenziazione didattica per l'inclusione*. Trento, Italy: Erickson.

d'Alonzo, L., & Caldin, R. (Eds.). (2012). *Questioni, sfide e prospettive della Pedagogia speciale*. Napoli, Italy: Liguori.

Galanti, M. A. (2019). Images of intellectual disability: the pedagogical gaze and the neuropsychiatric gaze. In M. A. Galanti (Ed.), *Disturbi del neurosviluppo e dell'apprendimento in un'ottica inclusiva*. Numero monografico, *Nuova secondaria ricerca*, 7(XXXVI), 27–35.

Galanti, M. A., & Sales, B. (2017). *Disturbi del neurosviluppo e reti di cura. Prospettive neuropsichiatriche e pedagogiche in dialogo*. Pisa, Italy: ETS.

Goffman, E. (1961). *Asylums: Essays on the social situation of mental patients and other inmates*. Garden City, NY: Anchor Books.

Goffman, E. (1963). *Stigma: Notes on the management of spoiled identity*. Englewood Cliffs, NJ: Prentice-Hall.

Goussot, A. (2007). *Pedagogie dell'uguaglianza: Saggi di pedagogia politica e filosofica*. Foggia Decreti Delegati: Edizioni del Rosone.

Ministry of Education. (1974). *Decreti Delegati*.

MIUR. (1977, August 4). Law 517, Norme sulla valutazione degli alunni e sull'abolizione degli esami di riparazione nonché altre norme di modifica dell'ordinamento scolastico, G.U. n. 224 del 18 agosto 1997.

MIUR. (2011). Criteri e modalità per lo svolgimento dei corsi di formazione per il conseguimento della specializzazione per le attività di sostegno, ai sensi degli articoli 5 e 13 del decreto 10 settembre 2010, n. 249.

MIUR. (2015, July 13). Law 107, Riforma del sistema nazionale di istruzione e formazione e delega per il riordino delle disposizioni legislative vigenti.

Pavone, M. (2010). *Dall'esclusione all'inclusione. Lo sguardo della pedagogia speciale.* Milano, Italy: Mondadori.

Trisciuzzi, L. (2005). *Manuale per la formazione degli operatori per la disabilità.* Pisa, Italy: ETS.

UN. (2006). *Convention on the rights of persons with disabilities.*

WHO. (2007). *International classification on functioning of disability and health: Children and young version.* Geneva, Switzerland: WHO Press.

Zappaterra, T. (2017). Ridisegnare il curricolo formativo dell'insegnante specializzato per il sostegno. Tra esigenze culturali e di inclusione. In G. Domenici (Ed.), *La formazione iniziale e in servizio degli insegnanti* (pp. 73–76). Roma, Italy: Armando.

Zappaterra, T. (2018). Valutare la formazione dell'insegnante specializzato. In S. Ulivieri (Ed.), *Le emergenze educative della società contemporanea Progetti e proposte per il cambiamento* (pp. 1131–1135). Lecce, Italy: Pensa.

CHAPTER 7

Art and Inclusive Initial Education: An Exploratory Research

Loredana Perla and Virginia Grazia Iris Magoga

Abstract

The languages of art, whose relevance is underlined at international level by the educational policies (European Commission, 2006; United Nation, 2011; United Nations Educational, Scientific And Cultural Organization, 2010) and scientific studies (Art Education Partnership, 2004; Eisner, 2008; Derby, 2012) promote active teaching methodologies useful for the formation of future teachers; through art it is possible to experiment with inclusive educational courses fed by edutainment used in the workshops of the Children's Museums (Dodd-Sandell, 2001; Hooper Greenhill, 2003). Within the framework of the teaching innovation of high-education (Felisatti-Serbati, 2017; Perla, 2018a), a research-training project was set up involving a target population of 100 university students. We present the results of a survey of 3 training workshops for pre-school and primary school teachers, conducted at the University of Bari (Italy). The hypothesis is that art constitutes an effective mediator to train future teachers for inclusion.

The methodological protocol of collaborative research (Perla, 2014) and with the intervention of three 'practitioners' (a sculptor, an expert in art and a photographer) – has foreseen: a training/laboratory phase with experimentation of playful and manipulative aimed at the production of artefacts on the theme of inclusion; a second phase with the administration of closed-question questionnaires on the impact of art in the development of teachers' inclusive skills; a third analytical phase on artifacts.

The results demonstrate the effectiveness of educational itineraries based on playful and interactive laboratory methodologies linked to art in inclusive teacher education.

Keywords

art and creativity – teacher formation – inclusion

© KONINKLIJKE BRILL NV, LEIDEN, 2020 | DOI: 10.1163/9789004432048_007

1 Introduction

In order to face the complex challenges in professional development and improve the quality of the school system, today it is important to direct reflection on the effectiveness of university teaching interventions and give relevance to the inclusive training for primary school teachers.

> The teacher's work is rapidly changing. Let's think about the complexity of class management, the impact with youth culture and the digital world, the new forms of learning and communication, the erosion of authority in the educational relationship between generations ... It is crucial to take note of these changes and to give an account of them in a precise description of the expected professional standards, which cannot include only the usual disciplinary, methodological, didactic, relational aspects, which are basically contained in employment contracts and in the legal status. This profile certainly involves new forms of initial preparation. (MIUR, 2017, p. 4)

> The University is in a phase of repositioning to design planning trajectories and new models for teaching staff training ... The two main cores around which the meaning of professional quality is knotted by acting as a teacher are: the first is the quality of the teacher personal identity, including the ethical depth of her/his behaviour (the so-called "teacher-Master" witness of a vision of teaching rooted in values); the second, professional quality acted out, expressed by an expertise who is capable of responding to changes in the contexts of contemporary education and training. It is from these two meanings that the ongoing work on the expected professional standards derives. From the meanings cited above also derives the work on the construct of "mediation aimed" at the professional learning of the teacher, according to diversified models, many of which in the process of experimentation. (Perla, 2018b, p. 311)

The quality of the educational system depends on many factors, among which there are some fundamental ones: training, preparation and professional competence of teachers, based on synergistic relationships between theoretical knowledge and professional practice (Attard, Madalińska, & Michalak, 2018). In order to form teachers who are aware of their actions, it is important to address directly the people involved, getting used to develop a research habit (Rossi, 2011). To create, strengthen and keep skills updated, it will be important to ensure adequate and innovative preparation. In particular, it is widely recognized the pedagogical value of laboratories in university training courses for future teachers of kindergarten and primary schools (Agrati, 2008; Dozza & Ulivieri, 2016; Eurydice, 2006; Federighi & Boffo, 2014; Nigris, 2004; Paquay, Charlier, Altet, & Perrenoud, 2001; Perucca & Paparella, 2006; Zaniello, 2012; Timperley, Wilson, Barrar, & Fung, 2007; Cappuccio 2016; Ellis & Mcnicholl, 2015).

In the laboratories, by strengthening training and updating teaching skills, teachers can improve the design and organization of different learning situations; give emphasis in class to the relationship between teaching strategies and disciplinary content; customize learning paths; know how to promote innovative education. The teacher will thus become a subject attentive to the personal development of students and will allow a better learning. Therefore, training in this area becomes necessary to adapt to recent research in the pedagogical and methodological field, in order to have a clearer understanding of the strategies appropriate to the different learning styles and times.

A place for the exchange of knowledge, which create innovation, reflection, education, the laboratory does not aim at acquiring mere operational skills but at merging declarative and procedural knowledge, transforming them into smart skills (Frabboni & Giovannini, 2009, Bertagna, 2012). This is even more the case in university teaching courses for the training of future teachers. In the Degree Courses in Primary Education Sciences, what it is stressed is the need to develop essential skills of inclusive education: attention to inclusion and diversity has to be understood as a "normal" professional attitude, capable of "modulating" the intervention in relation to the individual characteristics of each student.

The definition of the profile of an inclusive teacher requires the consideration of several areas of competence, with respect to which indicators and possible operational descriptors should be referred: personal; relational; psycho-pedagogical; teaching; organizational; epistemological (Miur, 2018, p. 314).

The pedagogical-didactic laboratories are therefore configured as structured training devices in line with the disciplinary subjects and topics, with planning and implementation strategies of an educational plan, the methodologies to encourage learning and to actively involve students.

Therefore, this contribution is part of the studies dedicated to the pedagogical-didactic space of the laboratory as a specific place for educational research from an inclusive perspective. In fact, here it is analysed an exploratory survey on the Laboratories carried out at the University of Bari, in the Faculty of Primary Education Sciences, focusing on the educational value of contemporary expression and artistic languages to identify innovative teaching, and to overcome inclusive challenges. The aim of the research is to evaluate the effectiveness of the artistic-creative laboratory space intended as a mediator for teacher training for inclusion (Panciroli 2012; Bresler, 2007; Dallari, 2005; De Bartolomeis, 2003).

2   The Visual Art as a Mediator to Train Future Teacher for Inclusion

The paradigms that have inspired this research have been those of Research-Action-Training (Altet, 2000–2012; Magnoler, 2012; Perrenoud, 2002) and Education Through Art (Dewey, 1951; Eisner, 2004, 2008; Read, 1954). Using the collaborative approach (Perla, 2014), the process has involved researchers, experts in relating fields (a sculptor, an artist-photographer, an expert art-manager) and students in the fifth year of the degree course in Didactics and Special Pedagogy: a course that trains prospective nursery and primary teachers. In this research the artistic content was conceived from the perspective of Education Through Art which supports a conceptual and educational position of art as a flexible tool for dealing with all contents, not only those specific of their disciplinary field but also those related to other disciplines with transdisciplinary possibilities (Eisner, 2002), also for the teachings of Disability Studies (Derby, 2012) and for research and teaching of disability (American Educational Research Association., 2004). In the vast panorama of educational research it is possible to find several examples to support the use of different forms of art within educational processes (Wasserman, 1958; American Educational Research Association, 2004; Burnaford, Brown, Doherty, & Mclaughlin, 2007; Marshall, 2016; Punzalan, 2018).

Especially all contemporary artists catch the changes of the increasingly complex society and create scenarios in which the public is invited to participate. Today visual authors abandon the production of objects which are typically aesthetic and create devices capable of activating the creativity of the user, transforming the art object into an instrument of dialogue, debate and relationship in which the process, the discovery of the other and the meeting become central. This new approach in making art directly involves the public in the creative process, allowing people to become a co-authors as well as observers of the work itself, thus revealing potential of are: the ability to create social value through collective performances. The interactive and participatory artistic work becomes the spark of the engine of social development and artistic and cultural initiatives become advocates of collective growth processes. Today, the philosophy of art claims that public art is able to develop a sense of community, a sense of civic identity, promote social change and tackle social exclusion by activating discussion processes, proposing solutions to enrich the territory, by offering a real social change (Bourriaud, 2004, 2010).

The theories of Education Through Art and the research produced by the Museum Studies stresses the importance of perceptive and sensorial education, capable of encouraging and developing inclusive skills. The innovative research carried out during these last few years supports a conceptual-educational position of art and its languages as flexible tools to:

- support the learning process and strengthen the cognitive, sensory, emotional, fantastic and creative dimensions, expressiveness and inventiveness, by mediating the relationship between teacher and student (Damiano, 2013), allowing the teacher to communicate knowledge by stimulating different codes;
- favour the integral development of the person and of the integrated and harmonic expression of himself;
- stimulate attention, analysis and synthesis abilities, the development of self-reflexive and self-assessment thinking;
- create an aesthetic-educational mediating dimension, a partnership ground, an opportunity to approach youth contexts (Kemperl, 2013; Kuttner, 2015; Kang, Mehranian, & Hyyatt, 2017).

In these specific studies it is possible to recognize the potential of creative and artistic processes in supporting and improving the teaching-learning process; unfortunately, this also draws attention the lack of models of creativity in university teacher education programs. This lack of models of creativity in university training rooms inevitably leads to a lack of creativity in teaching, planning activities, tasks and assessments.

This has negative effects on learning too, since people know well how the creative learning process occurs only when students try to make sense of a new experience in light of what they already know and believe. If successful, the creative combination of the new experience and the student's previous knowledge will result in a new and meaningful personal understanding.

This argument is in agreement with a long series of creative scholars and learning theorists who state that every time you learn something new and personally meaningful it means that a creative process has intervened in learning (Guilford, 1967; Littleton & Mercer, 2013; Piaget, 1973; Sawyer, 2012; Vygotsky, 1967/2004).

Teacher training programs containing significant creative education paths allow people to develop skills to help students take advantage of their creativity. Creativity as part of teacher education programs is therefore essential, and, in particular, it is essential to understand what students can experience, discover, see and learn to do through creativity (Barone, Berliner, Blanchard, Casanova, &

McGowan, 1996; Korthagen, Kessels, Koster, Lagerwerf, & Wubbels, 2001; Loughran, 2006).

This theoretical framework has led to the choice of placing the artwork and the process of creative operations at the centre of the workshops, providing for the contamination of learning methods and tools to train different *formae mentis* and social interaction among the participants, in order to enrich personal knowledge. Thus, the laboratory is a didactic device "useful and indispensable within the teaching training paths as a tool for professional learning ... and a main instrument of formation in practical knowledge ... a form of knowledge alternative to the formal, a universal and decontextualized one" (Agrati, 2008, p. 101). Considered "as one of the most suitable ways of teaching to teach ... a mental place before being a physical place, in which practice becomes theory, experience becomes the object of conceptual analysis, notions turn into knowledge" (Laneve, 2003, pp. 154–155).

In fact, it has guided the reflection of the University of Bari and the Department of Educational Sciences on the formative functions of art in contemporary society and on the design plans of university teaching for the training of future teachers who have a mediation training body in the laboratory context as their starting point. The University of Bari (UNIBA) carried out the experiment, trying to identify an innovative training intervention strategy, aimed at outlining aspects and educational implications of the mediation of languages, contemporary art and the widespread museum creative space for the development of the skills of future teachers and to assess the effectiveness of the artistic-creative laboratory space as a mediator for teacher training towards inclusion.

3   The Methodological Protocol of Collaborative Research the Design of the Creative Laboratory

The methodological research protocol was established according to a collaborative approach (Desgagné, Badnarz, Couture, Poirier, & Lebuis, 2001; Perla, 2014). The main cognitive aim was to investigate the beliefs and attitudes of the participants regarding: the importance of using arts in teaching practice, the contribution of visual disciplines, the promotion of using artistic means and tools to strengthen inclusive skills. The survey made it possible to give voice to the participants of the laboratories and to verify the effectiveness of the model, as well as to experiment solutions which are consistent with a training course as professional as possible. The design of the laboratories was planned to correlate the theoretical resources of the participants (specific and transversal knowledge and skills, Perla, 2013; Canevaro, 2007, 2008, 2009; Caldin, 2013; Bozzo, De Pietro, & Valenti, 2016) with practical-operational resources, enabling students to experience new approaches of teaching. In particular, experiential learning methodological strategies have been tested (Kolb, 1984; Nigris, Negri, & Zuccoli, 2007; Trehan & Pedler, 2011; Melacarne, 2012; Zuber-Skerritt, 2009; Di Nubila & Fedeli, 2010). The project lasted 6 months and it was carried out in three phases:

– a phase of laboratory training with experimentation of playful and manipulative methods aimed at producing artefacts for inclusive environments;
– a second phase with questionnaires made up of yes-and-no questions on the role of art in the development of teachers' inclusive competences;
– a third analytical and interpretative phase of the evidence of the surveys.

Specifically, the 10 hours of each of the 3 laboratories, (held from October 2018 to January 2019) were structured through:

– an initial meeting to introduce the external expert in the field and the topics which would have been discussed in the laboratory. The conversation with the expert included the vision of some works of art, shown either directly or in digital reproduction, exercises in visual creative reading, digital vision of museum routes or art galleries, collaborative organization of laboratory activities, choice of methodologies and materials to be used, identification of working groups.
– a second meeting, an operational phase, in which each group, thanks to the support and help of the expert, carried out the creative production activities; it has documented the artifacts created, through photography and video and shared them on social media; it has also been analysed in an open debate on project carried out individually or in group
– a third meeting, dedicated to the administration of anonymous questionnaires with yes-and-no questions, to detect students' opinions on the educational effectiveness and on the skills acquired in the laboratories. All the students enrolled in the Special Didactics, Special Education and Environmental Education course of Educational Sciences were involved in the survey (100 students).

The survey tool included 24 yes-and-no items and was divided into three main parts: in the first section, information elements are gathered to reconstruct the degree of appreciation for contemporary art, the students' opinions about the usability of contemporary art and the work of art in the knowledge of disciplinary contents as a professional resource; in the second part, the perceptions of the respondents are investigated, and the focus is on: the paths of art education, expressed through workshop; the synergy between museum, school and university; the role of teaching of visual art in the construction of teaching and inclusive skills; the possibility to experience inclusive educational paths through visual creativity; playful-expressive laboratory methods in learning processes of students with special educational needs, the possibility of taking full advantage of using artistic languages as didactic mediators in future teaching activities with impact on didactic postures; in the third part, the focus is on the perceptions concerning the evaluation of didactic activities. The data that have been collected focus on the perception of significant incentives in relation to the overall experience lived in the laboratories; the evaluation overall experience and degree of satisfaction rate; the usefulness of art laboratories in the training path of a future teacher; the increase in the level of interest and curiosity.

The thematic areas chosen for the questionnaire were:

- the perception of the implications of the skills possessed in carrying out the laboratory;
- personal reflection on the promotion of interactive teaching aimed at promoting learning;
- educational value of laboratory management and skills enhanced during the workshops;
- personal reflection on the skills future teachers should have;
- the acquisition of didactic transposition skills and building up design skills.

4   The Research Findings of the Education Project

For research purposes, it has been decided to report the data relating to the whole group of respondents: 100% of the participants filled in the questionnaires. The results of the survey show that 79% of the participants appreciate contemporary art and identifies its different properties: it constitutes a concrete evidence of a precise cultural moment, a paradigm of human complexity, a bridge between backward perspective that allows and helps to understand its elements. As to contemporary works of art, the data collected highlight the agreement to give it an educational value as a "text" which helps to read the message of the author-artist, but also as an opportunity to take on an aesthetic attitude towards reality and an opportunity for the different cultures to meet. More than 70% of students considered the work of art an educational material par excellence, an effective teaching tool for their creativity features and important to develop the necessary sensitivity to understand the world around them, useful both for that specific disciplinary contents and the contents concerning other subjects. Most participants agree to recognise the importance that visual teaching plays in the construction of teaching skills (a total of 75%);

in particular, 37% fully agree and 50% agree in supporting the effectiveness of playful-expressive laboratory methods for the development of inclusive skills for future teachers. The contribution of art and visual languages was rated in a positive way by 55% as regards the learning processes of people with special educational needs; more specifically, 36% completely agree and 46% agree with the importance to experience inclusive educational paths (Table 7.1).

In addition, 37% recognized the usefulness of the laboratory training experiences of art and inclusion, against a generally sacrificed art teaching in the curriculum of a future teacher, according to 88% of the students. Compared to the skills developed or strengthened thanks to the participation in paths of art education expressed in laboratory form, the analysis of answers has identified how many positive elements are favoured: collective dialogue, socialization,

TABLE 7.1   Frequency distribution of students' answers

Question	Strongly agree	Agree	Slightly agree	Disagree	Strongly disagree
The teaching of visual art plays an important role in the construction of teaching skills beyond the "briefcase" of the teacher.	25	51	19	3	2
Through the languages of contemporary visual art it is possible to experiment with inclusive educational paths.	36	46	16	1	1
The play-expressive laboratory methods are effective for the development of the inclusive skills of future teachers.	37	50	11	2	0
Contemporary works of art can represent a professional resource that offers the teacher the possibility of using creative teaching characterized by imagination and imagination.	36	46	17	1	1

operational planning, manipulative experimentation of the student and, in particular, the development of the imagination and creative empowerment, as indicated in Table 7.2.

As to the future teaching practice, over 70% of those attending laboratories believe that what they have learned will have a safe and positive impact on their future teaching practice; it also highlighted a greater propensity to use artists' languages as mediators teaching. Finally, it should be underlined that, in terms of general satisfaction, the 3 laboratories had a high level of satisfaction: the "yes" answers are mainly placed in the values "satisfied" and "fairly satisfied". In addition, 70% stated that the topics of the workshops have aroused interest and curiosity, with an overall positive assessment; only 4% report dissatisfaction, while 36% is satisfied and 38% of students very satisfied.

As to the future teaching practice, over 70% of those attending laboratories believe that what they have learned will have a safe and positive impact on their future teaching practice; it also highlighted a greater propensity to use artists' languages as mediators teaching. Finally, it should be underlined that, in terms of general satisfaction, the 3 laboratories had a high level of satisfaction: the "yes" answers are mainly placed in the values "satisfied" and "fairly satisfied". In addition, 70% stated that the topics of the workshops have aroused interest and curiosity, with an overall positive assessment; only 4% report dissatisfaction, while 36% is satisfied and 38% of students very satisfied.

TABLE 7.2   Frequency distribution of students' answers

The paths of art education expressed in laboratory form favour	Strongly agree	Agree	Slightly agree	Disagree	Strongly disagree
Collective dialogue	26	37	28	6	3
Manipulative experimentation	24	37	33	5	1
Socialization	26	44	18	11	1
Operational planning	30	32	35	3	0
Imagination	47	37	12	3	1
Creative empowerment	47	32	13	8	0

5   New Perspectives and Emerging Guidelines

The educational profession is extremely complex and, in order to be properly addressed, it requires: a solid education, a consolidated experience and the ability to be always questioning one's own work. Being a teacher not only requires knowledge of the contents of the acquisition of methodologies and teaching strategies, but also a strong motivational involvement and a deep emotional sensitivity towards the learner.

Thus, from the careful analysis of the data, it can be stated that the activities of the art laboratory of having created an effective space of interaction between theory and practice, between training design and experience of creative experimentation in the initial training of those attending the Didactic and Special Pedagogy course. We can therefore state that, from the point of view of curricular innovation, the art workshop for inclusion has fully responded to expectations. Among the elements of interest emerged, what deserves to be reported is the overall positive judgment on the relapse that participation in art didactic paths expressed in laboratory form, that contributed to develop and strengthen collective dialogue, socialization, operational planning and increased the development of fantasy and creative empowerment. Art workshops seem to promote individual reflection on the complex profile of a professional teacher, on actual teaching and learning practices, also helping to build a new repertoire of laboratory practices. Therefore, it is possible to conclude by recognizing the importance of art and its cultural heritage, its powerful communicative functionality and the innovative value that its artistic practice mainly owns for inclusive purposes. The experimentation of art laboratories has allowed us to build a repertoire of possible practices and opened university teaching to new research paths.

So, the hope is that it can propose integrated training models, build a repertoire of functional practices and training opportunities for the construction of knowledge and training of teachers aware of their actions, by exploiting the potential of contemporary art, the process of creative operation and the communicative possibilities of the museum device – which consider the mind embodied in the subject, rooted in the environment and dependent on social relations.

Furthermore, the possibilities offered by the relationship between educational laboratories and realities outside the university (in this case artistic institutions, museums, art studios, photographic studios or design galleries etc.), are certainly a valid opportunity to define forms of bidirectional communication: to offer students the opportunity to carry out experiences that put them in relation with figures outside the university context and to avoid forcing the training proposal in a rigid curriculum, rather to proceed towards a "creative" reorganization of university teaching. Experimentation of art laboratories has allowed to build a repertoire of possible practices and opened university teaching up to new research paths.

Note

This chapter is the result of a shared project. However, Loredana Perla is the author of Sections 1–2, Virginia Grazia Iris is the author of Sections 3–5.

References

Agrati, L. A. (2008). *Alla conquista del sapere pratico. Il laboratorio nella formazione degli insegnanti.* Roma, Italy: Carocci.

Alberici, A., Catarsi, C., Colapietro, V., & Loiodice, I. (2007). *Adulti e università. Sfide ed innovazioni nella formazione universitaria e continua.* Milano, Italy: FrancoAngeli.

Altet, M. (2000). L'analyse de pratiques. Une demarche de formation professionnalisante? *Recherche & Formation, 35,* 25–41.

Altet, M. (2012). L'apporto dell'analisi plurale delle pratiche didattiche alla co/formazione degli insegnanti. In P. Rivoltella & P. G. Rossi (Eds.), *L'agire didattico* (pp. 291–312). Brescia, Italy: La Scuola Editrice.

Arts Education Partnership. (2004). *The arts and education: New opportunities for research.* Retrieved January 1, 2019, from www.aep-arts.org/wp-content/uploads/New-Opportunities-for-Research.pdf

Attard, T., Madalińska, M. E, & Michalak, J. (2018). *Teacher education: Policy and practice.* International Perspectives and Inspirations. Warsaw, Poland: FRSE.

Barone, T., Berliner, D. C., Blanchard, J., Casanova, U., & Mcgowan, T. (1996). A future for teacher education: Developing a strong sense of professionalism. In J. Sikula (Ed.), *Handbook of research on teacher education* (2nd ed., pp. 1108–1149). New York, NY: Macmillan.

Bertagna, G. (2012). *Fare laboratorio.* Brescia, Italy: La Scuola Editrice.

Berthoz, A. (2011). *La semplessità.* Torino, Italy: Codice.

Bertin, G. M. (1978). *L'educazione estetica.* Firenze, Italy: La Nuova Italia.

Bourriaud, N. (2004). *Postproduction. Come l'arte riprogramma il mondo.* Milano, Italy: Postmedia.

Bourriaud, N. (2010). *Estetica relazionale.* Milano, Italy: Postmedia.

124

PERLA AND MAGOGA

Bozzo, G., De Pietro, O., & Valenti, A. (2016). An experimental approach for science laboratories in the contest of science of primary education degree course. *Form@ re, 16*(2), 194–212.

Bresler, L. (Ed.). (2007). *International handbook of research in arts education.* Dordrecht: Springer.

Burnaford, G., Brown, S., Doherty, J., & Mclaughlin, H. J. (2007). *Arts integration frameworks, research-practice. A literature review.* Washington, DC: Arts Education Partnership.

Caldin, R. (2013). Current pedagogic issues in inclusive education for the disabled. *Pedagogia Oggi, 1,* 11–25.

Canevaro, A. (2007). *L'integrazione scolastica degli alunni con disabilità.* Trento, Italy: Erickson.

Canevaro, A. (2009). *L'integrazione scolastica di alunni con disabilità dal 1977 al 2007: risultati di una ricerca attraverso lo sguardo delle persone con disabilità e delle loro famiglie.* Bolzano, Italy: Bozen University Press.

Cappuccio, G. (2016). La riflessione sulla pratica didattica in laboratori dei tutor di Scienze della Formazione Primaria. *Formazione & insegnamento, European Journal of Research on Education and Teaching, 14*(3), 409–420.

Castoldi, M. (2011). *Progettare per competenze. Percorsi e strumenti.* Roma, Italy: Carocci.

Conway, P., Murphy, R., Rath, A., & Hall, K. (2009). *Learning to teach and its implications for the continuum of teacher education: A nine-country cross-national study.* Report commissioned by the Teaching Council, University College, Cork, Ireland.

Cristini, C., & Ghilardi, A. (2009). *Sentire e pensare: Emozioni e apprendimento tra mente e cervello.* Milano, Italy: Springer.

Dallari, A. (1997). *A regola d'arte.* Firenze, Italy: La Nuova Italia.

Dallari, A., & Francucci, C. (1998). *L'esperienza pedagogica dell'arte.* Firenze, Italy: La Nuova Italia.

Dallari, M. (2005). *La dimensione estetica della padeia. Fenomenologia, arte, narratività.* Trento, Italy: Erikson.

Damiano, E. (2013). *La mediazione didattica.: Per una teoria dell'insegnamento.* Milano, Italy: FrancoAngeli.

Darling-Hammond, L., & Sykes, G. (2001). *Teaching as the learning profession: Handbook of teaching and policy.* San Francisco, CA: John Wiley &Sons.

De Bartolomeis, F. (2003). *L'arte per tutti. Conoscere e produrre.* Bergamo, Italy: Edizioni junior.

Derby, J. (2012). Art education and disability studies. *Disability Studies Quarterly, 31*(1).

Desgagne', S., Badnarz, N., Couture, C., Poirier L., & Lebuis, P. (2001). L'approche collaborative de recherche en éducation: un rapport nouveau à établir entre recherche et formation. *Revue des sciences de l'éducation, XXVII*(1), 33–64.

Dewey, J. (1951). *L'arte come esperienza.* Firenze, Italy: La Nuova Italia.

Dewey, J. (1986). *Come pensiamo.* Firenze, Italy: La Nuova Italia.

Di Nubila, R. D., & Fedeli, M. (2010). *L'esperienza: quando diventa fattore di formazione e di sviluppo. Dall'opera di David A. Kolb alle attuali metodologie experiental learning.* Lecce, Italy: Pensa Multimedia.

Dodd, J., & Sandell, R. (2001). *Including museums: Perspectives on museums, galleries, and social inclusion.* Leicester: RCMG.

Eisner, E. W. (2002). From episteme to phronesis to artistry in the study and improvement of teaching. *Teacher and Teaching Education, 18*(4), 375–385.

Eisner, E. W. (2004). What can education learn from the arts about the practice of education? *International Journal of Education & the Arts, 5*(4).

Eisner, E. W. (2008). What education can learn from the arts. *LEARNing Landscapes, 2*(1), 23–30.

Ellis, V., & Mcnicholl, J. (2015). *Transforming teacher education: Reconfiguring the academic work.* London: Bloomsbury Academic.

European Commission. (2006). *Le raccomandazioni del Parlamento Europeo e del Consiglio del 18 dicembre 2006.* Brussels, Belgium: European Commission. Retrieved January 1, 2019, from https://eur-lex.europa.eu/legal content/IT/TXT/?uri=celex%3A32006H0962

European Commission. (2006). *Eurydice 2006. L'assicurazione di qualità nella formazione degli insegnanti in Europa.* Brussels, Belgium: European Commission. Retrieved January 1, 2019, from http://www.indire.it/eurydice/content/index.php?action=read_cnt&id_cnt=1836

European Commission. (2013). *Supporting teacher competence development. For better learning outcomes.* Brussels, Belgium: European Commission. Retrieved January 1, 2019, from http://www.schoolleadership.eu/portal/resource/supporting-teacher-competence-development-better-learning-outcomes

Fabbri, L., & Melacarne, C. (2016). Didattica dell'innovazione e innovazione didattica. L'apprendimento come condizione per il cambiamento. In M. Fedeli, V. Grion, & D. Frison (Eds.), *Coinvolgere per apprendere. Metodi e tecniche partecipative per la formazione* (pp. 319–339). Lecce, Italy: Pensa Multimedia.

Fabbri, L., & Romano, A. (2018). *Metodi per l'apprendimento trasformativo. Casi, modelli, teorie.* Roma, Italy: Carocci.

Federighi, P., & Boffo, V. (Eds.). (2014). *Primaria oggi. Complessità e professionalità docente.* Firenze, Italy: Firenze University Press.

Felisatti, E., & Serbati, A. (2017). *Preparare alla professionalità docente e innovare la didattica universitaria.* Milano, Italy: FrancoAngeli.

Flores, M. A. (2017). Editorial. Practice, theory and research in initial teacher education: International perspectives. *European Journal of Teacher Education, 40*(3), 287–290.

Frabboni, F., & Giovannini, M. L. (2009). *Professione insegnante. Un concerto a più voci in onore di un mestiere.* Milano, Italy: FrancoAngeli.

Fry, H., Ketteridge, S., Marshall, S. A. (2003). *Handbook for teaching and learning in higher education enhancing academic practice* (3rd ed.). London: Taylor & Francis.

Gallagher, S., & Zahavi, D. (2009). *La mente fenomenologica.* Milano, Italy: Raffaello Cortina.

Glenberg, A. M., & Kaschak, M. P. (2002). Grounding language in action. *Psychonomic Bulletin & Review, 9*(3), 558–565.

Goisis, C. (2013). *Lo sviluppo professionale dell'insegnante. Un'indagine sul ruolo delle competenze tacite.* Milano, Italy: Vita e pensiero.

Goldman, N. (1991). *Arte e linguaggio.* Milano, Italy: FrancoAngeli.

Grion V., & Maretto M. (2017). Student Voice e didattica partecipativa: un valore aggiunto per l'innovazione. *Form@re, 17*(3), 174–187.

Hansen, D. T. (2005). Creativity in teaching and building a meaningful life as a teacher. *Journal of Aesthetic Education, 39*(2), 57–68.

Hooper Greenhill, E. (2007). *Museums and education: Purpose, pedagogy, performance.* London: Routledge.

Iavarone, M. L. (2011). *Abitare la corporeità. Nuove traiettorie di sviluppo professionale.* Milano, Italy: Franco Angeli.

Kold, D. (1984). *Experiential learning. Experience as the source of learning and development.* Englewood Cliff, NJ: Prentice-Hall.

Korthagen, F. A., Kessels, J., Koster, B., Lagerwerf, B., & Wubbels, T. (2001). *Linking practice and theory: The pedagogy of realistic teacher education.* London: Routledge.

Lakoff, G., & Johnson, M., (1999). *Philosophy in the flesh: The embodied mind and its challenge to western thought.* New York, NY: Basic Books.

Laneve, C. (2003). *La didattica fra teoria e pratica.* Brescia, Italy: La Scuola.

Lave, J., & Wenger, E. (2006). *L'apprendimento situato. Dall'osservazione alla partecipazione attiva nei contesti sociali.* Trento, Italy: Erickson.

Lieberman, A., & Miller, L. (2001). *Teachers caught in action: Professional development that matters.* New York, NY: Teachers College Press.

Little, J. W. (2006). *Professional community and professional development in the learning centered school.* Washington, DC: National Education Association.

Little, J. W. (2007). Teachers' accounts of classroom experience as a resource for professional making. *The 106th Yearbook of the National Society for the study of Education, Part I, 106*(1), 217–240.

Loughran, J. J. (2006). *Developing a pedagogy of teacher education: Understanding teaching and learning about teaching.* London: Taylor & Francis.

Magnoler, P. (2012). *Ricerca e formazione, la professionalizzazione degli insegnanti.* Lecce-Brescia, Italy: Pensa MultiMedia.

Magnoler, P., Notti, A., & Perla, L. (2017). *La professionalità degli insegnanti. La ricerca e le pratiche.* Lecce, Italy: Pensa Multimedia.

Margiotta, U. (2014). *Teorie dell'istruzione. Finalità e modelli.* Roma: Anicia.

Marshall, J. (2016). A systems view: The role of art in education. *ArtEducation, 69*(3), 12–19.

Melacarne, C. (2012). Action learning e action oriented research. Una ricerca sul turnover organizzativo. *Educational Reflective Practices, 2*(2), 59–82.

Mezirow, J., & Taylor, W. (2011). *Transformative learning: Theory to practice. Insights from community, workplace, and higher education.* San Francisco, CA: John Wiley.

Michelini, M. (2018). *Riflessioni sull'innovazione didattica universitaria. Interventi alla tavola rotonda GEO.* Udine: Forum. Retrieved January 10, 2019, from https://geo.uniud.it/fileadmin/user_upload/TR_Innovazione_Didattica_Universitaria__DEFINITIVO.pdf

MIUR. (2017). *Sviluppo professionale e qualità della formazione in servizio documenti di lavoro.* Retrieved January 10, 2019, from http://www.flcgil.it/files/pdf/20180417/dossier-miur-sviluppo-professionale-e-qualita-della-formazione-in-servizio-del-16-aprile-2018.pdf

Nigris, E. (Ed.). (2004). *La formazione degli insegnanti. Percorsi, strumenti, valutazione.* Roma, Italy: Carocci.

Nigris, E., Negri, S. C., & Zuccoli, F. (Eds.). (2007). *Esperienza e didattica. Le metodologie attive.* Roma, Italy: Carocci.

OECD. (2013). *PISA 2012 results; What makes schools successful? Resources, policies and practices* (Vol. IV). Paris, France: OECD Publishing.

Oreck, B. A. (2004). The artistic and professional development of teachers: A study of teachers' attitudes toward and use of the arts in teaching. *Journal of Teacher Education, 55*(1), 55–69.

Oreck, B. A. (2006). Artistic choices: A study of teachers who use the arts in the classroom. *International Journal of Education & the Arts, 7*(8), 1–15. Retrieved January 10, 2019, from https://www.researchgate.net/publication/234605539_Artistic_Choices_A_Study_of_Teachers_Who_Use_the_Arts_in_the_Classroom

Panciroli, C. (2012). *Le arti visive nella didattica.* Verona, Italy: Quiedit.

Paparella, N., & Perucca, A. (Eds.). (2006). *Le attività di laboratorio e di tirocinio nella formazione universitaria.* Roma, Italy: Armando.

Paparoni, D. (2003). *Il corpo parlante dell'arte. La nuova scena internazionale: linguaggi, esperienze, artisti.* Roma, Italy: Castelvecchi.

Paquay, L., Charlier, E., Altet, M., & Perrenoud, P. (Eds.). (2001), *Former des enseignants professionnels.* Brussels, Belgium: De Boeck.

Perla, L., & Riva, M. G. (2016). *L'agire Educativo,* Brescia, Italy: La Scuola.

Perla, L. (2015). Lo sviluppo professionale dell'insegnante. Ipotesi per una modellistica in fieri. *Mizar. Costellazione di pensieri, I,* 9–21.

Perla, L. (2018a). Formare il docente alla didattica universitaria: il cantiere dell'innovazione. In M. Michelini (Ed.), *Riflessioni sull'innovazione didattica universitaria. Interventi alla tavola rotonda GEO (30 giugno 2017)* (pp. 79–88). Udine, Italy: Forum.

Perla, L. (2018b). La formazione degli insegnanti primari e secondari. In S. Ulivieri (Ed.), *Le emergenze educative della società contemporanea* (pp. 311–314). Lecce, Italy: Pensa editore.

Perla, L. (Ed.). (2013). *Per una didattica dell'inclusione. Prove di formalizzazione.* Lecce, Italy: Pensa Multimedia.

Perla, L., & Martini, B. (2019). *Professione insegnante.* Milano, Italy: FrancoAngeli.

Perrenoud, P. (2002). *Dieci nuove competenze per insegnare.* Roma, Italy: Anicia.

Pinto Minerva, F., & Frabboni, F. (2013). *Manuale di pedagogia e didattica.* Roma, Italy: Laterza.

Punzalan, F. J. (2018). The impact of visual arts in students' academic performance. *International Journal of Education and Research, 6*(7), 121–130. Retrieved January 10, 2019, from https://www.ijern.com/journal/2018/July-2018/10.pdf

Read, H. (1954). *Education through art.* Milano, Italy: Ed. di Comunità.

Richardson, V. (2001). *Handbook of research on teaching* (4th ed.). Washington, DC: American Educational Research Association.

Righetti, M. (2007). *Organizzazione e progettazione formativa.* Milano, Italy: Franco-Angeli.

Rivoltella, P. C. (2012). *Neurodidattica. Insegnare al cervello che apprende.* Milano, Italy: Raffaello Cortina.

Rivoltella, P. C. (2014). *La previsione. Neuroscienze, apprendimento, didattica.* Brescia: La Scuola Editrice.

Robasto, D., & Trinchero, R. (2019). *I mixed methods nella ricerca educativa.* Milano, Italy: Mondadori.

Rossi, P. G. (2011). *Didattica enattiva. Complessità, teorie dell'azione, professionalità docente.* Milano, Italy: FrancoAngeli.

Rossi, P. G. (2015). *L'agire didattico. Manuale per l'insegnante.* Brescia, Italy: La Scuola.

Sancho-Gil, J. M., Sánchez-Valero, J.-A., & Domingo-Coscollola, M. (2017). Research-based insights on initial teacher education in Spain. *European Journal of Teacher Education, 40*(3), 310–325.

Schreiber, J. B. (2018). Creativity and pre-service teacher education: What you see is what you get. *Global Education Review, 5*(1), 5–19.

Shepherd Knowles, M., Holton E. F., Swanson, R. A., & Holton, E. (2005). *The adult learner: The definitive classic in adult education and human resource development.* Amsterdam: Elsevier.

Sibilio, M. (2014). *La didattica semplessa.* Napoli, Italy: Liguori.

Siegel, D. (2001). *La mente relazionale. Neurobiologia dell'esperienza interpersonale.* Milano, Italy: Raffaello Cortina.

Sini, C. (2012). *Il silenzio e la parola. Luoghi e confini del sapere per un uomo planetario.* Milano, Italy: IPOC.

Sorzio, P. (2011). *Apprendimento e istituzioni educative: Storia, contesti, soggetti.* Roma, Italy: Carocci.

Sossai, M. R. (2017). *Vivere insieme. L'arte come azione educativa.* Palermo, Italy: Torri del Vento.

Timperley, H., Wilson, A., Barrar, H., & Fung, I. (2007). *Teacher professional learning and development: Best evidence synthesis iteration.* Wellington: Ministry of Education. Retrieved January 10, 2019, from http://www.oecd.org/education/school/48727127.pdf

Trehan, K., & Pedler, M. (2011). Action learning and its impact. *Action Learning: Research and Practice, 8*(3), 183–186.

United Nations. (2011). *Dichiarazione sull'educazione e la formazione ai diritti umani.* Retrieved January 10, 2019, from https://www.ohchr.org/EN/Issues/Education/Training/Pages/UNDHREducationTraining.aspx

United Nations Educational, Scientific and Cultural Organization. (2010). *L'agenda di Seul: obiettivi per lo sviluppo dell'educazione artistica.* Retrieved January 10, 2019, from http://attiministeriali.miur.it/media/200765/agenda_seul.pdf

Villegas-Reimers, E. (2003). *Teacher professional development: An international review of the literature.* Paris: UNESCO.

Von Glasersfeld, E. (1988). Introduzione al costruttivismo radicale. In P. Watzlawick (cur.), *La realtà inventata.* Milano, Italy: Feltrinelli.

Wasserman, B. (1958). The role of art education in public school programs for adult learning. *Art Education, 11*(5), 10–19.

Zaniello, G. (Eds.). (2012). *La didattica nel Corso di laurea in Scienze della Formazione Primaria.* Roma, Italy: Armando.

Zuber-Skerritt, O. (2009). *Action learning and action research.* Rotterdam, The Netherlands: Sense Publishers.

CHAPTER 8

Design of a Mobile App to Digitalize Teachers' Professional Journals in the Practicum

Paula Martín-Gómez, María Luisa García Rodríguez, Juanjo Mena and Gang Zhu

Abstract

The teaching practicum is probably the most genuine period of professional training at the teaching degree. The use of tools such as the teacher's professional journal helps to reflect and systematize the experience of the teacher in training. This chapter includes the design of a mobile application to facilitate the use of the teacher's professional journal through its digitalization in order to experience the benefits it brings as a tool that favors the teacher's own practice and professional development. An analysis of the content of 20 teacher journals written by students of Infant Education at the University of Salamanca was made with the aim of extracting the main reflection topics.

The result was a carefully produced indexing tree that has been used as an analysis tool in the NVIVO12 software for the study of qualitative data. The tree allowed extracting a significant and complete categorization of the teacher's professional journal that makes possible its analysis and constitutes the starting point for the design of the prototype of the mobile application in a paper, which will be developed.

The digitization of the professional teachers' diary based on the most frequent topics of the teachers themselves in practice shows the relevance of the diary since it is based on a thematic index that arises from practice, not theory. This will favor its implementation both by teachers in training and by active professionals contributing to their professional development.

Keywords

analysis – design – indexed tree – journal – tool – professional development – teaching practice – reflection

© KONINKLIJKE BRILL NV, LEIDEN, 2020 | DOI: 10.1163/9789004432048_008

1   **Introduction**

It is necessary to become aware of the necessity of continuous training
for teachers to face the challenges of today's society (Rivas, 2004; Bilbao &
Monereo, 2011). One of the proposals to improve teaching practice is using
resources as, for example, the teacher's professional journal. The traditional
version requires to sit down after each class and then write down every reflection that the teacher considers relevant in respect of what occurred during the
whole school day. However, nowadays teachers do not have time enough to do
this activity, due to the different changes in the education system that have
taken place over recent decades (Marchesi, 2007). These changes have brought
with them a significant reduction of time that teachers have to schedule and
reflect on its own practice for the benefit of an increase of the bureaucratic
burden and of the classroom ratios (Hargreaves, 2005).

   On the other hand, the broad mass of the population nowadays does have
mobile devices with internet access, and they are thoroughly conversant with
the usage of mobile applications. Because of this reason, it has been considered
interesting to digitalize this methodological tool and implementing it with a
categories system which makes it easier to use that tool in the school day-to-day.

2   **Background**

There are a number of challenges for teachers nowadays (Otero, 2012): High
student/teacher ratios, a large number of students with educational needs,
bureaucratization of teaching, and complicated family relationships. These
challenges significantly reduce the time devoted for specific training, research
and promotion (Ávalos, 2011).

   In light of this situation, teachers must be fully aware of their great responsibility to transfer their knowledge into practice, and mostly to their students'
learning (Ávalos, 2011). This requires cognitive and emotional implications, at
both collective and individual levels.

   One way to achieve it is through reflexive practice. Teacher's professional
journal becomes an excellent tool for self-assessment tool that evaluates the
practice itself incorporating main concerns, expectations and perceptions.
This is what differentiates it from a simple record of school activities. Bardají
(2008) states that:

> The reflective journal is an account about what happens in practical train-
> ing and contains descriptions, analysis, personal opinions and valuations

about the situation lived or worked there. It allows to take the own experience as a tool for reflection. Both the fact of writing about what is done
and reading about what has been done leads to achieve to see things (and
oneself too) from a distance perspective. (p. 52)

This methodological tool allows that teachers gather up all relevant landmarks
from the teaching-learning process, that they think about them, that they provide the basis for decision-making, establish links between theory and practice and allows the teacher to be aware of its own evolution and the evolution
of the group, always presented in a contextualized way. In addition, it favors
the development of descriptive, value and analytical-explanatory levels of the
reflection and research process of the teacher (Porlán & Martín, 1999; Trif &
Popescu, 2013).

In order to better understand this journal contextualization, the following
explanations outlined by Zabalza (2004) may be helpful:
- *It is not necessary to draft the journal every day.* This involves keeping a certain amount of continuity, preventing it from becoming irregular or spo-
  radic.
- *They are texts written by teachers, both in-service and pre-service.*
- *Any remark that the author may consider remarkable can be part of the journal.* Unless the issues have been previously defined, the content is, in general, opened.
- All the areas of teaching activity may be the spatial framework in which the
  narration is framed.

Additionally, Medina Millán (2001) describes a number of important characteristics in the use of a teacher's professional journal that are summarized in
Table 8.1.

Ultimately, the journal contributes to the improvement of the teaching role
through reflective practice. Reflection is a key aspect of professional development in order to offer quality, effective and fair education on the part of
teachers (Finefter-Rosenbluh, 2016). It is a widely studied concept in the last
thirty years (Brookfield, 1995; Dewey, 1993; Schon, 1987), whose implications in
current literature tilt towards notions as collaborations with colleagues, mentoring or critical reflection (Larrivee, 2000; Mercado & Baecher, 2014; Whit-
head & Fitzgerald, 2007). With respect to its characteristics: "Reflexive practice
is essentially heuristic, creative and it develops teacher's autonomy" (Trif &
Popescu, 2013, p. 1070). As Day states (2011), teachers always influence their
students' ways of thinking, feeling and behaving.

Furthermore, as has been shown in several studies, reflection on action is a
decisive aspect to develop professional competences (Clarke & Hollingsworth,

TABLE 8.1   Major contributions resulted from the use of the journal

Function	Description
Prediction-execution contrast	The journal is truly helpful in both ways: on one side, it's useful for retracing a certain programming, methodologies, curricula, etc. that had been previously established; on the other side, it is useful for recording its real practical implementation in class, considering problematic and spontaneous situations that may arise.
Intergroup contrast	When the same subject is taught in different groups, its reflection through the journal demonstrates the differences between both groups and the need to adjust educational practice as well as the programming, which was shared at the beginning, to the different levels and peculiarities.
Reconstruction	The analysis of the journal enables an understanding of the group class, the contents, and the methodological strategies used.
Alienation	The reconstruction described in the previous section enables the view of educational reality from a certain distance, and this allows to identify particular situations that otherwise could not be noticed.

SOURCE: MEDINA MILLÁN (2001)

2002; Mena, Sánchez, & Tillema, 2009). Therefore, elaborating a teacher's professional journal for the practicum is powerful tool to compress this process.

Professional practice during the practicum represents a very significant activity, since it offers pre-service students an initial contact with their future profession (Frabboni, 2006; Casas Vialta, 1984). García Rodríguez (2016) states that:

> The practicum is understood as the set of activities carried out by pre-service teachers during their university studies in two institutional frameworks: university and schools, with a view to achieving professional goals. (p. 123)

Therefore, the practicum subject constitutes an unparalleled opportunity for the pre-service teachers training in the use of the teacher's professional journal, so that they can incorporate it with guarantees once they begin to practice as education professionals.

Once the practicum period is over, the first teaching years are of special relevance in professional development because beginner teachers are to apply the pedagogical knowledge learnt in practice (Tynjälä & Heikkinen, 2011). It could certainly be assured that, in many cases, beginner teachers find it difficult the day-to-day school life because their training is perceived as insufficient, which results in high turnover rates during the first five years (Dicke et al., 2015; OCDE, 2005; Hebert & Worthy, 2001; Schmidt, Klusmann, Lüdtke, Möller, & Kunter, 2017).

3   The Main Focus of the Chapter

The purpose of this research is to design a mobile application (IOs mobile operating system) that constitutes a digitalized version of the teacher's professional journal ordered into categories. More specifically, a double aim is intended. On the one hand, we want to identify the topics that pre-service teachers write about in their practice journals in order to build an indexing tree that will also become an analysis tool and, on the other hand, favoring the use of the teacher's professional journal as a tool that promotes reflective practice and professional development.

3.1   *Methodology*

This research aims at designing a mobile application to digitalize the professional teaching journal that is currently elaborated in many teacher education programs. More specifically this study will analyze the different topics that teachers reflect on in their journals to reach an exhaustive categorization which will help to deploy the contents of the teaching professional journal online tool.

An interpretative paradigm and a qualitative design methodology (Creswell, 2013) was followed. Content analysis was used as a "... systematic evaluation of communicative material" (Flick, von Kardoff, & Steinke, 2004, p. 266). The research approach is based on the grounded analysis theory (Corbin & Strauss, 1997). No theoretical model regarding the content of the professional journal is assumed.

Three different stages were followed:

(a) *Categorization*. Once the researchers obtained the ethical consents, a description of the material collected was made according to ten parameters: extension, elaboration process, existence of categorization, nature of categorization, number of categories presented, periodicity, visual data, references, self-assessment, and final reflection. A first indexing tree had been developed based on the data obtained in this first approximation to the sample, from the reading of the specialized literature and from the corpus of data itself. It had been developed taking as unit "the textual unit", seen as each of the times when new information has been incorporated into the journal, and taking into account the general theme of each of these entries. After 15 different versions were completed, and widely discussed by the three authors (principle of saturation), a refined final version was submitted. Table 8.2 shows the triangulation process (Vallejo & Finol, 2009) which was carried out to develop the indexation tree.

The final version showed in Table 8.2 (number 15) was used as the categorizing system to analyze the journals with the software NVIVO12.

TABLE 8.2   Register of triangulation process for the indexation tree elaboration

Meeting number	Date	Modality	Participants	Subject matter
1	29-01-18	Email	Researcher 1 Researcher 2 Researcher 3	First draft of the indexation tree
2	03-02-18	Email	Researcher 1	Initial suggestions about the first draft
3	04-02-18	Email	Researcher 1 Researcher 2	Initial suggestions from Researcher 2 about the first draft
4	08-02-18	Skype	Researcher 1 Researcher 2 Researcher 3	Initial suggestions from Researcher 3 about the first draft
5	12-02-18	Email	Researcher 1 Researcher 2 Researcher 3	New indexation trees reworked from experts' suggestions revision. Elaboration of the first version of the indexation tree incorporating them.
6	16-02-18	Face-to-face meeting	Researcher 1 Researcher 2 Researcher 3	Last version of the indexation tree revision, which gives rise to a new proposal.
7	27-03-18	Face-to-face meeting	Researcher 1 Researcher 2 Researcher 3	Theoretical grounds of the tree from the theoretical framework of the thesis verification.

(cont.)

TABLE 8.2   Register of triangulation process for the indexation tree elaboration (*cont.*)

Meeting number	Date	Modality	Participants	Subject matter
8	28-03-18	Face-to-face meeting	Researcher 1 Researcher 2 Researcher 3	Subcategories inside main categories revision.
9	09-05-18	Email	Researcher 1 Researcher 2 Researcher 3	Proposal for a new version of the tree, in which the category "3.2. Professional tasks" is restructured.
10	06-07-18	Face-to-face meeting	Researcher 1 Researcher 2 Researcher 3	Indexation tree revision before starting the journal analysis with NVIVO12.
11	23-07-18	Face-to-face meeting	Researcher 1 Researcher 2 Researcher 3	Final restructuring of categories tree
12	1-8-18	Email	Researcher 1	Version emerged from changes made during analysis with NVIVO 12
13	11-10-18	Face-to-face meeting	Researcher 1 Researcher 2 Researcher 3	Introduction of a new subcategory and reorganization of the existing ones inside category "1. Context".
14	08-02-19	Email	Researcher 1 Researcher 2 Researcher 3 Professor and Researcher at the Technical North University, Ecuador Professor researcher at the University of Kurdistan Hewler	Study of the reliability of the indexation tree and restructuring of itself.

(*cont.*)

TABLE 8.2   Register of triangulation process for the indexation tree elaboration (*cont.*)

Meeting number	Date	Modality	Participants	Subject matter
15	15-02-19	Email	Researcher 1 Researcher 2 Researcher 3 External Researcher1 External Researcher 2	The reunification of categories and final version of the tree

Reliability tests were also conducted to check how replicable the system of analysis was. Two professors from different universities acted as independent raters: one professor and Researcher at the Technical North University in Ecuador, and the other one is a professor researcher at the University of Kurdistan Hewler (UKH). In both cases, three documents were provided: a) the final version of the indexation tree, b) the definition of the category system, and c) a random sample of 20 fragments from the journals to be categorized by the independent raters. The agreement percentage reached was of 80 and 85% respectively (see Table 8.3).

TABLE 8.3   Results of the reliability of the indexation tree

Independent raters	Agree	Disagree
PhD John Valle	17–85%	3–15%
PhD Andrew Miller	16–80%	4–20%

Note: Pseudonyms are used to name the independent raters

The final version of the indexation tree was used as the final category system to lastly analyzed the journals with NVIVO12.a.

(b) Market research. The purpose of the creation process of the indexation tree and the analysis of journals gave way to the design of the app Teacher's Professional Journal. The first step was to conduct a market research of 15 similar apps in order to check if there was an existing product with similar characteristics.

(c) Design of the app. From the data obtained a first paper prototype was designed that was presented and discussed with two computer engineers who are the developers, currently in process. The prototyping technique consisted of synthetically sketching the interface that is intended to be valued in different ordered sheets so that the user can interact with them and simulates their operation. A logo and a brand image were also designed to represent the app.

4   Results

The most important results coming from this study, according to the research questions and objectives proposed are presented below.

4.1   *Phase 1: Categorization of the Preservice Teachers' Journals*
The categorization followed several stages and was conducted with NVIVO v12.

In the first image we can appreciate how in the first version of the tree seven main categories were extracted, with its attendant subcategories, between three and four hierarchy levels:
1.   The educational center,
2.   Early childhood education,
3.   The educational figure,
4.   Classroom students (3-6),
5.   Complementary activities,
6.   Educational administration
7.   Reflection (see Figures 8.1 and 8.2).
In a second analysis, throughout consecutive meetings of the researchers, some changes were introduced, and so new versions of the tree did emerge.

General requirements of an indexation tree were reviewed. Categories were agreed to be well-balanced, that is, having the same hierarchy levels. Besides, categories must be exhaustive (all data must be collected in understanding categories) and selective (one category cannot include another, for example, "Pre-School Education" and "Students from 3 to 6 years").

This entailed a reformulation of the tree categories and, in some cases, the use of new category labels due to the nuances of meaning given by certain terms. The main changes could be synthesized as follows:

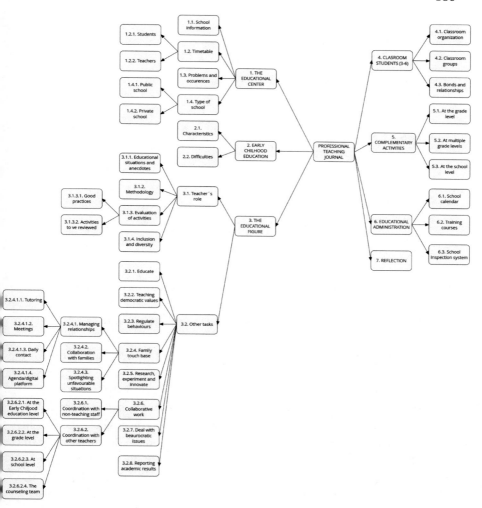

FIGURE 8.1   Full indexation tree. First version

- There were four main categories in which the categories already contained in the previous versions of the tree are relocated: educational context, teacher, and student. Category "families" was incorporated.
- The number of hierarchy levels was the same in all categories, but category "2. Teacher" which was the one that accounted a greater number of entries.
- "Category 1. Educational center": "1.1. School" and "1.2. Educational Level".
- "Category 2. Teacher": "2.1. Knowledge", "2.2. Tasks" and "2.3. Roles".

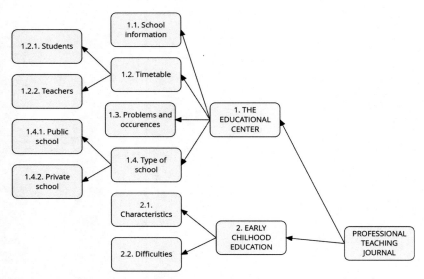

FIGURE 8.2   Detail of one category (e.g. professional teaching journal). First version

– "Category 3. Students": "3.1. Curriculum acquisition" and "3.2. Personal development".
– "Category 4. Family": "4.1. Characteristics" and "4.2. School-family relationships".

On the other hand, a number of agreements were reached. First of all, the title. To make it inclusive we omitted "of" and keep: "Teacher's professional journal". Furthermore, the order of the two first main categories was inverted. It was considered that it is more appropriate that the school appear in the first place, then the educational stage on which the journals focus on and, finally, the teaching figure that writes them. Finally, we proceed to verify the theoretical foundation of the indexation tree based on the postulates included in the theoretical framework.

The final version of the tree was eventually reached (see Figures 8.3 and 8.4) including the following changes:

– In the category "2.2. Tasks" a new subcategory appears: "2.2.5. Self evaluation and beliefs", in which reflections of the author about its own teaching practice are gathered. It is different from subcategory "2.2.1.3. Evaluating", in which results obtained and the suitability of the programming and activities.
– Inside subcategory "4.2. School-family relationships", belonging to category "4. Family", the following subcategories are created, for reasons of the analyzed information: "4.2.1. Personal contact and collaboration" and "4.2.2. Other methods".
– It was considered relevant to add the subcategory "1.1. Administration" to category "1. Context" because many entries led with legislative amendments, student-teacher ratio changes, etc.

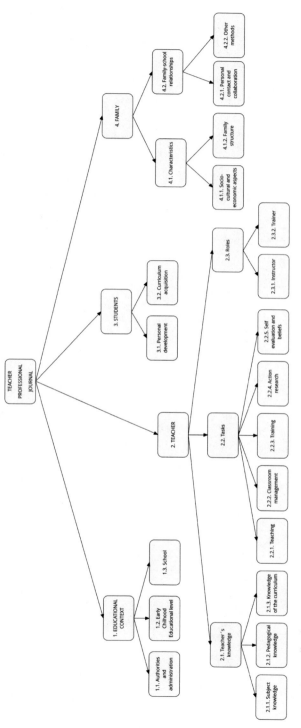

FIGURE 8.3   Full indexation tree. Final version

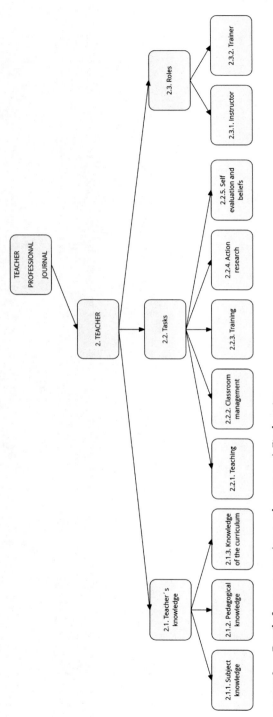

FIGURE 8.4   Detail of one category (e.g. teacher category). Final version

4.2   *Phase 2: Market Research*

Prior to the design of the application and according to the parameters set, a market research about 15 different mobile applications was conducted. Five indicators were used: description, user, sign, strengths, and weaknesses (see Table 8.4).

As shown in Table 8.4 only three mobile applications specifically addressed the teaching professional journal. Most of them are meant for classroom management rather than tools to collect and classify information by the teachers.

Out of the analysis, we consider that there are several aspects that could be considered to improve the functionality of a teacher's journal app:
– English version (and other languages).
– Creating, classifying and sharing information.
– Customizable and flexible.
– Attaching, importing, managing and storing resources and data.
– Being available offline.
– Possibility to store data in the cloud.
– Being compatible with different devices.
– Having the printing option for the content.
– Collect the journal's inputs in several formats: text, audio, image and video.
– Presenting a simple interface.
– Being available in two operating systems: iOS and Android.

Building on this market research, also identified several issues that are convenient to be avoided when designing the app:
– Not free access.
– Containing advertising in its demo version.
– Proving defective, not allowing saving the identified tasks.
– Having an excessively basic interface.

4.3   *Phase 3: Teachers' Professional Journal App Design*

From the whole process described so far, the hard-copy prototype of the app Teaching Professional Journal was designed as seen in Figures 8.5 and 8.6.

The logo and name of the app (still under the design process) will appear on the top line of the first screen. As we can see in Figure 8.1 the login can be done via email, via login with Facebook or via login with Google+. Once the account is created, the users can access it by their username and password. Please refer to Appendix A for more information.

The "Calendar" tab in the upper right frame in Figure 8.6, makes it possible to open a calendar that monitors the teaching activity over the class days.

In the main menu the users can find settings for timetable, calendar, journal and configuration. Under the "Timetable" tab, they can customize its own

TABLE 8.4   Apps' market research on teachers' journals

App	Parameters	Input
1. Aula profesores	Description	Application focused on the management of the classroom. It allows you to register incidences, absences, grades, communicating with students and families, arranging interviews and consulting events, schedules and interviews as well as share content.
	User	Teachers.
	Icon	Robotic-looking avatar.
	Strengths	It allows not only to organize the class but also to create content and sharing them.
	Weaknesses	It does not contain the teaching professional journal.
	What could be re-used?	It works offline.
	Operating system	iOS
2. Canvas teacher	Description	Application for classroom management which make teaching tasks easier. It focuses in three main categories: grades, communications and updating of content.
	User	Teachers.
	Icon	Round, white and orange mandala.
	Strengths	It is in English, it could be used by users from all over the world.
	Weaknesses	It does not contain the teaching professional journal.
	What could be re-used?	The classification into three main categories of content.
	Operating system	iOS and Android.

(cont.)

TABLE 8.4 Apps' market research on teachers' journals (cont.)

App	Parameters	Input
3. Teacher's logbook Additio	Description	This application constitutes a very complete tool for the organization of the class since it allows to manage the group (attendance, monitoring, other teachers, making complete customizable reports on the students, create a plan of the available to students in the classroom, contact students and their families, check the Schedule and calendar, export data from Excell or write all kinds of meetings and interviews).
	User	Teachers.
	Icon	White biretta on a red ground.
	Strengths	It is the most complete application of all that have been reviewed and are currently on the market, due to the wide range of organizational aspects that it incorporates. In addition, it is the only one which includes the teaching journal. Besides that, it is highly customizable, which makes it more attractive. It allows the user to attach, import, store and manage all kinds of resources and data.
	Weaknesses	The journal is basically focused on a mere register of data rather than on the collection of teacher's reflections; it is more focused on monitoring teacher programming. In fact, the teacher has got a journal for each group. It is not free.
	What could be re-used?	– The application can be used from any device (mobile, tablet, computer) since they are synchronized. Thus, although the mobile is used in the classroom, the subsequent analysis and reflection on the data could be carried out from a computer or a tablet. – It incorporates a classroom schedule and a calendar that would be useful to temporarily locate the reflections. – It can be used offline. – Vertical weekly view of the journal is useful as it would allow chronological monitoring or reflections.
	Operating system	iOS and Android.

(cont.)

TABLE 8.4 Apps' market research on teachers' journals (*cont.*)

App	Parameters	Input
5. Teacher's logbook	Description	Application for classroom management that allows: to record student grades and progress through different mechanisms (including rubrics), calculate final grades, register attendance, generate statistics, organize students' personal information, keep a class journal and generate reports.
	User	Teachers.
	Icon	Biretta and a notebook with a pen.
	Strengths	Great flexibility.
	Weaknesses	In order to remove advertising you have to make your accont premium.
	What could be re-used?	It is compatible with all devices and it also has backups in the cloud.
	Operating system	Android.
6. Daybook teacher	Description	Application that works as a daily planner for teachers and includes: journal, register of grades and behaviour, the option to share data with students, etc.
	User	On each daily entry you can add notes, reminders, evaluations, homework or even behavior.
	Icon	Teachers.
	Strengths	White sun shape with some clouds on a blue background.
	Weaknesses	It is developed in English; it could be used by users all over the world.
	What could be re-used?	It is too exhaustive regarding the information required about timing and schedule. It does not save indicated settings and sometimes it takes too long to process them.
	Operating system	It is a journal in the sense that allows you to collect information every day, but it does not refer to reflection or any type of categorization. It is available for iPad, iPhone and online. The online backup system allows you to save information or even printe. In addition, journal entries can be displayed daily, weekly or monthly. iOS.

TABLE 8.4   Apps' market research on teachers' journals (*cont.*)

App	Parameters	Input
7. Google classroom	Description	API (Application Programming Interfaces) from Google developers.
	User	Teachers can easily elaborate and manage tasks, collect them, provide feedback to their students, send notifications or communicate with students in real time. Individual folders are automatically generated for each student and his or her homework in Google Drive. Students can access the homework page to find out what they have to do. Once they have completed their task, they can send it or ask questions to their teachers and schoolmates.
	Icon	Administrators and developers of schools, companies, students and teachers.
	Strengths	A traditional blackboard with a group of students on it.
	Weaknesses	Since it is an API, non-Google services can take advantage of their tools and infrastructure. It facilitates the teaching work in aspects such as communication with students, the organization of sessions and saving time. Its interface is very similar to all Google components, and so it makes it easier to use it if you are familiar with them.
	What could be re-used?	It does not contain the teaching professional journal. It is an application aimed at working with students and programming.
	Operating system	Files can be shared via Gmail or Drive (or similar). iOS and Android.

(*cont.*)

TABLE 8.4   Apps' market research on teachers' journals (*cont.*)

App	Parameters	Input
8. Go Teach	Description	Application for the programming of classes and organization of the classroom: schedules, events and homework.
	User	Teachers.
	Icon	Clock shape on top of a book, in turquoise and white.
	Strengths	It is in English, it could be used by users from all over the world.
	Weaknesses	It does not contain the teaching professional journal. It is not free.
	What could be re-used?	It allows you to attach files to the written entries.
	Operating system	iOS.
9. ILD PRO	Description	It allows an observation and monitoring of each student and evaluate them using the mobile phone or tablet.
	User	Teachers.
	Icon	Sign and geometric drawing in white and blue tones.
	Strengths	It is in English, it could be used by users from all over the world.
	Weaknesses	It presents errors when entering username and password.
	What could be re-used?	The collected observations have different formats: text, audio, video or photo.
	Operating system	iOS and Android.

(*cont.*)

TABLE 8.4 Apps' market research on teachers' journals (*cont.*)

App	Parameters	Input
10. MeSchool	Description	Application intended to register and planning teachers' tasks.
	User	Teachers.
	Icon	Geometric shapes in Orange tones.
	Strengths	You can select any language.
	Weaknesses	It is too simple, it does not have schedules, calendars or any other record, other tan homework.
	What could be re-used?	The wide range of languages in which it is available.
	Operating system	iOS.
11. Mi ayudante de aula	Description	Application for classroom management. Its utilities include: the organization of tasks, the storage of information in different formats, attendance control, monitoring, recording of academic results and obtaining average marks.
	User	Teachers.
	Icon	Notebook in which notes are registered and a pencil.
	Strengths	The main menu is distributed in recognizable categories: classes, students, assessments, assistance, utilities and help.
	Weaknesses	The interface is too basic and dark.
	What could be re-used?	Information is stored in different formats: photography, personal data, documents, etc.
	Operating system	Android.

(*cont.*)

TABLE 8.4   Apps' market research on teachers' journals (*cont.*)

App	Parameters	Input
12. Plan de clase	Description	It's a planner in which teachers can register their sessions and have a monitoring system.
	User	Teachers.
	Icon	A calendar.
	Strengths	The planning of activities can move from one day to another in an easy way in order to adapt it to the programming.
	Weaknesses	It is not free. It is a tool that only focuses on the programming of sessions.
	What could be re-used?	A PDF of the sessions can be generated and printed. It has a backup in Dropbox or Drive.
	Operating system	iOS and Android.
13. Profesor ayudante	Description	Application for classroom management that allows to: register attendance, grades, observations, student disposition in the classroom, communicate with families, prepare progress reports in PDF and identify students who could be facing difficult situations.
	User	Teachers.
	Icon	An exam with the highest grade on a folder.
	Strengths	The interface is simple and similar to Google's therefore the user is generally familiar with it. It is available for both operating systems iOS and Android.
	Weaknesses	It does not contain the teaching professional journal. Also, not all of its utilities are available for free.
	What could be re-used?	It allows to compose a map based on the distribution of the students in the classroom. This could help us to recreate some of the situations in the journal and understand them better.
	Operating system	iOS and Android

(*cont.*)

TABLE 8.4 Apps' market research on teachers' journals (*cont.*)

App	Parameters	Input
14. Teacher assistant	Description	Application for classroom management. It allows the teacher to communicate with families and with students.
	User	Teachers.
	Icon	White biretta on a blue background.
	Strengths	It is in English, it could be used by users from all over the world. It is available for both operating systems iOS and Android.
	Weaknesses	Interruptions are constant during its use due to advertising. To eliminate it, it is necessary to pay 10,99 euro.
	What could be re-used?	It allows synchronization between devices. The data is protected by a PIN or by touch ID and it has a backup in Dropbox.
	Operating system	iOS and Android.
15. Profes en apuros Agenda	Description	Application for classroom management. Its utilities include the agenda itself in which you can write down events, schedule, meetings, birthdays, tutorials, etc. In addition, it collects the results of the evaluation according to the fields that are considered appropriate and the groups.
	User	Teachers.
	Icon	Sign on a blue background.
	Strengths	It is simple and intuitive.
	Weaknesses	It is not free.
	What could be re-used?	Registration can be done directly through Facebook without creating a new account.
	Operating system	iOS and Android.

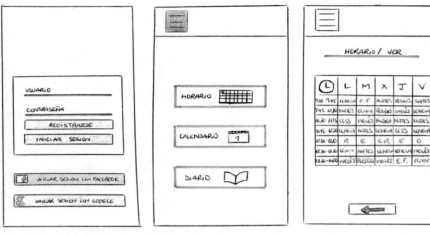

FIGURE 8.5   Design of the app Professional Teaching Journal. Access with username and
password, main menu and timetable tab

FIGURE 8.6   Calendar settings and journal in the app Teaching Professional Journal. Calendar;
Access to professional journal; Display entries; New journal entry

work schedule, according to several classrooms, subjects and the school opening hours.

Finally, from the "Journal" tab the users can access the main categories
established in the indexation tree and, once the category is located, they have
the option to see these entries made so far or to introduce a new entry that, in
addition to text, can incorporate audio, image or video.

On the right you can see how in each category you can check the available
entries, edit them or enter a new one. This option is the key to the exercise of
reflective practice, since not only you can access to every available entry inside

a category to monitor it, but also you can incorporate new reflections at any time.

5   Future Research Directions

Prospectively, the challenge is to continue working on the design of the application and developing it. It will be necessary to maintain constant communication with educators and technicians in order to determine its functionality and definitive characteristics of the application. The tool will be tested using the *INvision* digital tool set to transform the hard-copy prototype into an interactive prototype that users will be able to use and so we can obtain and incorporate the corresponding feedback.

The app will be validated by five skilled professionals who are currently teaching, by means of an interview after using the application. Further on, it is intended that preservice teachers at the undergraduate degrees can use the application during the practicum. Finally, a questionnaire is going to be designed to compare the traditional writing of the journal vs. the digital version log. Afterwards, an analysis of the responses obtained will be made to see the degree of agreement on some dimensions of the application use: easiness of use, utility, importance of the content, if it is useful (or not), etc. This agreement will be subjected to the W-Kendall statistical.

6   Conclusion

In this chapter, the creation of an indexation tree has been proposed based on the study of the content of teaching professional journals written by students during the practicum, as well as the promotion of using the methodological tool of the teaching professional journal by means of its categorization and digitalization through an app.

The objectives have been met. Regarding the categorization process, the descriptive study, as well as the triangulation process carried out have resulted in a category system, which is exhaustive and complete. Thus, the indexation tree has become an optimal tool for analyzing the content of teaching professional journals through NVIVO12 software, since it presents an inductive categories index.

Secondly, regarding the market research, the purpose of analyzing the different existing apps was to refine the characteristics of the product and to confirm that not many mobile applications offer an inductive category system to organize each journal input. Ordinarily, the prevailing functionality of most of the applications consulted was the classroom management. Only three of them offered the possibility of writing a journal but, unlike the purpose of the app presented, it was limited to open registration of entries with no categorization.

Thirdly, regarding the design of the app, it is found that in many practicum programs in both national and international universities a professional journal or portfolio is a requisite. For instance, the use of portfolios as part of the evaluation methods in Educational Technology and Learning Sciences bachelor's degrees is common practice (Sánchez, 2005). In the same way the creation of the NETWORK e-portfolio by the Spanish Ministry of Education has established relevant connections between teachers and allows developing an observatory and a database on its implementation throughout the country registering up to seventy ongoing projects during its first year (Barberá, Barujel, & Illera, 2009).

However, this type of tasks is not always digitalized, which would be convenient in the knowledge society. This is why the design and the subsequent use of an app based on a Teaching Professional Journal might easy teachers' work regarding reflective practice, and also encourages pre-service teachers' motivation.

The innovative aspect of the app prototype might improve pre-service teachers' professional learning, accommodating the "thinking and rethinking practice" processes to the new information era. This is in line with what Acosta, Leyva and Licea (2018) state with regard to incorporate ICTs to university education, due to the socio-cultural and economic evolution that has taken place in the last years:

> The emergence of virtuality as an alternative for training, based on the replacement or alternation of traditional physical spaces by virtual environments, which do not demand the direct physical concurrence of their actors and in which their participation time is assumed flexibly, imposes to the formative reality of contemporary universities the challenge of taking advantage of such potentials in order to complement and consolidate their fundamental processes and functions. (p. 159)

Nowadays, both teachers and students need to be open to the use of technologies in the teacher education programs. García (2013) thinks that the creation of virtual educational spaces complementing face-to-face teaching is the way of facing the challenge of the increase in university students that has taken place since the 60s. The application will allow to obtain reflection reports with all the entries issued by each teacher, will offer a wide database with professional information, solutions to the different difficulties that daily arise in the classroom, teaching experience, peer consultations or specialized theories of literature. The inherent responsibility of the teaching figure is immense with a view to improve the social reality, apart from the wide range of possibilities available to extend its educational action, since the platform to which it is addressed is very wide.

Data resulted from the use of the application, once validated, will allow identifying style profiles (grouping of large categories), calculate the reflexive coefficient of teachers, and share the information with other teachers of the training programs.

It is important to take into account that the optimization of teaching learning processes favours a social positive transformation, since it works to the benefit of the whole community from the most basic levels. The app would make this reflexive exercise faster and also it would make possible for lots of professionals currently working to use this methodological resource. Accepting the value of good educational practices leads to the importance of offering quality initial training; the better formed the future teachers are, the greater their contribution to the improvement of society will be and, in better conditions, they will be able to cope with social and technological changes.

References

Acosta, J. Z., Leyva, A. L., & Licea, M. R. M. (2018). La virtualidad como alternativa de formación universitaria. *Didasc@ lia: Didáctica y Educación, 9*(2), 159–178.

Avalos, B. (2011). Teacher professional development in teaching and teacher education over ten years. *Teaching and Teacher Education, 27*, 10–20.

Barberá, E., Barujel, A. G., & Illera, J. L. R. (2009). Portafolios electrónicos y educación superior en España: Situación y tendencias. *Revista de Educación a distancia*.

Bardají, T. (2008). El diario reflexivo como herramienta de autoaprendizaje en la formación de enfermería. *Nursing, 26*(7), 52–55.

Brookfield, S. D. (1995). *Becoming a critically reflective teacher*. San Francisco, CA: Jossey Bass.

Day, C. (2011). *Pasión por enseñar. La identidad personal y profesional del docente y sus valores*. Madrid, Spain: Narcea.

Dewey, J. (1933). *How we think*. Madison, WI: University of Wisconsin Press.

Finefter-Rosenbluh, I. (2016). Behind the scenes of reflective practice in professional development: A glance into the ethical predicaments of secondary school teachers. *Teaching and Teacher Education, 60*, 1–11.

Flick, U., von Kardoff, E., & Steinke, I. (Eds.). (2004). *A companion to qualitative research.* Thousand Oaks, CA: Sage.

Frabboni, F. (2006). *El libro de la Pedagogía y la Didáctica.* Editorial popular.

García, H. M. (2013). La educación universitaria en el bolsillo, aplicaciones y entornos virtuales/The university's education in the pocket, applications and virtual environments. *Estudios sobre el mensaje periodístico, 19*(Special Issue), 319.

García Rodríguez, M. L. (2016). El prácticum en la formación inicial del maestro. In S. Nieto Martín (Ed), *Competencias del profesional docente* (pp. 121–132). Madrid, Spain: Dykinson S. L.

Larrivee, B. (2000). Transforming teaching practice: Becoming the critically reflective teacher. *Reflective Practice, 1*(3), 293–307.

Medina Millán, J. L. (2001). El diario del profesor, un reflejo del aula. *Cuadernos de pedagogía, 305,* 67–70.

Mercado, L. A., & Baecher, L. (2014). Video-based self-observation as a component of developmental teacher education. *Global Education Review, 1*(3), 63–77.

Porlán, R., & Martín, J. (1999). El diario como instrumento para detectar problemas y hacer explícitas las concepciones. *EL DIARIO del profesor: un recurso para la investigación en el aula, 7,* 18–42.

Sánchez, R. B. (2005). El Portafolio, metodología de evaluación y aprendizaje de cara al nuevo Espacio Europeo de Educación Superior. Una experiencia práctica en la Universidad de Sevilla. *Revista Latinoamericana de Tecnología Educativa-RELATEC, 4*(1), 121–140.

Schön, D. (1987). *Educating the reflective practitioner.* San-Francisco, CA: Jossey-Bass.

Snyder, C. (2003). *Paper prototyping: The fast and easy way to design and refine user interfaces.* Burlington, MA: Morgan Kaufmann.

Strauss, A., & Corbin, J. M. (1997). *Grounded theory in practice.* Thousand Oaks, CA: Sage.

Trif, L., & Popescu, T. (2013). The reflective diary, an effective professional training instrument for future teachers. *Procedia – Social and Behavioral Sciences, 93,* 1070–1074.

Vences, N. A. (2009). Las redes sociales como herramienta educativa en el ámbito universitario. *RELADA-Revista Electrónica de ADA-Madrid, 3*(3).

Whitehead, J., & Fitzgerald, B. (2007). Experiencing and evidencing learning through self-study: New ways of working with mentors and preservices in a training school partnership. *Teaching and Teacher Education, 23*(1), 1–12.

Zabalza, M. Á., & Beraza, M. Á. Z. (2004). *Diarios de clase: un instrumento de investigación y desarrollo profesional* (Vol. 99). Madrid, Spain: Narcea Ediciones.

Appendix A

In this appendix some images of the paper-copy prototype of the Teachers'
Reflective Journal app are shown.

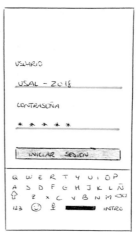

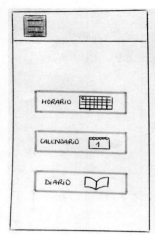
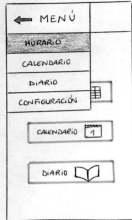
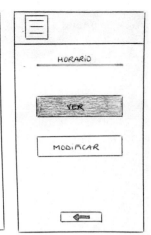

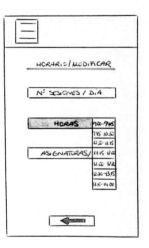

Teaching Media Literacy and Critical Thinking to Countering Digital Misinformation

Minodora Salcudean and Raluca Muresan

Abstract

This chapter attempts to analyze the opinions of Romanian teachers regarding the necessity of studying and understanding the phenomena generated by new media (social media/digital media), especially online digital misinformation, in schools. As we were interested in finding out if teachers believe that introducing a media literacy class can contribute to countering this complex phenomenon, that has been extremely amplified these days by new communication technologies, we have established a brief theoretical exposure and several definitions of the term *fake news*, a term widely circulated in the academic environment and between media practitioners. We have developed a survey that we have applied online to 156 teachers from secondary and upper secondary education in Romania and analyzed their opinions regarding our set out issue. The results of this research show that, although most teachers are in favor of the introduction of media education in schools, the serious problems such an endeavor brings to light – that require a more extensive research – are related to human resources, to the training of the teachers who would take on this class and to the most appropriate way to integrate this discipline in the school curricula, either interdisciplinary or in specific school subjects. Accepting the idea that the internet is both a source of information and misinformation for students, the teachers questioned in this study believe that the digital misinformation phenomenon can be diminished by developing media skills and by practicing critical thinking.

Keywords

media literacy – digital literacy – media education – media culture – fake news – teaching – digital misinformation

© KONINKLIJKE BRILL NV, LEIDEN, 2020 | DOI: 10.1163/9789004432048_009

1   Introduction

In the context of the international debate regarding an increase of misinformation phenomena, manipulation and propaganda through classic and social media, public figures and international and Romanian organizations try to find efficient solutions for countering the avalanche of false content and actions (clickbait, trolling, fake followers, etc.) carried out by political, economical or other actors, with intent to misinform and manipulate online users.

A legislative proposal that stipulates the introduction of *Media Education and Culture* in Romanian schools as a mandatory subject for 5th and 9th grades caught our attention. The initiator of this proposal argues that 'the development of the fake news phenomenon generates a crisis for contemporary society and threatens the proper functioning of liberal democracies' and claims that it is useful for young people to be familiar with the mediums they can access in order to acquire diversified information, to form a critical and analytical mechanism and to develop skills in order to differentiate between fake news and real information.

This initiative complies with a guideline that has developed worldwide during the last 50 years, namely acknowledging the important role of communication and media in democratic societies and granting a special importance to the development of media skills, considered to be a crucial qualification in today's society.

UNESCO advised already in 1982, through the Grünwald Declaration, that political and educational systems should initiate and sustain media educational programs, that would encourage critical thinking and the use of media as a means of expressing creativity.

Twenty-five years after the adoption of the Grünwald Declaration, another document has been adopted in Paris, containing twelve recommendations for actions meant to encourage the implementation of media education. This document has been drafted by experts, decision-makers in the field of education, teaching staff and researchers, representatives of non-governmental organizations and media professionals from around the world. The recommendations that were formulated maintain the four guidelines comprised in the Grünwald Declaration: the development of extensive media education programs at all levels of education; teacher training and the awareness of other participants from the social field; research and the dissemination of research; international cooperation in actions.

In its turn, the European Parliament recommend that media education be a part of formal education, available to all children and that it should be established as an important part of school curriculum in all stages of education

(European Parliament Resolution, 2008/2129 (INI)). It is also recommended that media education should be focused on practical aspects and correlated with economical, political, literary, social, artistic and tech/computer subjects.

To this end, this resolution suggested a solution for the development of media skills by creating a school subject called "Media Education", but also an interdisciplinary approach combined with extra-curricular projects. The European Commission also underlines the importance of media education in the digital environment, regarding it necessary for boosting the competitiveness of the knowledge economy and for the establishment of an integrative informative society (Recommendation of the European Commission 2009/625/CE).

In this context, we need to mention the initiative of the European Commission from 2010, which had the goal of mapping out the most relevant national and regional media literacy projects, with the purpose of identifying best practices in this field and encouraging knowledge transfer between the EU states. This initiative materialized in a report called *Mapping of media literacy practices and actions in EU-28* (2017), pointing out the most diverse and interesting media literacy projects carried out in 28 EU states, outside the school curricula. This report along with the EMEDUS Report on Formal Media Education in Europe (2014), that concentrated on highlighting carried out projects within national school programs, offer a correct and comprehensive image of the interest shown in the last 10–15 years for the implementation of projects intended to develop media literacy.

2   Formal Education in a Global, Multicultural and Digital Society

Under the massive impact of digital communication, media is in a perpetual transformation, expanding, shooting off in multiple directions; education should be equally flexible and open to change. Even more, when the generations of digital natives have different informational needs and methods of accessing knowledge (Prenski, 2001; Friedl & Tkalac Vercic, 2011; Tapscot, 2011; Thomas, 2011), the huge data quantity available to them, the multitude of opinions and online perspectives, the trends established by influencers from different areas etc. necessarily determine a new educational approach of online communication and interaction for the generations of children and teens who not only consume, but also produce public media content.

The corresponding concept of this reality, *produsage*, entered into circulation with the publication of the book *Blogs, Wikipedia, Second Life and Beyond: From Production to Produsage,* written by the Australian professor Axel Bruns. In a similar manner, the term *produser* became popular, a term that describes a person who is, at the same time, both consumer and producer of information (written or audio-visual) for the web.

In Romania's formal education, there is a critical necessity to meet the needs of the digital natives and to develop abilities like: an interrogative-skeptical approach of social media content, selectivity, the ability to distinguish between facts and opinions, the ability to interpret data, by stimulating critical thinking.

In the present public space in Romania, journalists, NGO representatives or politicians often raise the problem of the lack of content found in the school curricula provided by the public school system. Financial, entrepreneurial education, sustainability or sexual educations are the most cited directions of change, in line with the new challenges of the global world. Media education, however, despite being so crucial in the context of the fulminating evolution of new communication technologies, has not inspired the interest of the members of the government, regardless of their political color. In Romania, the public debate on this subject has grown due to the legislative initiative registered at the end of 2018, that introduced the school subject "Media education and culture" in secondary education curricula as a mandatory subject for students from grades IV to IX, with the purpose of developing their media abilities and critical thinking, but also thanks to projects implemented by the Center for Independent Journalism (CIJ) in schools and/or with groups of teachers. On the CIJ website, under *Media education and culture lab*, the purpose of such endeavors, that intend to introduce "media education elements in educational programs for high schools with humanist profile (Romanian, English, French, history, social sciences) and to create a set of instruments and materials meant to help students understand and respect the role of media in a democratic society, to recognize propaganda and to use social media responsibly", is specified.

In other corners of the world, although – as shown above – media education has always been a constant concern in solid democracies, the occurrence, evolution and interaction between traditional media and new media has reignited, more than a decade ago, the need for adopting a theme or a school subject that can provide insight regarding the functionality of the media/new media system, the mindful use of quality information and the accountability of online behaviors.

Nevertheless, "as communication systems and information flows become increasingly central components of social, economic and political activity at all levels, media education remains marginal within educational systems everywhere" (Masterman, 2005, p. 1).

Extensive research points out the necessity for formal education to adapt in order to meet the challenges of digitalization: "Today information about the world around us comes to us not only by words on a piece of paper but more and more through the powerful images and sounds of our multi-media culture. Although mediated messages appear to be self-evident, in truth, they use a complex audio/visual 'language' which has its own rules (grammar) and which can be used to express many-layered concepts and ideas about the world" (Thoman & Jolls, 2008, p. 8). For centuries the education system has been organized based on the principle of transferring knowledge from teacher to student and on demonstrating the correct assimilation of knowledge by passing tests. Today, this system is no longer relevant, as students need "to learn how to find what they need to know when they need to know it, from the best sources available – and to have the higher order thinking skills to analyze and evaluate whether the information they find is useful for what they want to know" (Thoman & Jolls, 2008, p. 9).

More and more experts draw attention to the fact that education has become more and more anachronistic "as it continues to prepare students for a society that no longer exists" (Gutierrez & Tyner, 2012, p. 32), not being able to keep up with the increasing global and digital demands of the society we live in, where emphasis is put on multiculturalism, fast access to information and social media, without taking into account spatial and temporal limitations and which pleads for a complete revision of the mission of education.

3 Less Media Literacy More Fake News: Concepts and Theoretical Framework

Although in the common language the meaning of the word literacy is very clear, as it refers to learning to read and write, the modern sense in which it is used today was extended in order to encapsulate present concepts like literacy, digital literacy, visual literacy, computer literacy or social networking literacy. In other words, literacy is understood today as a concept that is "vibrant and dynamic and constantly evolving" (Gutierrez & Tyner, 2012, p. 36).

In the scientific literature there has been a particular interest in clarifying and establishing the meanings of these multiple literacy notions, with the purpose of eliminating possible confusion and misunderstandings. For that reason, we also regard some terminological clarifications and conceptual delimitations as necessary in the present chapter, moreover because today the terms media literacy and media education are considered to be interchangeable.

Thus, in a definition proposed by UNESCO in 2005, the term *literacy* is defined as the ability to identify, understand, interpret, create, communicate, and compute, using printed and written materials associated with varying context. Literacy involves a continuum of learning in enabling individuals to achieve his or her goals, develop his or her knowledge and potential to participate fully in community and wider society. (UNESCO, 2005, p. 21)

Alongside the concept of *media literacy*, another two notions that are closely interrelated with it, are very often invoked in scientific literature, respectively the concepts of *digital literacy* and *information literacy* (Koltay, 2011, p. 215). Although most authors admit the existence of a strong connection between the three notions, there is no consensus, in scientific literature, regarding the ground each of them covers or the relation between them.

From numerous definitions suggested for *media literacy*, we have chosen the one provided by W. James Potter (2019, p. 23), who identifies in it "a set of perspective that we actively use to expose ourselves to the mass media to process and interpret the meaning of the messages we encounter". We motivate our choice because of the key subtlety made by the author when conceptualizing the term media literacy, referring to the acquisition of hermeneutical skills and relating proactively to media messages.

A complex definition of *digital literacy* refers to "the ability to define, access, manage, integrate, communicate, evaluate and create information safely and appropriately through digital technologies and networked devices for participation in economic and social life" (Teng, 2018). Given the fact that, as (traditional and current) media professors and researchers, we are preoccupied by the subject of education and the development of skills that are not exclusively professional but also transversal, we value this perspective that stresses ("safely and appropriately") a responsible online behavior in a digital environment, understood as a space of co-participation.

For *information literacy*, a term frequently used in the US in the 90s, numerous professional and educational organizations have suggested definitions that incorporate common elements, however, all these definitions have been formulated "prior to the astonishing rise of social media and collaborative online communities and do not fully address the information knowledge required to participate in these new environments" (Mackey & Jacobson, 2011, p. 63).

For example let's regard the definition provided by the UNESCO guide „Towards Information Literacy Indicators", according to which *information literacy* represents "the capacity of people to: (1) recognize their information needs; (2) locate and evaluate the quality of information; (3) store and retrieve information; (4) make effective and ethical use of information, and (5) apply information to create and communicate knowledge" (Catts & Lau, 2008, p. 7).

As a worldwide promoter of media education, UNESCO proposes the use of a single concept, called *media and information literacy* (MIL), considered to be more comprehensive and to sum up all these numerous related literacy notions like library literacy, news literacy, digital literacy, computer literacy, Internet literacy, freedom of expression and freedom of information literacy, television literacy, advertising literacy, cinema literacy, games literacy or social networking literacy, although without providing a detailed taxonomy of different notions related to media and information literacy (Grizzle & Calvo, 2013, pp. 53–54). Therefore, according to the definitions suggested by UNESCO, *media and information literacy* (MIL) refers to that basic knowledge set "about (a) the functions of media, libraries, archives and other information providers in democratic societies, (b) the conditions under which news media and information providers can effectively perform those functions, and (c) how to evaluate the performances of these functions by assessing the content and services they offer" (Grizzle & Wilson, 2011, p. 16).

The integration of the two concepts into one is underpinned by the recognition of the fact that "aim of both is to support the compendium of skills, competencies and attitudes that children, youth and other citizens need to function and thrive in a digital society" (Gutierrez & Tyner, 2012, p. 35).

This perspective is, however, not unanimously accepted, as some studies insist on a strict separation of the two areas, media literacy and information literacy, seeing more differences than similarities between them (Lee & So, 2014, p. 143) or suggesting the use of a more general concept, *meta-literacy*, a concept which "provides a conceptual framework for information literacy that diminishes theoretical differences, builds practical connections, and reinforces central lifelong learning goals among different literacy types" (Mackey & Jacobson, 2011, p. 76).

At this point we need to note that, according to Buckingham (2003, p. 4), the use of the concept *media education* refers to "the process of teaching and learning about media". A complex concept, media education intends "to develop both critical understanding and active participation. It enables young people to interpret and make informed judgments as consumers of media; but it also enables them to become producers of media in their own right, and thereby to become more powerful participants in society. Media education is about developing young people's critical and creative abilities" (Buckingham, 2003, p. 4).

There is a connection between the (lack of) media/digital education and fake news. The fact that media education made a comeback to public attention, in politics as well as in academia and NGOs, is directly connected to the magnitude of the phenomenon of digital disinformation.

In this context, focusing on media education can be regarded as an important strategy for combating what we generically call today *fake news*. For this purpose, the Media Literacy Index/2018 is very relevant, as it points out the contrasts between established democracies that "have higher resilience potential to fake news with better education, free media and high trust between people" and Balkan countries (among which Romania is also cited), that "are most vulnerable to the adverse effects of fake news and post-truth, with controlled media, deficiencies in education and lower trust in society" (Lessenski, 2018, p. 1).

Furthermore, *The Eurobarometer on Fake News and Online Disinformation* (2018), created by the European Commission, is also relevant, as over 80% of the respondents perceive the phenomenon of fake news as a danger to democracy.

Only in the last two years, many studies (Peters, 2017; Fletcher & Park, 2017; Fletcher et al., 2018; Newman, 2018; Vosoughi et al., 2018; Bittner, 2019) reflect both the interest of the academic environment for *fake news* and the preoccupation of non-governmental organizations to capture the magnitude and the specificity of online misinformation; this subject is also a priority on the public agenda of states and international organizations. In order to find solutions, practitioners and theoreticians involved in fighting the misinformation phenomenon suggest two courses of action: on the one hand, the intensification of interdisciplinary research in the fields of humanities, social and computer studies, in order to assert the dynamics of the production, reception and viralization of potentially misinformative content as well as studying digital behavior, man-machine interaction, artificial intelligence etc. (Vosoughi et al., 2018; Bargaoanu, 2018); on the other hand, educating the users – (*produsers* – producers and users of digital content) on understanding the operating mode of media and new media, as well as on the accountability of their digital behavior (Wardel, 2016, 2017; Menczer et al., 2018; Bargaoanu, 2018).

Fake news, the expression of the year in the Collins dictionary, publicly established and made famous during the US presidential election campaign, is actually improper and semantically limitative. Wardle (2017) has considered it "misleading and unhelpful", as it denotes "a multitude of sins – crystallizing audience concerns about biased and shoddy journalism, political spin, misleading online advertising, as well as deliberately fabricated stories distributed via social media" (Newman, 2018, p. 16).

In an European Commission report from 2018, prepared by an international group of experts (High Level Expert Group on Fake News and Online Disinformation Report, 2018, p. 10), it is stressed that the term misinformation actually expresses the phenomenon that is amplified by new media. Essentially, we cannot speak only of *fake news*, but of an entire spectrum of digital content likely to generate informational chaos:

> This includes relatively low-risk forms such as honest mistakes made by reporters, partisan political discourse, and the use of click bait headlines, to high-risk forms such as for instance foreign states or domestic groups that would try to undermine the political process in European Member States and the European Union, through the use of various forms of malicious fabrications, infiltration of grassroots groups, and automated amplification techniques.

Digital News Report from the Reuters Institute for the Study of Journalism (2018, p. 38), one of the most used and credible sources for media practitioners and theoreticians, pays special attention to the conceptualization and understanding of the online misinformation phenomenon, suggesting waiving off the coined term *fake news*, as it is often used in political conflicts and replacing it with terms like misinformation and disinformation. "The global debate over so-called 'fake news' has changed a lot in the last year. What began as concern over the narrow problem of completely made-up news stories has since sparked a renewed interest in the much broader issue of online misinformation".

Although the term *fake news* is widely in use at present, it must be understood in a much wider sense than merely referring to made-up articles or media fiction. Thus, in academic research, the term *fake news* is mostly correlated with these two terms: *misinformation*, as in "the inadvertent sharing of false information", and *disinformation* or "the deliberate creation and sharing of information known to be false" (Wardel, 2016, 2017).

4   What Do Romanian Teachers Think about Introducing the Subject *Media Education and Culture* in School Curricula

Based on the finding that, although recent studies show the magnitude of the misinformation phenomenon in the new media era and although the generations of digital natives massively eat up online content – with youngsters becoming easy victims of digital misinformation – present Romanian school curricula do not include the study of phenomena associated with media and new media, we have elaborated a questionnaire, aiming to access the opinions of school teachers regarding these issues.

These were the objectives of the research:

- What do Romanian teachers think about introducing the subject *Media education and culture* in school curricula and what would be the most appropriate way to introduce it;
- What are the opinions of Romanian teachers regarding the students' media knowledge and skills provided by the present education system;
- What are the skills the subject *Media education and culture* would develop within students;
- What do Romanian teachers think about the fake news phenomenon and about the possibility of countering it by introducing the subject *Media education and culture.*

Teachers from secondary and upper secondary education in Romania were invited to take an online survey. The participation was voluntary and anonymous, and the authors of this study didn't have a formal relationship with the teachers in question or with the schools they work in. For two weeks (4–17 March 2019), 156 surveys were completed. The 156 survey participants were tenured teachers (81.8%), substitute teachers (18.2%), the majority with over fifteen years of experience (60.8%), who teach various school subjects: Romanian language or foreign languages (51%), humanities and social sciences (29.7%), mathematics and science (14.8%) and technological education (4.5%).

Less than half of the respondents, namely 42.9%, knew about a legislative proposal for the introduction of *Media education and culture* as a mandatory subject for classes VI and IX. Nevertheless, over 70% of the respondents consider this a good initiative, while a very small percent of the teachers (1.9%) are against such an endeavor. The majority of respondents believe that this subject would be useful (48.1%) or very useful (35.3%) for Romanian students. The majority of the teachers (58.3%) believe that communication and media graduates would be best suited to teach this subject. Other options would be, in order of preference, social studies teachers (31.4%), Romanian language teachers (25.6%), history teachers (10.9%) and philosophy teachers (7.7%). Over two-thirds of the respondents (71.8%), have shown interest in participating in training sessions for teachers who will eventually teach this subject, in the eventuality that such training be organized. Asked about the type of preparatory activities they consider attractive, most teachers would choose training sessions with experts in the field of media education (60.9%), followed, according to preferences, by classroom training or online courses. Only 9.6% of the teachers find the organization of training during summer schools, appropriate.

Although the legislative proposal intends for this subject to be mandatory, the teachers don't consider this the best way of introducing a school subject in the curriculum. Over half of the respondents believe that this subject should be integrated into the school curriculum within existing subjects (31.4%), studied during occasional activities (21.1%) or only in upper secondary education (2.6%). Of the 35 teachers who agree with introducing *Media education and culture* as a mandatory subject, only 8 believe that this subject should replace an existing subject, the rest would introduce it in addition to the other school subjects.

The respondents believe that the present education system develops students' media knowledge and skills too little or not at all (see Table 9.1).

Asked about the benefits for students as a consequence of the introduction of media education in schools, teachers mentioned most often: students' development of critical thinking and of the capacity of filtering information; developing skills for recognizing different kinds of media content and identifying *fake news*; recognizing risks and online safety measures management and awareness about the social, political and economical implications of media content (news, stories, coverage etc.).

Over 78% of the teachers believe that the internet is a source of both information and misinformation for youngsters, but they also believe that fake news and digital misinformation can be countered through media education. Almost three-quarters of the respondents (73.2%) consider the claim that

TABLE 9.1   Romanian teachers' opinions regarding the students' media knowledge and skills provided by the present education system

The present education system develops cognitive skills related to the media system and the ability of students to think critically about the received information		The present education system develops abilities and digital skills through which youngsters can produce online content responsibly		According to present school curricula, students are provided with knowledge about media (media, digital media, social networks)	
				Very good	1.9%
Too much	3.8%	Too much	1.3%	Good	17.3%
About right	7.7%	About right	15.4%	Neither good nor bad	21.8%
Too little	76.3%	Too little	72.4%	Poor	38.5%
Not at all	10.9%	Not at all	9%	Very poor	14.7%
I don't know/ No answer	3.8%	I don't know/ No answer	1.9%	I don't know/ No answer	5.8%

uneducated people are – to a greater extent – responsible for sharing false content online, to be true and more than half of these (54.5%), believe that the information provided by Romanian media is only in a minor way credible and relevant for the public.

5   Media Education Is Required in Schools, but How and by Whom
         Will It Be Taught? Discussions and Dilemmas

Although media education in schools is present in Western countries with a democratic tradition, in Romania, except for some non-governmental organizations like the Center for Independent Journalism (CJI), or Active Watch Romania, who have initiated and conducted programs for countering fake news and misinformation by holding workshops with students and teachers, but only in a few schools, there are no national media literacy policies. Thus, the 2004 project, that has introduced the optional subject "Media competence" into the national school curricula for high-school students is not the result of national, proactive policy, but exclusively the outcome of the efforts invested by the organization Active Watch Romania.

     This project is highlighted in the Media and Information Literacy Policies in Romania (2013) as one of the few notable efforts made in our country for introducing media education in schools: "as far as policy is concerned Romania took some steps to develop media literacy but it has understood the need for media education in its wider understanding. To this it adds the lack of a strong civil society voice to lobby for media education and almost no academic interest to deliver research and training in the field of media education" (Stanila & Fotiade, 2014, p. 18).

     Our study is the first one to approach the problem of media education in Romanian schools, from the teachers' perspective, and we wish it to be a first step in the achievement of a more broader research, as the sample for the present research is rather small and concentrated in the proximity of the city of Sibiu, in the center of Romania. However, the achieved results are very relevant, especially where the percents reveal opinions widely spread among teachers. For example, over 85% of the teachers believe that media knowledge and critical thinking abilities in relation to the use of digital information or skills to produce digital content responsibly are not taught in Romanian schools.

     If the necessity of teaching media education in schools is agreed upon by most of the teachers, an issue that deserves further discussion concerns the human resource that could teach either integrated topics or the subject itself. There are studies that show that the teachers themselves increasingly understand the relevance of media and new media in society and the need of an approach based on understanding the phenomena they generate. "Many administrators and educators would agree that one of the main goals of education is to help youth develop critical thinking abilities" (Scull & Kupersmidt, 2012). Regardless if it will be taught in separate subjects or interdisciplinary, media education entails a long-term investment, according to Nicoleta Fotiade, Media Literacy Expert/Founder Mediawise Society (Peticila, 2018). Media education should be included in the initial as well as on-going training of teachers, and, although, at first glance, this can be perceived as a costly process, "long term effects that will occur from not offering this type of training for children and teens will be more expensive" (Peticila, 2018).

From a different perspective, a recent, conceptually and bibliographically highly articulate, study (Druick, 2016), proposes a diachronic perspective regarding the implementation of media education, while insisting on a cautious approach regarding it, stressing the correlation between the evolution of capitalism and the spreading of neo-liberal ideology and media education. The author points out the risk of political interference in the implementation of media education programs, which should make us vigilant for possible governmental interests. Moreover, the EMEDUS Report on Formal Media Education in Europe (2014), which has studied the way in which media literacy has been introduced in the school curricula of multiple European countries, has proven that where formal media education isn't introduced due to a constructive dialogue between political and professional groups, but imposed by politics "from the top", chances of implementation are slim because of the lack of qualified teachers in the area, negative attitudes towards pedagogic reforms or the lack of long term funding (2014, p. 10).

6   Conclusions

Regarding the present research, the main conclusion that has emerged from the interpretation of the questionnaire and from the consulted studies, articles and reports, is that (new) media education represents an efficient strategy for counteracting fake news, because it can develop critical thinking skills and can highlight the characteristics of a responsible digital behavior.

Romania, similar to other young democracies in the world, has a hard time understanding and managing the general and incorrectly called phenomenon of fake news, while politicians, representatives of the public and teachers support the introduction of a new subject, starting with middle school, about the role of media in the age of social media, about journalism and the freedom of speech, about democratic press models, about having access to information and globalization etc., by presenting current content that is relevant for the generations of digital native consumers and online content creators par excellence.

Accepting, in a high rate, the idea that the internet is both a source of information and disinformation, the questioned teachers in our study believe that a higher level of education, generally, and media education, specifically, will reduce the phenomenon of digital disinformation.

An alternative, but by no means less important, conclusion points out the connection between the role of a trainer and filter between professional press and education. According to The Eurobarometer on Fake News and Online Disinformation, journalists are perceived as "the main responsible for stopping the spread of fake news", by 45% of European correspondents, while the country percentage isn't much different in Romania (2018, p. 24). The collaboration between schools and media could start here in order to support educational projects adapted to the digital world and its challenges.

While media practitioners and theoreticians plead for the production of responsible content, considering that in the digital era, it is vital for journalism to preserve its role of acting for the general good and in the public interest, to build trust relying on fact-checking and on promoting credible sources and that the press should act as "an antidote for information disorder, countering the informational chaos with reliable information" (Bittner, p. 18), researchers, teachers, politicians and NGOs regard the raising level of media education as an efficient solution for countering misinformation in the digital environment. Media and critical thinking skills can be efficient solutions for enhancing resilience against the present informational chaos, while the teachers who understand the phenomena generated by new media can become information vectors for the digital natives, who are keen online content consumers.

Accepting, in a high percentage, the idea that the internet is both a source of information and misinformation, the questioned teachers believe that a higher level of education, generally, and media education, specifically, will reduce the phenomenon of digital misinformation.

References

Bargoanu, A. (2018). *#Fake News. Noua cursa a inarmarii* [*#Fake news. The new arming race*]. Bucuresti, Romania: Evrika Publishing.
Bergel, H. (2017). Oh, what a tangled web: Russian hacking, fake news, and the 2016 US presidential election. *Computer, 50*(9), 87–91. doi:10.1109/MC.2017.3571054

Bittner, A. K. (2019). *EFJ report digital journalism and new business models.* Retrieved from https://www.lamira.cat/documents/02-2019-efj-report-digital-journalism-and-new-business-models.pdf

Buckingham, D. (2003). *Media education. Literacy, learning and contemporary culture.* Cambridge: Polity Press.

Catts R., & Lau, J. (2008). *Towards information literacy indicators.* Paris: UNESCO.

Center for Independent Journalism. *Laboratory of education and media culture.* description Retrieved from https://www.cji.ro/laboratorul-de-educatie-si-cultura-media/

Ciampaglia, G. L., Mantzarlis, A., Maus, G., & Menczer, F. (2018). Research challenges of digital misinformation: Toward a trustworthy web. *AI Magazine, 39*(1), 65–74.

Druick, Z. (2016). The myth of media literacy. *International Journal of Communication, 10,* 1125–1144.

European Audiovisual Observatory. (2017). *Mapping of media literacy practices and actions in EU-28.* Strasbourg. Retrieved from https://www.epra.org/news_items/mapping-of-media-literacy-prectices-and-actions-in-eu-28-eao-report

European Commission. (2018). *Flash Eurobarometer 464 – Fake news and disinformation online.* Retrieved from https://ec.europa.eu/commfrontoffice/publicopinion/index.cfm/survey/getsurveydetail/instruments/flash/surveyky/2183

Fletcher, R., Cornia, A., Graves, L., & Nielsen, R. K. (2018). *Measuring the reach of "fake news" and online disinformation in Europe.* Reuters Institute & University of Oxford. Retrieved from https://reutersinstitute.politics.ox.ac.uk/our-research/measuring-reach-fake-news-and-online-disinformation-europe

Fletcher, R., & Parks, S. (2017). The impact of trust in the news media on online news consumption and participation. *Digital Journalism, 5,* 10. https://doi.org/10.1080/21670811.2017.1279979

Friedl, J., & Tkalac Vercic, A. (2011). Media preferences of digital natives' internal communication: A pilot study. *Public Relations Review, 37*(1), 84–86.

Grizzle, A., & Calvo, M. C. T. (2013). *Media and information literacy: policy and strategy guidelines.* Paris: UNESCO.

Grizzle, A., & Wilson, C. (2011). *Media and information literacy curriculum for teachers.* Paris: UNESCO.

Gutierrez, A., & Tyner, K. (2012). Media education, media literacy and digital competence. *Comunicar, 38,* 31–39.

Ito, M., Horst, H., Bittanti, M., Boyd, D., Herr-Stephenson, B., Lange, P. G., Pascoe, C. J., & Robinson, L. (2008). *Living and learning with new media.* The John D. and Catherine T. MacArthur Foundation Reports on Digital Media and Learning.

Jenkins, H. (2006). *Confronting the challenges of participatory culture: Media education for the 21st century.* The John D. and Catherine T. MacArthur Foundation Reports on Digital Media and Learning.

Koltay, T. (2011). The media and the literacies: Media literacy, information literacy, digital literacy. *Media, Culture & Society, 33*(2), 211–221.

Lee, A., & So, C. (2014). Media literacy and information literacy: Similarities and differences. *Comunicar, 42,* 137–146.

Lessenski, M. (2018). *Common sense wanted resilience to 'post-truth' and its predictors in new media literacy index 2018.* Open Society Institute Sofia. Retrieved from http://osi.bg/downloads/File/2018/MediaLiteracyIndex2018_publishENG.pdf

Mackey, T. P., & Jacobson, T. E. (2011). Reframing information literacy as a metaliteracy. *College & Research Libraries, 72*(1), 61–78.

Masterman, L. (2005). *Teaching the media.* London: Routledge, Taylor & Francis E-Library.

Newman, N. (2018). Journalism, media, and technology trends and predictions. Reuters Institute & University of Oxford. Retrieved January 2018 from https://reutersinstitute.politics.ox.ac.uk/our-research/journalism-media-and-technology-trends-and-predictions-2018

Peters, M. A. (2017). Post-truth and fake news. *Educational Philosophy and Theory, 49*(6), 567. https://doi.org/10.1080/00131857.2017.1288782

Peticila, M. (2018). *Educatia media in scoala, proiect Mediawise Society* [*Media education in school, mediawise society's project*]. Retrieved from https://www.edupedu.ro/educatia-media-in-scoala-proiect-mediawise-society-elevii-n-ar-trebui-sa-fie-protejati-de-mesajele-de-propaganda-ci-lasati-sa-le-analizeze/

Potter, J. W. (2019). *Media literacy* (9th ed.). Los Angeles, CA: Sage.

Prensky, M. (2001). Digital natives, digital immigrants. *On the Horizon, 9*(5), 3–6.

Scull, T. M., & Kupersmidt, J. B. (2011). An evaluation of a media literacy program training workshop for late elementary school teacher. *The Journal of Media Literacy Education, 2*(3), 199–208.

Stanila, C., & Fotiade, N. (2014). *Media and information literacy policies in Romania.* Paris: TRANSLIT.

Tandoc Jr., E. C., Lim, Z. W., & Ling, R. (2018). Defining "fake news". *Digital Journalism, 6*(2), 137–153. doi:10.1080/21670811.2017.1360143

Tapscott, D. (2011). *Crescuti digital.* Bucharest, Romania: Editura Publica.

Teng, J. X. (2018). *Digital literacy and beyond.* Paris: UNESCO.

Thoman, E., & Jolls, T. (2008). *Literacy for the 21st century: An overview & orientation guide to media literacy education.* Center for Media Literacy. Retrieved from http://www.medialit.org

Thomas, M. (2011). *Deconstructing digital natives: Young people, technology, and the new literacies.* London: Routledge, Taylor & Francis Group.

UNESCO. (2005). *Aspects of literacy assessment: Topics and issues from the UNESCO expert meeting.* 10–12 June 2003. Paris, France: UNESCO.

Vosoughi, S., Roy, D., & Aral, S. (2018). The spread of true and false news online. *Science,*
359(63801), 1146–1151.

Wardel, C. (2016). [*M/D*]*isinformation reading list*. First draft. Retrieved from
https://firstdraftnews.org/misinformation-reading-list/

Wardel, C. (2017). *Fake news. It's complicated*. First draft. Retrieved from
https://medium.com/1st-draft/fake-news-its-complicated-d0f773766c79

CHAPTER 10

Innovative Practices in Teacher Education: Why Should We? How Can We?

Paulien C. Meijer

Abstract

This chapter describes a rationale for developing innovative practices in teacher education and for teacher education. It departs from the idea that education, in general, needs to equip children to purposefully shape (future) society together. Teachers and teacher educators need to model the type of learning that is needed to address this basic idea. Describing insights from research on creativity in education and on adaptive expertise, this chapter provides inspirations for teacher educators to develop innovative practices for their student teachers, and for the professionalization of teacher educators.

Keywords

teacher education – innovation – creativity – expertise – teacher educators – practices – professional development

1 The Function of Education in Society

This chapter starts from the idea that global changes demand that all people, more than ever before, work together in creating a better world. Teachers have a crucial role to fulfill here, as they work with the people who will create future society: children. They also have to deal with society's rapid technological developments, and need to address an increasingly diverse student population. In addition, societal, global and environmental challenges, all contribute to an insecure future for all, and this is particularly felt by our youth. In essence, more than ever, teachers are challenged to address the "five Ps" which the United Nations identified as core in "transforming our world" in their 2030 agenda for sustainable development: People, planet, prosperity, peace, partnership. In this chapter, I will depart from an exploration of what this challenging task means

© KONINKLIJKE BRILL NV, LEIDEN, 2020 | DOI: 10.1163/9789004432048_010

for teachers. Subsequently, I will particularly focus on teacher education. A focus on teacher education is one that is often ignored, but when one considers the crucial role of teachers for student learning, it is not far-fetched to state that teacher educators have an equally crucial role in teacher learning. As not much is written about the role of teacher educators in addressing new challenges in teaching, part of this chapter will be about teacher educators' role.

But I will start with the children. Throughout the world, we see children and young people standing up to ask attention to issues they are concerned with. For example, Swedish Greta Thunberg demands attention for climate change, Nobel peace prize winner Malala Yousafzai fights for accessible education for girls and women, and David Hogg, who survived the Parkland school shooting, is now fighting for gun control. They are illustrative for a generation that not only asks, but demands that we change society, and that we do so not only for them but also with them. They represent a generation that demands that we reconsider how we have formed and organized our society today and that we reconsider the values we base our society on. And their demands are by no means odd or incomprehensible. They demand peace, safety, inhabitable earth, education, to name but a few, in ways that would require fundamental changes to present-day society. How can we meet their demands? Not by merely passing on the knowledge that society has produced so far, or by assimilating them into present society. Both would mean that they should accept and adapt to present society, while they make absolutely clear that it is exactly the knowledge that society has produces so far, and how society has come to organize itself, has lead to the very problems they are addressing. It would also imply that their demands and their voices would be silenced.

This chapter intents to recognize children's demands in a way that challenges present-day society. I take the stance that teacher education, educating future teachers, can have a crucial role to fulfill here. This is not only a political statement, but also a moral appeal. We cannot leave teacher education as it is. We would fail our youth.

Addressing our youth's demands means that we first need to (re)consider our vision on the function of education in society. For long, many have claimed that the basic function of education is to prepare children 'for the labor market'. In addition, people claimed that education needs to prepare children for 'participating in society'. And lately, people have come to emphasize that children need to get ready 'for a future we do not know yet', and 'professions that do not yet exist'. However, considering the demands and challenges as described above, all these perspectives are limited and in danger of biases, because in essence, they see children as passively undergoing education. I propose the following perspective:

The function of education in society is to equip children to purposefully shape (future) society together.

In this perspective, children do not only need to develop thorough knowledge, understanding, and a large range of skills, but also a willingness to engage in a shared responsibility, in order to decide and give shape to how society (including the labor market) and the future develops. This requires a critical stance, responsibility for each other, and active involvement. The consequence of all this for pupils, teachers, and schools is that attention should not be limited to conventional ways of acquiring knowledge and skills. In one way or another, this needs to merge with the cultivation of innovative ways of thinking. This would mean, for example, that attention to the process of creating, of finding and shaping new opportunities, and of analyzing what we – in collaboration – wish for, needs to fuse in. It also means that concepts such as imagination, courage, mutual respect, embracing uncertainty, and responsibility for each other should take a more central position. If we wish to accomplish this in pupils, teachers need to model the type of learning and actions we expect from students and, even further, teacher educators need to model the type of learning and actions we expect from pupils as well as from teachers.

In this three-double layer (pupils, teachers, and teacher educators) this chapter focuses on teachers and teacher educators, using two perspectives: (a) creativity and (b) adaptive expertise. I think that these perspectives are particularly interesting since research in these areas has provided insights that might help in addressing the inclusion of (the cultivation of) innovative ways of thinking as described above. Any genuine and heartfelt innovation requires "creativity" of everyone involved, in this case: of pupils and teachers and teacher educators. In addition, finding and keeping your balance between innovation and routine – this balancing being the core of adaptive expertise – deserves attention, since it prevents us from focusing disproportionately on either routines, or innovation.

In the following, I will suggest some ways in which (student) teachers might develop creativity and adaptive expertise. Next, I will discuss some consequences for teacher educators.

2   Creativity

Creativity is included in the list of the "4 C's" that make up the so-called 21st-century skills, together with Critical thinking, Collaboration, and Communication. Looking through recent and ancient history, however, it is evident that these skills were relevant in all centuries: no Chinese wall, Egyptian or Maya pyramid, moon landing, or the World Wide Web would have been possible without such skills (and, evidently, without content knowledge). But it seems that nowadays, with big global challenges, these skills are more urgent to develop for people, and there is growing call-out to schools to address these. Recently, the OECD launched a report in which they developed and tested instruments for teaching creativity and critical thinking (Vincent-Lancrin et al., 2019) as an answer to the growing demand they perceived for paying attention to both in education.

Many books have been written about creativity in all forms in education, from kindergarten to university (e.g. Robinson, 2017; Beghetto, Kaufman, & Baer, 2015; Craft, Jeffrey, & Leibling, 2001; Sternberg, Jarvin, & Grigorenko, 2015) and many will undoubtedly follow. Also, a multitude of models about creativity was developed, such as the "four-C model" of Helfand, Kaufman and Beghetto (2016). All these books and models are meant to help teachers pay more attention to the development of creativity in their lessons. Many teachers acknowledge the value of creativity, but research also shows that they are struggling: they feel ill-equipped and they feel that they lack time (e.g., Lucker, Beghetto, & Dow, 2004).

So, creativity is seen as important by teachers, but it is seen so little in the classroom. Why is that? One explanation is the underestimation of what the inclusion of creativity in the classroom would really entail (Oosterheert & Meijer, 2017). To understand this explanation, let us first have a look at a definition of creativity, which is often used in the context of education (Cadle, 2015, p. 174):

> Creativity is the interaction among imagination, cognitive presence, ego-strength, conation, aptitude, process, domain engagement, and environment by which an individual or group follows the creative process to produce an accepted product that is both novel and useful as defined within a personal or social context.

This is a complicated definition, which pays attention to the process of creativity, the people involved and the creative product as well. Without going too deep into all components in the definition (see Cadle, 2015 for this), it is interesting to explore what it would mean in relation to the vision on the purpose of education as described earlier: "We need to equip children to purposefully shape (future) society together". Together, this vision and Cadle's definition lead to a *movement*, which can best be described as follows. We need to move:
– from a focus on individual learning towards also including collective learning;

- from narrow goals towards also including broad goals;
- from re-activity towards also including pro-activity;
- from simple towards also including complex tasks;
- from fragmented subject matter(s) to integration.

Interestingly, in his essay on "the nature of creativity", Sternberg (2006) pointed out that creativity follows from an active decision to think along new lines. In order to include creativity in the classroom, an active decision to start such a movement needs to be made on all levels – so not only by pupils, but also by teachers, teacher educators, school administrators, and researchers. For teachers this means, among other things, that they need to understand not only their subject matter content, but also understand this in a broader context: connected to other contents and to the purpose of education in general. It also implies that they need to take up shared responsibility for student learning in the broad range (not only in their own subject) and for own and each other's learning. On a more personal level it implies that teachers are (more) flexible, imaginative, they tolerate uncertainty and even embrace and actively seek uncertainty, and everything we ask from our pupils. Framed somehow differently, it implies that teachers decide to sometimes "travel without a destination", and enjoy it.

From this description, it follows that when teachers decide to include creativity in their classroom, adding some creative assignments will not suffice. It requires a reconsideration of one's own role as a teacher, in relation to one's pupils, colleagues, subject, and the purpose of education (including society). How can teachers start or advance in this?

Learning to pay attention to creativity is not just acquiring a skill. A reconsideration of one's own role and one's relations to others asks not only for skill development and knowledge acquisition, but also for learning processes that relate to identity development (e.g., Illeris, 2009). For *student teachers*, this means that all these components of such a learning process should be organized in an integrated way. Another chapter in this book describes a "course" I developed with two of my colleagues in my teacher education institute, labeled "Teaching for creativity" in which we attempted to set this up.

For *experienced teachers*, UNESCO goes as far as to state that we need to "retrain them". What would this entail? Several studies have shown that curriculum change requires a "re-culturing of the classroom", in which all those involved need to reposition themselves. For example, Overman, Vermunt, Meijer, and Brekelmans (2019) described this for teachers and pupils, and concluded that for such a re-culturing to succeed, one can best take the perspective of a dialogue, with oneself and with others. In many curriculum reforms, this dialogue is overlooked, and implementing reforms is often seen as the introduction of new books, literature or assignments, which can be handed down to the teacher, and consumed by pupils (Overman et al., 2018). But if one acknowledges that learning to teach for creativity requires a reconsideration of one's own role and one's relations to others and to subject matter content, it is immediately clear that this will not suffice. Teachers will need to ask themselves what it means to pay attention to creativity in the classroom, and how that relates to subject matter. They need to be flexible, imaginative and have to be able to deal with the uncertainties that come with the "traveling without a destination".

In an earlier essay (Oosterheert & Meijer, 2017) we described, based on a literature review, the partial domain-specificity of creativity; the multifaceted nature of the full creative process; and the vulnerability of creative functioning in an education context. These characteristics not only play out for pupils but also for teachers. Particularly the vulnerability aspect can be difficult for teachers, and Overman et al. (2019) found that most of the experienced teachers they have studied, appeared to avoid this. These teachers, working with innovative ways of science teaching, felt that this affected their ways of working with pupils, and reverted to their usual routines, which felt more comfortable.

3   Adaptive Expertise

This brings us to the issue of adaptive expertise. When incorporating attention to creativity in their teaching, for both new and experienced teachers it is important to explore how they find (and keep) their balance between innovative ways of working (such as paying attention to creativity) and other parts of teaching. If teachers feel that there is too much innovation and not enough attention to developing routines (for new teachers) or for respecting their carefully constructed routines (for experienced teachers), an unbalance might crop up. A way to look at this balance or unbalance is through the lens of "adaptive expertise", depicted in Figure 10.1.

In the late eighties, Hatano and Inagaki (1986) studied expertise and found two "types" of experts, which they labeled as routine experts, and adaptive experts (see Figure 10.1). The first rely most on routines they have developed over years of experience and are able to do their work very efficient. The latter also have developed such routines but, next to that, are also keen on innovation if a situation should require this, or if they themselves seek out. Among others, Schwartz et al. (2005) described that adaptive experts are able

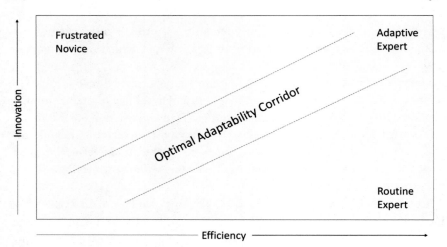

FIGURE 10.1   "Adaptive expertise" in relation to innovation and efficiency (adapted from
Cutrer et al., 2016)

of "drawing on their knowledge to invent new procedures for solving unique
or fresh problems."

An essential characteristic of adaptive experts is that they balance routines and innovation, by functioning in a so-called Optimal Adaptability
Corridor, as depicted in Figure 10.1. Particularly in the context of education,
there are many routines, which aim to provide structure to pupils, teachers
and all other people engaged in schools. These routines are important and
need to create peace and quiet to be able to teach and learn. For teachers,
the importance of maintaining a balance between routines and innovation is
evident.

In an earlier section of this chapter, I discussed some ideas about how to
delve into the creative exploration (top left of Figure 10.1), and what this might
mean for teachers, such as for their flexibility, imagination and tolerance for
uncertainty. But if routines predominate over innovation and creative ideas,
these routines might need to be reconsidered. These routines can be one's
own routines as an experienced teacher. But they can also pertain pupils', colleagues', or others' routines. And even if one decides that some routines have
lost their function or even are counterproductive, it sometimes is not so easy
to give them up. Literature suggests some strategies that support the breaking
down of routine behavior (e.g., Illeris, 2013; Mezirow, 2006; Meijer, Oolbekkink,
Pillen, & Aardema, 2014):

– Embrace dilemmas, professional tensions and (internal) conflicts as potential learning opportunities;

- Use or create 'critical incidents', and examine these in light of the development of new expertise;
- Create and engage in professional dialogue with colleagues and pupils.

All of these strategies provide learning opportunities that very much invite teachers to reconsider routines by opening up opportunities for creative explo-rations, big or small.

4   Consequences for Teacher Educators

For teacher educators, this means that they need to "move" as well. They need to model the learning and teaching they expect from student teachers and experienced teachers. They need to delve into creative explorations and break-down routines to develop new practices. And they need to develop profession-ally in order to be able to do so. I will elaborate on these three aspects below and provide some examples of how this might work out in practice.

4.1   *Modelling*

First, teacher educators need to model the learning and teaching that is expected from (student) teachers (cf. Lunenberg, Korthagen, & Swennen, 2007). They need to show that they are learners themselves, and that they keep on questioning their routines even after many years of experience. How do they connect (new) content and practice? How do they (continue to) deal with uncertainty? How do they find and keep a balance between routines and cre-ative exploration?

In a blogpost, Wells (2017) stresses the importance of modelling for teacher educators, particularly if they want to stimulate that their student teachers experiment with creative pedagogies in their teaching. He frames this as fol-lows and I could not have said it better:

> As teacher educators, we need to model creative pedagogy with our pre-service colleagues. We need to develop teachers who have the criti-cal expertise to appreciate the need for progress measures and outcome accountability, but not at the expense of creative, 'outside of the box' learning approaches. We need to encourage our trainee teachers to fos-ter the skills required to become transformational agents of change in their future classrooms and schools. We need to develop recognition that a 21st-century 'classroom' no longer needs to mimic its Victorian ancestry and that our pupils may demand their learning is contextualized and

approached through alternative pedagogies. ... teacher education needs to be developing creativity, risk-taking and criticality in our pre-service teachers that enables our pupils' thinking to be challenged. Our teacher education courses also need to be reflective of learning contexts and pedagogical approaches that will enhance creativity and engagement in the classroom and therefore support the expertise that our young people require to successfully connect with their 21st-century futures. (Wells, 2017)

4.2   *Developing Practices*

Second, teacher educators need to develop practices. Such practices include attention for creativity and innovation in teacher education in such a way that it connects to the vision and movement described earlier in this chapter. Teacher educators cannot just pass down the curriculum, but also cannot impose "disruptive innovations" (cf. Ellis, Souto-Manning & Turvey, 2019) that lack a clear purpose and ignore the development of routines. Their practices have to support the search for a balance between creative explorations and the development of routines. Such practices need to include attention for working together with schools to emphasize workplace learning (Leeferink, Koopman, Beijaard, & Ketelaar, 2015). This workplace learning should not boil down to mere socialization in the school, but newcomers need to feel welcome to bring innovative ideas and practices so that the "workplace" (all those surrounding the new teacher) learns as well.

Many books have been written about innovative practices in teacher education, often in terms of 'pedagogies'. Of particular interest here is the edited book "International teacher education: promising pedagogies", edited by Lily Orland-Barak and Cheryl Craig (2014). Also, the 2017 SAGE *Handbook of Research on Teacher Education*, edited by Jean Clandinin and Jukka Husu, contains a section that is labeled Learning Through Pedagogies in Teacher Education, edited by Juan José Mena Marcos. This section contains several chapters that report about innovative practices in teacher education, which teacher educators can use as inspiration for their own practice. In addition to practices described in SAGE Handbook, Table 10.1 contains an example of an innovative practice in which my own university is involved. It initiated from the point of view that student teachers and experienced teachers should learn together and not, as is the conventional way, in separate trajectories or courses.

TABLE 10.1   Example of innovative practice in teacher education

The "Leeratelier" ("hybrid learning lab")

In a joint effort to connect student teacher learning and experienced teacher learning, and to rethink and further develop student teachers' placement leaning, a "hybrid learning lab" was set up. This lab blended in the regular curriculum of one-year post-master teacher education program. During this year, every Tuesday morning, six groups of student teachers, experienced teachers and teacher educators came together and collaboratively designed their own learning by, for example, doing research together, collaborative lesson design and evaluation, or inviting guests. By working this way, individual learning and collective learning are supposed to be connected. A prerequisite is that all involved see themselves as learners, including the teacher educators. In addition, participation is on equal level: newcomers' innovative ideas and practices are as much as welcome as those of experienced teachers and educators.

Each group focused on two questions: what and how do we want to learn and develop together? What and how do we want our pupils to learn and develop together? These seem to be simple questions, but are inherently complex, and assume a pro-active mindset and a shared responsibility for each other and for pupils.

For teacher educators participating in these labs, it meant that they needed to rethink their role as teacher educator as they are, next to their role as educators, co-learners and co-workers. This implied that also they needed to reconsider their routines, undergo the uncertainty that goes along with that, and develop, together with their co-participating teachers and student teachers, new practices they would never have been able to develop in their more "conventional" setting. Interestingly, as they were also working in the conventional setting, doing their regular teacher educator tasks, they started to rethink these as well, and sometimes included elements, or pedagogies, which originated from the learning labs, in these tasks as well. New questions arose, such as:

- How can 'learning' best be understood in such a context of 'expansive knowledge construction'?
- How to facilitate that the creation of each individual's learning environment is approached as a collaborative responsibility?
- How can the integration of content and practice best be conceptualized and enacted?

TABLE 10.2   Example of innovative practice for teacher educators' professional development

The Summer Academy of the International Forum of Teacher Educator Development (InFo-TED)

A one-week Summer Academy, embedded in a virtual learning platform, was launched and attended by 45 experienced teacher educators from seven European countries. During this week, these teacher educators teamed up and worked in groups on shared projects that they themselves designed, executed and evaluated. The Academy was set up and carried out by a team of well-established teacher educators from the seven participating countries. These educators participated as learners as well. They worked from a carefully constructed framework and planning, leaving explicit space for sharing practices, development of projects and identity work. Pedagogies included:
– "Zipping" theory and practice (Kelchtermans, 2018) to integrate elements of a conceptual model (Kelchtermans, Smith & Vanderlinde, 2017) and teacher educators' own practices, in order to further develop both model and practices;
– Storyfication as a means to examine the various pathways of becoming a teacher educator and the journey in the profession itself;
– Modelling on all levels, including "modelling of modelling", such as voice-over teaching (Oldeboom, 2018) to develop awareness of the levels of learning and learners involved in the practice of teacher educators;
– Building on past experiences towards future-oriented collaboration of participants;
– Unknown end-products: tolerating uncertainty and experience the joy that follows from that.
The summer academy started with the concept of "how I teach is the message" (Kelchtermans, 2009). During the week, however, this concept evolved into "how *we* teach is the message". Participants had a wide range of backgrounds, not only coming from various countries, but particularly because their pathways into teacher educators had been different (e.g., first being a high school teacher, or first being an academic researcher) as well as their tasks within teacher education. This profoundly influenced the way they approached their work. Exploring this together made the participants realize that such a range of background is a huge benefit for student teachers, as it is for pupils to have a range of different teachers during their time in schools. If we want our student teachers to take up a shared responsibility for educating pupils, we should explicitly model this. Hence, how *we* teach is the message. New questions arose, such as:
– How are we, as teacher educators, part of each other's stories?
– What professional identity do we share as teacher educators?
– What is needed to educate new teacher educators who are attentive to innovative teaching practices?

4.3   *Professional Development*

Third, addressing student teachers' creativity and adaptive expertise has consequences for teacher educators' professional development. They need to learn all the above in trajectories that reflect the new pedagogies and practices, which means that learning through dialogue in (international) collaboration, doing research, and revisiting one's professional identities become much more central. It also entails that they need to be prepared to take up the shared responsibility for preparing teachers for their collaborative task. Teacher educators can only do this together, as a team. Table 10.2 contains an example practice for teacher educators' professional development, which we developed as a group of experienced teacher education. In this practice we experimented with a range of innovative ideas regarding teacher education and the education of teacher educators throughout Europe.

Examples of innovative practices that aim at the development of teacher educators are scarce. Certainly, a challenge that awaits us in the near future is to develop such practices.

5   Conclusions

When we reconsider the question: Innovative practices in teacher education: why should we? The answer cannot be other than: "Because we owe this to future generations" and "because our youths demand this". Many children do not want knowledge transmitted that has until now produced conflict, guns, oppression, and an uninhabitable earth. If teacher education teaches teachers to transmit that knowledge, we fail our children and, as such, future generations.

The next question, Innovative practices in teacher education: how can we? requires a longer answer. First, we need to develop pedagogies from the understanding that teacher educators, as well as teachers, contribute to how our children give shape to (future) society. Second, we need to model. It is not just the pedagogies we use, it is also the pedagogy we are. If we feel that education needs to equip children to purposefully shape (future) society together, children do not only need to develop thorough knowledge, understanding, and a large range of skills, but also a willingness to engage in a shared responsibility, in order to decide and give shape to how society and the future develops. This requires active involvement and not passively undergoing a fixed curriculum.

It is exactly this, that teacher educators need to model for (future) teachers. Hence, not only do teacher educators need knowledge, understanding and a large range of skills, they also need to be willing to engage in shared responsibility and to do this explicitly and openly. Accordingly, they cannot pass on, or work according to a fixed curriculum. They need to explain, for (future) teachers, what they are doing, and why. Also for teacher educators, there should be more attention to the process of creating, of finding and shaping new opportunities and of analyzing what we wish for. To model this explicitly, we should do this all in collaboration. Again parallel to the consequences for pupils, teachers and teacher educators need to be aware of the idea that, alongside knowledge and skills, their imagination, courage, mutual respect, embracing uncertainty, and responsibility for each other should take a central position as well. For some teacher educators this might mean that they need to engage in creative exploration, for others it might mean that they also need to focus on the breaking down of routines and for others it means that they need to keep a better balance between innovation and routines. It is clear that modeling all this explicitly for student teachers (or teachers: for their pupils) is a very powerful practice to show what we expect from learners.

So, the three-double layer teacher educators need to attend to, means that the most powerful way of getting pupils to learn, is that educators in the other layers need to explicitly model that they are learners as well, and set the stage for the type of learning that we expect from our pupils. If we want to address their demands for global and profound changes, we cannot stick to passing on the existing curriculum. We need to include teacher educators, in such a way that they can be the educators that our youth needs.

References

Beghetto, R. A., Kaufman, J. C., & Baer, J. (2015). *Teaching for creativity in the common core classroom.* New York, NY: Teachers College Press.

Cadle, C. R. (2015). A completion mindset: Bridging the gap between creative thinking and creativity. *Psychology of Aesthetics, Creativity, and the Arts, 9*(2), 172–177.

Clandinin, D. J., & Husu, J. (2017). *The Sage handbook of research on teacher education.* Los Angeles, CA: Sage.

Craft, A., Jeffrey, B., & Leibling, M. (2001). *Creativity in education.* London: Continuum International Publishing Group.

Cutrer, W., Miller, B., Pusic, M., Mejicano, G., Mangrulkar, R., Gruppen, L., Hawkins, R., Skochelak, S., & Moore, D. (2016). Fostering the development of master adaptive learners: A conceptual model to guide skill acquisition in medical education. *Academic Medicine, 92*, 1.

Ellis, V., Souto-Manning, M., & Turvey, K. (2019). Innovation in teacher education: Towards a critical examination. *Journal of Education for Teaching, 45*(1), 1–13.

Griffin, D. (2016). *Education reform: The unwinding of intelligence and creativity.* Dordrecht: Springer.

Hatano, G., & Inagaki, K. (1986). Two courses of expertise. In H. W. Stevenson, H. Azumam, & K. Hakuta (Eds.), *A series of books in psychology. Child development and education in Japan* (pp. 262–272). Freeman/Times Books.

Helfand, M., Kaufman, J. C., & Beghetto, R. A. (2016). The four-c model of creativity: Culture and context. In V. P. Glaveanu (Ed.), *The Palgrave handbook of creativity and culture research*. London: Palgrave.

Illeris, K. (2009). *Contemporary theories of learning*. London: Routledge.

Kelchtermans, G. (2009). Who I am in how I teach is the message: Self-understanding, vulnerability and reflection. *Teachers and Teaching: Theory and Practice, 15*(2), 257–272.

Kelchtermans, G. (2018). Zipping as professional learning [Blog post]. InFoTED: International Forum for Teacher Educator Development.

Kelchtermans, G., Smith, K., & Vanderlinde, R. (2017): Towards an 'international forum for teacher educator development': An agenda for research and action. *European Journal of Teacher Education, 41*, 120–134.

Leeferink, H., Koopman, M., Beijaard, D., & Ketelaar, E. (2015). Unraveling the complexity of student teachers' learning in and from the workplace. *Journal of Teacher Education, 66*(4), 334–348.

Lunenberg, M., Korthagen, F., & Swennen, A. (2007). The teacher educator as a role model. *Teaching and Teacher Education, 23*(5), 586–601.

Meijer, P. C., Oolbekkink, H. W., Pillen, M., & Aardema, A. (2014). Pedagogies of developing teacher identity. In L. Orland-Barak & C. Craig (Eds.), *International teacher education: Promising pedagogies*. Bingley: Emerald.

Meijer, P. C., & Oosterheert, I. E. (2018). Student teachers' identity development in relation to "teaching for creativity". In P. Schutz, J. Y. Hong, & D. Cross Francis (Eds.), *Research on teacher identity: Mapping challenges and innovations* (pp. 121–130). Springer.

Mezirow, J. (2006). An overview of transformative learning. In P. Sutherland & J. Crowther (Eds.), *Lifelong learning: Concepts and contexts* (pp. 24–38). New York, NY: Routledge.

Oldeboom, B. (2018). *'Voice over teaching' for teacher educators*. Blogpost at InFoTED: International Forum for Teacher Educator Development.

Oosterheert, I. E., & Meijer, P. C. (2017). What it takes to cultivate creativity in education. *Pedagogische Studiën, 94*(3), 196–210.

Orland-Barak, L., & Craig, C. (2014). *International teacher education: Promising pedagogies*. Emerald.

Overman, M., Vermunt, J. D., Meijer, P. C., & Brekelmans, M. (2019). Teacher–student negotiations during context-based chemistry reform: A case study. *Journal of Research in Science Teaching, 56*(6), 797–820.

Robinson, K. (2017). *Out of our minds: The power of being creative*. North Mankato, MN: Capstone.

Schwartz, D. L., Bransford, J. D., & Sears, D. (2005). *Efficiency and innovation in transfer. Transfer of learning from a modern multidisciplinary perspective*. Greenwich: Information Age Publishing.

Sternberg, R. J. (2006). The nature of creativity. *Creativity Research Journal, 18*(1), 87–98.

Sternberg, R. J., Jarvin, L., & Grigorenko, E. L. (2015). *Teaching for wisdom, intelligence, creativity, and success.* New York, NY: Skyhorse.

United Nations. (2015). *Transforming our world: The 2030 agenda for sustainable development.*

Vincent-Lancrin, S. (2019). Fostering students' creativity and critical thinking: What it means in schools. In *Educational research and innovation.* Paris: OECD Publishing. http://doi.org/10.1787/62212c37-en

Wells, D. (2017). 21st century creative pedagogy: Its importance in teacher education [Blog post]. Retrieved from https://info-ted.eu/21st-century-creative-pedagogy-its-importance-in-teacher-education/

PART 3

Teaching in a Multicultural World

∵

CHAPTER 11

Educating Refugee Students: Global Perspectives and Priorities

Snežana Obradović-Ratković, Vera Woloshyn, Kari-Lynn Winters,
Neelofar Ahmed, Christos Govaris, Stavroula Kaldi,
Christiana Deliewen Afrikaner and Feyza Doyran

Abstract

The number of refugees and asylum seekers are expected to rise over the next few decades, leading to increased concerns about their education, resettlement, and wellbeing. However, there are limited studies that systematically explore the unique needs and schooling experiences of refugee students from a global, evidence-based perspective. In this chapter, we discuss the potential impacts of trauma on refugee students' well-being, describe the nature of student-responsive educational programming across a series of host countries, and provide recommendations for administrators, policy developers, and educators. We encourage all the stakeholders in education to develop critical reflexivity and cultural competencies as well as local and global policies, programs, and partnerships.

Keywords

refugee students – trauma-informed education – arts-based education – student-responsive education – cultural competencies – global perspectives

1 Introduction

In 2018, the number of refugees, asylum-seekers, and internally displaced people around the world reached a staggering 70.8 million, resulting in unprecedented migration and resettlement patterns across the globe (UNHCR, 2019). Among these displaced people, nearly 25.9 million are refugees, with many of these persons coming from Syria, Afghanistan, and South Sudan. The majority of these refugees are under 18 years of age, with many journeying as unaccompanied minors.

The primary definition of a refugee that applies to different countries and is contained in Article 1(A)(2) of the 1951 Convention, as amended by its 1967 Protocol (UNHCR, 2011), defines a refugee as someone who:

> Owing to well-founded fear of being persecuted for reasons of race, religion, nationality, membership of a particular social group or political opinion, is outside the country of his nationality and is unable or, owing to such fear, is unwilling to avail himself of the protection of that country; or who, not having a nationality and being outside the country of his former habitual residence, is unable or, owing to such fear, is unwilling to return to it. In the case of a person who has more than one nationality, the term 'the country of his nationality' shall mean each of the countries of which he is a national, and a person shall not be deemed to be lacking the protection of the country of his nationality if, without any valid reason based on well-founded fear, he has not availed himself of the protection of one of the countries of which he is a national. (p. 14)

While most refugees hope to return to their home countries, repatriation is an unrealistic possibility for many due to ongoing persecution, violence, and other acute threats. As a result, the number of international refugees has increased steadily, with countries like Canada, Turkey, Pakistan, Uganda, Lebanon, Islamic Republic of Iran, Germany, Bangladesh, and Sudan hosting large numbers of displaced persons (Rasmi, 2019; Yousif, 2019). The United Nations High Commissioner for Refugees (UNHCR, 2019) reported that Canada resettled nearly 30,000 refugees in 2018, exceeding the number of refugees resettled in any other country (Falconer, 2019; Yousif, 2019). Germany continues to receive the highest number of asylum applications in the European Union (Trines, 2019). One-third of the asylum seekers that arrived in 2015 and 2016 were under the age of 18. Although the number of asylum applications in Germany has dropped in 2018, the total number of people seeking asylum or other forms of protected status has reached 1.7 million. Pakistan is one of the top leading refugee-hosting countries in the world welcoming refugees from countries such as Bangladesh, India, Bosnia and Herzegovina, Burma, Somalia, and Afghanistan. Pakistan currently hosts more than 1.4 million registered Afghan refugees (UNHCR, 2018). Turkey has hosted a staggering 3,079 914 Syrian citizens since 2011 (UNHCR, 2017). Greece has officially welcomed approximately 62,000 refugees including 20,000 children (0–18 years old), of which 3,150 were unaccompanied minors (Euronews, 2017), while the number of refugees and migrants in Serbia has oscillated between 4,800 and 8,000 since 2017 (Government of Serbia, 2019).

Of great concern, the number of refugees and asylum seekers are expected to rise over the next few decades (UNHCR, 2017, 2019), leading to increased concerns about how to effectively and systematically respond to the needs of these vulnerable individuals:

> The lack of effective information-sharing systems for refugees and migrants, as well as physical barriers between countries, have left refugee and migrant children and their families facing great uncertainty. The steady increase in the numbers of refugees and migrants and the longer periods of stay created additional needs for services for children. (UNICEF, 2017, p. 2)

Many refugees experience protracted intervals of displacement, ongoing resettlement, insecurity, and uncertainty. Ultimately, many refugees seek integration in their host countries through permanent residency or naturalizing processes. Increased migration and resettlement patterns have resulted in immediate economic strain, heightened national security and identity concerns, and humanitarian fatigue within some host countries, including those that neighbor conflict zones. These concerns, in part, have prompted some countries and regions to implement border restrictions, barriers, and closures, and have given rise to anti-refugee and anti-immigration sentiments. Such restrictions and negative attitudes work to intensify the distress and suffering of those who are forced to flee their homes (Kakissis, 2018; Matlin, Depoux, Schütte, Flahault, & Saso, 2018; Yitmen & Verkuyten, 2018).

Although there is substantial literature documenting the experiences of newcomers, immigrants, and subsequent language learners, there are relatively few studies that systematically explore the unique needs and schooling experiences of refugee students from a global, evidence-based perspective while acknowledging the limitations and challenges associated with such educational programming. To contextualize and understand the psycho-social needs of refugee students, we conducted a systematic literature review on the topic. We begin the chapter with an overview of the potential impacts of trauma on students' well-being. We then describe the nature of student-responsive educational programming across a series of host countries, emphasizing the situational and contextual realities of students who attend these programs. We close the chapter by providing recommendations for administrators, policy developers, and educators.

2   Trauma

Many refugee children and adolescents have directly or indirectly experienced trauma, either before their arrival to their host country and/or following it. The American Psychological Association (2013) defines trauma as "exposure to actual or threatened death, serious injury, or sexual violence" (p. 271) where individuals either directly experience events; witness them as they occur to others; learn that such events have occurred to a close family member, care provider, or friend; or experience "repeated exposure to adverse details of such events through lived experiences" (p. 271). This understanding of trauma has been critiqued as limited for not including references to highly upsetting events that are not life-threatening or injurious, such as psychological abuse (e.g., degradation, humiliation, and coercive non-violent sexual experiences), emotional abuse, and/or major losses or separations (Briere & Scott, 2015). For these reasons, many educators and health-care professionals have adopted a broader working definition of trauma to include those events that extremely upset individuals; work to overwhelm individuals' internal resources, sense of control, connectedness and overall ability to cope (short and/or long term); and result in lasting psychological impacts (Briere & Scott, 2015; Horsman, 1999).

Common pre-migration and resettlement traumatic experiences include maltreatment, violence, disaster, war, illness, accidents/injuries, displacement, loss and separation, and relational aggression (Esses, 2017; Stewart, 2012). In some instances, these experiences are acute and short-lived. In other instances, especially those involving interpersonal trauma, these experiences are repetitive and cumulative (Esses, 2017; Record-Lemon & Buchanan, 2017; Tavares, 2012). Many children and youth, especially unaccompanied and/or orphaned minors, may continue to experience neglect, abuse, and acculturation distress and challenges post-migration.

Children and adolescents vary in their response to traumatic events, with some demonstrating resilience and growth in contexts of adverse experiences. In these instances, protective factors that promote resilience among refugee children – social support from friends and community, a sense of belonging, a positive attitude towards education, a positive attitude, family connectedness, and connections to home culture – tend to be strong, present, and abundant (Pieloch, Mccullough, & Marks, 2016). More often, however, children's resilience is compromised. In these instances, adversity tends to be high and protective factors are few, absent, or nonexistent. In such contexts, refugee children and youth who attend school present a vulnerable student population (MacNevin, 2012; Stewart, 2012).

3   Trauma and Education

Children and adolescents who experience trauma typically show acute and/ or chronic symptoms of psychological and social-emotional distress. Trauma has been associated with mental health concerns including anxiety disorders, depressive disorders, substance use disorders, posttraumatic stress disorder (PTSD), and other trauma-related disorders (Briere & Scott, 2015). These children may experience difficulties with emotional regulation, including intense feelings of anger, fear, sadness, anxiety, and stress. They may also experience profound uncertainty, social isolation, and loneliness. Many experience ongoing interpersonal challenges with peers and others, as well as lack of trust that often extends to adult authority figures including educators and community helpers (MacNevin, 2012; Record-Lemon & Buchanan, 2017; Stewart, 2012, 2017).

Refugee children and adolescents often experience multiple and layered learning challenges. Cognitive difficulties related to focus, memory, and concentration may be present (MacNevin, 212; Orsam, 2015; Stewart, 2012, 2017). Many refugee students (and their families) also face linguistic challenges associated with subsequent language learning. These challenges are often exacerbated by disrupted or non-existent schooling experiences. For instance, the majority of Syrian refugee students resettling in Turkey have not attended school over the last two to four years (Dorman, 2014). According to the 2016 European Civil Protection and Humanitarian Aid Operations (ECHO), such children "remain at risk of becoming a lost generation" (ECHO; cited in Aydin & Kaya, 2019, p. 47). Moreover, refugee children and their families may be unfamiliar with school norms and behavioral expectations, leading to additional stress.

Many children and adolescents report experiences of marginalization, racism, and/or discrimination from peers, educators, and/or community members (Noh, Beiser, Kaspar, Hou, & Rummens, 1999; Carranza, 2009; Guo, Maitra, & Guo, 2017). Guo, Maitra, and Guo (2017) argued that educational institutions often replicate "minority – majority tensions and become places where exclusion and discrimination are experienced at different levels by refugee children" (p. 6), leading to "higher degrees of isolation, alienation, segregation, depression, and concomitant stress among minority youth" (Baker, 2017, p. 9). Processing their own traumatic experiences, parents and caregivers may be limited in their ability to support their children's school-related activities due to language, acculturation, and financial challenges and concerns. For instance, many adult refugees experience unemployment or underemployment, which precipitate financial uncertainty and hardships including food and housing insecurity. Children and adolescents in these contexts may seek out employment and/or assume additional household and childcare responsibilities to assist their families. Collectively these factors may limit refugee students' focus on academic pursuits and lead these students and their families to perceive the school environment as hostile and unwelcoming (Kovacevic, 2016; Oxman-Martinez & Choi, 2014; Saklan & Erginer, 2017). Despite the concerns and challenges encountered by refugee students in the resettlement process, the majority of refugee students and their families perceive education as hope for new beginnings and future possibilities (Kovačević, 2016; Stewart, 2017).

4   The Critical Role of School

Schools have the potential to play a significant role in the emotional healing of children and youth newcomers who have experienced trauma (Gladwell, 2019). Not only are educators some of the first professionals whom refugee families will meet, but also school policies and programs of care are vehicles of inclusion, connecting people who are available and ready to offer support in times of crisis and post-crisis. For example, schools in Greece familiarize students with formal school environments as well as support efficiencies in everyday communications and tasks of daily living as experienced within Hellenic and European cultures (Ministry of Education, Research and Religious Affairs, 2019). Greek educational policies and programs (from kindergarten up through high school) aim to address all refugee children without discrimination (Fouskas, 2019). Research demonstrates that school-wide strategies such as these, including the presence of a caring adult over time (a teacher) and sustained programming that meets their needs, allow asylum-seeking children opportunities to thrive (Gladwell, 2019).

North American school districts have developed welcoming initiatives and policies to support refugee students and families, mandating interactive sessions for staff and community members serving newcomers. Here, school staff learn about migrant students' resettlement processes and hear first-hand stories from refugee families (Rozier, 2017). Teachers and staff are then encouraged to use the acquired information in order to reevaluate and transform curricula and pedagogical practices for their district.

Like in other Canadian provinces, establishing a welcoming environment has become a priority in Labrador and Newfoundland in order to help newcomers adjust to local culture and end discrimination towards migrants (Li, Que, & Power, 2017). In addition to federal and provincial government policies being established, community readiness services and academic programs were implemented for students to promote cross-cultural awareness in the communities and to bridge refugees' education gaps, preparing them to join mainstream classes (Li et al., 2017). Schools, identified as having insufficient numbers of teachers from culturally and linguistically diverse backgrounds, developed inter-cultural programs and more robust ESL programs (Sarma-Debnath & Castano, 2008). Recreational/leisure and homework support groups were also established in Newfoundland's capital city.

In Ontario Canada, the Thames Valley School District has been thoughtful and proactive about helping families that settle into their area. In order to assist with the students' transition, the schools have implemented welcoming programs where teams of people network with community members, parents, and incoming students, ensuring full transparency and creating a sense of safety and community for those in need. Their aim to create discrimination-free environments of openness and equity that encourage a climate of respect for all students.

In Canada, Newfoundland and Ontario have developed the most policies and resources related to addressing refugee student needs. Resources included guides for classroom teachers, language teachers, and administrators (Ratković et al., 2017). For example, the Ontario Ministry of Education has developed an eight-page monograph for teachers entitled "Capacity Building K-12: Supporting Students with Refugee Backgrounds, Special Edition #45", which was released in July 2016, after the Syrian refugee resettlement had taken place. The monograph introduces a framework for responsive practices based on six main goals: refugee students are simultaneously developing academic English and learning the curriculum, students see themselves in the learning environment, teachers encourage refugee students to invest their identities in learning, students are supported in acquiring the confidence they need to express their opinions, teachers have high expectations for refugee students, and teachers help refugee students achieve their hopes and aspirations. This monograph outlines the first steps in developing asset-based programming for refugee students in Ontario and beyond.

Internationally, policymakers and educators are implementing interventions in support of asylum-seeking youth. School districts in the US, for example, are manifesting changes in curricula, offering family involvement opportunities, exploring community partnerships, and developing manuals for working with refugee students (Edwards, 2017). Alternatively, the Greek government is working in collaboration with UNHCR and several NGOs to create Reception Facilities for Refugee Education and Reception Classes in major cities and islands throughout the country (Iefimerida, 2017; UNHCR,

2018). Similarly, UNHCR collaborates with the Pakistani government to facilitate Afghan refugees' access to health and education through local service providers. These refugees are settled in 54 villages across Pakistan and children are provided free education in 153 Pakistani public schools (UNHCR, 2019). Government policymakers in England, Scotland, and Wales are also seeking to build diversity awareness and improve networking for professionals working in educational systems with asylum-seeking youth (Gladwell, 2019). Educators and related professionals (e.g., counselors and psychologists) across the world work to provide programming in local schools and/or refugee accommodation structures.

5   Educational Programming

There is no universal approach to educating refugee students. The need for varied and flexible programming is reflective, in part, of the dynamic and often uncertain nature of refugee migration and resettlement processes. For instance, many refugee students and their families live in temporary accommodations. In these instances, educational programming may need to begin before the acquisition of permanent residency or landed immigrant status, or as refugee students and their families continue to journey to their final destinations (i.e., during an ongoing migration and resettlement process).

Refugee students in Namibian refugee camps, for example, have access to pre-primary, primary, and secondary schools. The Namibian government utilizes the expertise of refugees to render essential services in the schools, camps, and surrounding areas. Qualified refugees receive training in a variety of disciplines including the arts, sciences, and technical subjects, and are then employed as educators.

According to Trines (2019), refugee children resettling in Germany, are required to complete nine or 10 years of school until they reach the age of 18. Most refugee children first attend German language integration classes before they join regular classes. In 2016, the refugee student integration into the school system was successful with 95% of refugee students attending school.

More than 57,000 Afghan refugee children are attending primary and (in some regions) secondary schools in Pakistan. In this way, the state provides the opportunity for Afghan refugee children to develop solidarity with local children and, at the same time, eliminates the risks inherited in a dual educational system. Tertiary-level scholarships are also offered to Afghan refugee students to continue their higher education in Pakistan (UNHCR, 2019).

The Greek government has taken important actions and measures concerning migration, protection, and support of asylum-seekers. Programs have been developed to improve the conditions of reception centers, avoid conflicts, simplify complicated processes of relocation and resettlement, protect unaccompanied minors, safeguard local communities, and develop integration policies to overcome social disadvantages that migrants face (Fouskas, 2019). Providing access to early education for immigrant and refugees' young children is one of the strategies Greece is using to enable smoother transitions into the Greek educational systems while combating discrimination.

Host countries like Canada and Serbia have adopted ongoing, long-term multifaceted programming approaches to refugee education. For instance, refugee students in Serbia are enrolled most of the day in regular classes while spending part of their school time in supplemental language classes. Students also engage in extra-curricular programming intended to support acculturation experiences, promote positive peer relationships, and overcome trauma-related challenges (Government of Serbia, 2019). In Canada, educational programming may vary from the delivery of manualized, evidence-based psychotherapies (Record-Lemon & Buchanan, 2017) to the implementation of collaborative and restorative linguistic and pedagogical programming (Lee, 2017).

Creative, musical, dramatic, embodied, and art-based programming is also being increasingly used to support refugee students' learning and acculturation experiences. Research from Denmark and Canada demonstrates that creative approaches to educational programming, such as those that use the arts, help refugee children build bridges with local children by giving them opportunities to express themselves within safe spaces and in less traumatic ways (Chayder, 2019). According to Canadian music educator Jenny Skidmore (2016), music is a class where refugee children can succeed despite language barriers because of the focus on physical performance rather than language skills. She suggests that well-structured music programs "can offer so much more than a break from the classroom routine" (p. 10) and help refugee students emotionally and cognitively by building their cultural awareness while contributing to the vitality of the community as a whole: "Students can use instruments to 'orchestrate' a variety of emotions present either in pictures, words, poetry, or stories, and can participate in the activity in small groups or as one large ensemble" (Skidmore, 2016, p. 10).

Integration of non-verbal forms of communication, as seen in music, dance, drama, and the visual arts, may also provide refugee students with multiple opportunities for expression and connection, and more readily relate to birth-country learning and pedagogical styles and preferences, such as oral history traditions. Research demonstrates the arts can be a healing and empowering process for refugee children and adolescents, working to promote students' sense of solidarity, tolerance, and resilience while compensating for the loss of familiar supports and communities (Obradović-Ratković, Kovačević, Ahmed, & Ellis, in press; Ratković et al., 2017; Stewart, 2012; Tavares, 2012). Through collaborative practices, mentorship, and ongoing professional development across the arts, educators can become more adept at developing inclusive and culturally-responsive educational practices that may support refugee youth and their local peers (Skidmore, 2016).

In these ways, host countries and educators utilize multidisciplinary approaches that work to address the immediate and/or long-term needs of refugee students in the context of their lived experiences and situational circumstances (Farmakopoulou, Triantafyllou, & Kolaitis, 2017).

Ideally, these educational programs and curricula are delivered by educators who are well versed in trauma-informed practices and who demonstrate cultural competencies and sensitivities.

6   Situational and Contextual Realities

Beyond simply implementing inclusive policies and curricula, school boards and schools are also charged to think about language and communication programs, transportation, health and mental wellness supports, social and informational sessions, after-school programs, welcoming behaviors from the whole community, as well as provide informational sessions for host communities. Despite best efforts and good intentions, host schools and communities continue to experience tensions and challenges. For example, Labrador and Newfoundland's immigration rates are relatively low (only 0.34% of Canada's total entry of immigrants); however, the growing population of refugees in these regions still causes gaps in services such as education, mental health care, language translation, and community awareness programs (Li, Que, & Power, 2017).

Another example of situational tensions is present in Namibia. In 2015, Namibian school enrolment for Osire Primary School stood at 750 learners with 26 teachers of whom the majority were refugees from Burundi, Democratic Republic of Congo, Rwanda, Angola, and Zimbabwe (New Era, 2015). Yet many of these teachers left for resettlement countries, such as the United States and Canada, decreasing the number of qualified teachers in the school and hindering refugee students' learning and resettlement experiences. School districts also lack adequate teaching and study materials, such as books. The exam results of the high school are amongst the best in the country; however, relatively few refugees complete their professional degrees due to limited aid from the state and financial strains associated with tertiary education.

In Germany, refugee children's education is complicated by teacher shortages and refugee students' diverse backgrounds, including student age and academic experiences (Trines, 2019). Some children are too old for their respective grades, and most are enrolled in lower-level schools. In such a context, there is the danger of promoting a segregated and inferior school education for the refugees.

In developing countries like Pakistan, one of the major challenges in education is the increasing ratio of out of school students with gender disparity of more girls out of schools than boys (National Educational Policy Framework, 2018). UNHCR (2015) estimates that more than 80% of Afghan refugee children are out of school. Most of these children are girls. This low percentage of girls attending school is due to Afghan's socio-cultural traditions of not sending girls to school or sending them only to classrooms administered by female teachers. Literacy among Afghan women refugees is about 7.6%, which leads to a shortage of Afghan female teachers teaching in public schools and furthers the challenge of Afghan girls' access to education.

In Greece, a part of the educational community supported the full integration of refugee students into formal public schools; however, some parents expressed xenophobic attitudes and threatened to occupy schools. Reception Facilities for Refugee Education (RFREs) were established in schools based on a system of informal request and consent, which portrayed some schools as "refugee-friendly" and others as "refugee-hostile" (Simopoulos & Alexandridis, 2019). Refugee education in Greece also faces challenges due to the lack of systematic social policies and consequently educational policies concerning refugees both in the country and in the European Union. Some of these challenges include the status of the teaching staff, many of whom are not permanent class teachers or fully equipped to address refugee children's educational needs, irregular school attendance, or dropouts, as well as low public awareness of refugee needs. The evidence of the contribution refugees can make to their host communities is not widely understood or accepted (Ager & Strang, 2008). Often, time pressure and the difficulty of the tasks to be accomplished limit the objectives of refugee education and the design of appropriate curricula. Refugees are hosted in camps outside towns and cities and they often feel isolated or trapped as their destination countries are in central Europe. Within this framework, educational initiatives remain fragmented and ineffective in terms of social inclusion. In addition to schooling challenges, refugee children, who have been admitted at the "Aghia Sophia" Children's Hospital in Athens since 2010, have demonstrated traumatic new-onset symptoms, such as PTSD symptoms and sleeping disorders as well as pre-existing problems, including autism spectrum disorders and psychosis (Farmakopoulou, Triantafyllou, & Kolaitis, 2017). Farmakopoulou et al. (2017) recognized that "the management of such cases becomes even more difficult because of communication difficulties due to language barriers" (p. 1).

In Turkey, the Ministry of National Education (MoNE) is responsible for ensuring that all refugee children have access to education. In 2016, the number of Syrian children enrolled in temporary education centers (TECs) increased to almost 500,000 (UNHCR, 2017). Refugee children registered with the Turkish government authorities can register in schools free of charge (UNHCR, 2017). MoNE approved the establishment of temporary education centers (TECs) for Syrian refugee children. TECs offer instruction in Arabic, implement a modified form of the Syrian curriculum, and employ Syrian volunteer teachers. In 2016, MoNE has approved over 350 TECs to operate in urban areas hosting large numbers of Syrian refugees. Since then, MoNE has increased the number of hours of Turkish language teaching in TECs and placed greater emphasis on the inclusion of Syrian children in Turkish schools. However, challenges continue to arise. For example, the Turkish government has not accredited the schools due to the low quality of teaching. According to Doyran (2019), this low quality of teaching is attributed to the instruction in the Arabic language and lack of teachers' professional training. The author analyzed the needs of refugee students attending schools in Istanbul from the perspectives of teachers and school administrators. The initial findings revealed that the major challenges the refugee students face are language barriers and psychological struggles, in part, due to the trauma of being forced to leave Syria and live in Turkey. Despite the challenges, the educators participating in Doyran's (2019) study expressed their commitment to helping Syrian refugee students overcome their psychological problems and integrate with the society.

School systems across the globe have been challenged with addressing the educational needs of refugee children and youth. Financially, school districts struggle to keep up with the ongoing support that is needed. Insufficient educator training and lack of educational pedagogies and resources are also particularly challenging (İçduygu, 2015; Pigozzi, 2018; Ratković, et al., 2017). Some administrators worry about added expenses to school systems and burdens on local host communities. Moreover, politically, anti-immigrant movements stir up narratives of fear and terrorism. UNHCR is working with refugee-receiving countries to develop educational programming and to support newcomers' integration into societies internationally but faces challenges in terms of human and financial resources. Dryden-Peterson (2011) outlines some of the challenges associated with the education of refugee children and youth:

Education is one of the highest priorities of refugee communities. Yet there is insufficient support to UNHCR to guarantee the right to education for refugee children and young people. The lack of high quality and protective education for refugees stands in the way of meeting Education for All goals, of achieving durable solutions, and of sustainable development and reconstruction of home and host countries. (p. 6)

Dropout rates for refugee children pose another challenge across the globe. Although education is a basic human right, half of primary school children who are refugees and 75% of adolescent refugees are out of school (Moskal & North, 2017; UNICEF, 2017). Thus, there is a critical need for educators to understand factors that work to support refugee students' schooling experiences, as well as those that may impede their engagement in educational studies. Such negative factors may include economic or social disadvantages associated with students' refugee backgrounds and/or belief systems as well as in-school factors, such as lack of safety, insufficient school infrastructure, and inadequate instruction (Pigozzi, 2018). Especially concerning, some local country residents, potential host families, and educators hold inaccurate, negative, and/or discriminatory beliefs and attitudes against refugee students and their families, which can undermine these students' self-esteem, social competence, and academic achievement, ultimately compromising their social, economic, and political integration in the host society (Oxman-Martinez & Choi, 2014; Saklan & Erginer, 2017). Thus, it is vital for school boards, administrators, and educators to recognize and overcome these challenges to promote effective teaching, learning, and resettlement processes.

7   Recommendations

Increased forced migration challenges national education systems across the globe. Some of the challenges include educating and resettling unaccompanied minors; engaging students who are on the move (e.g., students who are heading from Greece and Serbia to Western Europe); teaching students with traumatic disorders; assessing refugee students' learning; and educating teachers for strength-based, trauma-informed, art-based, and culturally-responsive pedagogies.

To support unaccompanied minors, a person who knows each refugee's language and culture should supervise the students. Additionally, giving permanent residency and access to education would enhance the unaccompanied minors' learning, wellbeing, and social integration. Quality of placements (e.g., safe houses, foster care, and adoption) provided to these young people is critical. In their UK-based study, Brownlees and Finch (2010) found that unaccompanied children in foster care receive more support and are more likely to access and succeed in education than those in other placements. However, foster care is not appropriate for all children; some children might prefer living independently, rather than living with strangers. Article 20 of the United Nations Convention on the Rights of the Child (1990) states that, when considering children's placements, "due regard shall be paid to the desirability of continuity in a child's upbringing and to the child's ethnic, religious, cultural and linguistic background" (para. 52).

Instead of supporting a dual system of education, we recommend immediate enrollment of refugee students in regular schools and classes (when possible) because students' long-term enrollment in RFREs and reception classes may limit students' academic achievements and social integration. For example, without interaction with the host community, refugee students' language skills can be hindered, decreasing students' motivation to learn and reinforcing the public's perception of refugee students as people in transit. As suggested by Simopoulos and Alexandridis (2019), greater numbers of morning reception classes within public school hours should be scheduled and supported by teachers and social workers. Institutional support for schools and teachers through training and access to language interpreters is a priority.

It is increasingly recognized that education delivered in a safe environment can provide recovery, healing, and empowerment for the vulnerable, forcefully displaced people. In this area, much of the international focus has been on the practical difficulties of delivering education, such as providing access to schooling, building temporary classrooms, and recruiting and training teachers (Bubbers, 2015). More attention should be paid to the educational experiences and outcomes of migrants and refugees, and the issues of discrimination and social injustice (Moskal & North, 2017). A matter of refugee education is a matter of inclusion, social justice, and equity.

Teacher pre-service education and in-service professional development must be proactive, ongoing, and rooted in strength-based, trauma-informed, and arts-based pedagogies as well as cultural competencies. Teachers and teacher candidates should implement and advocate for refugee education and integration in order to facilitate public awareness of and sensitivities towards diversity and coexistence.

It is well recognized that teachers' intra- and inter-cultural competencies, attitudes and beliefs are powerful influencers of refugee student success (Hanover Research, 2014; Nordgren, 2017). Given that as many as 85% of the world's refugees remain in their host nation (Nordgren, 2017), these nations must facilitate refugee integration in the educational system, economy, and society. To integrate refugee students in the school and society, schools must have culturally competent teachers and administrators (Banks, 2002; Diller & Moule, 2004). Key elements of cultural competence are relationship building and communication (Lindsey et al., 2009). Close and trusting relationships between teachers and students not only enhance learning but also empower students to become life-long learners as well as responsible and contributing citizens (Darling-Hammond, 2010). In response, many countries have initiated professional development programming to support the development of educators' cultural competencies, sensitivities, compassion, and active listening skills (Stewart, 2017). Cultural competency is defined as:

> a set of behaviours, attitudes, and policies that enable a system, agency, or individual to function effectively with culturally diverse consumers and communities; it requires recognition and an understanding of how economic conditions, race, culture, ethnicity, social context, and the environment define health and disability, and in turn, their influence on the provision of services. (Jezewski & Sotnik, as cited in Kanagaratnam, Pain, McKenzie, Ratnalingam, & Toner, 2017, p. 108)

Building on this definition, teachers' cultural competence is defined as teachers' abilities to recognize their own world views, understand and embrace the cultural diversity of their students, and challenge their own biases and assumptions when engaging with culturally diverse students and their families (Banks 1994; Bennett; Gillette & Boyle-Baise, 1995; Nieto & Rolon 1995). More specifically, culturally competent teachers practice self-assessment, learn about and consider students' cultures in their teaching practice, employ a culturally responsive pedagogy, foster respect and cultural sensitivity in the classroom, and involve families and communities in their children's education.

The development of proactive educational programming by culturally competent teachers is vital for supporting refugee children and youth. These approaches and programs shape teachers' sense of self, their social locations, and their pedagogies, providing safe and inclusive spaces for students. To value diversity and adopt culturally-responsive teaching practices in their classroom, teachers must value their students' cultural backgrounds, customs, traditions, histories, and ways of communication.

To understand cultural competence at a global, transnational level, Koehn and Rosenau (2013) provide a helpful four-dimensional multicultural competence framework. This structure could be considered to develop educators' and community members' analytic, emotional, creative, and behavioral competencies. The authors (2013) summarize the framework as follows:

Analytic competence refers to the ability to transform cognitive resources (i.e. culture-general and culture-specific knowledge) into comprehension and to learn effective cross-cultural interaction strategies through reflection upon experiences. Emotional competence focuses on the affective aspect that requires one to have an open mind for diversity and multiple identities and be self-confident in cross-cultural interactions. Creative competence refers to "the ability to synthesize diverse cultural perspectives in problem solving, to envision mutually acceptable alternatives, and to tap into diverse cultural sources for inspiration" (110). Behavioral competence entails skills that promote "communicative facility" and "functional adroitness" (113). (Koehn & Rosenau, as cited in He, 2013, p. 57)

Building teachers' cultural competence in increasingly diverse classrooms is critical to challenge the cultural-deficit mindset in teacher education (Banks 1994; Villegas & Lucas, 2002).

In the context of forced migration, cultural/intercultural competencies are needed as core qualifications and professional competences within educational institutions (both in schools and universities as well as in extracurricular pedagogical spheres). Based on the current scientific discourse and her personal experience, Esser (2019) suggests the concept of intercultural competence and intercultural pedagogy-founded on stereotypes, culturalizations, and artificial homogenizations. Mecheril (2013) clearly demonstrates that concepts must be fundamentally rethought and reformulated. The core question is: How should a concept for further development of intercultural competence be formulated such that inclusion is promoted in social settings and educational institutions? The guiding interest is thus to reformulate the concept of intercultural competence that targets the further development of individual competence profiles and the professionalization of educators.

The key skill reflective competence, concerning personal interpretative behavior, will become a relevant key area in the reformulation of the concept of intercultural competence, which can be described as reflexive, diversity-conscious intercultural competence. The relevant key skill area of reflective ability, which is being developed here, relates to the ability to critically self-reflect, understand structure and society in the context of forced migration, and contextualize education in flux or hybrid situations and contexts.

Equity in education enhances social cohesion and trust (OECD, 2008). Currently, policymakers are engaging with the issues of refugee integration into society, education, and job markets (Crul, Keskiner, Schneider, Lelie, & Ghaeminia, 2017; Ratković et al., 2017). Systematic, inter-sector approaches, rather than "bandage" approaches, to refugee education have emerged as effective approaches to forced migration, resettlement, and responsible national and global citizenship. Without sufficient resources, cultural competencies, and transnational collaboration, however, the responsibility for large-scale refugee movements and resettlement will not be properly planned or shared, which will hinder children's access to quality education.

8   Conclusion

Refugee children and adolescents often experience multiple challenges that may be exacerbated due to disrupted or non-existent prior schooling experiences as well as ongoing marginalization, racism and/or abuse from peers, educators, and community members, (Kovačević, 2016; Oxman-Martinez, & Choi, 2014; Saklan & Erginer, 2017). Many refugee children and youth continue to encounter psychological, social, emotional, learning, and resettlement struggles due to their background experiences or belief systems, and in-school factors including lack of safety, school infrastructure and resources, and culturally-responsive instruction. We argue that it is critical for educators and refugee communities to recognize and overcome these challenges through the implementation of creative, strength-based, asset-based, inclusive, and holistic approaches to education. To this end, educators should be encouraged and supported in developing critical reflexivity, cultural competencies, and an understanding of education in the context of forced migration. Moreover, educational researchers, administrators, policymakers as well as host and refugee communities across the world must work together to develop systematic local and global education policies and programs concerning refugee students' and their families' resettlement and wellbeing.

Further research is required to contextualize and understand refugee student education and wellbeing locally and internationally. Providing teachers, policy makers, refugee families, researchers, and communities with the culturally-responsive practices and resources as well as ongoing professional development opportunities will enhance student transition, empower refugee students, and inform policy (Ratković et al., 2017). Additionally, researchers are encouraged to explore holistic and creative approaches to education and resettlement from the perspective of the refugee students (Bešić, Paleczek, & Gasteiger-Klicpera, 2018). Educating refugee children and youth across the globe is critical and possible when communities prioritize students' feelings and experiences, and then work together for future and positive solutions. Proactive, ongoing, and culturally-responsive programming will generate timely knowledge and sustainable practices, enhancing teaching and learning in a global classroom.

References

Ager, A., & Strang, A. (2008). Understanding integration: A conceptual framework, *Journal of Refugee Studies, 21*(2), 166–191. https://doi.org/10.1093/jrs/fen016

American Psychiatric Association. (2013). *Diagnostic and statistical manual of mental disorders* (5th ed.). Washington, DC: Author.

Aydin, H., & Kaya, Y. (2017) Educational needs and barriers for Syrian refugee students in Turkey: A qualitative case study. *Intercultural Education, 28*(5), 456–473.

Aydin, H., & Kaya, Y. (2019) Education for Syrian refugees: The new global issue facing teachers and principals in Turkey. *Educational Studies, 55*, 46–71. doi: 10.1080/00131946.2018.1561454.

Baker, J. (2017). *The manifestations of prejudice in everyday life: An examination of racial microaggressions, ethnophaulisms, and integrated threats as observed by white post-secondary youth in St. John's, Newfoundland and Labrador.* St. John's, NL: The Harris Centre Memorial University. Retrieved from https://www.mun.ca/harriscentre/reports/BAKER-ARF-15-16.pdf

Balkan, B., & Tumen, S. (2016) Immigration and prices: Quasi-experimental evidence from Syrian refugees in Turkey. *Journal of Population Economics, 29*(3), 657–686.

Banks, J. (1996). The historical reconstruction of knowledge about race: Implications for transformative teaching. In J. A. Banks (Ed.), *Multicultural education, transformative knowledge, and action: Historical and contemporary perspectives* (pp. 64–87). New York, NY: Teachers College Press.

Bešić, E., Paleczek, L., & Gasteiger-Klicpera, B. (2018). Don't forget about us: Attitudes towards the inclusion of refugee children with(out) disabilities. *International Journal of Inclusive Education.* https://doi.org/10.1080/13603116.2018.1455113

Briere, J. M., & Scott, C. (2015). *Principles of trauma therapy: A guide to symptoms, evaluation, and treatment* (2nd ed.). Thousand Oaks, CA: Sage.

Carranza, M. E. (2009). What is keeping Latino/a students out of school? Some possible explanations. In D. Schugurensky, D. Mantilla, & J. F. Serrano (Eds.), *Four in ten: Spanish-speaking youth and early school leaving in Toronto* (pp. 32–35). Latin American Research Education and Development Network (LARED) and the Transformative Learning Centre, Ontario Institute for Studies in Education of the University of Toronto.

Chayder, L. A. (2019). Art as a bridge-builder: A program for young refugees. *Journal of Museum Education, 44*(1), 69–80. https://doi.org/10.1080/10598650.2018.1550610

Darling-Hammond, L. (2010). Teacher education and the American future. *Journal of Teacher Education, 61*(1–2), 35–47. https://doi.org/10.1177/0022487109348024

De Jager, J. (2012). *Working paper on Namibia's refugee legislation.* Retrieved from http://www.refugeerights.uct.ac.za/usr/refugee/Working_papers/Working_Paper_1_of_2012.pdf

Dorman, S. (2014). *Educational needs assessment for urban Syrian refugees in Turkey.* Istanbul, Turkey: YUVA Association Press.

Doyran, F. (2019, July 1–5). *Empowering refugee students in Turkey.* Paper presented at the 19th ISATT Conference, Sibiu, Romania.

Diller, J., & Moule, J. (2004). *Cultural competence: A primer for educators.* Belmont, CA: Wadsworth Publishing.

Dryden-Peterson, S. (2011). *Refugee education: A global review.* Geneva, Switzerland: UNHCR. Retrieved from https://educateachild.org/explore/barriers-to-education/refugees

Edwards, T. K. (2017). Refugees and inclusive school practices in the face of tolerance. *The High School Journal, 100*(4), 223–225.

Esser, S. (2019, July 3). *Professionalization of teachers in the context of forced migration.* Paper presented at the Educating Refugee Children: Global Perspectives and Priorities Symposium, ISATT Conference, Sibiu, Romania.

Esses, V. M., Hamilton, L. K., & Gaucher, D. (2017). The global refugee crisis: Empirical evidence and policy implications for improving public attitudes and facilitating refugee resettlement. *Social Issues and Policy Review, 1*, 78.

Farmakopoulou, I., Triantafyllou, K., & Kolaitis, G. (2017) Refugee children and adolescents in Greece: Two case reports. *European Journal of Psychotraumatology, 8*(4), 1351179. https://doi.org/10.1080/20008198.2017. 1351757

Fouskas, T. (2019). Overcoming social disadvantage and inequality in social integration of migrants through education: Social policy and access to early childhood education for immigrant and refugee children in Greece in times of crisis. *Current Politics & Economics of Europe, 30*(1), 145–168. Retrieved from http://search.ebscohost.com/login.aspx?direct=true&db=buh&AN=1372589 97&site=ehost-live

Gillette, M., & Boyle-Baise, M. (1995). *Multicultural education at the graduate level: Assisting teachers in developing multicultural perspectives.* Paper presented at the annual meeting of the American Education Research Association, San Francisco, CA.

Gladwell, C. (2019). Accessing and thriving in education in the UK. *Forced Migration Review, 3*(60), 43–46.

Government of Pakistan. (2018). *National education policy framework 2018.* Retrieved from http://planipolis.iiep.unesco.org/en/2018/national-education-policy-framework-2018-6524

Government of Republic of Serbia. (2019). *Education of migrant students in Serbia 2018/2019*. Retrieved from http://www.mpn.gov.rs/wpcontent/up loads/2019/05/2019-Education-of-migrants-in-Serbia.pdf

Guo, S., & Maitra, S. (2017). Revisioning curriculum in the age of transnational mobility: Towards a transnational and transcultural framework. *Curriculum Inquiry, 47*(1), 80–91.

He, Y. (2013). Developing teachers' cultural competence: Application of appreciative inquiry in ESL teacher education. *Teacher Development, 17*(1), 55–71. https://doi.org/10.1080/13664530.2012.753944

Horsman, J. (1999). *Too scared to learn: Women, violence, and education*. Toronto: McGilligan.

İcduygu, A. (2015). *Syrian refugees in Turkey: The long road ahead*. Washington, DC: Migration Policy Institute Press.

Iefimerida. (2017, October 23). *Reception Classes (RC) in order to educate 7.000 refugee children aged 4–18 years old*. Retrieved from http://www.Iefimerida.gr/news/370142/7000-ta-prosfygopoyla-poy-tha-pane-fetos-sholeio-stin-ellada)

Kakissis, J. (2018, May 9). *"Europe does not see us as human": Stranded refugees struggle in Greece*. Parallels: npr. Retrieved from https://www.npr.org/sections/parallels/2018/03/09/589973165/europe-does-not-see-us-as-human-stranded-refugees-struggle-in-greece

Karakuş, M. (2018). The moderating effect of gender on the relationships between age, ethical leadership, and organizational commitment. *Journal of Ethnic and Cultural Studies, 5*(1), 74–84.

Koehn, P. H., & Rosenau, J. N. (2002). Transnational competence in an emergent epoch. *International Studies Perspectives, 3*(2), 105–127. https://doi.org/10.1111/1528-3577.00084

Kovačević, D. (2016). *Yugoslavian refugee children in Canadian schools: The role of transformative leadership in overcoming the social, psychological, and academic barriers to successful integration* (Major research paper). Retrieved from http://dr.library.brocku.ca/bitstream/handle/10464/10821/Brock_Drag ana_Kovačević_2016.pdf?sequence=1

Lee, K. (2017). Using collaborative strategic reading with refugee English language learners in an academic bridging program. *TESL Canada Journal, 34*, 97–108.

Li, X., Que, H., & Power, K. (2017). Welcome to "the rock": Service providers' views on newcomer youth integration in Newfoundland and Labrador. *Journal of International Migration and Integration, 18*(4), 1105–1122. https://doi.org/10.1007/s12134-017-0520-6d

MacNevin, J. (2012). Learning the way: Teaching and learning with and for youth from refugee backgrounds on Prince Edward Island. *Canadian Journal of Education/Revue Canadienne de l'éducation, 35*(3), 48–63.

Matlin, S. A., Depoux, A., Schütte, S., Flahault, A., & Saso, L. (2018). Migrants' and refugees' health: Towards an agenda of solutions. *Public Health Reviews, 39*, 27. doi:10.1186/s40985-018-0104-9

Mclellan, D. (2017, August 4). *10 facts about refugees in Namibia*. Retrieved from https://borgenproject.org/about-refugees-in-namibia/

Mecheril, P. (2013): Interkulturelle Pädagogik (Intercultural competence, professionalization). In G. Auernheimer (Ed.), *Interkulturelle Kompetenz und pädagogische Professionalität: Ausgabe 4*. Darmstadt, Germany: Wissenschaftliche Buchgesellschaft.

New Era. (2015, June 17). *Refugees need school feeding scheme*. Retrieved from https://reliefweb.int/report/namibia/refugees-need-school-feeding-scheme

Nieto, S., & Rolon, C. (1995, November). *The preparation and professional development of teachers: A perspective from two Latinas*. Paper presented at the invitational conference on Defining the Knowledge Base for Urban Teacher Education, Emory University, Atlanta, GA.

Noh, S., Beiser, M., Kaspar, V., Hou, F., & Rummens, J. (1999). Perceived racial discrimination, discrimination, and coping: A study of south east Asian refugees in Canada. *Journal of Health and Social Behaviour, 40*, 193–207.

Obradović-Ratković, S., Kovačević, D., Ahmed, N., & Ellis, C. (in press). Educating refugee students in Canada: Towards a pedagogy of healing. In B. Sethi, S. Guruge, & R. Csiernik (Eds.), *Understanding the refugee experience in the Canadian context*. Newcastle upon Tyne: Cambridge Scholars Publishing.

Orsam. (2015). *Ortadoğu Stratejik Araştirmalar Merkezi. Suriyeli Siğinmacilarin Türkiye'ye Etkileri*. Rapor No:195. Ocak.

Oxman-Martinez, J., & Choi, Y. R. (2014). Newcomer children: Experiences of inclusion and exclusion, and their outcomes. *Social Inclusion, 2*(4). http://dx.doi.org/10.17645/si.v2i4.133

Paperny, A. M. (2018, November 16). Refugee claims to Canada on track to hit highest levels in nearly 30 years. *Global News*. Retrieved from https://global news.ca/news/4671586/canada-refugee-claims-2018-highest-levels/

Parliament, Republic of Namibia. (1990). *Namibia refugees (recognition and control) Act 2 of 1990*. Retrieved from https://laws.parliament.na/annotated-laws-regulations/law-regulation.php?id=334

Pieloch, K. A., McCullough, M. B., & Marks, A. K. (2016). Resilience of children with refugee statuses: A research review. *Canadian Psychology/Psychologie canadienne, 57*(4), 330–339.

Pigozzi, M., J. (2018). *Reducing risk factors: Helping children stay in school*. Retrieved from https://educateachild.org/library/publications/reducing-risk-factors-helping-children-stay-school---occasional-paper-4

Rasmi, A. (2019, January 31). The caveats behind Canada's feel-good refugee numbers. *Quartz*. Retrieved from https://qz.com/1536578/canadas-refugee-policy-in-context/

Ratković, S., Kovačević, D., Brewer, C. A., Ellis, C., Ahmed, N., & Baptiste-Brady, J. (2017). *Supporting refugee students in Canada: Building on what we have learned in the past 20 years.* Report to the Social Sciences and Humanities Research Council of Canada, Brock University, St. Catharines, ON. Retrieved from https://espminetwork.com/new-report-supporting-refugee-students-in-canada-building-on-what-we-have-learned-in-the-past-20-years/

Record-Lemon, R. M., & Buchanan, M. J. (2017). Trauma-informed practices in schools: A narrative literature review. *Canadian Journal of Counselling & Psychotherapy/ Revue Canadienne de Counseling et de Psychothérapie, 51*(4), 286–305.

Rozier, A. (2017, February 27). High line schools teach staff how to help refugees. *King5.* Retrieved from http://www.king5.com/news/local/highline-schools-teach-staff-how-to-help-refugee-students/415411812

Saklan, E., & Erginer, A. (2017). Classroom management experiences with Syrian refugee students. *Education Journal, 6*(6), 207–214. doi:10.11648/j.edu.20 170606.17

Sarma-Debnath, K., & Castano, A. (2008). *Responding to the educational challenges of newcomer students and families.* St. John's, NL: Multicultural Women's Organization of Newfoundland and Labrador.

Save the Children. (2018). *Safe and enabling elementary education environment for refugee and asylum seeking pupils.* Belgrade, Serbia: Save the Children North West Balkans, Field Office Serbia and Balkans Migration and Displacement Hub. Retrieved from https://resourcecentre.savethechildren.net/library/safe-and-enabling-elementary-education-environment-refugee-and-asylum-seeking-pupils

Sheehy, I. (2014, October 15). *Refugees need access to higher education.* Retrieved from https://www.universityworldnews.com/post.php?story=20141015204738526

Simopoulos, G., & Alexandridis, A. (2019). Refugee education in Greece: Integration or segregation? *Forced Migration Review, 60,* 27–29. Retrieved from https://www.fmreview.org/education-displacement/simopoulos-alexan dridis

Skidmore, J. (2016). From discord to harmony: How Canadian music educators can support young Syrian refugees through culturally responsive teaching. *Canadian Music Educator, 57*(3), 7–8.

Smit, U., & Dafouz, E. (2012). Integrating content and language in higher education. An introduction to English-medium policies, conceptual issues and research practices across Europe. *AILA Review, 25,* 1–12.

Stechyson, N. (2018, January 15). Refugee children face unique mental health risks, Canada's doctors say. But they're also incredibly resilient. *Huffington Post.* Retrieved from https://www.huffingtonpost.ca/2018/01/15/refugee-mental-health_a_23333754/

Stewart, J. (2012). Transforming schools and strengthening leadership to support the educational and psychosocial needs of war-affected children living in Canada. *Diaspora, Indigenous, and Minority Education, 6*(3), 172–189. doi:10.1080/15595692.2012.691136

Stewart, J. (2017). A culture of care and compassion for refugee students. *Education Canada, 57*(1), 20–25. Retrieved from http://search.ebscohost.com.myaccess.library.utoronto.ca/login.aspx?direct= true&db=eue&AN=121609519&site=ehost-live

Tavares, T., et al. (2012). *Life after war: Education as a healing process for refugee and war-affected children.* Winnipeg: Manitoba Education. Retrieved from https://www.edu.gov.mb.ca/k12/docs/support/law/full_doc.pdf

Trines, S. (2019, August 8). The state of refugee integration in Germany in 2019. *World Education News + Reviews.* Retrieved from https://wenr.wes.org/2019/08/the-state-of-refugee-integration-in-germany-in-2019

UNESCO. (1997). *Refugee education: More Afghan girls in school.* Retrieved from http://www.unesco.org/education/educprog/emergency/casestudy/pakistan.htm

UNESCO. (2000). *EFA FORUM statistical document.* World Education Forum Dakar. Paris, France: UNESCO.

UNHCR. (1990). *Convention on the rights of the child.* Retrieved from https://www.ohchr.org/en/professionalinterest/pages/crc.aspx

UNHCR. (2011). *Convention and protocol relating to the status of refugees.* Geneva, Switzerland: UNHCR. Retrieved from https://www.unhcr.org/protection/basic/ 3b66c2aa10/convention-protocol-relating-status-refugees.html

UNHCR. (2015). *Breaking the cycle.* Retrieved from https://www.unhcr.org/nansen/ breaking_the_cycle_report_2015.pdf

UNHCR. (2016a). *Aiming higher – The other one percent.* Retrieved from https://www.unhcr.org/afr/aiming-higher.html

UNHCR. (2016b). *Missing out: Refugee education in crisis.* Retrieved from https://www.unhcr.org/missing-out-state-of-education-for-the-worlds-refugees.html

UNHCR. (2017). *Turkey facts sheet.* Retrieved from https://reliefweb.int/report/turkey/ unhcr-turkey-location/113

UNHCR. (2018a, June 19). *Figures at a glance: Statistical yearbooks.* Retrieved from https://www.unhcr.org/figures-at-a-glance.html

UNHCR. (2018b, September 13). *Report part II global compact on refugees: General Assembly official records seventy-third session supplement No. 12.* Retrieved from https://www.unhcr.org/gcr/GCR_English.pdf

UNHCR. (2019a). *Figures at a glance: Statistical yearbooks.* Retrieved from https://www.unhcr.org/figures-at-a-glance.html

UNHCR (2019b). *The UN Refugee Agency Pakistan: Education.* Retrieved from https://unhcrpk.org/education/

UNHCR. (n.d.). *For the office of the high commissioner for human rights' compilation report. Universal periodic review: 2nd cycle, 24th Session.* Retrieved from https://www.refworld.org/pdfid/5a12da042.pdf

UNICEF. (2017). *Fact sheet: 27 million children out of school in conflict zones*. Retrieved from https://www.unicef.org/media/media_100857.html

Vertovec, S. (2007). Super-diversity and its implications. *Ethnic and Racial Studies, 30*(6), 1024–1054. http://dx.doi.org/10.1080/01419870701599465

Villegas, A. M., & Lucas, T. (2002). Preparing culturally responsive teachers: Rethinking the curriculum. *Journal of Teacher Education, 53*(1), 20–32. https://doi.org/10.1177/0022487102053001003

Yitmen, Ş., & Verkuyten, M. (2018). Positive and negative behavioural intentions towards refugees in Turkey: The roles of national identification, threat, and humanitarian concern. *Journal of Community & Applied Social Psychology, 28*, 230–243. https://doi.org/10.1002/casp.2354

Yousif, N. (2019, January 23). Canada's resettlement of refugees highest in the world for first time in 72 years, new data show. *The Star Edmonton*. Retrieved from https://www.thestar.com/edmonton/2019/01/23/canadasresettlement-of-refugees-highest-in-the-world-for-first-time-in-72-years-new-datashows.html

CHAPTER 12

EFL Writing in Romania: Reflections on Present and Future

Estela Ene and Sydney Sparks

Abstract

Many global contexts remain largely unexplored, and thus unable to inform the shaping of an accurate picture or theory of second language (L2) writing around the world. Romania is such a context. This study investigates the attitudes and perceptions of 52 in-service K-12 English teachers from Romania, and represents an expansion of prior research conducted by the researcher. Using a survey, data were collected about the teachers' attitudes and perceptions about EFL writing in Romania. The findings illustrate the teachers' persistent positive attitudes towards the English language and English-speaking countries/cultures as well as further need for professional development in the area of pedagogy and EFL writing.

Keywords

teacher training – development – EFL writing – L2 writing – Romania

1 Introduction

The number of studies about second language (L2) writing in English as a Foreign Language (EFL) contexts has been on the rise. This development is well justified, since efl is more widely spread than English as a Second Language (ESL), and ignoring what happens in the EFL world can leave large gaps in our understanding of L2 writing (something we have known at least since Silva, Leki, & Carson, 1997). Additionally, the needs and processes of EFL writers can be quite different from those of ESL writers. Chapters in Manchón (2011) illustrate EFL situations in which English language learners write-to-learn language or content through English writing more than learning-to-write for the sake of developing writing skills in English. Looking at Eastern and Central

© KONINKLIJKE BRILL NV, LEIDEN, 2020 | DOI: 10.1163/9789004432048_012

Europe, Harbord (2010) notes that writing there tends to be taught primarily as a means to develop linguistic proficiency. It is encouraging, therefore, that the research has been expanding to more global contexts that were previously unexplored.

In an older meta-analysis, Ortega (2009, pp. 233–235) had found that about a third of the empirical research articles in major international journals such as the *Journal of Second Language Writing* and *TESOL Quarterly* were about EFL writing, but focused almost exclusively on Japan, Hong Kong, and China. Since then, more work about EFL writing in a wider range of countries has been published, including in Cimasko and Reichelt (2011), Manchón (2009, 2012), Ruecker and Crusan (2018), Seloni and Henderson (2019), and You (2010). In the European context, there are large, corpus-based, comparative studies which describe the local writing cultures and EFL writing practices of multiple countries from both Eastern and Westen Europe (for example, EUWRIT is described in Chitez, Kruse, and Castelló (2015) – about Romania, Ukraine, Macedonia, Switzerland, Germany, and Spain; and Kruse, Chitez, Bekar, Doroholschi, and Yakhtonova (2018) describe the LIDHUM project, in which reforms of writing were implemented at universities in Switzerland, Romania, Macedonia, and Ukraine).

A subset of the existing research on EFL writing examines writing teacher preparation and other teacher-related factors, such as attitudes and perceptions. The rationale for investigating teacher-related factors is based on the crucial role that teachers play in shaping the teaching-learning process. Such research not only reflects the specific differences among contexts but also suggests reasons for those differences, illustrating that approaches to L2 writing pedagogy cannot be a one-size-fits-all approach. Casanave (2009) argues that an ecological framework to EFL writing is advisable because "this view emphasizes the complex, messy, interrelated and contextually situated (or local) nature of all learning, including language learning (Larsen-Freeman, 2002; Tudor, 2003; Van Lier, 2002, 2004) and writing (Casanave, 1995b)" (p. 257).

Studies that are mindful of the ecological perspective have pinpointed a number of factors that matter in the way that EFL writing is taught and practiced in different countries. For example, some important differences have been found across EFL contexts in the type and amount of teacher preparation and professional development. EFL teachers can be classically trained in language and literature as well as primarily self-taught as pedagogues, clamoring for more professional development (Ene & Mitrea, 2013, about Romania); they can be trained in multiple rhetorical traditions and not necessarily as teachers of writing (Kruse, Chitez, Bekar, Doroholschi, & Yakhtonova, 2018, about Switzerland, Romania, Macedonia, and Ukraine; Reichelt, 2005, about Poland; and Reichelt, 2009a, about Germany); or they have to be deliberately challenged to observe and reflect on pedagogical practices in order to innovate their traditional ways (Lee, 2010). Teachers often face difficult working conditions with huge workloads, large classes, low pay, and few resources (Ene & Hryniuk, 2018, about Poland, Mexico, and China; Ene & Mitrea, 2013, about Romania; Lee, 2010, about Hong Kong; see also chapters in Manchón, 2009). Sometimes they are disempowered in hierarchical, traditional systems (Casanave, 2009, about Japan). In many countries, national and standardized assessments exert overwhelming pressure on daily classroom activities (see chapters in Ruecker & Crusan, 2018).

Teacher attitudes towards the target language and/or associated cultures can interact with the many practical factors listed above, and – in turn – they can influence what a teacher is able or willing to do in the classroom. In recent work about teachers from Poland, Mexico, and China, Ene and Hryniuk (2018) reported teachers' reservations about their students' true need to master English, and particularly writing in English. In prior work conducted in Poland, Reichelt (2005) had found that Polish teachers and students had a very positive attitude towards EFL and did not see English as a threat to their individual or cultural identity. In Turkey, Clachar (2000) noted that four of the seven teachers included in the study felt that Western, process-oriented writing methodologies were not appropriate for Turkish students because they were at odds with students' expectations for authoritative, traditional instruction. Arikan (2011), in a much larger study of 412 prospective teachers from Turkey, found that the teachers had positive attitudes about the target language but not about the target culture, and this was interpreted as an aspect that could diminish the teachers' ability to promote cross-cultural understanding. Furthermore, Gürsoy (2013), in a survey of 200 Turkish teachers, found mildly positive attitudes towards English, and female teachers having more positive attitudes than males. In the Basque country in Spain, Ipiña and Sagasta (2017), reported that prospective teachers in their longitudinal study did not feel that English was a threat to their identity. The examples here illustrate that teacher attitudes vary greatly and in somewhat unexpected ways, depending on the linguistic and cultural distance between the teachers' first language and culture and English, political relationships, but also teacher experience and research methods employed by different researchers.

In research which is specifically about Romania – a less researched EFL context – Ene and Mitrea (2013) used data from surveys, written reflections, a focus group and four teacher interviews to examine what 41 K-12 EFL writing teachers in Romania believed about L2 writing theory and pedagogy, as well as how they formed and applied their knowledge base. The study found that the participants were primarily self-taught in the area of EFL writing pedagogy, and were heavily influenced in their practices by the textbooks used, the national curriculum, standardized assessments, and heavy teaching workloads. Process-based writing that incorporated multiple drafts, peer review, and self-assessment was rare compared to focus on grammar and vocabulary, but many functional and even some creative genres were taught (as also noted by Chitez et al., 2015, and Kruse et al., 2018). Focus on functional genres increased in the grades that preceded national assessments. For the most part, the teachers from the 2013 study did not think that they were greatly affected by globalization, although they acknowledged the increased access to authentic English-language materials. The teachers were critical of national policy changes without explicitly connecting them to global changes.

The purpose of this study is to expand the knowledge base about EFL writing in Romania and capture developments since Ene and Mitrea (2013), particularly as related to teacher attitudes and perceptions that can influence the teaching of English writing. By filling in this knowledge gap, the chapter aims to contribute to the better understanding of EFL writing and teacher preparation around the world.

2   Research Questions

The research questions that guide this inquiry are:
– What are Romanian K-12 English teachers' attitudes and perceptions towards the English language and English-speaking cultures?
– How have attitudes evolved since the earlier 2013 study by Ene and Mitrea?
The chapter will discuss the implications of teachers' attitudes for the teaching of EFL writing.

3   Study Design

3.1   *Context*
Romania, a European Union member since 2007, has a population of around 19.4 million, with around 3 million students in K-12. English is the main foreign language taught to students from preK-12; students participate in national assessments for English at the end of their 4th grade year and at the end of high school. High-performing students who aim to study abroad take the TOEFL, IELTS, and other certificates.

Traditionally, language teachers are graduates of language and literature studies (for example, English teachers graduate with degrees in English

Language and Literature). During their studies, teachers receive training in linguistics, literature, and pedagogy. In recent years, courses on academic or research writing have been introduced, especially for MA students.

Data for this study were collected via an online survey distributed to K-12 teachers of English in a variety of areas of Romania in all of its three main geographic regions. While the 2013 study was conducted in a single location and tapped into the teacher population from only Sibiu county, the current study reached teachers from other counties as well.

3.2   *Participants*

Fifty-two K-12 teachers of English, all female, participated in this research. All but six of the teachers received their Bachelor's degree 1980–2017. The other six participants were pursuing degrees at the time of the study; one was in the process of receiving a BA, four their MAs, and one a PhD. The institutions from which the teachers had graduated included all of the major Romanian universities from Bucharest, Cluj, Iași, Sibiu, Timișoara, Craiova, and Ploiești; half of the participants had graduated from the Lucian Blaga University of Sibiu. The teachers were all between the ages of 24 and 60, with 23 (44%) of them in their thirties. Thirteen (25%) of the participants had been teaching for 11–15 years and another 13 (25%) for 16–20 years. Eleven (21%) had taught for 6–10 years, 10 (19%) for more than 20 years, and the remaining 5 (9%) for less than 5 years.

Twenty-four (46%) of the teachers taught grades 9–12 and 10 (19%) taught grades 5–8; the remaining participants taught several different grade groupings in the K-12 range. The teachers' schools were from the following areas: 27 (51%) from Sibiu, 8 (15%) from Iași and 3 (5%) from rural areas near Iași, 6 (11%) from Craiova and 4 (7%) from the area, 2 (3%) from Brașov, 1 from Galați, 1 Timișoara, 1 Bucharest, and 1 from Mureș. On average, 36 (69.2%) of the teachers had between 20–30 students/pupils in each group/class; 5 (9%) had 30 or more students and 8 (15.4%) had between 10–20 students in each group or class. Thirty-eight (73%) of the teachers spent between 20 hours a week or less teaching. The remaining 14 (26%) teachers spent more than 20 hours teaching each week.

3.3   *Methods*

A fifty-two-question survey was distributed to the participants. The first 16 questions were designed to collect demographic information. The remaining 36 questions pertained to English writing and reading practices and beliefs within the teachers' classrooms, the teacher's comfort with teaching, beliefs about English teaching practices, and English teaching and professional development in Romania. The survey consisted of a mixture of open-ended, Lykert-type scale and yes/no questions. The responses were quantified when appropriate; open-ended answers were analysed qualitatively, by identifying themes and ordering them from the most to the least frequent. Some open-ended answers consisted of several sub-parts that were related to more than one theme. Due to the space limitations of this venue, only the section of the survey that focused on teacher attitudes will be analysed and discussed particularly relative to the Ene and Mitrea (2013) study.

4   Results/Findings

– Q: What is your attitude (emotion, feelings) about the English language? Fifty-one (98%) of the respondents indicated that they had a positive attitude about the English language, while only one respondent indicated a negative attitude. Thirty-one (59%) participants provided a comment as to why. Seventeen (54%) of these 31 responses connected a positive attitude for the English language with a positive attitude for the respondent's job or a desire for students' best learning outcome: "I love what I do and the English language is the tool that helps me do it", and "Because I totally love it, I love teaching it, and I believe that it is really helpful for my students' future". Seven (22%) of the respondents provided an answer that was a simple statement of positivity, such as, "I have always loved this subject". Four (12%) cited the usefulness of English for their positive attitude for the language; one of these answers explained, "I strongly believe that English is a language that allows lots of liberty in thinking and expressing yourself". Two (6%) respondents cited their reason for having a positive attitude toward English as being the global status of English, calling the language "universal" and saying "it is international and no longer belongs to a specific nation".

TABLE 12.1   Teacher attitudes for English

Reason for attitude	Theme frequency
Positivity toward job/desire for students' best learning outcome	54% (17)
Usefulness	22% (7)
Global status of English	12% (4)

- Q: What is your attitude (emotion, feelings) about English-speaking countries/cultures?

The teachers' positive attitude applied to not only the English language but also English-speaking countries. Fifty (96%) of the 52 participants answered that they had a positive attitude about English-speaking countries; 2 answered that they had a neutral attitude. Twenty-eight (54%) of the 52 respondents provided a written answer expressing their reasoning, and 1 answer fit in two of the below categories; 5 (17%) of the answers were unclear or irrelevant and were not used in the analysis.

Of the 28, 7 (25%) of the answers were related to a positive view of the culture of English-speaking countries, though it was not clear which English-speaking countries and cultures the respondents were referring to specifically: "Great culture"; "I like their culture and mentality"; "I appreciate their culture and mentality". Six (21%) of the answers expressed a general mood of positivity, such as, "They are interesting" and "Somehow I feel a connection". Five (17%) respondents connected their positive attitude toward English speaking countries with a positive attitude toward the English language. Four (14%) of the answers made a connection to the writing classroom in some way. Three responses showed that the respondents felt that English-speaking countries contribute positively to their teaching. One teacher said, "[English-speaking countries] provide authentic materials for the English class" while another teacher wrote, in contrast, "They should invest more in facilitating access to materials/courses etc". Two (7%) answers are worth noting because of the connections they drew between appreciating English-speaking countries/cultures and the higher values of diversity and global understanding. One comment said, "We can learn if we communicate with the other communities as well" and the other said, "I love diversity".

- Q: How does the way you feel about English and English-speaking countries affect what or how you teach in your English class?

TABLE 12.2   Teacher attitudes for English-speaking countries/cultures

Reason for attitude	Theme frequency
Appreciation of target culture	25% (7)
General positivity	21% (6)
Positivity toward English language	17% (5)
Writing classroom connections	14% (4)

Forty-nine (94%) of the 52 respondents said that their attitude for English and English-speaking countries helped what or how they teach in their English classes, while 3 (5.8%) said their attitude did not affect their teaching at all. Eleven (21%) of the teachers indicated in their open-ended answers the belief that their own enthusiasm and confidence about the English language and associated cultures was bound to have a positive effect on their students' desire to learn English. One (2%) shared the opinion that teachers have a responsibility to cultivate appreciation for other languages and cultures. The remaining 40 (77%) teachers did not provide additional answers.

- Q: If you could change something about how English is taught in Romania, what would it be and why?

Forty-four (84%) out of the 52 teachers responded to this question. However, some respondents provided multiple examples of aspects of English teaching they would like to change. Of the 44 respondents, 9 (20%) teachers said there was a need for more and/or longer English classes. Eight (18%) said they would change the materials and technology available to them, including the textbook. Teachers wanted materials and technology that are more attractive to students and more funding for teaching materials. One teacher pointed out that investing in technology would give students access to a wider variety of materials. Another teacher said she would "introduce a lot of genuine British or even American English materials instead of the ones made by Romanians, which are pretty old and outdated". Seven (15%) teachers said they would change the teaching approach, with some stating they would like a more "communicative approach" rather than "the exam-oriented approach". Six (13%)

TABLE 12.3   Teacher desires for change of English teaching in Romania

What the teacher would change	Theme frequency
More/longer classes	20% (9)
Materials and technology	18% (8)
Teaching approach	15% (7)
National curriculum/syllabus	13% (6)
Smaller class sizes	13% (6)
Relevance of materials	11% (5)
Freedom in teaching	9% (4)
More interaction	6% (3)
Nothing	6% (3)
Irrelevant answer	4% (2)
Professional development for teachers	2% (1)

said they would change the national curriculum or syllabus. Six (13%) also said they would have smaller class sizes. Five (11%) of the teachers said they wanted to make their classes and materials more relevant to their students, including more of a focus on "real life" situations. Four (9%) answers had to do with a desire for more freedom, be it in choosing materials or choosing class-room content. Three (6%) wanted more interaction in their classrooms, with other English language learners or with native English speakers. Three (6%) said they would not change anything, two (4%) answers were irrelevant, and one answer pertained to providing teachers with professional development to motivate them.

– Q: If you could change something about how WRITING in English is taught in Romania, what would it be and why?

Of the 40 (76%) respondents for this question, 8 (20%) said they would change the writing textbooks or materials used in class. Eight (20%) also said they would change assignment requirements, meaning the types of assignments required of students and/or the number of assignments required. Six (15%) said they wanted classes, assignments, or materials to be more relevant to their students. Another six (15%) teachers said they would change nothing. Four (10%) of the teachers said they wanted more writing classes, class time, or practice time. Three (7%) said they wanted to teach more practical lessons or require more practical assignments of their students. Finally, one (2%) teacher wanted to implement professional development for teachers.

TABLE 12.4 Teacher desires for change of English writing teaching in Romania

What the teacher would change	Theme frequency
Textbooks/materials	20% (8)
Assignment requirements	20% (8)
Relevance of classes, assignments, or materials	15% (6)
Nothing	15% (6)
More or longer classes	10% (4)
Practicality of lessons/assignments	7% (3)
Professional development	2% (1)

5   Discussion

The attitudes of the 52 K-12 English teachers from Romania towards the English language and English-speaking countries and cultures was overwhelmingly positive. The reasons behind these positive attitudes varied from simply liking the language and culture(s) to seeing the utility of English as a global language of international communication. The combination of aesthetic, integrative and practical, instrumental reasons for having positive attitudes is rather unique. Other EFL studies have found that teachers' strong instrumental (rather than integrative) motivation towards English as a means of international communication can nurture positive attitudes towards the target language and culture(s) (Gürsoy, 2013). However, the participants in this study also displayed interest in and openness towards the target language and culture(s).

Furthermore, the absence of specific negative attitudes is overall similar to the findings in the Ene and Mitrea (2013) study, in which the participating teachers also affirmed the usefulness of the English language and some positive effects of globalization in terms of easier access to a wider variety of authentic language and teaching materials. In the 2013 study, a couple of participants had expressed concerns about the globalization of Western writing conventions due to the spread of English, as well as about the increased incidence of plagiarism facilitated by the internet. In the present study, no one expressed such concerns or reservations. On the contrary, the teachers wanted more access to technology, native speakers, and authentic materials. Thus, there is no overall change in the general attitude of the teachers over time. In addition, because the current study included more areas of Romania than Ene and Mitrea (2013), we can now see that the positive attitude shared in 2013 by the English teachers from Sibiu county is, in fact, more widely-spread.

Almost all of the participating teachers also reported that their own positive attitude towards the English language and English-speaking countries or cultures helped them in the classroom by giving them confidence and joy, and by making it possible to transmit those feelings to their students. This connection between positive attitudes and motivation (Gardner & Lambert, 1972) is often the very reason why attitudes are explored in research. Sercu, Garcia, and Prieto (2005, p. 489) have also posited that teachers' "perceptions will, undoubtedly permeate their lessons, determining the way the foreign culture/s is/are presented and dealt with". This study presents evidence that teachers themselves appreciate the motivating power of a positive attitude for themselves as professionals as well as for their students. The current study is limited to establishing what the Romanian teachers' attitudes were. The translation of those attitudes into practice will be explored in the future using other sections of the survey used for this study.

As far as the teachers' wishes for how the teaching of English in general and of English writing in particular could improve in Romania, the strongest theme that emerged had to do with wanting more authentic teaching materials and more relevant materials that the students could identify with. Both of these relate to the comments about wanting more freedom from the national curriculum and designated textbooks. Other updates that were requested had to do with the use of more communicative and technology-supported ways of teaching, as well as simply having more time to teach instead of rushing to keep up with the curriculum. These findings, too, are similar to the prior study as well as to the findings of Ene and Hryniuk (2018) about Poland and China (and somewhat less about Mexico). In essence, what the Romanian teachers expressed in both studies is that a modernization of the teaching of English and EFL writing is needed, including in the sense that more professional development for teachers is necessary.

A contextual factor that is usually mentioned as a stressful, limiting factor of EFL contexts is about working conditions, specifically workload and class size (Ene & Mitrea, 2013; Ene & Hryniuk, 2018; Lee, 2010; Reichelt, 2005, 2009b). Interestingly, no explicit comments were made in the present study about the teaching loads of teachers in Romania, although it is notably high and was pointed out in the 2013 study as an obstacle for teacher preparation and the use of process-oriented writing. A small subgroup among the participants – only 13% of them, precisely – expressed the wish to have smaller classes, although 78% of them had more than 20 students per class. Further investigations can determine if this population simply accepts the fact that class size is unlikely to change, or there are other reasons for this result.

6   Conclusions and Implications

As noted above, the attitudes of Romanian teachers seem to have stayed overall positive over the past six years. The positive outcome of this may be that a generally positive attitude may make it easier for the teachers to teach and help their students achieve their learning goals, as motivation theory predicts. English's global status served as a source of instrumental motivation. Uniquely, the Romanian EFL teachers also displayed integrative motivation in the form of openness to the target language and culture. As in the past, the teachers were more critical of the internal, national conditions surrounding the teaching of English rather than any potentially threatening aspects of the spread of English in the world. This suggests that such teachers would be able to model and cultivate a positive attitude towards intercultural communication and understanding. While critical theorists (Canagarajah, 1999; Pennycook, 1999) advocate for questioning the globalization of English and its conventions, EFL teachers often get caught in the immediacy of just teaching (Ene & Mitrea, 2013; Manchón, 2011).

The findings and conclusions presented here are based on a single section of the survey given to the 52 participating teachers. Future analyses of the complete survey – which cannot be done in the confines of this venue – may illuminate further connections between the attitudes of the teachers and their reported classroom practices.

References

Arikan, A. (2011). Prospective English language teachers' perceptions of the target language and culture in relation to their socioeconomic status. *English Language Teaching, 4*(3), 232–242.

Canagarajah, A. (1999). *Resisting linguistic imperialism.* Oxford: Oxford University Press.

Casanave, C. P. (1995). Local interactions: Constructing contexts for composing in a graduate sociology program. In G. Braine & D. Belcher (Eds.), *Academic writing in a second language: Essays on research and pedagogy* (pp. 83–112). Norwood, NJ: Ablex.

Casanave, C. P. (2009). Training for writing or training for reality? Challenges facing EFL writing teachers and students in language teacher education programs. In R. Manchón (Ed.), *Writing in foreign language contexts: Learning, teaching, and research* (pp. 256–277). Buffalo, NY: Multilingual Matters.

Chitez, M., Kruse, O., & Castelló, M. (2015). The European writing survey: Background, structure, implementation, and some results. *Working Papers in Applied Linguistics, 9.*

Cimasko, T., & Reichelt, M. (2011). *Foreign language writing instruction: Principles and practices.* Anderson, SC: Parlor Press.

Clachar, A. (2000). Opposition and accommodation: An examination of Turkish teachers' attitudes toward Western approaches to the teaching of writing. *Research in the Teaching of English, 35*(1), 66–100.

Ene, E., & Hryniuk, K. (2018). Worlds apart but in the same boat: How macro-level policy influences EFL writing pedagogy in China, Mexico, and Poland. In T. Ruecker & D. Crusan (Eds.), *International political contexts of second language writing assessment* (pp. 15–28). London: Routledge.

Ene, E., & Mitrea, A. (2013). EFL writing teacher training, beliefs and practices in Romania: A tale of adaptation. *The European Journal of Applied Linguistics and TEFL, 2*(2), 117–138.

Gardner, R. C., & Lambert, W. E. (1972). *Attitudes and motivation in second-language learning.* Rowley, MA: Newbury House.

Gürsoy, E. (2013). Prospective ELT teachers' attitudes toward the English language in an EFL context. *Journal of International Education Research, 9*(1), 107–114.

Harbord, J. (2010). Writing in Central and Eastern Europe: Stakeholders and directions in initiating change. *Across the Disciplines, 7.*

Ipiña, N., & Sagasta, P. (2017). Teacher students' attitudes towards English in a multilingual context. A longitudinal study. *International Review of Applied Linguistics in Language Teaching, 55*(1) 61–92.

Kruse, O., Chitez, M., Bekar, M., Doroholschi, C. I., & Yakhtonova, T. (2018). Studying and developing local writing cultures: An institutional partnership project supporting transition in Eastern Europe's Higher Education. In M. Chitez, C. I. Doroholschi, O. Kruse, L. Salski, & D. Tucan (Eds.), *University writing in Central and Eastern Europe: Tradition, transition, and innovation* (pp. 29–44). Dordrecht: Springer Nature.

Larsen-Freeman, D. (2002). Language acquisition and language use from a chaos/complexity theory perspective. In C. Kramsch (Ed.), *Language acquisition and language socialization: Ecological perspectives* (pp. 33–46). New York, NY: Continuum.

Lee, I. (2010). Writing teacher education and teacher learning: Testimonies of four EFL teachers. *Journal of Second Language Writing, 19*, 143–157.

Manchón, R. M. (Ed.). (2009). *Writing in foreign language contexts: Learning, teaching, and research.* Buffalo, NY: Multilingual Matters.

Manchón, R. M. (Ed.). (2011). *Learning-to-write and writing-to-learn in an additional language.* Philadelphia, PA: John Benjamins Publishing Co.

Manchón, R. M. (Ed.). (2012). *L2 writing development: Multiple perspectives.* Boston, MA: De Gruyter Mouton.

Ortega, L. (2009). Studying writing across EFL contexts: Looking back and moving forwward. In R. Manchón (Ed.), *Writing in foreign language contexts: Learning, teaching, and research* (pp. 233–235). Buffalo, NY: Multilingual Matters.

Pennycook, A. (1999). *English and the discourse of colonialism.* New York, NY: Routledge.

Reichelt, M. (2005). English-language writing instruction in Poland. *Journal of Second Language Writing, 14*, 215–232.

Reichelt, M. (2009a). Learning content in another context: English-language writing instruction in Germany. *Issues in Writing, 18*(1), 25–52.

Reichelt, M. (2009b). A critical evaluation of writing teaching programmes in different foreign language settings. In R. Manchón (Ed.), *Writing in foreign language contexts: Learning, teaching, and research* (pp. 183–206). Buffalo, NY: Multilingual Matters.

Ruecker, T., & Crusan, D. (Eds.). (2018). *The politics of English second language writing assessment in global contexts.* New York, NY: Routledge.

Seloni, L., & Henderson Lee, S. (Eds.). (2019). *Second language writing instruction in international contexts: Language teacher preparation and development.* Bristol: Multilingual Matters.

Sercu, L., Garcia, M. C. M., & Prieto. C. (2005). Culture learning from a constructivist perspective: An investigation of Spanish foreign language teachers' views. *Language and Education, 19*(6), 483–495.

Silva, T., Leki, I., & Carson, J. (1997). Broadening the perspective of mainstream composition studies. *Written Communication, 14*(3), 398–428.

Tudor, I. (2003). Learning to live with complexity: Towards an ecological perspective on language teaching. *System, 31*(1), 1–12.

Van Lier, L. (2002). An ecological-semiotic perspective on language and linguistics. In C. Kramsch (Ed.), *Language acquisition and language socialization: Ecological perspectives* (pp. 140–164). New York, NY: Continuum.

Van Lier, L. (2004). *The ecology and semiotics of language learning: A sociocultural perspective*. Dordrecht: Kluwer Academic Publishers.

You, X. (2010). *Writing in the devil's tongue: A history of English composition in China*. Carbondale, IL: Southern Illinois University Press.

CHAPTER 13

Teacher Practical Reasoning When Implementing Curriculum Reforms: A Case Study from Singapore

Heng Jiang, Terence Titus Chia, Ria George Kallumkal and Malathy Krishnasamy

Abstract

In this chapter, we trace teachers' "practical reasoning ladders" based on their heuristic goal system and rational laddering, which plays important mediating roles between knowledge, beliefs, and contextual demands. The main argument of this chapter is that studying teacher "practical reasoning" can contribute to a better understanding of how teachers respond to the "Teach Less Learn More" initiative in Singapore. We would further argue that the tensions among different dimensions of reasoning (instructional, pragmatic, and reflective) create dilemmas for teachers in their classroom practices. These arguments are grounded in the qualitative analysis of classroom teaching of six English language teachers in four primary schools in Singapore. In these cases, we show how teachers' "practical reasoning ladders" can serve as a frame for a deeper understanding of teacher responses to curriculum reforms. Although this study is situated in Singapore, it touches upon the fundamental issues, such as curriculum implementation, teacher practical reasoning, and teacher agency that educational researchers, practitioners, and policymakers are concerned within many other contexts.

Keywords

curriculum implementation – teacher practical reasoning – primary school teachers – Singapore educational reforms

1 Introduction

Research has substantially advanced our understanding of the process of implementing educational reforms worldwide. However, teachers do not implement educational change as proposed by policy but enact, translate, mediate it, filtered via existing professional knowledge, dispositions, and beliefs (Braun, Maguire, & Ball, 2010; Craig, 2010). This has been powerfully demonstrated by the work on teachers' "practical knowledge" (Elbaz, 1981, 1983; Gholami & Husu, 2010; Meijer, 1999), "personal practical knowledge" (Clandinin & Connelly, 1992), "practical argument" (Fernsternmacher & Richardson, 1993), and so on. This study concerns a typical case of mediated curriculum implementation from the teachers' perspectives. Six primary school teachers in Singapore are involved in the two-year research project that examined how teachers implemented the student-oriented curriculum reforms in Singapore in the past decade. Specifically, the research question is, "What can we understand teachers' practical reasoning when they respond to the curriculum reforms in Singapore?" All participant teachers attempted to enact student-oriented teaching for primary 3–5 students. In their teaching, the key ideas of the innovation in teaching did not adhere to full fidelity. However, the influence of the reform initiatives and teachers' efforts to reconstruct their practices could be evidenced by the teachers' practical reasoning in their teaching.

2   Literature Review

Much research has been done around the question of why the tension persists between what is proposed as educational change and what is implemented in the classroom. The underlying theme that frequently lurks behind this tension is the juxtaposition of reforms and change against teachers' personal interpretations of the reform, practical considerations, resistance, and/or deficiencies in knowledge or beliefs. There are two opposing views to explain this issue, namely, a *matching* paradigm and another *adaptation* paradigm.

The first kind of view goes along with decades of educational policies that have actively de-professionalized teachers through highly prescriptive curricula and strict regimes of inspection and control (Priestley & Philippou, 2018). It posits that the prescribed and actual curriculum should "match", continues to create one of education's most difficult policy problems. In this "matching" scenario, teachers, who necessarily stand between reform and pupils (Fullan, 2007), are seen to persist in their rigidity or recalcitrance, thus preventing change from occurring in schools. Not surprisingly, there is a vast literature on the many dimensions of teacher competence – knowledge, beliefs, dispositions, experiences – and how teacher change can be achieved by interventions in these areas (Verloop, van Driel, & Meijer, 2001). Nevertheless, the issue persists: Reformers propose, and teachers dispose.

The alternative view that "curriculum", however, defined and presented, should be seen as a "potential" (Ben-Peretz, 1975) to be expressed in different ways in classroom situations. This vision accompanies the new curriculum reforms in many countries that regard teachers as active curriculum developers in classroom practices (Priestley et al., 2015). Thus, the research focused on "curriculum potential" does not view the discrepancy as an inadequacy, as implementation research is inclined to do, but rather, is concerned to credit the legitimately different uses to which the curriculum is actually put (Connelly & Lantz, 1990, p. 17). When the intentions of educational change are introduced into classroom practices, adaptations are often involved, which are not in themselves problematic (Cohen, 2011; Doyle & Rosenbury, 2012). This view encourages the attitude that curricular adaptations in practice are reflections of local ability to accommodate to the community, to the teacher, and to student needs.

Practically speaking, whether the "matching" view or the "adaptation" view is adopted, there will never be ultimate control over ends. Westbury (2002) argued that the problem of the low impact of curriculum reform could be seen as gaps that occur when reform visions are compromised as a curriculum moves through its various levels: institutional, programmatic, and classroom. Ideas and design principles are translated into teaching materials, which are to be interpreted and implemented by teachers, which in turn produce varied learning experiences for their students (Deng & Gopinathan, 2016; Remillard & Heck, 2014). In this process, the teacher's practical knowledge (defined as the teacher's understanding and conceptions of the meaning of how and what to do in their practices of teaching as well as knowledge mediated by practice) plays an important role (Connelly & Clandinin, 1990). When meaning is the "underlying motivation behind thoughts, actions and even the interpretation and application of knowledge" (Krauss, 2005, p. 763), it makes sense to examine the almost real-time interpretation teachers have, in light of their practical knowledge, of the educational reforms that they encounter in order to explain and reason through their instant decision-makings in the classroom. It is conceivable that their interpretation in the form of practical reasoning (Janssen et al., 2013) may differ from what those educational concepts are intended for, thus contributing to the divergence between theory and practice. Thus, the emerging literature on teachers' moment-to-moment reasoning about their implementation of the curriculum reforms is of tremendous value to understanding the creation and influence of such divergence.

In this chapter, we follow the second line of research to examine how teachers make sense of policy shifts and reform practices by tracing teachers' practical reasoning, defined as the reasoning aimed at deciding what to do and how to do it. Practical reasoning is based on Greek "'practical philosophy' which aims at developing the kind of context-based practical reasoning that is employed in the conduct of a wide range of morally informed human activities" (Carr, 2004, p. 61). It is different from theoretical reasoning, which ends in knowledge. Fenstermacher and Richardson (1993) define practical reasoning as "the process of thought that ends in an action or an intention to act ... [and] pertains to the thinking done in anticipation of or following an action, as well as the relationship that obtains between this thinking and the action itself" (p. 102). However, practical reasoning is not void when action is taken. Stout (2019) reviewed philosophical tradition of practical knowledge and practical reasoning to suggest "identifying the content of practical knowledge not with the conclusion but with a premise of practical reasoning – a kind of practical reasoning that occurs *within* [italics added] rather than before action" (Stout, 2019, p. 564). That is, practical reasoning can also be a process of verdict *within* action, which draws upon the practical knowledge. Audi (2006) delineated the structural flow of practical reasoning with three basic elements: *purposive premise* (I want G, where G is a goal), *instrumental premise* (A-ing will achieve G), and a *practical conclusion* (e.g., I should A).

To understand teachers' practical reasoning in practice, we use lesson observation and stimulated recall interviews to make explicit their "practical reasoning ladder" to examine their almost real-time decisions made in conducting the lesson, which plays an important mediating role between knowledge, beliefs and contextual demands. "Practical reasoning ladder" is based on the notions of heuristic goal system and rational laddering (Janssen, Westbroek & Doyle, 2014) to show the layers of reasoning in the intentions that undergird the teaching tasks, which reflect the three elements of the practical reasoning above.

3   The Singaporean Context

Singapore's superior performance in international student tests has attracted much attention worldwide. Teachers in Singapore are found to teach in 'the traditional way' because of their traditional pedagogical beliefs and practice, which are supported, regulated, and constrained more by a prescribed national curriculum, high-stakes examinations, and an examination-based meritocracy ideology (Grunert & Grunert, 1995; Lim & Tan, 2018). With the vision of educating the young generation for the future world characterized by globalization, knowledge innovation, and uncertainties, the Ministry of Education (MOE) in Singapore has initiated waves of educational reforms to foster student-oriented pedagogy and better curriculum integration and relevance for critical and higher-order thinking, problem solving, creativity, and positive attitudes with the meaningful use of new technologies since 1990s.

Notwithstanding multiple reform initiatives to encourage the "Thinking Schools, Learning Nation (TSLN)" and "Teach Less, Learn More (TLLM)" pedagogical vision for student-centeredness, pedagogical practice in Singapore's classrooms has remained largely traditional, directed toward curriculum content delivery and examination performance (Hogan et al., 2013). Teaching is largely driven by content coverage and preparing students for semester-end and high stakes examinations, with the primary focus on the transmission of knowledge and skills contained in the national curriculum (represented by teaching and examination syllabi). There is little evidence of teaching for high-order thinking, meaningful use of learning technologies, students' constructing knowledge, and interdisciplinary learning (Deng, Gopinathan, & Lee, 2013; Hogan, 2014). Researchers suggested that the limited or lack of impact on pedagogical practice has to do with teachers' traditional beliefs about knowledge, teaching, and learning. In Singapore, teachers conventionally tend to view knowledge as a body of ready-made facts or factual information contained in the national curriculum, upon which students are tested during examinations. Their teaching rarely deviates from a logic of curriculum coverage, knowledge transmission, and assessment (Hogan et al., 2013). Accordingly, classroom teachers tend to rely on whole class forms of lesson organization, with whole-class lectures and Initiate-Response-Evaluate sequences (IRE) as the dominant methods. When teachers make limited use of constructivist-pedagogical methods such as checking prior knowledge, monitoring understanding, and providing feedback, they largely do so to get students to know the correct answers (Deng & Gopinathan, 2016).

Thus, across the different educational reform movements that have emerged over the past thirty years in Singapore, this gap between intention and practice in curriculum reforms merits closer attention especially when the MOE announced a reduction of standardized examinations for Primary schools (especially the removal of the exams for P1 and 2). However, most extant studies do not delve into teachers' thinking and reasoning to find out how teachers respond to the educational change via moment-to-moment reasoning in practice and what influences teachers' reasoning. Teachers are advised to encourage student interactions in class and lessen teacher talk. As described below, we will present six English language teachers' practical reasoning in their classroom practices in this chapter.

4   Methods

This study draws upon data from a larger two-year research project involving ten primary schools and over 100 teachers in Singapore. In this particular study, we focus on six English language teachers for Grade 3–5 in four neighborhood primary schools. Along with three research assistants, we observed the participants' lessons at least once and conducted the one-hour interview in the first free period the teacher had on the same day. Two of them are teacher leaders, two are experienced teachers with more than five years of service, and two are novice teachers. They participated on a voluntary basis and agreed to the ethically approved procedures in the study. Table 13.1 shows the profiles of the participants.

Although there is an array of tools to find out what teachers enact in the classroom, we have found that a combination of lesson observation and post-lesson interviews supported with the laddering method provides possibilities to make explicit teacher practical reasoning in practice. As we mean it here, the laddering method is both a method of data collection and a tool for data analysis. In short, the laddering method is a contextualized tool intended to lay out the holistic scenario of a lesson (varying between 50–70 minutes), including its sequence of classroom activities, the intentions behind designing these activities, and underlying values and beliefs that guide their teaching. To construct the teacher's goal system representation, we adapted the widely used laddering method (Grunert & Grunert, 1995; Veledo-de Oliviera et al., 2006) for co-constructing the teacher's goal system (Janssen et al., 2013) to understand their practical reasoning about their choices of actions in the class. The laddering method, which originated in clinical psychology, is a well-established procedure in several fields for constructing personal goal-means structures to

TABLE 13.1   Participants' profiles

	Status/school	Gender	Ethnicity
Mr. S	Teacher leader (Senior Teacher), School 1	Male	Indian
Mr. P	Teacher leader (Level Head), School 2	Male	Chinese
Mdm. L	Experienced teacher, School 3	Female	Chinese
Mdm. R	Experienced teacher, School 2	Female	Malay
Mr. F	Novice teacher, School 3	Male	Malay
Ms. X	Novice teacher, School 4	Female	Chinese

predict and influence behavior (Reynolds & Olson, 2001) and has been previously used to construct teacher s' goal systems for teaching (Janssen et al., 2013, 2014). The procedure consists of the following steps:

a. First, we observed the participants' lessons and made detailed observational notes. The participants were informed that they were not being evaluated, and we hoped to observe a normal lesson that they would conduct as if not being observed.

b. Next, during the post-lesson interview, each teacher was asked to write down the sequence of the teaching and learning activities on separate post-its.

c. Next, each teacher was asked the following questions: What is the lesson objective? What is the intention behind each activity? How is each intention served by different activities? How is the lesson objective connected to the intentions and activities discussed earlier? Their answers were written on another set of post-its and placed above the respective activities or intentions. See for example Fig. 1 for teacher P's heuristic laddering.

d. Finally, the teacher was asked to evaluate the lesson and validate his/her laddering representation. Were goals missing that need to be added? Were goals adequately connected to other goals and the lesson objective(s)? Were there connections missing that need to be drawn? Should you have the opportunity to teach this lesson again, what would you change?

The laddering method resulted in a visual representation of each teacher's goal system, i.e., each teacher's perception of the "what" and "why" of teaching a

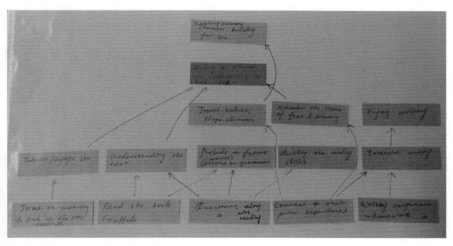

FIGURE 13.1   An example of laddering

lesson (see, for example, Figure 13. 1). When analyzing the data, we adapted the Coding Scheme for Classroom Discourse in Singapore (Luke et al., 2005) to tease out (1) teacher-oriented activities (including whole-class lecture/mono-logue, whole-class answer checking[1]), (2) student-oriented activities (such as individual student work; small group work) and (3) teacher-student knowl-edge building (whole class open discussions). Two of the team members inde-pendently coded the teaching videos for inter-rater reliability checking and later discussed discrepancies in their coding. The final Kappa indices for each coded lesson are in a substantial range between 0.7651–0.9778. The collection of the laddering systems also allowed us to explore the intentions behind these activities. The sub-categories for the intentions were derived from the inter-views with the teachers and further be grouped into three major categories, as indicated in Table 13.2.

TABLE 13.2   Teachers' intentions

Categories	Sub-categories	Examples
Instructional reasoning	Comprehend the critical aspect of the content for teaching	"Now I'm beginning to make more connection with the things that they're exposed to and make purposeful or what do you say, obvious links".
	Focus of lesson activities (concept, skills, memorization)	"I give them a hinge question. So, during this hinge question, I actually related it to how passive voice is being used in news headlines".
	Engage students	"I love group activities, so I always make a point to do group activities. Because it is a time for students to talk to each other and learn from each other".
	Instill values	"I'll want to get them to think more about "care" hence the video that has this element of care in it".
	Ongoing assessment for students	"And my assessing of their understanding was on like if they if they said that they understood the passage then I wanted to ask these questions to really check whether they understood".
	Manage the classroom	"But he has been making a nuisance of himself so this is my arrangement with him until he's ready to go back".

(cont.)

TABLE 13.2   Teachers' intentions (*cont.*)

Categories	Sub-categories	Examples
Pragmatic reasoning	Cost (e.g. time, teaching materials)	"Because today I have time constraint, I tweak it a little bit. So I do this thing called the opening read and opening write".
	Congruent	"I actually wanted to give more examples but I was very mindful because I know kahoot, I'm doing it for the first time on an ipad in my class the last two periods, there would be some problem".
	Clarity and easiness	"I felt that reading the whole passage and annotating was very tiring for them. So this time round, I tried doing only 1 passage, 1 short passage for each student".
	Effectiveness (often for exams)	"Because at the back of my mind, I know that the oral exam is will be coming up in term 2. ... And I don't want to wait until then to address so."
Reflective	Instrumental reflection for future teaching/reflective	"I was mindful based on my learning in the previous lesson".
	Deep and broad reflections to challenge prior assumptions	"So I reflected maybe it is the way I teach, maybe is the way I'm teaching that he is not getting interested, it's for him I have to engage him differently, in a different way".

The first type of intention is *pedagogical* intentions, including representing the content of the subject knowledge, engaging students (and checking students' understanding and providing feedback), and managing the classroom. The second type includes *pragmatic* intentions, which purported the teachers to enact easier plans in congruence with the valued purposes in the specific context, considering the constraints of resources and cost. Preparing for exams stands out as an important pragmatic intention that motivates teachers in decision making. The third is the *reflective* intention, which directs towards teachers themselves and their teaching for improvement. Next, these results are discussed.

5   Findings

The findings show that teachers still apply teacher-oriented teaching more than student-oriented activities in their lessons, in terms of the time allowed for teacher talk, student talk, and teacher-student dialogue. Among the three types of teachers with different years of experience, teacher leaders used open discussion to build knowledge together with students and intended to incorporate students' responses to adapt the follow-up teaching. But the beginning teacher and experienced teachers in this study opted to lead students in the whole class answer checking and guide student group/individual work. When being probed further, the teachers shared their *pedagogical, pragmatic,* and *reflective* intentions to guide their reasoning to choose mostly teacher-oriented practices during the lesson.

5.1   *Teacher Oriented Teaching*

Participants preferred to use the teacher-oriented approach to teach in class, which are represented as whole class lecture/monologue and whole-class answer checking. As Table 13.3 shows, the teachers used 41.55% of the lesson time on whole-class lecturing and 15.38% on whole-class answer checking. This corresponds to the earlier research on the Singaporean teachers' teaching regime (Hogan, 2014). However, the results show that some teachers also skillfully used more group work in their teaching. For instance, Mr. F, a novice teacher in his third year of teaching, has a coherent plan to have students work in "home groups" and "expert groups". In the observed lesson, his students seemed to be familiar with the group work system and worked fairly well with peers.

Only the teacher leaders, Mr. S, and Mr. P, used some time to discuss with students on open-ended questions. Mr. P spent quite some time on discussing with students with open-ended questions. For instance, when co-reading the story-book of "Gruffalo", Mr. P. raised questions to guide students' understanding of the text. He did not use all the basic information questions (i.e., What did mouse say to the fox?) as suggested by the teachers' guidebook, but raised questions to stimulate students' discussions, such as "What do you think of the mouse? ... Why?" The students were very engaged in thinking along with the story plot.

Many of the teachers used small group work during the lesson. They mostly had students to work in pairs or groups of 4–5 to discuss the assigned tasks, such as discussing the questions in worksheets or annotating reading materials together.

In general, the sequence of the lesson activities follows the pattern of "I do, we do, you do" model (Fisher & Frey, 2007): Whole class lecture – "I (meaning the teacher) do it", Guided whole class activity or group work – "We do it", and Independent – "You do it alone". Teachers quoted this pattern of teaching from what they had learnt during school professional development programs and tried to apply it in their teaching. The role of a teacher seemed to gradually release the control of the class. That is, they would like to support the students as much as they can in the beginning, later allow students to apply what is learned in pairs and eventually let students work independently. However, with much focus on teachers' guidance and time spent on the explicit lecturing and whole class answer checking, the classrooms observed in this study remain largely teacher oriented.

5.2 Practical Reasoning for Teaching: Pedagogical, Pragmatic, and Reflective Intentions

In these teacher-oriented classrooms, teachers still tried hard to strike a balance between what was demanded by the curriculum reforms and what they considered as important. During the post-lesson interviews, teachers delineated the intentions behind their choices of the lesson activities and layered the valued their reasons in their laddering system. It is found that there are three main reasons driving their lesson design and implementations: *pedagogical, pragmatic,* and *reflective* intentions. These three intentions intertwined together to inform the teachers' decisions and actions in classroom.

As indicated by the participants, *pedagogical intentions* pertain to the purposes of (1) representing the content, (2) focus of lesson activities; (3) engaging students, (4) instilling values, (5) ongoing assessment of student learning, and (6) managing the classroom. Teacher-oriented activities discussed in the section above were often backed with the intention to "represent the content" and "preparing for the exams". The student-oriented activities, such as group work, were often associated with "engaging students" and "instilling values" of learning from each other.

These *pedagogical intentions* were often mediated by the *pragmatic intentions,* which involved (1) cost, (2) congruence, (3) clarity and ease, and (4) effectiveness (often for standardized exams). This aligns with what Doyle (1977) delineated as the practicality that directs teacher decision making when adopting educational innovations. The participants would consider time as the cost when they decided to use less student group work. They would consider it important to cover the required curriculum content in the lesson. Also, the participants constantly think if the use of certain teaching would be congruent with the immediate context of the classroom. For instance, Ms. X opted to start the lesson with a game of "finding bananas" to engage students as she found that her students seemed to be tired after the PE lesson and needed "something exciting" to tune into the lesson. When the participants decide to use a new student-oriented approach in teaching, such an approach was usually clear and easy to use when serving the valued purposes. Such an approach was often subject to the teacher's adaptation. For instance, Mr. S adopted a quick-write strategy (i.e. having students to write with non-stop within a few minutes) as suggested during one of his professional development programs to help students' express themselves in writing. Mr. S found this strategy easy to use, and he added a "loop" (rounds of revisions) to the quick-write procedure. When asked why he made such an adaptation, he said:

> S: Looping has dual objectives. One is to uncover a writer's block, when a writer is faced by a block, by forcing yourself to write, you might discover things that you never write about. You have to write; in that process, something might pop out. ... Second, looping would mean that I revisit it, but to look for certain things that are interesting to you and I take that to do the writing. In that way, the writing becomes more and more focused. ... Once you loop twice, the third loop is something close to what you really want to write about. Only after this then we can talk about how you can write better, that would be the writer's craft. (Transcript of the interview with Mr. S., 13 February, 2019)

In this quote, Mr. S considered quick write an easy approach for him to administer and for students to "uncover a writer's block". He also added "looping" to it which aims at cultivating "writer's craft". However, in this lesson, he decided to have students do "quick write" (5 minutes of writing in response to the theme of "care" set by the teacher) instead of loops of free-write "because ... time was one thing and the objectives are different". In addition to time (pragmatic) and lesson objective (pedagogical), he also considered the standard examinations when choosing between more teacher-guided "quick write" and student-initiated "free write", or sometimes combine both:

> I really want to move away from this very Singaporean thing of writing for examinations... because they only want to write because there is a compo exam at the end of the year and you cannot create writers like that, you need to open their minds. Ya so ... uh but on the other hand I know that I cannot go completely off tangent and just do creative writing. There is a goal at the end and they are in P5, a very important year before their PSLE next year, so I try, I am trying, what I am trying to do is to marry both. (Transcript of the interview with Mr. S., 13 February 2019)

As a matter of fact, effectiveness for preparing students for the standardized exam is a major pragmatic concern for all the participant teachers. For instance, novice teacher Mr. F pointed out the tensions between the standardized exams

TABLE 13.3 Classroom discourse analysis patterns

	Teacher oriented			Students oriented		Teacher-student knowledge building	Miscellaneous
	Whole class lecture/monologue	Choral repetition or oral reading	Whole class answer checking	Individual student seatwork	Small group work	Whole class open discussion	
Miss X	713	34	1639	549	0	356	249
Mdm R	1492	0	0	805	859	56	0
Mr F	1761	0	162	593	1459	0	0
Mr S	2057	0	394	0	676	48	95
Mdm L	562	1346	739	0	62	447	94
Mr P	2041	0	260	0	0	1107	106
Total: seconds	8626	1380	3194	1947	3056	2014	544
Total: percentage	41.55	6.65	15.38	9.38	14.72	9.70	2.62

and the need to cater to the students' individual learning. They tried to use the discourse of the student-oriented teaching, such as "facilitating" and "self-regulated learning", to improve their current practices, and in the meantime check on student learning to prepare them for high-stakes exams without "holding the water for too long" (in Mr. F's words).

Teachers not only have *pedagogical* and *pragmatic* considerations when trying to choose between teacher-oriented activities and having students take the lead, but also engaged themselves in the effort to improve their teaching as manifested in their *critical intentions*. There are two types of critical intentions: one is reflective for future changes in teaching, the other is more of challenging their former assumptions on teaching and learning. The former is prevalent in the participants whilst the latter is relatively rarer.

As stated earlier in the method section, we have asked the teachers to identify the moments during which they were especially aware of their thoughts and decisions. With this general guidance, we nevertheless found that most of the episodes teachers brought up were motivated by the *critique* about the success or failure of their practices rather than by an awareness of their in-the-moment deliberations. Teachers shared that they had spent too long on one segment, had failed to see a student whose hand was raised or were glad they had remembered to attend to a particular detail. They recognized the gap between their teaching and what they understood as "student-oriented" teaching. For example, experienced teacher, Mdm. L, described her change in teaching vocabulary from explicit definition to using the contextual clue in the text to guess the meaning of the words:

> I feel a lot of these strategies that I have been applying right, would be more on building vocabulary and then, more on, testing their understanding after I explicitly tell them the meaning. So it's like, they, on their part, they don't have to do anything. They just listen. ... *So I realise, wah, my seven years seem like, I always focus on this strategy. I want to make a change.* And yes I did say, I did tell them that sometimes, okay when we are doing comprehension, you don't know this word right, you look at the clues. (Transcript of the interview with Mdm. L, 29 September 2018)

However, as it is shown, the purpose is for "comprehension", the short term for the comprehension section in the standard exams. Mdm L's reflection on her prior teaching and changes made to help students actively draw meanings from the contextual clues was to help students perform well in comprehension tests. The prevalence of these *pedagogical-pragmatic-reflective intentions* in tensions suggests that teachers do routinely review and change their own practices. However, we did not find many instances when teachers were engaged in critiquing their prior assumptions about teaching and learning. As the quotes from Mr. S and Mdm. L suggested, most teachers tended to accept the overall examination-oriented and teacher-directed teaching, although they also reflected and tried to make changes to their current practices.

6   Discussion and Conclusions

We focus on the challenge of effectively implementing student-oriented teaching in traditional teacher-dominated Singaporean classrooms and expose the intricate nature of the teacher's practical reasoning that goes on 'in the moment' of classroom teaching. Using the tool of laddering method, we make visible six English teacher's practical reasoning in response to the student-oriented curriculum initiatives. Additionally, through stimulative recall interviews, the teachers were able to (re)construct a more fully articulated understanding of the rationale behind their teaching activities. It shows that teachers mulled over *pedagogical, pragmatic,* and *reflective* intentions to design their teaching, although the open-ended interactions and students' construction of knowledge remain limited in their lessons as described in the other studies (Deng & Gopinathan, 2016; Hogan, 2014; Tan, 2008).

The main argument of this chapter is that studying teacher "practical reasoning" can contribute to a better understanding of how teachers make sense of the "Teach Less Learn More" initiative in Singapore. We further argued that the tensions among different dimensions of reasoning (instructional, pragmatic, and reflective) create dilemmas for teachers in their classroom practices. With the qualitative analysis of six English teachers' classroom teaching, we show how a teacher's practical reasoning ladder can serve as a frame for a deeper understanding of teacher responses to student-oriented curriculum reform.

Overall, this research provides evidence that the teachers were able to develop a more nuanced and more conscious awareness of their own instructional responses to student-oriented curriculum reforms. When articulating their rationales, there are tensions between what they think about their actions and what they think is required by the reforms. They tried to approach the latter and make use of it to justify what they are doing. However, they also noticed that gaps remain, and questions are left for future resolutions. This makes a compelling case for professional development interventions that pay attention to the intricacies of the teacher's practical reasoning that goes on in the activity of actual teaching.

Moreover, a major contribution of this study is to study, and document classroom teaching practices entail in terms of teacher intentions and decision-making. Although this study is situated in Singapore, it touches upon the fundamental issues, such as curriculum implementation, teacher practical knowledge, and teacher agency, that educational researchers, practitioners, and policymakers are concerned within many other contexts. That which was ultimately learned in the classroom as the curriculum was implemented has always been a subject of systematic control in a centralized educational system in Singapore. But the question remains, of course, how practical reasoning directs teachers' decision-making and gives rises to (changed) teaching practices in the classroom.

Note

1   Two teachers incorporated choral reading in their lessons. However, they inserted the guiding questions to elicit students' answers while reading, as requested by the STELLAR syllabus. We combined these choral reading activities with the whole class answer checking.

References

Audi, R. (2004). Reasons, practical reason, and practical reasoning. *Ratio: An International Journal of Analytic Philosophy, 17*(2), 119–149.

Audi, R. (2006). *Practical reasoning and ethical decision*. London: Routledge.

Ben-Peretz, M. (1975). The concept of curriculum potential. *Curriculum Theory Network, 5*(2), 151–159.

Cohen, D. (2011). *Teaching and its predicaments*. Cambridge, MA: Harvard University Press.

Connelly, F. M., & Clandinin, D. J. (1990). Stories of experience and narrative inquiry. *Educational Researcher, 19*(5), 2–14.

Connelly, F. M., & Lantz, O. C. (1990). Definitions of curriculum: An introduction. In A. Lewy (Ed.), *The international encyclopaedia of curriculum*. New York, NY: Pergamon.

Deng, Z., & Gopinathan, S. (2016). PISA and high-performing education systems: Explaining Singapore's education success. *Comparative Education, 52*(4), 449–472.

Doyle, W., & Rosemartin, D. (2012). The ecology of curriculum enactment: Frame and task narratives. In T. Wubbels, P. den Brok, J. van Tartwijk, & J. Levy (Eds.),

Interpersonal relationships in education: An overview of contemporary research (pp. 137–147). Rotterdam, The Netherlands: Sense Publishers.

Elbaz, F. (1981). The teacher's "practical knowledge": Report of a case study, *Curriculum Inquiry, 11*(1), 43–71.

Fenstermacher, G. D., & Richardson, V. (1993). The elicitation and reconstruction of practical arguments in teaching. *Journal of Curriculum Studies, 25*(2), 101–114.

Fisher, D., & Frey, N. (2007). Implementing a schoolwide literacy framework: Improving achievement in an urban elementary school. *The Reading Teacher, 61,* 34, 36. Retrieved from http://www.hsigarland.org/ReadingRoost/resources/research%25 20articles/implementing%20a%20schoolwide%20litearcy%20framework.pdf

Fullan, M. (2007). *The new meaning of educational change* (4th ed.). New York, NY: Teachers College Press.

Grunert, K. G., & Grunert, S. C. (1995). Measuring subjective meaning structures by the laddering method: theoretical considerations and methodological problems. *International Journal of Research in Marketing, 12,* 209–225.

Hargreaves, A., & Fink, D. (2006). *Sustainable leadership.* San Francisco, CA: Jossey-Bass.

Hogan, D. (2011, May–June). *Culture and pedagogy in Singapore: An institutionalist account of the fate of the teach less learn more policy initiative.* Paper presented at the 4th Redesigning Pedagogy: Transforming Teaching, Inspiring Learning International Conference, National Institute of Education, Nanyang Technological University, Singapore.

Hogan, D. (2014). Why is the Singapore school system so successful, and is it a model for the west? *The Conversation.* Retrieved from http://theconversation.com/why-is-singapores-school-system-so-successful-and-is-it-a-model-for-the-west-22917

Hogan, D., Chan, M., Rahim, R., Kwek, D., Aye, K. M., Loo, S. C., ... Luo, W. (2013). Assessment and the logic of instructional practice in secondary 3 English and mathematics classrooms in Singapore. *Review of Education, 1*(1), 57–106.

Janssen, F., Doyle, W., & van Driel, J. (2013). How to make innovations practical. *Teachers College Record, 115*(7), 1–42.

Janssen, F., Westbroek, H., & Doyle, W. (2014). The practical turn in teacher education: Designing a preparation sequence for core practice frames. *Journal of Teacher Education, 65*(3), 195–206.

Krauss, S. E. (2005). Research paradigms and meaning making: A primer. *The Qualitative Report, 10*(4), 758–770.

Lim, L., & Tan, M. (2018). Meritocracy, policy and pedagogy: Culture and the politics of recognition and redistribution in Singapore. *Critical Studies in Education,* 1–17.

Luke, A., Freebody, P., Lau, S., & Gopinathan, S. (2005). Towards research-based innovation and reform: Singapore schooling in transition. *Asia Pacific Journal of Education, 25*(1), 5–28.

MOE. (2010). *Teaching and learning resources – English language.* Retrieved from https://www.moe.gov.sg/education/syllabuses/resources

Priestley, M., Biesta, G. J. J., Philippou, S., & Robinson, S. (2015). The teacher and the curriculum: Exploring teacher agency. In D. Wyse, L. Hayward, & J. Pandya (Eds.), *The Sage handbook of curriculum, pedagogy and assessment.* London: Sage Publications.

Priestley, M., & Philippou, S. (2018). Curriculum making as social practice: Complex webs of enactment. *The Curriculum Journal, 29*(2), 151–158. doi:10.1080/09585176.2018.1451096

Reynolds, T. J, & Olson, J. C. (2001). *Understanding consumer decision making: The means-end approach to marketing and advertising strategy.* Mahway, NJ: Lawrence Erlbaum Associates.

Richardson, V., & Placier, P. (2001). Teacher change. In V. Richardson (Ed.), *Handbook of research on teaching* (pp. 905–947). Washington, DC: American Educational Research Association.

Stout, R. (2019). Practical reasoning and practical knowledge. *Canadian Journal of Philosophy, 49*(4), 564–579, doi:10.1080/00455091.2018.1463839

Supovitz, J. A. (2008) Implementation as iterative refraction. In J. A. Supovitz & E. H. Weinbaum (Eds.), *The Implementation gap: Understanding reform in high schools* (pp. 151–172). New York, NY: Teachers College Press.

Veledo-de Oliveira, T., Ikeda, A. A., & Campomar, M. C. (2006). Discussing laddering application by the means-end chain theory. *The Qualitative Report, 11*, 626–642.

Verloop, N., Van Driel, J. H, & Meijer, P. (2001). Teacher knowledge and the knowledge base of teaching. *International Journal of Educational Research, 35*, 441–461.

CHAPTER 14

Understanding What, How, and Why Teacher Educators Learn through Their Personal Examples of Learning

Cui Ping, Gonny Schellings and Douwe Beijaard

Abstract

This study aims at gaining a deeper understanding of what, how, and why teacher educators learn about their work. It is a follow-up study of a questionnaire study into teacher educators' professional learning. Through an interview, eleven teacher educators were asked for their personal examples with regard to what they have learned for their work as well as how and why they have learned that. These examples were then analyzed for themes related to the content of learning, learning activities, and reasons for learning. Reported examples of learning content cover a diverse range of professional knowledge themes with a focus on knowledge of pedagogy and experience-based knowledge. Reported examples of learning activities concern mainly personal informal initiatives to learn; the teacher educators reported only a few examples of formal learning opportunities. Reported examples of reasons for learning range from personal interest to meeting job demands. These findings indicate that teacher educators' work is a profession with an own knowledge base, that it is important to value informal learning activities and to offer teacher educators the opportunity to decide to participate in formal learning activities. Teacher educators' intrinsic drive to learn appears to be inherent in their work with student teachers – seeing the value of their work.

Keywords

teacher educator – professional learning – interview study

© KONINKLIJKE BRILL NV, LEIDEN, 2020 | DOI: 10.1163/9789004432048_014

1   Introduction

Teacher educator professional learning is an emerging field of interest. Its significance is rather self-evident in discussions about the quality of the whole education system (Cochran-Smith, 2003) on the one hand, but the professionalism of teacher educators is lacking clarity (Buchberger, Campos, Kallos, & Stephenson, 2000) on the other. So, questions regarding who teacher educators are, what they do in their work as educators, and how they professionally learn are very relevant research questions (Berry, 2013; White, 2018).

In a previous study, we explored what constituted teacher educator professional learning by means of a literature review (Ping, Schellings, & Beijaard, 2018). In this review study, 75 research articles were reviewed resulting in a comprehensive list of main categories and subcategories regarding the content of teacher educators' learning, their learning activities, and their reasons for learning. It concluded that teacher educators' professional learning is rather diverse instead of being fixed. In a follow-up study, the main categories and the text fragments these categories were based on, were used to construct a digital questionnaire to confirm the professional learning topics found in the review study and to explore the extent to which teacher educators perceived the professional learning topics as relevant to their work in practice. The questionnaire resulted in nine professional learning topics which teacher educators perceived as highly relevant to their practice. A brief description of the nine professional learning topics is provided in the theoretical background section below. As a follow-up study of the literature-based questionnaire, the current study mainly aims at gaining a deeper understanding of teacher educators' professional learning by investigating their personal examples of learning.

TABLE 14.1   Foci and topics of the current study

Foci	Topics of professional learning
Content of professional learning	Pedagogy of teacher education
	Research
	Curriculum
Activities of professional learning	Learning through academic engagement
	Learning through reflective activity
	Learning through getting input from others
Reasons for professional learning	External requirement
	Personal ambition
	Professional role transition

2 Theoretical Background

The theoretical background of this study is based on our previous research results (Ping et al., 2018) with a focus on the content of teacher educators' professional learning, their learning activities, and their reasons for professional learning. Each focus appeared to consist of three professional learning topics (see Table 14.1).

2.1 Content of Professional Learning

Of the learning content, the topic "pedagogy of teacher education" refers to the professional knowledge of learning about teaching and teaching about teaching. Learning about teaching mainly relates to learning the knowledge and skills about how to teach and about how student teachers learn to teach. Learning about how to teach includes curriculum instruction, teaching strategies, and the integration of ICT into teaching practices (Jacobs, Assaf, & Lee, 2011). Learning about how student teachers learn to teach relates to the knowledge and skills needed for teaching learners and supporting their learning (Loughran, 2014). Teaching about teaching emphasizes on making pedagogical reasons or assumptions underlying teacher educators' own practices explicit and meaningful for themselves and their student teachers (e.g., Willemse & Boei, 2013). The topic "research" entails the knowledge and skills of doing research by teacher educators themselves. Research knowledge, for example, refers to methodological knowledge regarding methods and techniques for the collection and analysis of data (Kosnik et al., 2015). The skills of conducting research include skills like the development of a research design and the construction of research methods (Harrison & Mckeon, 2010). The "curriculum" as a topic deals with the knowledge and skills of designing a curriculum or modifying course modules to meet student teacher learning needs. It generally refers to the knowledge about the teacher education program and curriculum materials used within the program (Castle, 2013; Cheng, Tang, & Cheng, 2014).

2.2 Activities of Professional Learning

Of the learning activities, the topic "learning through academic engagement" contains research-related activities, including conducting academic/practitioner research and attending an academic conference. For example, Griffiths et al. (2010) found that teacher educators highly value conducting a PhD research project with formal supervisory support. Another example concerns teacher educators improving their practice by conducting practitioner research. Han et al. (2014) conducted a collaborative self-study in order to understand the concept of cultural responsiveness and to implement it in their teaching practices. The topic "learning through reflective activity" refers to teacher educators critically examining their own teaching practices or other relevant aspects of their work either individually or collaboratively. For example, White (2011) reflected on her teaching practice by successively reflecting on the theory implicit in her teaching, reflecting on the teaching process to see whether the implicit theory was clear for her student teachers, and reflecting on the comments or feedback from student teachers. "Getting input from others" as a topic pertains to teacher educators discussing the difficulties met in their teaching or exchanging ideas related to their work with significant others, usually their colleagues. Selkrig and Keamy (2015), for example, reported that teacher educators invited their trusted colleagues as critical friends to comment on their teaching, and through the conversations with their critical friends, they adjusted their teaching.

2.3   *Reasons for Professional Learning*

Of the reasons, the topic "personal ambition" includes teacher educators' personal interest in learning and professional responsibility of keeping on learning about their work. For example, Peeraer and Van Petegem (2012) found that teacher educators with a strong interest in learning ICT applied it into their lessons more frequently and in more diverse ways than other teacher educators who were in the same training program. The "external requirement" as a topic refers to updating knowledge or capacities due to the changes happening in teacher education policy/programs or as a result of assessments of research (and education) of the teacher education institute. For example, Jónsdóttir, Gísladóttir, and Guðjónsdóttir (2015) found that the extension of a teacher education program from a three-year bachelor to a five-year master program led to changes for teacher educators; as a consequence it was necessary for them to learn doing research and supervising student teachers doing research task. The "professional role transition" as a topic pertains to updating knowledge or developing skills due to the new demands after their role transition, such as from a secondary school teacher to a teacher educator in higher education. For example, Reichenberg et al. (2015) found that teacher educators, either having a school teaching background or a research background, hardly received professional training to learn to become a teacher educator. As a result, it took a while for teacher educators to learn the knowledge, develop the skills, and develop a professional identity as a teacher of teachers after having started to work as a teacher educator.

The above research findings gave us insights into what matters regarding what, how, and why teacher educators learn their work in general. In this study, we aim at gaining a deeper understanding of these three foci by asking teacher educators for their personal examples of what they have learned about their work, the learning activities they undertake for that, and their reasons for learning. The research question for this study is as follows: What do teacher educators' professional learning look like from their own examples of learning?

3   Method

3.1   *Participants*

Of the Dutch participants of the survey questionnaire (N = 218), 75 teacher educators volunteered to be interviewed. Of this group, 15 teacher educators were purposefully selected by two criteria: (1) having high mean scores on the questionnaire items of the content that they have learned and (2) having predominately defined themselves as a teacher of teachers. As such, we have selected teacher educators who, to a large extent, have learned about their work in a more diverse way. Four teacher educators could not be interviewed because of their lack of time. Eleven teacher educators agreed to participate in the interview study and gave informed consent. Table 14.2 displays an overview of the participants' general background information. Seven female and four male teacher educators participated in our study. Their ages ranged from 35 to 55 years old and their working experiences as a teacher educator ranged from 7 to 20 years. Nine interviewees worked as subject teacher educators (e.g.,

TABLE 14.2   Background information of the eleven teacher educators

Gender	Type of institute	Subject they teach	Working experience as a teacher educator
Female	RU	Chemistry didactics	7 years
Female	UAS	Geography didactics	7 years
Female	UAS	Research skills	8 years
Male	Both	History didactics	10 years
Male	UAS	Physics didactics	10 years
Female	RU	English didactics	13 years
Male	UAS	Chemistry didactics	16 years
Female	Both	Biology didactics	17 years
Female	RU	General pedagogy	18 years
Male	UAS	Philosophy didactics	20 years
Female	RU	Chemistry didactics	20 years

Note: RU = Research University; UAS = University of Applied Science; Both = Research University and University of Applied Science physics), one as a general pedagogy teacher educator, and one as a teacher educator teaching research skills to student teachers. Five of them worked in a research university, four in a university of applied science, and two in both types of universities. In the Netherlands, in general, a research university offers teacher education programs for upper secondary education, and a university of applied science provides educational programs for primary and lower secondary and vocational education (Snoek, 2011).

Six participants followed a path to become a teacher educator in higher education that used to be common in the Netherlands: as experienced school teachers they left their schools and began to work as a teacher educator. Three participants followed another path: they reached a PhD degree in their subject and entered the profession as a teacher educator. The remaining two had a different career before they became a teacher educator, one worked in a company doing chemistry research and the other worked as a nurse. Our participants' main tasks covered a wide range: seven participants were mainly involved in teaching student teachers subject didactics, five in supervising student teachers during their internships, four in conducting research projects, and one mainly as a course director of the professional master programs – *learning and innovation*.

3.2   *Data Collection*

A semi-structured interview was constructed including three main sections: (1) questions about background information of the participants, for example, how they had become a teacher educator; (2) questions about their main tasks as teacher educator in their current institute; and (3) questions about personal examples of their professional learning pertaining to what they learned, how they learned, and why they learned. The interview questions were open-ended to elicit teacher educators' personal examples. For example, with regard to what they had learned, we asked: "could you please give some examples of what you have learned during your work as a teacher educator?" After our participants have given their answers, we usually summarized their answers in order to check whether we understood these correctly. We also asked follow-up questions to know more about the examples given or to ask for more examples regarding what they have learned. In the same way we asked for their personal examples of how and why they have learned during their work as a teacher educator. A try-out interview with a teacher educator took place to check whether the interview questions were understandable and would result in elaborate answers, and also to test the duration of the interview. This only resulted in some reformulations of the wording of the questions.

Eleven interviews were conducted in a face-to-face form in English by the first author at the interviewees' workplace. All interviews were audio recorded and transcribed. On average, the interview lasted about 45 minutes ranging from 20 to 65 minutes and took place from October to December 2018.

3.3   Data Analysis

The data analysis consisted of the three steps described below.

Step 1: Summarizing interview transcriptions and displaying summaries into a matrix

For each interview question, participants' answers were summarized. For example, one participant's answer about what she had learned was:

> I think what adds to my professional learning is that I started thinking and paying more attention to the rationale behind my teaching. When I was teaching in secondary school, I did a lot of things because I know it worked well based on my past teaching experiences. But now I give more thorough thinking to the theory behind my teaching and try to explain it clearly to my student teachers.

The first author summarized this piece of interview transcription as "focusing on the why behind teaching". A matrix was designed to display summaries per teacher educator systematically. In this matrix, the row represented summaries of participants' answers to each interview question, and the column represented the teacher educators. The matrix thus provided a concise overview of summaries from eleven teacher educators' answers to interview questions, regarding examples of learning content, examples of learning activities, and examples of reasons for learning. Representative quotes were added to the summaries. This process took place in close consultation with the other two authors.

Step 2: Labelling summaries and combing labels into themes

A label was assigned to each summary in the matrix. A label represented the meaning of a summary. All labels with similar meanings were combined into one theme. The following is an example to illustrate Step 2. It is an example of one teacher educator's answers to the interview question about how she has learned about her work. Her answers were summarized into two phrases: "learning from supervising teachers' research project" and "learning by experimenting new insights into my teaching". A label of "learning from doing tasks" was given to the summary of "learning from supervising teachers' research project"; a label of "learning from personal experiment" was given to the summary of "learning by experimenting new insights into my teaching". Thereafter, the two labels were combined into the theme "practicing and testing".

Step 3: Checking the accuracy of the data analysis

To ensure the accuracy of the analysis of the data, an external researcher, a colleague of the authors though with different research expertise, was invited to check the data analysis procedure. We sent her a file including data summaries, labels, themes, and the representative quotes belonging to the summaries. Based on her readings of the materials, she concluded that the data analysis procedure, in general, has been adequate, but she commented on the similarity between the themes in the focus of learning content. We decided to reorganize those themes in order to make them more distinguishable based on her suggestions. The following example illustrates the adjustments made in the themes: the label "pedagogy knowledge" was originally put under the theme "subject matter knowledge", but has been valued as one separate theme of learning content after a discussion with the two other authors. A report including the file that we sent to the external researcher and adjustments in themes can be requested from the first author.

4   Results

The main results are displayed in Tables 14.3–14.5, each consisting of themes and descriptions of the themes, followed by representative quotes. Below each table, the themes are explained more in-depth.

4.1   *Content of What Teacher Educators Learn*

The eight learning themes and their descriptions in Table 14.3 show a wide range of what teacher educators learn during their work. The learning themes represent knowledge areas which were seen by them as important to learn about their work. As shown by Table 14.3, most examples they gave pertain to the pedagogy knowledge and the knowledge gained from their own teaching experiences as a teacher educator.

The theme "subject knowledge" refers to content knowledge of subjects such as physics. Our participants expressed that they were well-prepared for the content knowledge of their subject, and now as a subject teacher educator, they consider subject knowledge as important to keep updated with. For example, one participant explained:

TABLE 14.3   Themes of professional learning content

Theme	Descriptions of themes	Examples of quotes
Subject knowledge	The knowledge of the subject matter that student teachers will teach in secondary schools.	"I learned the chemistry content knowledge".
Pedagogy knowledge	Three kinds of knowledge that are all pedagogical in nature. One is general educational knowledge, like educational psychology theories. One is PCK, the didactic knowledge of making subject matter teachable. The last one is knowledge about the schools, e.g., school development and what happens in schools.	"I learned about educational psychology". "I started to learn more subject specific didactics about what it means to teach chemistry". "I learned a lot about how teaching at schools actually looks like. Students at schools differ a lot, how students behave differ a lot, and teaching in a real classroom is always more complex than in theory. It is nice to have both a theoretical and a practical view of how teaching takes place at school".
Student teacher learning	The knowledge about how student teachers learn, including their learning needs and development level.	"I always keep in mind what student teachers need to learn". "As a teacher educator, I gradually noticed that it is important to make my student teachers see the connection from the beginning of their study to the moment that they can graduate and become a teacher at school. Usually, student teachers spend about one and a half years of learning in this institute, and my job is to help them make that connection".

(cont.)

TABLE 14.3   Themes of professional learning content (*cont.*)

Theme	Descriptions of themes	Examples of quotes
Experience based knowledge	The knowledge that they learn from their own teaching experiences and observations. It mainly refers to the practical knowledge of teaching PCK, including the changes in their focus of teaching, linking theory and practice, and the role modeling capacity. It furthermore includes the pedagogical instrumental skills of planning and preparation of courses, designing instructional programs, and assessing student teacher learning.	"My didactics has changed from that I am the one who knows and tells a lot about chemistry as I did in the school beforehand, to that student teachers are active adult learners and we are going to work together". "When I started working here as a teacher educator, I focused on telling my own experiences that worked well in my teaching and explained it in a certain way. But now I could explain my teaching in-depth, more explicit, and richer in helping my student teachers make choices in their teaching. So, I could bring more knowledge from theory into my explanation of teaching". "I firmly believe that how I behave as a professional teacher educator also reflects on student teachers who should become a professional teacher. I want to be transparent in that". "I learn to internalize the general goals of our teacher education program into my own course". "I learn to do more formative assessment in my teaching, like asking and giving more feedback to my student teachers".

(*cont.*)

TABLE 14.3   Themes of professional learning content (*cont.*)

Theme	Descriptions of themes	Examples of quotes
Coaching	The knowledge and capacity of supporting student teachers to reflect on the issues they meet in their internship and invoke them to think deeply about what it means to develop their identity as a teacher.	"As a supervisor, I learn to be open-minded, willing to listen to student teachers' concerns, and being adaptive to student teachers' learning needs".
Research	The knowledge and skills of how to do research, for example regarding research methods.	"I really learned the skill to observe and apply it to my teaching now. When I give courses to my student teachers, I always combine observing what they do with what they say instead of only focusing on what they say".
Management and leadership	Taking the leadership in developing, implementing, and evaluating teacher education programs for the institute.	"I have been working in this institute for 18 years as a teacher educator. It becomes quite normal for me to develop into an expert in my field. And now I get more opportunity to do management tasks than teaching. For example, I am taking the responsibility of developing a new curriculum for our institute".
Professional identity	Developing a professional role as a teacher of teachers.	"I realized that I am here not just like a biology teacher, instead, I am getting into the role of a teacher of teachers".

Learning chemistry content knowledge is such a small part in my learning, because I think I have already acquired sufficient chemistry knowledge. However, I still keep updated with the chemistry content knowledge, when it relates to the new developments in chemistry subject happening in the school context.

The theme "pedagogy knowledge" relates to our participants' learning of pedagogical aspects. Under this theme, teacher educators particularly refer to three kinds of knowledge they have learned: (1) learning general education knowledge, (2) subject didactic knowledge (PCK), and knowledge about schools, although this latter was not often reported by the participants. With regard to general knowledge about learning and teaching, for example, one participant reported that he learned more about educational psychology at the beginning of his career as a teacher educator. Being educated as a historian, he was not aware of the relevance of the teacher-student relationships as well as how to motivate student teachers' learning. Taking another example, a chemistry teacher educator learned a lot about conceptual change theory in his educational master study, and now he uses it when he prepares and teaches his courses. The didactic knowledge of how to teach a certain subject to student teachers was reported by many participants as part of their main expertise they did not gain before working as a teacher educator. It seems as it takes some time for teacher educators to become capable of teaching subject didactics. For example, a physics teacher educator talked about his struggle in teaching subject didactic especially at the beginning of his career:

> As a teacher educator, I always remind myself that it is not enough to only teaching the subject, I also need teaching student teachers how to teach that subject. In the beginning, I found it extremely hard to combine these two in my teaching, because it was already hard enough to get student teachers to the subject content. And then when my experiences grow, it becomes a little bit easier to take the teaching of that subject into account. Also because I read more literature and I become more aware of the part where student teachers experience difficulty in their learning. It gets slightly easier for me to integrate or at least to make connections between teaching subject content and subject didactic". Another participant expressed that learning subject didactics for her is more about learning what it means to teach chemistry. The knowledge about schools is added to this theme. Our participants implied that keeping updated with what happens at secondary schools helps them to make a connection between theory and practice. For example, one geography teacher educator said: "I kept my network with geography teachers from different secondary schools. I have learned a lot about the current things happening at schools, the kind of issues these teachers encountered at schools. In this way, I shared this practical knowledge about schools with my student teachers and it helped my teaching to be more relevant to student teachers' learning.

The theme "student teacher learning" refers to the knowledge about understanding student teachers' learning needs as well as their student teachers' development level. For example, one participant indicated her knowledge changed from focusing on what she could teach to what student teachers need to learn. "*Now I transferred my focus in teaching into what student teachers need to learn and what is the most effective way for them to learn*". Another participant reported that he became more aware of the importance of making student teachers being active learners.

> I want to make my student teachers curious about learning. I think it is important in my teaching to make my student teachers to know their own development level. For example, they should learn to know in what they are good and in what they are not, how to take these consideration into account in order to develop a lifelong learner.

The theme "experience based knowledge" refers to the knowledge about teaching in practice. Our participants expressed much about the changes that occurred in their teaching as a result of their growing teaching experiences, which we mention here as their practical knowledge. The first kind of practical knowledge they expressed is about the change in their focus in their teaching: from teacher-centered to student-centered teaching. For example, one participant reported her change in teaching, namely transferring responsibility to student teachers, as follows:

> In my didactic teaching part, student teachers practice a lot instead of me as a teacher educator who tells them what to do. For example, I am now teaching a didactic subject about collaborative learning. I make my student teachers think about what is important in their classroom teaching, and how and why they should make groups of pupils in one classroom ... And in the end, they make their own lessons, perform, and explain those lessons.

The second kind of practical knowledge is about the change in which our participants paid more attention to the theory behind their teaching and started searching theory or empirical evidence to support their teaching. For example, one participant depicted her knowledge change as follows:

> When I taught in secondary school, I did many things because I knew it worked well based on my experiences. Now as a teacher educator, I think more about the theory behind my teaching to connect theory with

practice. I also try to explain that theory clearly to my student teachers in my teaching.

The third kind of practical knowledge pertains to the role of modeling in teaching. Many participants indicated that it takes a while for them to give attention to the double layers in their teaching, i.e., role modeling how to teach while they are teaching. For example, one participant reported that she became more purposeful in role modeling:

> Being a teacher educator, I gradually realize that student teachers are looking at me how I instruct them and what kind of assignments I give them. So, I firmly believe that how I behave as a professional teacher educator also influences student teachers who learn to become a professional teacher.

All the above examples concern changes directly relating to teaching, but they mentioned also changes in their course preparation and the assessment of student teachers' learning. For example, one teacher educator said: "I paid attention to the curriculum issues more broadly. In preparing my lessons, I am not only considering the goal of my own lesson, but also thinking about what my other colleagues' goals of their subject teaching are". Another participant said: "I learned many things about how to assess student teachers' learning, for example not only about making good questions but also considering the rationale behind the assessment".

The theme "coaching" pertains to providing guidance to student teachers, especially when they meet difficulties. One participant has been involved in coaching student teachers for many years, and she said that there are always some tensions in student teachers' learning to teach. She gave one example concerning student teachers' dilemmas in learning to teach.

> My student teachers are very smart students in their subject study. If they study hard in one subject, they get a good score at the end of the term. When they come here to learn to become a teacher, everything changes fundamentally. They study hard, but sometimes it does not guarantee that they can become good teachers when they go to the real classroom during internships. Sometimes, they can be very emotional.

As a teacher educator, her task is not so much giving hands-on solutions, instead, it has to be more about guiding student teachers to reflect on the tensions they meet and help them to analyze these and move forward by themselves. For example, she described what she tried to do in supervision meetings:

> In classes, we often have reflection exercises in a group. I try to engage my student teachers in conversations about what it means for them to be a teacher. What they need to become a better teacher. I also provide them with the theory and ask them what they could use. I would like to discuss different learning styles with them.

The theme "research" refers to the knowledge and skills of doing research. Participants' answers implied that conducting research is helpful to their professionalization when it closely relates to their daily practice. For example, one participant benefited from doing her PhD research and said:

> I really learned the skill to observe and apply it to my teaching now. When I give courses to my student teachers, I always combine observing what they do with what they say instead of only focusing on what they say.

The theme "management and leadership" refers to teacher educators taking a leadership role in developing a new curriculum or managing some tasks for the institute. For example, one teacher educator said: "I am responsible for leading a master physics program in my institute. It involves many organization tasks, for example, making sure that teacher educators are responsible for different courses".

The theme "professional identity" was not so often referred to by the participants. For example, one teacher educator indicated the change in how she saw herself as a teacher educator:

> Gradually I know the difference between being a teacher and being a teacher of teachers. I am aware that I am a role model for student teachers, I have to explain and explicate the theory behind my teaching practice to them.

4.2   Activities of How Teacher Educators Learn

Formal and informal learning activities can be distinguished; where formal learning activities are systematically organized with more or less structured support, informal learning activities are not. As Table 14.4 indicates, teacher educators undertake more types of informal learning activities than formal ones.

TABLE 14.4   Themes of professional learning activities

Theme	Examples of quotes	
Informal activity	Informal learning activities are based on teacher educators' personal initiatives. Learning activities that could be distinguished pertain to: learning from practicing and testing, learning from interacting and discussing with others, learning from reading sources, learning from reflective activity, and learning from encountering difficulties, dilemmas, and mistakes that happened in their practice.	"I have learned by doing, by teaching different groups of student teachers with different experiences". "When I encountered difficulty in practice, I discussed it with colleagues to see how they deal with it if they were in the same situation. So I learned a lot from colleagues who were more experienced in it than me". "I purposely read a lot, for example, a theory about curriculum development. Because I think it is important for a teacher educator to know something about curriculum development or curriculum design". "After each course I give, I reflect on what should I learn and what is a more effective way of teaching. If I am happy with my teaching, then I just keep it. But if I am not really happy with that and I think it could change and be more effective next time ... I always make notes and next time I know that I am going to change that part". "I am learning from making mistakes and failure".

(*cont.*)

TABLE 14.4   Themes of professional learning activities (*cont.*)

Theme	Examples of quotes	
Formal activity	The formal activities include well-organized programs like professional development programs and doing a study in the field of education, or by pursuing a PhD study in subject-specific didactics.	"I took a course in video interaction. It is quite an extensive course in guiding you how to use videos and images to have a reflection exercise with your student teachers". "At this moment, I really learn a lot by doing my PhD research".

The theme "informal activities" include many types of activities which teacher educators engage in for solving a problem in their practice or gaining growth in their expertise.

The first type of informal activity that can be distinguished is practicing and testing. Our participants reported that they learned a lot from just doing tasks because they hardly received support from a formal preparation program to learn to be a teacher educator. For example, one participant reported that she learned much by coaching student teachers.

> Obviously I learned a lot by doing. When I started here as a teacher educator, I got the task of coaching student teachers. I had no experience with coaching and did not take a course in advance. So, I just have to do it and meanwhile, of course, I learned a lot from doing it.

Besides, participants reported that they learned much by experimenting, for example by purposefully experimenting with a new didactic method in their teaching. One participant had the habit of reflecting on the course she gave and made a note on the part that she wanted to change next time. When the new course came, she purposefully experimented in her course with the adjusted idea.

The second type of informal activity is interacting and discussing with others. Most participants reported that they frequently discussed the issues they met in their work or exchanged the information or ideas of the new development in the field with their colleagues. For example, one participant said that there is a formal meeting day in her institute to discuss certain topics with colleagues: "We have a fixed date where my colleagues and I sit together to discuss one specific aspect for our professionalization as teacher educators". Another participant said that it is very normal for him to talk with colleagues about the work, for example when there was a report coming he just read it and discussed it with colleagues. Our participants also indicated that they learned through receiving feedback from colleagues or from their student teachers. The feedback could be critical about aspects not having performed well but also rewarding aspects that are going well. For example, one participant learned from her colleague's feedback that her subject didactics is doing well.

> My colleague told me that he learned so much about teaching teachers from me. He observed what I did and how I approached the questions those student teachers asked and how I shaped the interaction with them. I am learning from the feedback that I am doing well in my teaching.

Collaborative working or joint work is seen as one valuable informal learning activity by our participants. For example, one experienced teacher educator valued that she learned much from writing a book together with experienced teacher educators at the beginning of her career. Another participant indicated that she learned a lot from preparing a course together with experienced teacher educators. Observing colleagues what they are doing also appears a valuable learning activity. For example, one participant reported that she learned a lot from observing colleagues what they did and how they interacted with student teachers.

The third type of informal learning activity is learning from reading. Our participants reported that they sometimes purposefully selected research articles or books to learn one specific area of knowledge or to solve one specific issue about their work. Sometimes it just happens that they read something that inspires them or relates to their work, for example, newsletters received from their workplace email. For instance, one participant always tries to make a connection between what she reads with her own work as a teacher educator: "When I read, I always have the question in my mind, like what is its relation to my work and how can I use it in my teaching?"

The fourth type of informal learning activity is learning from reflection which seems so much intertwined with our participants' work. They usually reflect after each course by considering what they are (not) satisfied with either on their way home or making notes on the parts (teaching) which need to be improved next time. Few of them also share their reflection on teaching with student teachers. For example, a teacher educator said:

> I always share my reflections with my student teachers. Like what my goals are for this lesson, how I try to achieve these goals, and why I think that I am doing it ok in this way instead of another way. How do you [student teachers] think about it?

The fifth type of informal learning activity is learning from encountering difficulties in practice, like learning from dilemmas, mistakes, and the discrepancies happening in their teaching. One participant, for instance, said to have learned much about effective teaching from experiencing tensions in her teaching.

> I met discrepancy in my teaching. On the one hand, student teachers want me as a teacher educator to tell them what they should do in the classroom so that it is a kind of guarantee that what I tell will always work for them in practice. On the other hand, I know that I cannot give them a one-size-fits-all method, because every school differs and the classroom varies as well. So how to balance and make my teaching more effective is still quite challenging.

The theme "formal activity" refers to structured programs with systematic support. Attending professional development programs, like taking a course or joining a workshop about one certain topic, is seen as an important way to learn by our participants. For example, participants reported that they followed a course about assessment to get a certification. "As a teacher educator in my institute, we all have to get a certification for how to make good exams organized by my institute".

Attending conferences is appreciated by our participants as an opportunity to enrich their network and to get new insights into one certain topic. This theme also refers to pursuing a formal study, namely learning with systematic guidance like a PhD study in a subject didactic area. For instance, one participant highly appreciated that he followed a Master study in educational sciences three years ago. He said that he did not receive sufficient educational training beforehand, so following this educational master study really gave him new insights. He was inspired by the knowledge he read from the books and the insights he got from the conversations with teachers and peers.

4.3   *Reasons Why Teacher Educators Learn*

The themes and their descriptions in Table 14.5 show that teacher educators' reasons for professional learning range from an internal drive for learning to an external drive through job inspiration and external requirements. Of these reasons, teacher educators' personal interests and their appreciation of the

TABLE 14.5   Themes of reasons for professional learning

Theme	Descriptions of themes	Examples of quotes
Individual reasons	These reasons pertain to the personal attitude and personal interest regarding learning.	"Learning and developing is important for me. I always want to do new things and I am very curious and eager to learn. I think it is my disposition to be curious about learning new things". "Learning is a sort of magical thing. It is fascinating and interesting. I want to learn more"
Reasons related to the job	These reasons refer to feeling professionally responsible for keeping on learning about the profession, the intrinsic reward of the work based on seeing the value or meaning of the work, and the demands and challenges required from the job.	"I teach my student teachers about what learning is and also instruct them how to learn. In order to do that, I should have experience of how I learn, and also keep on learning continuously about my profession". "I think for me that (professional learning) is the way to love my job". "Only 10% of the reasons come from the changes taking place in my work. Because something changes, I have to do something for it as a response".

value and the meaning of the job are more often referred to than the external job demands.

The theme "individual reasons" refers to teacher educators' personal attitude of why they find it important to keep on professional learning. One reason relates to their personal characteristics, like having a curious personality. For example, one participant said: "I would get bored if I do the same thing every day. I am always looking for the possibility of improving my current teaching becoming better and better, and I am eager to learn more about my profession". Another reason relates to their deep interest in learning. One participant, for instance, said: "I like learning. This is the reason why I like teacher education, because in the end it is about learning and developing".

Part of the theme "reasons related to the job" is that teacher educators are feeling responsible for learning about their work and also want to be a role model for their student teachers in this respect. For example, one participant expressed: "For me, being a professional teacher educator means keeping on learning. Because my student teachers learn from my teaching every day, and it is my responsibility to learn professionally and also model this for them". Another example is: "I commit to my work, so I take the responsibility of making it better myself. I am responsible for my own professional learning instead of what other people tell me to do or ask me to do". Another part of the reasons comes from the rewarding of teacher educators' work, namely that they love their work and would like to learn more about it. For example, one of the participants expressed: "I like my job very much. I have the idea that I can do it better and better". Few reasons come from their job demands, namely having to learn due to the requirements from their work. For example, one participant said: "Only 10% of the reasons come from the changes taking place in my work. Because something changes, I have to do something for it as a response".

5   Discussion

5.1   Discussion about Main Findings

In addition to the review and questionnaire studies, this study provides a deeper understanding of Dutch teacher educators' professional learning based on the concrete examples of their learning experiences in their own practices. Semi-structured interviews were conducted with eleven Dutch teacher educators about what they have learned for their work, their learning activities, and their reasons for learning. Eleven teacher educators' examples of their learning experiences directly showed the diversity in their professional learning and indirectly the multiple aspects of their work.

A wide range of learning themes, namely what teacher educators learn about their work could be identified in the interview data. It is noteworthy to state that although eight learning themes were identified, this does not necessarily mean that these themes were isolated from each other; on the contrary, some of them were interconnected. For example, the themes "pedagogy knowledge", "student teacher learning", and "experienced based knowledge" are related to each other. This supports our research result of the interconnectedness among professional learning topics in a previous study. Given that the interview study aimed at showing what teacher educators learn about their work, we decided to categorize learning themes as much as possible. The eight learning themes identified in this study (as well as those in our previous studies) can be seen as a contribution to substantiate the statement by Berry (2016) that teacher educators' work requires professional knowledge and to her plea to uncover the unique body of knowledge which comprises teacher educators' work (in a Dutch context) for more teacher educators. In this context Berry (2016, p. 46) wrote: "there is a pressing need for more teacher educators to recognize and know that a unique body of knowledge comprises their work and they can learn or develop such knowledge on the job". The eight learning themes in our study indicate multiple facets of teacher educators' work. This is, to some degree, in line with a review study conducted by Lunenberg, Dengerink, and Korthagen (2014), who identified six professional roles of teacher educators: teacher of teachers, coach, researcher, curriculum developer, gatekeeper, and broker. Five professional roles, except for the role of a broker, were represented by our participants' examples of learning content. The learning themes "pedagogy knowledge", "student teacher learning", "experienced based knowledge", and "subject knowledge" can be explicitly seen as belonging to the professional roles as distinguished by Lunenberg et al. This also counts for the learning theme "research" that links with the professional role of a researcher and the learning theme "coaching" that connects with the professional role as a coach. The professional role of a curriculum developer as distinguished by Lunenberg et al. connects with the learning theme "experience based knowledge" in our study, because this theme includes the knowledge and skills regarding the planning and preparation of courses and designing instructional programs. The professional role of a gatekeeper that Lunenberg et al. distinguish connects with the learning theme "student teacher learning", because this theme includes the understanding and taking into account of student teachers' development level as found in our study. The role of being a gatekeeper, namely, implies being responsible for admitting student teachers to the profession of teacher (Lunenebrg et al., 2014, p. 21). What teacher educators have learned about their work or the expertise they developed seem to depend on how they perceive their professional roles and tasks in their institute. For example, a teacher educator primarily responsible for teaching subject didactics emphasized at least to some extent other learning themes than a teacher educator who is responsible for supporting student teachers' internships and reflection on these. The different aspects of teacher educators' work that our study indicate may lead to the following question: how do teacher educators in the Dutch context perceive the multiple aspects of their work? Recent studies have shown that there are tensions between maintaining high-quality teaching and facing the increasing demand of conducting research, experienced by higher education teacher educators in diverse contexts (Smith & Flores, 2019). However, such tension might also imply that these different tasks complement each other. For example, a recent study by Maaranen, Kynäslahti, Byman,

Jyrhämä, and Sintonen (2019) showed that Finnish teacher educators see research as part of their teacher educator work, and being a researcher is a relevant part of their identity. Since we did not interview our participants about their perceptions of different working tasks, we do not yet know the answer to the above-mentioned question.

We categorized teacher educators' learning activities into a formal and informal theme. This categorization of learning activities did not necessarily mean that our participants only used single activities; instead, their reported learning activities consisted of a mix of activities. For example, the "reflective activity" is often followed by the learning activity "interacting and discussing with others". We found that the diversity and frequency of informal learning activities mentioned by our participants outweighed the formal ones (see Table 14.4). The eleven teacher educators' examples of learning activities in our study support the general conclusion from studies on workplace learning: a majority of professionals informally learn about their work in and from the workplace (Eraut, 2004; Tynjälä, 2008). A study conducted by Dengerink, Lunenberg, and Kools (2015) showed that teacher educators with seven or more years of working experiences prefer to learn in an informal way, such as discussing with colleagues; they feel less interested in participating in courses. This result may help us understand the informal learning activities frequently reported by teacher educators in our study. Of the informal learning activities, we found that our participants frequently mentioned "learning from practicing and testing" and "learning from interacting and discussing with others" as ways of how they learned about their work. This finding is in line with the result of another study by Van Eekelen, Boshuizen, and Vermunt (2005), in which they found that higher education teachers frequently reported learning by doing and learning in interaction as their learning activities. Similarly, another study into experienced teachers' learning activities also found "experimenting", "considering one's own teaching experience", "getting input from others", and "learning by doing" as the learning activities happening in their workplace (Hoekstra, Brekelmans, Beijaard, & Korthagen, 2009). These four types of learning activities also appeared in our study as teacher educators' learning activities. Of the formal learning activities found in our study, attending conferences and following professional development programs, for example, attending a workshop have been reported on most by the eleven participants. This result is similar with the result of a recent survey by Tank, Valcke, Rots, Struyven, and Vanderlinde (2018), who pointed to formal professional development activities for Flemish teacher educators generally organized as workshops on a voluntary basis. Besides the professional development programs, pursuing a Master or Doctoral study is another formal learning activity found in our study. These activities can be interpreted as research related learning activities. Research related activities are generally seen as important ways to improve teacher educators' professional development (Maaranen, Kynäslahti, Byman, Jyrhämä, & Sintonen, 2018). Among research related activities, especially self-study is widely seen as an important research activity which teacher educators use to improve their professional learning (e.g., Loughran & Berry, 2005; Zeichner, 2007). Self-study did not appear to be a professional learning activity for teacher educators in our interview. This finding confirms one result of our questionnaire study, namely that Dutch teacher educators score low on being involved in conducting self-study as their learning activity.

Our participants seemed to have a strong internal drive to learn by seeing the value of their work as an important reason for keeping on learning about their work. In general, adult learners are more motivated to learn by internal than external factors (Beavers, 2009). Their strong internal drive to learn could also be seen as triggered by what they do on a daily basis – supporting and working together with students who learn to become a teacher. They want their students to become good teachers, so they themselves also want to be seen as good teachers by their students. It is the responsibility inherent in their work with student teachers that obviously inspires them to learn. Our participants' strong professional responsibility is in line with a result from a study by Meeus, Cools, and Placklé (2018) who found that teacher educators' shared responsibility for the learning process of their student teachers is the key to learn in a community. If we look at the research field of workplace learning, one of the important factors influencing professionals to actively engage in learning in the workplace is to appreciate the value of their work together with feeling a commitment to learning (Eraut, 2004). This factor is also found in our study, namely teacher educators see the value of their work and feel a commitment to learning and making their work better. Eleven teacher educators indicated that personal professionalization, in their institutes, is compulsory, but they have the autonomy to decide about what and how of their own professional learning. This might explain why our participants have such a strong intrinsic drive for professional learning. Given that our participants were all experienced teacher educators, we wonder what beginning teacher educators' motivations are to becoming and being engaged in professional learning. Future research could address this question.

5.2   *Implications for Professional Learning*

In the introduction of this study, we mentioned the lack of clarity about what comprises teacher educators' profession. Our study, though being small-scaled, contributes to making this profession more visible by exemplifying what, how and why teacher educators learn during their work. Given the multiple facets of their work and the different ways in which they learn their profession, our study provides some suggestions for supporting their professional learning. Firstly, it would be useful to offer a wide range of professional learning topics, which could help teacher educators, especially beginning ones, to becoming and being aware of the diversity of topics relevant for their profession and assisting them to make their own choices regarding what they want or need to learn. Secondly, teacher education institutes need to explicitly value informal learning activities at the workplace, especially for experienced teacher educators, and provide the necessary support for that, for example by arranging a fixed time for them to talk with and learn from each other. At the same time, the variety of formal learning opportunities need to be provided as well, but not be in a compulsory way. Thirdly, it might be necessary for teacher education institutes to keep teacher educators intrinsically motivated to learn, namely by seeing the value of their work and feeling a commitment to learning.

5.3   *Limitations of the Study*

There are some limitations to take into account when interpreting the results of this study. Firstly, our participants might look biased: more subject teacher educators than general pedagogy teacher educators participated. We selected teacher educators based on their scores in our questionnaire study. Secondly, in our interview study only a small number of teacher educators participated. More participants could give more examples of their learning and therefore lead to stronger and more valid results. Thirdly, the interview data is self-reported. Future research can use observation methods to add more details next to what teacher educators report about their learning. Fourthly and lastly, there might be a cultural bias in the results because of the language and background of the first researcher, who used non-native language to interview Dutch teacher educators, which may have brought a language barrier in the interviews, and who analyzed the data through her own 'lens'. Nevertheless, the participants explained very specifically their examples whenever the researcher had any doubt or found something unclear in their answers.

6   Conclusions

Based on our research findings we formulate three conclusions. Firstly, through what teacher educators report they have learned about their work, it becomes clear that their work is a profession with its own knowledge base. Secondly, valuing informal learning activities at teacher educators' workplace, and providing them with the opportunity of deciding to participate in formal learning activities are both important to support their professional learning. Thirdly, it is inherent in teacher educators' work with student teachers that they are intrinsically motivated to learn about their work in practice. This seems to be a strong starting point for giving more structural attention to teacher educators' professional learning.

References

Beavers, A. (2009). Teachers as learners: Implications of adult education for professional development. *Journal of College Teaching and Learning, 6*(7), 25–30.

Berry, A. (2016). Teacher educators' professional learning: A necessary case of "on your own"? In B. De Wever, R. Vanderlinde, M. Tuytens, & A. Aelterman (Eds.), *Professional learning in education – Challenges for teacher educators, teachers and student teachers* (p. 229). Gent, Belgium: Academia Press.

Buchberger, F., Campos, B., Kallos, D., & Stevenson, J. (2000). *Green paper on teacher education in Europe: High quality teacher education for high quality education and training*. Umea University, Sweden: Thematic Network for Teacher Education in Europe (TNTEE).

Castle, K. (2013). The state of teacher research in early childhood teacher education. *Journal of Early Childhood Teacher Education, 34*(3), 268–286.

Cheng, M. M. H., Tang, S. Y., & Cheng, A. Y. N. (2014). Differences in pedagogical understanding among student-teachers in a four-year initial teacher education program. *Teachers and Teaching: Theory and Practice, 20*(2), 152–169.

Cochran-Smith, M. (2003). Learning and unlearning: The education of teacher educators. *Teaching and Teacher Education, 19*(1), 2–28.

Dengerink, J., Lununberg, M., & Kools, Q. (2015). What and how teacher educators prefer to learn. *Journal of Education for Teaching, 41*(1), 78–96.

Eraut, M. (2004). Informal learning in the workplace. *Studies in Continuing Education, 26*(2), 247–273.

Goodwin, A. L., Smith, L., Souto-Manning, M., Cheruvu, R., Tan, M. Y., Reed, R., & Taveras, L. (2014). What should teacher educators know and be able to do? Perspectives from practising teacher educators. *Journal of Teacher Education, 65*(4), 284–302.

Griffiths, V., Thompson, S., & Hryniewicz, L. (2010). Developing a research profile: Mentoring and support for teacher educators. *Professional Development in Education, 26*(1–2), 245–262.

Han, S. H., Vomvoridi-Ivanović, E., Jacobs, J., Karansha, Z., Lypka, A., Topdemir, C., & Feldman, A. (2014). Culturally responsive pedagogy in higher education: A collaborative self-study. *Studying Teacher Education, 10*(3), 290–312.

Harrison, J., Mckeon, F. (2010). Perceptions of beginning teacher educators of their development in research and scholarship: Identifying the "turning point" experiences. *Journal of Education for Teaching, 36*(1), 19–34.

Hoekstra, A., Brekelmans, M., Beijaard, D., & Korthagen, F. (2009). Experienced teachers' informal learning: Learning activities and changes in behavior and cognition. *Teaching and Teacher Education, 25*(5), 663–673.

Jacobs, J., Assaf, L. C., & Lee, K. S. (2011). Professional development for teacher educators: Conflicts between critical reflection and instructional-based strategies. *Professional Development in Education, 37*(4), 499–512.

Jónsdóttir, S., Gísladóttir, K. R., & Guðjónsdóttir, H. (2015). Using self-study to develop a third space for collaborative supervision of master's projects in teacher education. *Studying Teacher Education, 11*(1), 32–48.

Kosnik, C., Menna, L., Dharamshi, P., Miyata, C., Cleovoulou, Y., & Beck, C. (2015). Four spheres of knowledge required: An international study of the professional development of literacy/English teacher educators. *Journal of Education for Teaching, 41*(1), 52–77.

Loughran, J. (2014). Professionally developing as a teacher educator. *Journal of Teacher Education, 65*(4), 271–283.

Loughran, J., & Berry, A. (2005). Modelling by teacher educators. *Teaching and Teacher Education, 21*(2), 193–203.

Lunenberg, M. Dengerink, J., & Korthagen, F. (2014). *The professional teacher educator: Roles, behaviour, and professional development of teacher educators.* Rotterdam, The Netherlands: Sense Publishers.

Maaranen, K., Kynäslahti, h., Byman, R., Jyrhämä, R., & Sintonen, S. (2018). 'Do you mean besides researching and studying?' Finnish teacher educators' views on their professional development. *Professional Development in Education.*

Maaranen, K., Kynäslahti, h., Byman, R., Jyrhämä, R., & Sintonen, S. (2019). Teacher education matters: Finnish teacher educators' concerns, beliefs, and values. *European Journal of Teacher Education, 42*(2), 211–227.

Meeus, W., Cools, W., & Placklé, I. (2018). Teacher educators developing professional roles: Frictions between current and optimal practices. *European Journal of Teacher Education, 41*(1), 15–31.

Peeraer, J., & Van Petegem, P. (2012). The limits of programmed professional development on integration of information and communication technology in education. *Australasian Journal of Educational Technology, 28*(6), 1039–1056.

Ping, C., Schellings, G., & Beijaard, D. (2018). Teacher educators' professional learning: A literature review. *Teaching and Teacher Education, 75*, 93–104.

Reichenberg, R., Avissar, G., & Sagee, R. (2015). "I owe to my tutor much of my professional development": Looking at the benefits of tutoring as perceived by the tutees. *Professional Development in Education, 41*(1), 40–56.

Selkrig, M., & Keamy, K. (2015). Promoting a willingness to wonder: Moving from congenial to collegial conversations that encourage deep and critical reflection for teacher educators. *Teachers and Teaching, 21*(4), 421–436.

Smith, K. (2003). So, what about the professional development of teacher educators? *European Journal of Teacher Education, 26*(2), 201–215.

Smith, K., & Flores, M. A. (2019). Teacher educators as teachers and researchers [Editorial]. *European Journal of Teacher Education, 42*(4), 429–432.

Snoek, M. (2011). Teacher education in the Netherlands: Balancing between autonomous institutions and a steering government. In M. V. Zuljan & J. Vogrinc (Eds.), *European dimensions of teacher education: Similarities and differences* (pp. 53–82). Ljubljana: University of Ljubljana.

Tack, K., Valcke, M., Rots, I., Struyven, K., & Vanderlinde, R. (2018). Uncovering a hidden professional agenda for teacher educators: A mixed method study on Flemish teacher educators and their professional development. *European Journal of Teacher Education, 41*(1), 86–104.

Tynjälä, P. (2008). Perspectives into learning at the workplace. *Educational Research Review, 3*, 130–154.

Van der Klink, M., Kools, Q., Avissar, G., White, S., & Sakata, T. (2017). Professional development of teacher educators: What do they do? Findings from an explorative international study. *Professional Development in Education, 43*(2), 163–178.

Van Eekelen, I. M., Boshuizen, H. P. A., & Vermunt, J. D. (2005). Self-regulation in higher education teacher learning. *Higher education, 50*, 447–471.

Webster-Wright, A. (2009). Reframing professional development through understanding authentic professional learning. *Review of Educational Research, 79*(2), 702–739.

White, E. (2011). Working toward explicit modelling: Experiences of a new teacher educator. *Professional Development in Education, 37*(4), 483–497.

White, S. (2018). Teacher educators for new times? Redefining an important occupational group. *Journal of Education for Teaching, 45*(2), 200–213.

Willemse, T. M., & Boei, F. (2013). Teacher educators' research practices: An explorative study of teacher educators' perceptions on research. *Journal of Education for Teaching, 39*(4), 354–369.

Zeichner, K. (2007). Accumulating knowledge across self-studies in teacher education. *Journal of Teacher Education, 58*(1), 36–46.

CHAPTER 15

Exploring Teacher Educators' Professional Identity: The Role of Emotions and Teacher Educators' Professional Identity

Manpreet Kaur

Abstract

This research aimed to understand the emotional development of teacher educators and its influence on their professional identity, it is the report of an exploratory case study conducted on a sample of teacher educators in their initial years of profession. They were interviewed to reflect on emotional events of their classrooms and were asked how these emotions help in development of professional identity. The research question was how emotional events contribute in evolution of professional identity of teacher educators. Findings of this study might be used as a reference for a professional identity model that reflected the educators' understanding of self in relation to various emotional events. This study yielded four key signs of professional identity development: (a) identity beliefs, (b) emotional events and identity negotiation, (c) teachers' attributes and (d) adjustment. All participants stressed out that the role of emotional events is very important in developing professional identity. The study expounded that pleasing emotional events supported teacher educators' identities and unpleasing emotional events caused confrontation and modified their emerging identities.

Keywords

professional identity – teacher emotions – teacher educators

1 Introduction

Recent researches increasingly recognized the role executed by teacher educators in training of prospective teachers and this notion led to an important but emerging body of knowledge pool about the role of teacher educators.

© KONINKLIJKE BRILL NV, LEIDEN, 2020 | DOI: 10.1163/9789004432048_015

Development of professional identity and professional learning of teacher educators is not a sufficiently researched area and very less knowledge is available regarding the role of teacher educators and how & what needs to be done about their professional learning (Murray & Male, 2005; Loughran & Berry, 2005).

Ample research examining teacher's professional development and the factors associated with the evolution of teacher's professional identity of teacher is available but the quantum of research on identity issues of teacher educators who are the key actors in the area of quality education is relatively less. Teacher educators are a group of people "who provide instruction or give guidance and support to student teachers, and thus render a substantial contribution to the development of students into competent teachers" (Koster, Brekelmans, Korthagen, & Wubbels, 2005). According to Smith (2005), professional knowledge of teacher educator should ideally be more exhaustive, extensive and rich in terms of both specialized subject matter and knowledge of psychology, pedagogy and didactics. Teacher educators have to play a double role: as knowledge producer in education, producer of new techniques in learning and teaching, and to act as teacher of teachers. While educating teachers, they consciously as well as unconsciously act as a model in terms of teaching and value education (Loughran & Berry, 2005; Swennen, Jones, & Volman 2010). Thus, there is a need to define and to do extensive study on the professional identity of teacher educators in order to enhance the quality of teacher education in particular and education in general.

1.1   *Professional Identity*

Professional identity of teachers has developed as a specific field of research (Bullough, 1997; Knowels, 1992; Kompf, Bond, Dworet, & Boak, 1996). The notion of identity can be defined in many ways and it has also been expounded in various ways in teacher education. Some research studies found that the idea of professional identity is associated with teachers' images or concepts of self (Knowels, 1992; Nias, 1989) and it was asserted that these images or concepts of self firmly suggest the ways of teaching adopted by teachers, the ways they evolve and develop themselves as teachers, and adjust to developments in education.

Professional identity involves the process of interpretation and reinterpretation of experiences (Kerby, 1991) and is in line with the idea that teacher development is a continuous and lifelong learning process (Day, 1999; Graham & Young, 1998). The process of construction of professional identity includes answers to two basic questions "Who am I at this moment?" and "Who do I want to become?"

Klecka, Donovan, Venditti, and Short (2008) asserted that the identities of teachers, the identity of teacher educator is also structured with the help of various aspects or facets. Teacher educators are specialized professional group who maintain their own particular identity and professional development needs.

Teacher educators consist of a diversified group of learning professionals, occupied in diverse tasks, like teachers of teachers, coach, researcher, broker, gatekeeper, and curriculum framer (Lunenberg, Dengerink, & Korthagen, 2014). Therefore, the process involving the development of identity is far more complex in context of teacher educators. Murray and Male (2005) suggested that establishing a new professional identity of a teacher educator, experiencing challenges in different areas and becoming an active researcher takes two to three years.

1.2   *Teacher Emotions*

Teacher professional development research has been constantly focused on finding the rational factors (teacher skills, capacities and knowledge). But in the process of giving importance to these rational and basic facts, teacher emotions have been undermined and neglected to some extent (Crawford, 2011; Day, 2011; Hargreaves, 2001; Sutton & Wheatley, 2003) as a pertinent factor for teacher improvement and formation of identity initiatives.

Human emotions are mysterious phenomena in human psychology and that has puzzled many educationists for centuries. "Emotions are socially constructed, personally enacted ways of being that emerge from conscious and/ or unconscious judgments regarding perceived successes at attaining goals or maintaining standards or beliefs during transactions as part of socio-historical contexts" (Schutz, Hong, Cross, & Osbon , 2006, p. 344).

Recent researches on teacher emotions have gained focus since 1990's (Hargreaves, 1998; Marshak, 1996) and have garnered consideration in the last few years. These researches are inspired by factors like teacher behavior, teachers' teaching (Gong, Chai, Duan, Zhong, & Jiao, 2013; Trigweel, 2012), their professional identity (Lee, Huang, Law, & Wang, 2013), lives of teachers (Schutz, 2014; Taxer & Frenzel, 2015), pupil learning and behavior (Brackett, Floman, Achton-James, Cherkasskiy, & Salovey 2013; Jennings & Greenberg, 2009), and changes in education (Day, 2011) and these are influenced by teacher emotions (Becker, Goetz, Morger, & Ranellucci, 2014; Hagenauer & Volet, 2014). Teacher emotions include the dynamic mental state of a teacher self and respond to exterior stimuli to regulate emotions applying a synthesis approach. Emotions of teachers are not "internalized sensations that remain inert within the confines of their bodies but are integral to the ways in which they relate to and interact with their students, colleagues and parents" (Farouk, 2012, p. 491). Thus, emotions of teachers are dependent on the surrounding climate and have no individual existence independent of their climate, rather they comprise of interactions between person and environment (Schutz et al., 2006).

Understanding emotions gives educators an opportunity to educate teachers in such a manner that they do not just make a difference in their students' lives and their own lives but also improve their own effectiveness in teaching (Day, Sammons, Stobart, & Kington, 2007; Kelchtermans, 2005, 2011).

Bahia, Freire, Amaral, and Estrela (2013) asserted that emotions have potential to strengthen interpersonal relationships during classroom and broader contexts and create opportunities for teaching and learning in various situations.

Nias (1996) in his research findings suggested that teaching is not merely a technical job, but also involves an investment of the teacher's personal self in to his work. This comprises emotional events that give distinct information regarding an individual's developing identity commitments. It is a reciprocal relationship and not only the evolving identities of teachers influence emotions and actions but emotions and actions also have an influence on emergence and evolution of teacher's professional identity. Identity of teachers and their emotions are directly related through a process that is multidirectional, transactional and an ongoing process. When teachers undergo unpleasant emotions, they may challenge their own identities, which are related to personal beliefs and attitudes regarding teaching. Whereas pleasant emotional events point towards a confirmation of evolving identities (Cross & Hong, 2009), received identities (e.g. expectations regarding the role of teachers) may also have an impact on how forthcoming emotional feedback comes and is usually understood.

2   Research Aims

Although earlier research studies on teacher educators' professional identity provides a little about the role of emotions in evolution of their identities, this study is an effort to understand the connection between these two. Thus, the goal of this inquiry was to investigate pleasant and unpleasant emotional events in the beginning years of career of teacher educators and to examine how these emotional events help them in their professional identity development. Semi-structured open-ended interviews were conducted to ask educators to reveal emotional events and to understand the ways in which emotions contribute in emergence of identity processes. Zembylas (2003, p. 215) elucidated that teachers perceive these emotional events as lighthouse of their actual selves and these events become the fulcrums by which teachers commence reviewing and reconstructing their true self.

3 Method

This research used a qualitative method to explore the research question – how teacher educators in their induction year perceive emotional events in classroom and how these contribute in the evolution of their teacher identities.

3.1 *Participants*

Fifteen teacher educators in their induction year of profession working in seven different colleges of education of North India were the participants in this study. Their age ranged from 26 to 32 (average 29), including four males and eleven females. Data was collected using semi-structured interviews from novice teacher educators and interviews were continued around 45 to 60 min. In these interviews, teacher educators were inquired about pleasing and unpleasing emotional events of their induction year of career. For example, a teacher educator was asked to explain a recent incident when she was attentive towards her thoughts and emotions in the classroom, and 'how she thinks these emotional events affect her perception about herself as a teacher educator?' These interviews were intended to permit the educators to explain their past emotional experiences of the classroom and to deliberate on their feelings about how they feel as teacher educators and the role played by emotions in this situation.

3.2 *Data Analysis*

Participants' responses during interviews were recorded and assessed from two standpoints: within and across participants. The setup of the interview was semi-structured and helped comparing the responses of participants. Each participant was asked to discuss his/her emotional events (pleasant and unpleasant) during the classroom teaching and their responses to these events. In the second step, data were compared to the related studies on professional identity as well as teacher emotions. After several readings of the transcripts it was confirmed that the themes that emerged from the research reflected the overall setting (Groenewald, 2004; Le Compte & Preissle, 1993; Thompson, Locander, & Pollio 1989).

4   Results

The findings of the research provided a model of professional identity that suggested the educators' understanding and development of themselves in relation to different emotional events. This model comprises of four key indicators: (1) Identity beliefs, (2) Emotional events and identity negotiation, (3) Teachers' attributes and (4) Adjustment.

4.1   *Identity Beliefs*

Identity beliefs is a reference point used by teachers to define where they are now as compared to where they want to be. During the interviews, participants identified a variety of assertions that pointed towards some divergent expectations. For instance teacher educator 'A' (a 28-year-old female) exclaimed that: 'I never realized how difficult it is to be a teacher educator' suggesting that what she was experiencing was actually not what she expected. Teacher educator 'B' (a 26-year-old male) stated that: 'I know pedagogy but what is coming out is not matching what I need to do for them'.

In contrast, a few teacher educators expressed that perceived identity beliefs that were often not too far from what they experienced or how they expected to be in the classroom. For instance, Teacher educator 'C' (a 27-years-old female), stressed that she was not a 'conventional' teacher educator and she saw herself as 'enthusiastic and broad-minded'. She observed that students consider her as their 'friend' because she was 'so helpful'. In this example, her expectations helped her to emerge her identity as a good teacher educator. Teacher educator 'D' (a 26–year-old male) also saw himself as someone who is kind, not a dictator, and who tries to take feelings of his students into consideration.

Almost all participants passed through a struggle when they looked for techniques to reconcile incoming identity beliefs and expectations in actual teaching situation. Such matches and mismatches resulted in emotional events, which affect emerging identity and the emotional efforts of teacher educators associated with that identity beliefs.

4.2   *Emotional Events and Identity Negotiation*

Emotional event indicates to those emotions, which are triggered by some social interaction with teachers, students and administrators. Though not every emotional event has the potential stimulus to trigger the emerging identities of educators, there are instances when the significant emotional event appeared directly related to certain enduring identity negotiation. Participants said that these emotional events could be both unpleasant and pleasant. For instance, Teacher educator 'E' (a 26-year-old female) spoke about the 'pressure' she faced when she tried to capture the interest of every student in teaching. For teacher educator 'B' it was an overwhelming emotion to handle his 'challenging' class.

In contrast there are also some pleasant emotional events that may confirm some of educators' identities about themselves as teacher educators. In other classes of Teacher 'E' students were 'enthusiastic' and 'motivated'. Teacher educator 'F' (a 30-year-old male) stressed on the joy he experienced 'when students are really attentive and enthusiastic, it feels really good'. So, these emotional events either inclined to raise a question or confirmed educators' opinions of themselves as teacher educators.

4.3   Teachers' Attributes

The sample of the research showed varied attributes and claimed that both types of emotional events (pleasant and unpleasant) influenced teacher's attributes like flexibility, job satisfaction, awareness, understanding, enthusiasm, encouragement, and motivation.

Some participants reported that internal reasons (they are a bad/good teacher) and external reasons (they feel that they have no power over students) both are responsible for emotionally challenging events in teachers' life. External reasons appeared more prominent when they resulted into unpleasant events. For instance some teacher educators when asked about the struggle they faced indicated that students 'don't bother' and another teacher educator discussed conflicts experienced while trying to teach students who are 'not ready'. In such instances teachers feel unsatisfying emotional events in terms of reasons supposed to be outside of personal control (i.e. the problems lie in the environment, not within them) and influence their attributes.

However there were also instances where internal reasons are more prominent. For example, teacher educator 'G' (a 30-year-old male) talked about feeling frustrated and helpless as he said, ' don't know what to do to improve you'. He feels like is not doing a good job. Another educator 'H' (a 29-year-old female) believed that a teacher educator should be flexible and understanding. By endorsing these dispositions with the students, it invited experiences that challenged these beliefs leading her to question whether or not she should be harder with the students. She attributed failure to handle students due to lack of experiences. These educators were actively trying to better understand themselves, their control, and their role in teaching.

4.4   Adjustment

Teacher educators 'I' (28-year-old female) 'K' (26-year-old female) 'M' (32-year-old female) and 'O' (27-year-old female) also expressed that these emotional events offered valuable chances to learn what kind of modifications are needed to approach various situations and their perceptions regarding teaching. Most of the experiences focused on the management of classroom events.

Teacher educator 'J' (26-year-old female) was a very noteworthy example of a novice teacher educator who was thinking about questions like how to improve her identity as a teacher educator. She revealed a growing emotional conflict that compelled her to reflect on her identity as an educator. Her interactions with prospective teachers encouraged a profound feeling of empathy for problems of students and a desire to help them, but at the same time, it triggered a state of conflict with what meant to be a teacher educator of these prospective teachers. Teacher educator 'L' (a 29-year-old female) and 'N' (a 26-year-old female) revealed emotional struggle that forced them to reflect on their identity as teacher educator. They reported a deep conflict between an imaginary teacher identity and their survival teacher identity.

Teacher educator 'G' revealed that over the time his ideas of teaching and his beliefs about his capacity to be a good teacher were shaped by positive and negative experiences.

5   Discussion and Implications

Teacher educators identified emotional events as signs of evolving teacher identity and according to them the active process of construction and reconstruction of understanding of what is the meaning of a teacher educator is how one thoughtfully tackles the situations and product of some emotionally engaging events. Stress originated from the experience of lack of control, or perceptions that have a conflict with incoming expectations usually headed to evolution of identity (educators speculated what types of changes they required to cope or to create things differently during classroom teaching). Majority of participants expressed that the feelings of joy, happiness or satisfaction often complemented effective teaching occasions and they defined these occasions as when those students were fully engaged in the teaching learning process. In these instances, the positive emotions, which originate from the positive behavior of the students established the connotation of an 'effective' teacher, sometimes it is not dependent on their control on the situation. Teacher attributes and teacher adjustments both were also perceived in the processes of identity formation. Explanation of emotional events often headed to various struggles in the form of attribute development and possible adjustments.

Although these explanations seem to match with hypothesis of this study about the process of 'identity formation' for novice teacher educators (emotions, beliefs, attributes, adjustment), not every educator's reflections aligned this way, implying that these four qualities are multi-layered and have multi-directional connection. It may lead to the conclusion that evolving emotions have a greater role in stimulating future identity development processes. It is also found that the development of identity of teacher educators' comprises a more comprehensive area of experiences than what just occurs during the classroom teaching. The narrow view which states that only relevant teaching experiences and relationship with students play an important role in the life of a teacher, seems to oversee the wider contexts in teaching, which include relations with coworkers, teachers and policymakers to fulfill many externally imposed expectations. These may be the limitations of this study.

This research will add to existing body of literature that examines how teacher educators understand the importance of emotional events in shaping the teacher educators' identities. The research also suggests how emotional experiences conflicting with novice teacher educators' expectations trigger 'identity formation'. The study yielded a model including 'identity work' that involves (1) teacher identity beliefs, (2) pleasant and unpleasant emotional events, (3) teacher attributes and (4) adjustment. This model provides a reference for scholars to understand convergence and emergence of emotions and identity processes and also generates clues and ideas for future inquiry. The model points towards questions like: are emotional events the only source of identity adjustments? What is the role of pleasant and unpleasant emotional events in influencing identity-based attributes and adjustments?

This study also suggests ways for augmenting teacher education programs, particularly pre-service teacher training. The study highlights the importance of direct teaching experiences and emphasizes that prospective teacher educators should be made aware of the varied range of emotional struggles that they may encounter in classroom settings. The research suggests that they should regularly record diverse emotional experiences that they observe and undergo as student teachers. This could provide assistance to these educators with how to think and act through conflicting situations and emotional events of teaching.

References

Bahia, S., Freire, I., Amaral, A., & Estrela, M. T. (2013). The emotional dimension of teaching in a group of Portuguese teachers. *Teachers and Teaching: Theory and practice, 19*, 275–292.

Becker, E. S., Goetz, T., Morger, V., & Ranellucci, J. (2014). The importance of teachers' emotions and instructional behavior for their students' emotions – An experience sampling analysis. *Teaching and Teacher Education, 43*, 15–26.

Brackett, M. A., Floman, J. L., Ashton-James, C., Cherkasskiy, L., & Salovey, P. (2013). The influence of teacher emotion on grading practices: A preliminary look at the evaluation of student writing. *Teachers and Teaching: Theory and Practice, 19*(6), 634–646. http://dx.doi.org/10.1080/13540602.2013.827453

Bullough, R. V. (1997). Practicing theory and theorizing practice. In J. Loughran & T. Russell (Eds.), *Purpose, passion and pedagogy in teacher education* (pp. 13–31). London: The Falmer Press.

Crawford, M. (2011). Rationality and emotions. In C. Day & L. Chi-kin (Eds.), *New understandings of teacher education: Emotions and educational change.* LaVergne, TN: Springer.

Cross, D. I., & Hong, J. Y. (2009). Beliefs and professional identity: Critical constructs in examining the impact of reform on the emotional experiences of teachers. In P. A. Schutz & M. Zembylas (Eds.), *Advances in teacher emotion research: The impact on teachers' lives* (pp. 273–296). New York, NY: Springer.

Day, C. (1999). *Developing teachers, the challenge of lifelong learning.* London: The Falmer Press.

Day, C. (2011). *New understandings of teachers work: Emotions and educational change.* New York, NY: Springer.

Day, C., Sammons, P., Stobart, G., & Kington, A. (2007). Variations in the work and lives of teachers: Relative and relationship effectiveness. *Teachers and Teaching: Theory and Practice, 12*(2), 169e192.

Farouk, S. (2012). What can the self-conscious emotion of guilt tell us about primary school teachers' moral purpose and the relationships they have with their pupils? *Teachers and Teaching: Theory and Practice, 18*(4), 491–507.

Gong, S., Chai, X., Duan, T., Zhong, L., & Jiao, Y. (2013). Chinese teachers' emotion regulation goals and strategies. *Psychology, 4*(11), 870e877. http://dx.doi.org/10.4236/psych.2013.411125

Graham, R., & Young, J. (1998), Curriculum, identity and experience in multicultural education. *The Alberta Journal of educational Research, 44*(4), 397–407.

Groenewald, T. (2004). A phenomenological research design illustrated. Article 4. *International Journal of Qualitative Methods, 3*, 42–55.

Hagenauer, G., & Volet, S. E. (2014). "I don't hide my feelings, even though I try to": Insight into teacher educator emotion display. *Australian Educational Researcher, 41*, 261e281. http://dx.doi.org/10.1007/s13384-013-0129-5

Hargreaves, A. (1998). The emotional politics of teaching and teacher development: With implications for educational leadership. *International Journal of Leadership Education, 1*, 315–336.

Hargreaves, A. (2001). Emotional geographies of teaching. *Teachers College Record, 103*(6), 1056–1080.

Jennings, P. A., & Greenberg, M. T. (2009). The prosocial classroom: Teacher social and emotional competence in relation to student and classroom outcomes. *Review of Educational Research, 79*(1), 491–525. http://dx.doi.org/10.3102/0034654308325693

Kelchtermans, G. (2005). Teachers' emotions in educational reforms: Self-understanding, vulnerable commitment and micro political literacy. *Teaching and Teacher Education, 21,* 995–1006.

Kelchtermans, G. (2011). Vulnerability in teaching: The moral and political roots of structural conditions. In C. Day & J. C. K. Lee (Eds.), *New understanding of teacher's work: Emotions and educational change* (pp. 65e84). New York, NY: Springer.

Kerby, A. (1991). *Narrative and the self.* Bloomington, IN: Indiana University Press.

Klecka, C., Donovan, L., Venditti, K., & Short, B. (2008). Who is a teacher educator? Enactment of teacher educator identity through electronic portfolio development. *Action in Teacher Education, 29*(4), 83–91.

Knowles, G. J. (1992). Models for understanding pre-service and beginning teachers' biographies: Illustrations from case studies. In I. F. Goodson (Ed.), *Studying teachers' lives* (pp. 99–152). London: Routledge.

Kompf, M., Bond, W. R., Dworet, D., & Boak, R. T. (Eds.). (1996). *Changing research and practice: Teachers' professionalism, identities and knowledge.* London: The Falmer Press.

Koster, B., Brekelmans, M., Korthagen, F. A. J., & Wubbels, T. (2005). Quality requirements for teacher educators. *Teaching and Teacher Education, 21*(2), 157–176.

LeCompte, M. D., & Preissle, J. (1993). *Analysis and interpretation of qualitative data. Ethnography and qualitative design in educational research.* New York, NY: Academic Press.

Lee, J. C. K., Huang, Y. X. H., Law, E. H. F., & Wang, M. H. (2013). Professional identities and emotions of teachers in the context of curriculum reform: A Chinese perspective. *Asia-Pacific Journal of Teacher Education, 41*(3), 271–287.

Loughran, J., & Berry, A. (2005) Modelling by teacher educators, *Teaching and Teacher Education, 21*(2), 193–203.

Lunenberg, M., Dengerink, J., & Korthagen, F. (2014). *The professional teacher educator roles, behavior, and professional development of teacher educators.* Rotterdam, The Netherlands: Sense Publishers.

Marshak, D. (1996). The emotional experience of school change: Resistance, loss, and grief. *NASSP Bulletin, 80*(577), 72–77.

Murray, J., & Male, T. (2005) Becoming a teacher educator: Evidence from the field. *Teaching and Teacher Education, 21*(2), 125–142.

Nias, J. (1989). Teaching and the self. In M. L. Holly & C. S. McLoughlin (Eds.), *Perspective on teacher professional development* (pp. 151–171). London: The Falmer Press.

Nias, J. (1996). Thinking about feeling: The emotions in teaching. *Cambridge Journal of Education, 26,* 293–306.

Schutz, P. A. (2014). Inquiry on teachers' emotion. *Educational Psychologist, 49*(1), 1–12. http://dx.doi.org/10.1080/00461520.2013.864955

Schutz, P. A., Hong, J. Y., Cross, D. I., & Osbon, J. N. (2006). Reflections on investigating emotion in educational activity settings. *Educational Psychology Review, 18*(4), 343–360.

Smith, K. (2005). Teacher educators' expertise: What do novice teachers and teacher educators say? *Teaching and Teacher Education, 21*(2), 177–192.

Sutton, R. E., & Wheatley, K. F. (2003). Teachers' emotions and teaching: A review of the literature and directions for future research. *Educational Psychology Review, 15,* 327–358.

Swennen, A., Jones, K., & Volman, M. (2010). Teacher educators: Their identities, sub-identities and implications for professional development. *Professional Development in Education, 36*(1–2), 131–148.

Taxer, J. L., & Frenzel, A. C. (2015). Facets of teachers' emotional lives: A quantitative investigation of teachers' genuine, faked, and hidden emotions. *Teaching and Teacher Education, 49,* 78–88.

Thompson, C. J., Locander, W. B., & Pollio, H. R. (1989). Putting consumer experience back into consumer research: The philosophy and method of existential-phenomenology. *Journal of Consumer Research, 16,* 133–146.

Trigweel, K. (2012). Relations between teachers' emotions in teaching and their approaches to teaching in higher education. *Instructional Science, 40,* 607e621. http://dx.doi.org/10.1007/s11251-011-9192-3

Zembylas, M. (2003). Emotions and teacher identity: A poststructural perspective. *Teachers and Teaching, 9,* 213–238.

CHAPTER 16

Teaching Philosophy of Education to Undergraduates in the Deep Amazon

Ana Flávia Souza Aguiar

Abstract

This chapter looks at the experience of developing and teaching a course on philosophy of education to student teachers in Ipixuna, a city located in the heart of the Amazon rainforest, isolated between the limits of the Brazilian states of Acre and Amazonas. The discipline was part of a geography undergraduate program that focused specifically on the training of local people to become high school teachers. The city is located by the Jurua river, with an area of around 14,000 square km and a small population of around 28,000 people, according to the Brazilian Institute of Geography and Statistics. The first residents of the area established themselves during the Amazon rubber boom in the late nineteenth century and early twentieth century. The majority of the residences are located in the rural portion of the territory, around 63%. These communities are poor with people living in precarious situations: the city lacks basic infrastructure conditions and access to goods and services. The Amazonas State University started to offer training programs for teachers in 2018. This was the first time that local people had access to higher education studies in their hometown. Ipixuna has two high schools, none of which have licensed philosophy teachers. So this was also the first time students got in touch with someone who had academically studied philosophy. Here, I use the work of Paulo Freire and Stephen Brookfield to understand the emancipator power of education for both teacher and students considering the reality and the conditions of this territory.

Keywords

philosophy of education – early career – emancipator education

1   Introduction

This chapter aims to reflect on my experience as an early career teacher, teaching the subject philosophy of education to undergraduates in the city of Ipixuna, Amazonas, Brazil. In order to better comprehend and reflect upon my teaching experience in the isolated city of Ipixuna I turned to Paulo Freire's and Stephen Brookfield's concepts. Initially, I'll give a historical and geographical context of Ipixuna, and then briefly explain how the undergraduate course for future geography teachers offered by the Amazonas State University was structured. Next, I'll describe my perception on developing and teaching the course. After the experience, I reflected on some of Paulo Freire's and Stephen Brookfield's concepts to help me better comprehend the insecurities and feeling of failure that followed teaching the course in Ipixuna.

2   The City of Ipixuna

Ipixuna is a small town located by the Juruá River, it has around 28,000 people according to the 2010 Brazil's census. Poor people coming from Brazil's northeast originally set a camp in the area due to the rubber boom that stimulated economy and generated informal jobs. The first Amazon rubber boom dated from 1879 to 1912, and later from 1942 to 1945 there was another boost due to the Second World War. After the boosts, the rubber industry barons who explored the region left migrant workers behind to share the area with indigenous people that still visit the city. The rubber economy did not develop the region in any way. Ipixuna exists officially as an independent city since 1955; its human development index (HDI) is 0.481, which is considered to be very low. Brazil's HDI is 0.759. Due to its extended area, the city has a 1.85 average of habitant/km². The rural area of Ipixuna consists mainly of old rubber tree plantations.

In the second semester of 2018 the Amazonas State University began offering in Ipixuna 3 undergraduate courses focused on teachers' formation: geography, biology and math. The objective is to train people in the region so they're able to teach in their own local schools and region, which severely lacks teaching staff in all areas of knowledge. One of the students in my class had been a geography teacher for 8 years without any qualification to do so, which is common in the deep Amazon. Even though she was a teacher she had little domain of the formal written Portuguese language, as the majority of students did. They committed serious errors in writing activities, some of them even appeared to be functionally illiterates.

3 The Course

This was a geography undergraduate course coordinated by the Amazonas State University. High quality higher education in Brazil is public. It is accessible to all those who are interested and score well on a test. The results are ranked and the openings are filled with the best scoring students. This way, students who attend good schools are better prepared, which is why, recently, we have racial and social quotas on behalf of diversity and democratic access to public education. Public higher education in Brazil is also entirely free. Students have to afford their transportation, food and materials, but infrastructure and teachers are taken care of and paid by the government.

The courses offered in distant regions by the Amazonas State University are taught in the module scheme. That means that there is only one class for each of the undergraduate courses that last 4 years. Teachers travel to these cities from Manaus and teach their course on 12 days (5 hours per day summing up to 60 h). Each semester students have 8/9 modules. Students have 1–3 "free days" between modules. Teachers are required to evaluate students three times during the 12 days; two of the evaluations methods are up to the teacher to decide on how to grade them; it should be an essay, an oral presentation, any activity that the teacher seems fit, but the final test must be an individual written test given in the last day. If the students don't pass the exam, the teacher is required to prepare another test that the next traveling teacher applies. If, again, students don't pass the examination, they have one last chance on another final test. Failing the second test, they're expelled from the program; by this time they continued their studies, following subjects without knowing if they passed the class or not; students must study for these tests without the assistance of the teacher who taught the course.

I was invited to lecture the module on philosophy of education. The class started with 50 students selected between many candidates that took a multidisciplinary test. So, they were between the best in town. Philosophy of education was the second module that the students had. I found that to be strange because, in my experience, the subjects related to teaching and pedagogy usually come later on the courses, starting on the third and sometimes even in the fourth year of the undergraduate program. Why teach philosophies of education at the beginning of a course when students haven't even learned their main topic of study? I was left without an answer to this question. When I arrived in Ipixuna 3 students had already dropped out on the first module. At the end of my course, 2 others left the program. One of them had a health issue and had to look for treatment in another city. Another one said she couldn't keep up with the studies; she was out of school for over 5 years and didn't feel comfortable in the environment. She was a maid, one of the worst jobs a woman can have in Brazil, also one of the few work "options", reminiscent from slavery. It is common in middle-class Brazilian households to employ maids. We were the same age, something that shocked her (and me) deeply.

The students were mostly in their early 20's. Except for 2 older students, a woman who was 43 years old and an elder man, a Baptist Pastor who was 54 years old. The youngest student was 17. This was the first time that people from this town had the opportunity to study after high school in their own town. The daughters and sons of politicians and wealthy merchants were the only ones who could afford to travel and study in other cities. Before the Amazonas State University initiative there had been some boats in Ipixuna that traveled through the Amazon teaching work-related skills to poor riverside communities, like baking classes, manicure, woodworking, and others. These were short-term courses focused on skilled-labor; they didn't reflect on education or promote critical thinking.

4   Teaching the Course

I prepared and tried to develop a course giving students the historical background of educational philosophy in the first moment and then move on to getting students to think about the premises and basis of education; how different educational philosophies turn out into different teaching styles in the classroom. My main objective was to get students to become critical of the educational system that we have in Brazil. Which, despite Paulo Freire being the patron of education in Brazil, our country is still miles away from applying his ideas in our immense territory. Education in Brazil today, the way I see, is not far from what it was during Freire's years as a teacher, especially on concerns critical thinking students. It was challenging to criticize the system from inside the system and to talk about education in Brazil in a classroom that follows decades' worth of oppression and colonizing practices. It was clear to me that students saw the contradiction; the problem was that not only that it made them uncomfortable but it touched the core of their faith in education. It is the belief of many poor students that education is the only way that they can ascend in life; this course meant that they would be able to have better jobs and better lives. It didn't exactly matter what they were studying but the fact that they would have an undergraduate diploma. They look at schooling as the only way to change their lives. Apart from entering a religious mission to become priests or pastors, getting a diploma is the only way to distance these people from poverty. But, there I was telling them, or trying to reflect with them, that our educational system historically perpetuates poverty and sometimes alienates us from our reality. Even in the capital city higher education makes sure the industrial complex doesn't lack qualified workers. I wasn't saying that their lives wouldn't improve with this degree. But I wanted to think together about what that degree meant. These student teachers will be some of the few people in the region with a diploma. Their families rely on them to help out. Some of the students weren't studying because they wanted to, they were their families that bet into improving their lives through education. But their course lacks quality, lacks infrastructure. How can 47 students do their practicum if the city only has two local schools? When these students graduate where will they work? Will they have to move to even poorer communities?

Students found me odd. My identity was very different from theirs. Not only was I not a typical woman from the region, but I also studied in the extremely urbanized city of Sao Paulo. I'm someone who has been in touch with ideas such as feminism, atheism, racism, among many others that some students find it to be taboo. I couldn't avoid the colonizing white savior, oppressor felling. The way I saw it, my presence alone indicated that I had come to save them from their ignorance.

The students were focused on grades and were traumatized with oral presentations that they had to sustain in the previous course. All of the students were relieved that they wouldn't have to speak in front of the class this time. To my surprise, they weren't aware of the fact that they would become teachers in the future. When asked, most of them responded that they were not interested in geography at all, they chose that course because they found it to be the "easiest" one to choose in between biology and math, which were the currently available courses in the city at the time of the registration. Most of the students demonstrated a deep respect for teachers, but they also feared me, which later I understood was a hegemonic assumption, a habit that comes from studying a traditional disciplining teaching style all their lives.

I taught the course, changing it almost entirely after meeting the class. I wanted the students to be agents of their knowledge and for me to act as a facilitator, helping them with the challenges. In reality, I couldn't possibly do that in a room filled with students who had trouble reading and comprehending scientific texts, who had no domain over the Portuguese formal written language and who had trouble arranging ideas on paper. I devoted about 30 minutes at the beginning of each class to talk about writing essays properly and correcting the most common mistakes I found in written activities. Ethically, I didn't feel comfortable allowing these students to continue their studies without being able to write comprehensible simple texts. At the same time, I couldn't fail an entire class for it as well. I went full freestyle during some classes. Nothing had prepared me for that reality: 47 students with poor high school formation with a wide range of different hardships in life. I was the active agent, and the passive students had a lot more to learn than what I could offer on my 12 days' course, which was less on actual classes because I had to give them mandatory exams.

5   Reflecting on the Experience with Freire's and Brookfield's Concepts

The considerations that I present here are based on Paulo Freire's work, mainly *Pedagogy of the oppressed* (1993), *Pedagogy of hope* (2013), *Education, the practice of freedom* (1976) and *Education for critical consciousness* (1973); also, these look into Stephen Brookfield's book *Becoming a critically reflective teacher* (2017). Through Freire's and Brookfield's concepts I reflect upon my experience teaching in diversity and adversity. Brookfield knows Freire's work, he made an effort of applying it; with his experience he gives some contributions on thinking emancipatory education by discussing power dynamics and responsible use of power in classrooms. He understands Freire discusses the limitations he finds on applying theory to practice, some of which were the same problems I faced in Ipixuna. From Freire's work I get the philosophical and anthropological background, especially his concept of oppression and critical consciousness.

Paulo Freire defines himself as a critic of the Brazilian educational system. He worked as a teacher of illiterate poor people in Brazil's northeast. He understands that humans are naturally curious, we're incomplete and that we're connected to others through the ever-changing world (Freire, 1973). Freire has a Marxist background, his idea of education is student-centered, he focuses on social change and students' active participation. According to Freire, students should reflect on educational, family and work-related problems at schools, this is called the generative theme approach.

Freire considers that teachers should teach "for freedom" helping students reflect about society and themselves (1976). To Freire one must not only be conscious of the world by 'reading" it, but also to act, changing it. Our teaching should be emancipatory. As to how people can become conscious Freire says it's through dialogue. We must love the students as human beings equal as you and I. The co-teaching and co-learning that Freire defends refers to a position that teachers should learn from their students constantly, never placing themselves as the detainer of knowledge and the student as the empty vessel (Freire, 1993). We're both learning and we're both teaching since no one knows everything, and no one knows anything. The teacher-student should worry about the dialogue with the student-teachers.

Yet, in the classroom the application of Paulo Freire's ideas turned out to be a challenge, mostly for two reasons: 1. students expected me to speak from a position of power, and 2. Given the conditions, I didn't know how to abdicate from my authority figure and be (or act as an) equal to my students. I studied in a good university and did my masters on the acclaimed university that Paulo Freire worked from 1979–1997. I have to admit that aligning myself with the students and not putting myself above them was hard work. I tried and I'm sure I didn't succeed entirely. Although we speak the same language, our worldviews are profoundly different; there is also a clash of cultures. It wasn't particularly hard to bond with the students, it was hard to "read" their world and to humbly, truly believe that they could teach me something, or even anything. Eventually, I felt that a cultural genocide had been taken place. I felt that some of the students and people who I met during my stay weren't living life, they were surviving it. They had no access to cultural centers. Their world view came almost exclusively from TV and religious lectures. There was an absurd amount of gossip in town. Quickly I realized how full of prejudices I was, all of these thoughts came so naturally. How could I judge them if I was staying so little time in the city? How could I possibly break barriers and learn what they had to teach me if they didn't believe that they could teach me something? How to act as a co-learner if I'm the one evaluating and grading them? How to talk about action when they haven't embraced teaching as their future job? I felt that I had to prove that I had the best interest of these poor students in my teaching. I had to prove that I saw them as future colleagues and peers; after all, I had travelled all the way over there to train them into becoming teachers with a background on philosophy of education. The position of teacher and student in a class of future teachers, in my mind was clearly a temporary imbalance, because I tried to view us as co-learners and co-teachers. But they didn't. And 12 days couldn't change that. Students lacked self-esteem and evoked those feelings daily. Some of them had a defeated posture, going to school unmotivated, waiting for the day when they wouldn't pass the tests and would get expelled. To study in university was unthinkable growing up in Ipixuna. It wasn't on their horizon to have access to higher education. So, they weren't prepared to be there. Or at least their education so far wasn't preparing them to be there.

After the time I spent in Ipixuna I looked in literature for something that could help me understand what had happened during that course. I wanted to learn as much as could from that experience but I was still confused and feeling like I had failed immensely in putting Freire's ideas in action. Fortunately, I got in touch with Stephen Brookfield's ideas. He advocates for critical reflection among teachers. That is, reflection informed by the critical theory tradition, central to this philosophical tradition are two ideas: power and hegemony. Within hegemony, Brookfield works with the concept of hegemonic assumptions. He defines it as assumptions that "seem commonsense and serve us well but that actually work against our best interests" (Brookfield, 2017, p. viii). In *Becoming a critically reflective teacher* Brookfield analyses common hegemonic assumptions: the assumption that teachers use their charismatic singularity to motivate students, the idea that good teachers always have things under control, the belief that resistance to learning can be removed, the need to achieve perfect evaluation scores from students, the faith that someone somewhere has the answer to your teaching problems, and the certainty of feeling you can fix racism, sexism, and the other ills you see around you.

In order to critically reflect on our practice, and to be able to recognize hegemonic assumptions, Brookfield suggests that we analyze our actions as teachers through the four lenses of critical reflection: students' eyes, colleagues' perceptions, theory, and personal experience. In his words:

> The first of these lenses is the lens of students 'eyes, most often represented by classroom research and classroom assessment activities that give us reliable information on how students experience our classrooms. The second is colleagues 'perceptions, most commonly present when we team-teach but also available in support and reflection groups. The third is the lens of theory, comprising research, philosophy, and narrative descriptions of teaching in higher education. This literature can open up entirely new ways of thinking about familiar problems and dilemmas. And finally, the lens of personal experience provides a rich vein of material for us to probe. (Brookfield, 2017, p. viii)

The four lenses of critical reflection were the tools that I used to uncover assumptions about power and power dynamics in class. By reflecting on each of the four lenses I viewed myself from unfamiliar angles and that allowed me to respect my students, to take them more seriously. I was able to understand why students acted the way they did on many occasions. And, also, I understood the way I acted and the reasons that got me frustrated in class. By looking at myself from my student's eyes, combining it with theory and ruminating on my personal experience, especially as a student, I understood that students spent years internalizing the vision of teachers as a distant authoritarian punitive figure. I couldn't get their trust when there's clearly a power imbalance between teacher and students. I found that the hegemonic assumption that hurt me the most was assuming that I could motivate students. The way I saw it, I felt that students took advantage of my inexperience and saw me as a soft touch, someone they could take liberties with. So, what I did wasn't motivating them, they were just happy that they had an easy teacher and that they would certainly pass this subject. Still, to see the teacher as a punitive figure was a hegemonic assumption on their part. I don't have to be authoritarian and use my position of power the same way their teachers have done all through their lives. Even though I'm still full of energy and part of me believes that I can help students a lot with my teaching, it brings me peace that someone out there is trying to calm early teachers with the pains of not being able to motivate students. This sentence by Stephen Brookfield helped me immensely on getting in peace with my work in Ipixuna: "Burning out is a danger all activist-oriented teachers face as they try to effect social change from inside the academy" (Brookfield, 2017, p. 56). From this I understand that in an oppressive system like ours the social change from inside the academy is very limited.

Brookfield was also helpful in reflecting my ability to teach with an ethical and responsible use of power. I struggled with implementing Freire's ideas in class while trying to responsibly exercising my authority. I now understand that I can never let go of my position of power, what I can do is reflect on it and try to use it as ethically as possible. Brookfield helped me to go beyond my reading of Freire and to have my own opinions about my practice and on what's best for my students.

6   Final Thoughts

It was an impossible task to teach 47 students in 12 days for freedom and critical consciousness. I couldn't tune in the vocabulary-universe of my students. I was a foreigner in their land. I struggled to try to fit into the educator-educatee (co-teacher, co-learner) that Freire presents. My authority over the classroom was unrenounceable.

The life conditions in Ipixuna are precarious. Arriving there I felt extremely uncomfortable trying to dialogue about ideas of a white man to an audience of simple, common poor people living in extreme adversities, only to leave them 12 days later. Freire's work helped me to build my own sense of purpose on education and on what is my role in society, but reading him didn't prepare me for the reality of this poor rural riverside community in the Amazon region. Freire's work shaped me on becoming a teacher that works on getting students to realize that it is unacceptable to see the unjust system that we live in as natural. The exploration of natural resources to gain profit and develop Europe and America brought people and poverty to Ipixuna during the Amazon rubber boom. Our current model and system perpetuate the poverty that these students and their families live in. What was until around 100 years ago an isolated region in the Amazon rainforest, it is now a poverty pocket.

In Ipixuna, I found myself trying to reach out and bring critical conscious awareness to a few young minds. The module I taught gave them a chance to experience a new approach in teaching. Although I faced resistance, all of them were very transparent on the "nice surprise" my classes turned out to be. At the moment I didn't take their comments seriously. Only afterwards reflecting on the course I was able to respect what they said and to believe it. It was difficult to put myself in the position of co-teacher and co-learner, but in the process, I was compelled to try to find a way that I could do this and maintain my authority figure. I couldn't let go of my authority, students expected it. What I could do was to try to act on my authority differently, it didn't have to be a vertical authority, I could teach through a horizontal authority.

Among all the hardships in teaching in such an underdeveloped place, there was team spirit being nurtured, going against all odds students were autonomously working on group motivation. Almost daily they said they were in this together and that they would study together. They pared stronger students with weaker students to study together. There was no competition, they initiated autonomously a collaborative learning atmosphere. Still, this teachers initial training system lacks basic quality indicators. I wonder how do policy makers understand that it's better to have a bad course than no courses at all.

Even though I didn't feel that I gave those students the best course that they could have had. I can see that I tried my best on teaching for freedom, and that getting rid of hegemonic assumptions will be hard work in my career. I do believe that by recognizing them I'll become a better teacher. I'll try to teach so students can liberate themselves and not perpetuate oppressions. Maybe by watching my spontaneous classroom moments, students can find their own social emancipatory way through education. Maybe, they now see that a teacher doesn't necessarily have to be authoritarian. I am sure that I had a great impact on students' life. Even if they didn't get a lot of content I am sure that they understand that there are different ways that a teacher can act, other than what they have encountered all their lives. Through the lens of critical reflection, I learned that to the students I wasn't the colonizing white savior figure I saw myself as. To them, I was someone to be mirrored. They genuinely complimented my teaching daily, expressing gratitude and respect towards me and my work on promoting a different teaching style. At first I didn't trust their words, viewing it as dishonest. I wasn't taking their feedback seriously because I didn't trust them, and maybe because I didn't think that I could in fact learn something from them. It wasn't until I got back and reflected on what had happened that I accepted their words.

According to Freire, the oppressors don't have the strength to liberate themselves, the oppressed is the one who has the task of liberating themselves and the oppressors as well (Freire, 1993). When I looked at my practice through students' eyes, they set me free me of the failure I thought the course had been, and also, of my oppressor feeling. In my teaching I focused on being an example of how teachers can behave differently from what their hegemonic assumptions expected, i.e. I differed from traditional teaching methods. We created our lesson plans and timeline together. So, the work we developed and that I felt was too fragile and ineffective, especially given that I taught my module and left them in just 12 days, turned out to mean more to the students if I took their feedback seriously.

References

Brookfield, S. D. (2017). *Becoming a critically reflective teacher*. San Francisco, CA: Jossey-Bass.

Freire, P. (1973). *Education for critical consciousness.* New York, NY: Seabury Press.

Freire, P. (1976). *Education, the practice of freedom.* London: Writers and Readers Publishing Cooperative.

Freire, P. (1993). *Pedagogy of the Oppressed.* New York, NY: Continuum.

Freire, P. (2013). *Pedagogia da esperança: Um reencontro com a pedagogia do oprimido.* Rio de Janeiro, Brazil: Paz e Terra.

CHAPTER 17

Effects of Inquiry-Based Learning Cooperative Strategies on Pupils' Historical Thinking and Co-creation

Alexandra Stavrianoudaki and Antonis Smyrnaios

Abstract

Inquiry-based learning (IBL) is recognized as an instructional approach in teaching (Pedaste et al., 2015) that can result in improving different inquiry skills, such as identifying problems, formulating questions, analyzing and presenting data of an inquiry study (Alfieri et al., 2011). Previous research suggests that collaborative inquiry is an efficient method to foster historical thinking (Nilsen, 2016).

This study presents the practice of IBL among primary schoolchildren within the framework of teaching history aiming to investigate pupils' views about collaborative learning in an IBL environment. The method applied was a case study research design. Research methods included semi structured interview and pronounced thought methods to get insight into students' views and experiences. Participants were 14 year-4 class students. A 12-weeks program was implemented concerning the Classical Greece, artistic thought and culture. Data were analyzed with thematic analysis procedures.

The findings showed that students reformed historical habits of mind as well as their views about collaborative learning. More specifically students shaped positive attitudes toward co-working, developed their ability to self-construct flexible inquiry groups in their class and to co-create learning products which included remarkable decorative elements inspired by the classical historical period. A crucial theme that arose was that these elements were considered as facilitators for "doing history" and historical thinking.

Keywords

Inquiry-Based Learning – collaborative inquiry – historical thinking – doing history

© KONINKLIJKE BRILL NV, LEIDEN, 2020 | DOI: 10.1163/9789004432048_017

1   Introduction

Inquiry-Based Learning (IBL) is recognized as an instructional approach (Pedaste et al., 2015) that can result in improving different inquiry skills such as identifying problems, formulating questions, analyzing and presenting originated from an inquiry study (Alfieri et al., 2011). IBL is a constructivist and student-centered approach (Condliffe et al., 2016; Kuhlthau et al., 2015; Barron & Darling-Hammond, 2008) that enables and fosters students' motivation through their engagement in an authentic learning context (Deci & Ryan, 2016; Saunders-Stewart et al., 2015).

Recent research shows positive academic and achievement results for students engaged in IBL work. IBLs' approach is recognized as an effective framework for positive learning outcomes (Buck Institute for Education, 2017; Deci & Ryan, 2016). Where it is implemented, IBL allows students to make determinations about the problems, the challenges and the issues they investigate, moving them toward meaningful engagement and deeper learning. The main reason for this is that the development of knowledge occurs via an autonomous questioning and problem-solving process (Nunex & Leon, 2015; Small et al., 2014).

Although the specific choice of history as an epistemic field for this study was initially prompted by a personal research interest, there are several reasons that make history an appealing domain for IBLs' understanding and further investigation. From a research perspective, there is a potentially overlapping between epistemic IBL process and the ability of students to think historically, as suggested by the literature on historical thinking (Lee & Shemilt, 2003; VanSledright, 2002). Central to this approach is the fact that the skills demanded for applying an inquiry are related to the history content. More specifically historical thinking requires people to be aware of the nature of history, to generate historical arguments based on the evidence available, and to evaluate the strength of such arguments (Lee & Shemilt, 2003). In other words, we may assume that historical thinking necessarily includes the processes which people utilize to generate and evaluate historical arguments and estimate the limits of historical knowledge and the certainty of that knowledge (Maggioni, 2010). Within this learning framework we do not mean that students should be expected to do work at the same level as historians, but rather that they should learn to apply a conceptual understanding of how we know, explain, and give accounts of the past (Lee, 2011).

2   Theoretical Framework

The literature on IBL is based on Peirce's community of inquiry (Pedaste & Sara-puu, 2006). Peirce's rhetoric recommends a cooperative, communal process, involving certain normative structures of communication. Therefore, students communicate for the purpose of finding out new knowledge in a community and moving it toward a certain course of action (Colapietro, 2007; Pedaste & Sarapuu, 2006). With the phrase 'community of inquiry', Peirce introduces the origin of the idea about final consensus as a regulative ideal. He provides two reasons for this. First, Peirce assumes that external reality inevitably affects our thinking. Second, our individual beliefs about the external world will neces-sarily differ due to our different sensual experiences. Consequently, according to this theory, human beings acquire different beliefs, based on various expe-riences of external reality at different times and in different places. Thus, we cannot depend on our beliefs as immediate access to the world or to reliable knowledge. Our beliefs, valuable as they are, are nothing but tools that enable us to make the world immediately comprehensible. Therefore, ideas can be more productive, if they are established within a social context, where one learners' beliefs challenge and develop another's.

The field of ideas' sharing is closely related to peers' collaboration because through this process learners have the opportunity not only share their ideas but also challenge them and improve them. Thus peer collaboration is also identified as beneficial to the process of knowledge construction (Nilsen, 2016; Linn & Eylon, 2011). While some researchers claim that student collaboration assists in developing inquiry learning skills (Van Joolingen et al., 2007), others point to the role of collaboration in arguments' construction ability (Noroozi et al., 2013; Linn & Eylon, 2011; Littleton & Howe, 2010). On the other hand, researchers emphasize the learning environment that frames learners' collab-oration which should be configured in order to make their interaction more productive (Littleton & Howe, 2010; Mercer, 2010). Such effort appears worth-while, as several studies indicate that peer collaboration can improve students' conceptual understanding (Lee, 2011; Bell et al., 2007).

Concerning the demand for productive learning frameworks, there is con-siderable pedagogic potential in Inquiry-Based Learning theory. The main idea of IBL is that it is a process of collaborative knowledge construction based on investigating a genuine problem (Evenson & Hmelo 2000). As suggested by King and Ritchie (2012) the IBL is considered as the approach that mainly influ-ences students' capability to apply, relate and describe the knowledge accord-ing to their own collaborative thinking context. Similarly, Bruce and Davidson (1996) outline the characteristics associated with IBL: the recognition of the need for accurate information; the ability to ask salient questions as the basis for information searching; the skills for evaluating, organizing and integrating information; the ability to critically use information and problem solving.

Efforts to develop these skills have underlined the importance of IBL-activities, which requires students to form their own conclusions about the past, based on collaborative analysis of historical documents and other sources (Barton & Levstik, 2011; Kroll, 2005). This kind of activities enables students' involvement in disciplinary thinking and ideas sharing about History. Then as concerns to the History domain, previous research suggests that collaborative inquiry is an efficient method to foster historical thinking (Nilsen, 2016) that provides opportunities for students to build a deep knowledge of the content (Wiley & Voss, 1999). Moreover, VanSledrights' (2002) research shows that exposure to historical inquiry affects positively the increased use of intertextual comprehension strategies and the increased general motivation within the history content. The main reason for these profits of IBLs' implementation is that the learning framework of inquiry provides students the opportunity to make claims based on a disciplinary use of evidence, which means that these claims are advanced and evaluated according to criteria specific to the discipline of History.

Students' involvement in disciplinary historical thinking is considered very meaningful and influential (Hartzler-Miller, 2001) since apart from providing students the opportunity to build onto their own it improves their understanding of how historical knowledge is constructed (Lee & Ashby, 2000). This is why this process seems better aligned with the goals of promoting the development of historical thinking (Felton, 2009; Kroll, 2005) than simply memorizing historical facts.

Historical thinking (also referred to as historical reasoning or historical literacy) includes a set of disciplinary heuristics and attitudes that individuals utilize in the process of generating historical knowledge. The process specifically incorporates considering the criteria demanded to generate and evaluate historical arguments and evaluating the limits of historical knowledge and the certainty of that knowledge (Maggioni, 2010). Historical thinking is characterized by six components; asking historical questions, using sources, implementing contextualization, engaging in argumentation, using substantive concepts, and employing meta-concepts.

Therefore, question generation is an essential competency for historical thinking within the IBL framework. The basis of this construct is that collaborative question making enforces students formulate their own conclusions about the past, based on an analysis of sources (Levy, Thomas, Drago, & Rex, 2013). Students' interaction with historical material shows that question making not only fosters further questions' generation that may broaden the search but also works like a 'springboard' that enables students 'sieve' useful from useless or confusing information (Maggioni, 2010). In addition, as mentioned above inquiry collaborative methods are capable of challenging each other's beliefs. Thus it can be defended that via the interplay among learners and the historical material, question making process can be fostered in a manner that serves the educational goal of historical thinking development.

Hence it is not surprising that many researchers insist that simply memorizing historical facts is insufficient and highlight the significance of developing students' historical thinking and collaboration skills (Nilsen, 2016; Levy, Thomas, Drago, & Rex, 2013; Maggioni, 2010). It is also argued that these skills' development is important to be integrated into a collaborative inquiry and student-centered environment (Nilsen, 2016; Barton & Levstik, 2011; Magioni, 2010). It is also argued that discussion among students becomes more powerful and productive when the inquiry activity task requires peers' collaboration (Nilsen, 2016; Leijen et al., 2012). Alternative explanations are always possible, and research is needed to investigate how students' beliefs about inquiry and collaboration play out in collaborative learning frameworks.

However, translating these goals into practice turns out to be very unachievable for school systems that still insist on traditional approaches and narratives (Maggioni, 2010). This is why traditional teaching still remains the dominant strategy in teaching History (Nilsen, 2016; Barton & Levstik, 2011; Bell et al., 2010; Magioni, 2010). In schools, history is usually perceived as a domain heavily identified with reading and comprehension tasks. We can maybe interpret this phenomenon as a lack of awareness about the nature of knowledge acquisition theory and specifically about the nature of historical thinking. Therefore, there is a need to investigate further the nature of history and specifically students' perception about history in order to present completely their experience about participating in novel instructional approaches like IBL. This study also contributes to the current knowledge by exploring the relationship between IBL implementation and fostering co-working skills among students.

3   Methodology

The method applied was a case study research design. The main reason for the methodological selection is the fact that a case study can take an example of an activity, 'an instance in action' (Walker, 1974) and use multiple methods and data sources in order to explore it more deeply.

Previous research has shown that there are substantial differences in IBL across domains (Donovan & Bransford, 2005). Concerning the History domain typically involves the analysis of documents and artifacts to construct accounts of past events (Voet & De Wever, 2018). Apart from this, the present study aims to explore IBL within the History domain and provide a rich description of this 'instance in action' from the students' perspective. Furthermore, in view of the importance of promoting IBL skills in contemporary History education, this case-study aimed at examining IBLs' implementation for the purpose of promoting historical thinking and collaboration skills, within the framework of History education.

Qualitative research methods, such as semi structured interview and pronounced thought methods, were used to capture students' beliefs and appear to be particularly promising for capturing their richness (McCrum, 2013). Additionally, the combination of these research methods is expected to be beneficial for the presentation of the development of critical thinking, problem-solving skills, and improved collaboration skills (Johnson, Johnson, & Smith, 1998; Johnson & Johnson, 1999). On average, the interviews lasted about 25 minutes. As concerns to pronounced thought methods, it has been selected as a valuable methodological tool in order to get an insight of the cognitive processes that take place when students work collaboratively with History sources (Wineburg, 2001; VanSledright, 2002).

Participants were 14 year-4th grade students. A 12-week program was implemented concerning Classical Greece (civilization, most important thought and culture). This particular learning section has been selected because it provides variable learning opportunities for learners to assess historical persons' choices and improve their creativity and problem-solving skills within a very interesting historical framework.

The present study aims to explore students' perceptions of IBL-process within the framework of teaching History. The research questions are formulated as follows: What are primary students' views about
– the IBL in History classes?
– the contribution of IBL in fostering historical thinking?
– the contribution of IBL in fostering students' collaborative skills?
Data were analyzed with thematic analysis procedures. Thematic analysis has been selected as a realistic method, which reports experiences, meanings and the reality of participants. It is also considered as a constructionist method, which examines the ways in which events, meanings and experiences have arisen as effects of a range of discourses operating within society. For the purpose of this current research, Thematic analysis provides a contextualist framework, sitting between the two poles of essentialism and constructionism

(Willig, 1999), which acknowledge the ways individuals make their own meanings of their experience, and, in turn, the ways the broader social context disservices those meanings, while retaining focus on the material and other limits of reality. Therefore, thematic analysis can be a method that works both to reflect reality and to unpick the surface of reality.

4   Results

In choosing how to organize the reporting of the results of this study, we have to choose between several options. However, data analysis convinced us that the main contribution of the particular study to current theory and pedagogical practice lies in the descriptive richness of epistemic cognition it provides. In particular, the study contributes to reflect some key features of students' beliefs about historical thinking and how collaborative inquiry affects on this way of thinking. The results can be particularly useful to those educators and policymakers who strive to promote epistemic development in their students. Then, we focus on student epistemic beliefs and historical thinking, identifying the aspects of these constructs that emerged from the data as particularly significant. In this way, we can profit on students' description of their experience.

The results showed that the inquiry program had a positive impact on students' historical habits, on their beliefs about collaborative learning, and on their ability to self-construct flexible inquiry groups in their class. The rationale was students' engagement in an authentic scientific discovery process through following methods and practices similar to those of professional historians.

4.1   *Students' Views about IBL in History Classes*

Firstly, the IBL program has positive effects on students' beliefs about inquiry. All the participant students mentioned that they preferred doing history through inquiry. The rationale was the easy and pleasant way to participate in the learning process since students did not have to memorize dates or names. On one hand, we conceive this positive stance as result of students' excitement because of first exposure to collaborative inquiry processes. On the other hand, some participants claim that through this process they had the opportunity to learn more concerning the Hellenistic years. They claimed that inquiry offered them different classroom experiences, which focused on improving their conceptual understanding through active learning.

> This way is really exciting because we do so many things … It is like being
> a man who lives in ancient Greece and you have a particular life and a

job. It's like living their lives or like being a historian and you have to write about daily life ... Sometimes we face difficulties, but we enjoy it more. Some days ago we co-created a miniature of the ancient theatre of Diony-sus by following instructions. It was amazing. (Student 2)

However, for a few participants, the collaborative inquiry process was not a simple experience at all. Two of them stated that they found difficulties in understanding and analyzing written sources. These students appear to consider as difficulties a cluster of factors including their own inexperience in handling big text sources and their mates' consistency in filling the worksheets without taking into account the source text or without providing themselves enough time. It is not surprising that some student-participants claim that they found it hard to handle the tension into the inquiry group.

I found it difficult because everyone was acting without thinking. (Student 13)

Sometimes we argue because one of us wants to write one claim and another person from the group disagree and believes that it is not the right answer ... Then they get angry and we spend our time like this. (Student 14)

4.2   Students' Views about Historical Thinking

Regarding historical thinking, our research has shown that the epistemological beliefs of students concerning inquiry influence their historical thinking and task persistence. Moreover, students with more nuanced collaboration skills show a greater inclination to apply deep level strategies related to the discipline of History methods. More specifically data analysis offered three main results focused on how students externalize their improvement in historical thinking skills. The analyses to be presented reveal the complexity involved in students' group investigations with historical documents by drawing on an authentic learning context.

4.2.1   Better Understanding of Historical Content and Discipline History Methods

A better understanding of historical content and discipline history methods, focus on academic perspectives on analyzing historical documents. The IBL regards interest as a basic component of engaging students in real history situations and forging meaningful connections between domain knowledge and students' interests and experiences. In particular, the outcomes indicated that students had the opportunity to know, explain, and give accounts of the past by participating in real history situations like an excavation or decision-making processes in Ancient Greece.

4.2.2   Viewing History as a Resolution for Misconceptions

Drawing from our theoretical framework, one overarching goal was focused on students' ability to know, explain, and give accounts of the past. For this reason through the pronounced thought part we asked students to choose among some statues which they thought that belonged to the Classical period. They had to formulate arguments based on strategies and epistemological beliefs. Thus we identified some of the *misconceptions* they had. Specifically, some of the participants believed that classical is an amputee statue or a statue that they had seen at a museum. On the other hand, other participants were able to explain why a statute is classical or not based on historical argumentation (e.g. bodies' poise, statues size);

4.2.3   Viewing History as Creativity

Viewing history as creativity focuses on finding creative resolutions in genuine historical problems and co-creating learning products with remarkable decorative elements inspired by the classical historical period. As concerns to creative resolutions, IBL as a process of knowledge construction based on investigating a genuine problem is a capable framework for making learning a fun activity. Specifically, students improved their creativity through their engagement in real conditions of historians' or archeologists' work like organizing an excavation process or like electing the most appropriate person for an ambassadorship in ancient Greece.

Concerning the aspect of co-creating learning products inspired by the classical period, analysis of interviews with students allows an exploration of the role of peer collaboration aiming at completing a decorative element inspired by the classicism. What makes the co-creating process important right at the process of historical thinking within the framework of creating learning products? One way of interpreting this is that students enjoy working together and doing arts because they bring themselves loser to the classical ancient culture. Apart from this, we found out that co-creating builds common ground for further question making and ideas sharing.

> Firstly M. made by her own a small one (Erechtheion). She said Acropolis is not only Parthenon. I said "ok"! What else do we have to do? I looked for information and then we asked you to bring more sources. We construct Propylaia and Athena Nike. M. helped me remember that there are also these small temples apart from Parthenon. (Student 7)

Co-creating encourages the students to use their own ideas, remarks and observations to improve the final learning product. A crucial theme that arose was every learning task in the group investigation was recognized by the majority of participants as facilitator for "doing history" and historical thinking. Students incorporate and adjust new history information with their existing knowledge to construct the decorative elements and assessment games under the scheme of social interaction with their schoolmates and teachers.

> We had to learn some sources but not only this (…), the difficult one was to connect all of the ideas and all the parts to make Parthenon like it is. (Student 3)

4.3   Students' Views about Collaboration

Finally, for our analysis we focused on how IBL affects students' collaboration skills and we found that students shaped positive attitudes toward co-working, since they had the opportunity to recognize their classmates' competencies and attitudes which they had not noticed before.

> Me and M. are classmates for the last three years and we didn't have any connection. With this program we had to collaborate so even if we didn't want so, we met each other. It may seem doom but I feel that I didn't know what somebody can do. I didn't know my mates. (Student 7)

> … When you complete a sheet with another mate you have two brains. You have also two chances. If you write something wrong your peer can find out what is wrong and check it. (Student 6)

Concerning collaboration students seem that they have changed their beliefs from the beginning till the end of the program and through their interviews we distinguish four different levels of collaboration that are presenting in Table 17.1.

Firstly, during the whole-class discussions at the beginning of the program, most of the participants had not developed their collaboration skills and perceived themselves as very competent completing tasks individually. This implies that the classroom climate was very competitive (Level 1). However, evidence from the data showed that a challenging task that requires a kaleidoscope of skills is difficult to be accomplished by one person individually (Level 2). Consequently, students began gradually being less seclusive into the group investigation and developed their ability to self-construct flexible inquiry groups. Onto one small group, students had the opportunity to discuss their ideas not only about the context but also about each other's special skill

TABLE 17.1   Different levels of collaboration

Category level	Level 1	Level 2	Level 3	Level 4
	Not developed collaboration skills	Challenging tasks require on kaleidoscope of skills	Students began gradually being less seclusive into the group investigation	Three main student roles within the group were shaped and implemented: secretary facilitator presenter
	Students perceived themselves as very competent completing tasks individually	Difficulty to be accomplished by one person individually	Self-construction of flexible inquiry groups	
	Competitive classroom climate		Discuss ideas about each others' special skills & utilization into a particular learning task	

and decide how they could utilize everyone's' skill into a particular learning task (Level 3). Finally, all group members did a task that was interesting and pleasant for them without being isolated. Gradually, this process of evaluating everyone's skills and capacities into the community leads to the configuration of some particular roles that learners were taken on. Hence students created and implemented on their own one system of roles' shaping into the inquiry community. Every one of these roles has corresponds to the person that was able to complete one task better than the others in the community. Certainly, in this phase every separated task assigned to one person (role-person) was oriented at the fulfillment of the common groups' target (Level 4).

So, three main student roles within the group work were shaped and implemented. The interacting students' roles are shifting since students usually didn't want to have every time the same role and they had also had acquired the self-consciousness to quitclaim their role to a more appropriate peer for a specific task. The analysis also has shown that roles' shaping and implementation was not only a matter of improving student collaboration. Rather, roles' implementation and highly productive operation can be considered as the highest level of achieving historical thinking goals into the class based on students' collaboration skills. The roles shaped are:

4.3.1   Secretary
The person that completes the worksheets. The performed analysis indicates the contribution of the secretary to the fulfillment of the inquiry goals. Secretary's role includes a range of activities at every phase of the inquiry. Secretary had to find out not only the obvious but also the hidden information in a source and conjure an appropriate manner to embed this information into the groups' sheet.

4.3.2   Facilitator
Facilitators' main role was to make questions and share ideas about the activities. This role was about making questions that enforce the group investigation to come to conclusions about the historical challenge under study; It is very surprising that students characterize this role as "Lazy Job' since they consider it easy enough to share ideas, give explanations and make questions. Thus they used to choose this role when they were feeling tired. According to student 5:

> Facilitator does nothing at all. If you are 'Lazy Job', you just help and you share ideas but you are not obliged to write.

Another participant claims similarly:

> You can participate and help in worksheets but you don't have to present nor write anything. (Student 7)

Participants' claims about the role of the facilitator reveal two main aspects of co-working. Firstly, students tend to be more productive when they feel that they participate actively in one community of inquiry but they are not obliged to do so. The optional nature of facilitators' role has revealed as the key of success for students' release to think out of the box and enforce the investigation with fresh and innovative ideas. Secondly, and perhaps more profound, the exemption from writing and presenting, seems to be another reason for students' perfection to the role of facilitator. The majority of the participants support that understanding and finding information into a text source and

presenting the final learning product are considered difficult for them. One
alternative explanation is that some of the participant learners face learning or
language-oriented difficulties. In broad terms, data analyses conducted reveal
that participants that hold this role were were considered themselves able
enough to pose critical and meaningful questions to their group and help in
this way their peers to provide various occasions and explanations about every
particular task.

4.3.3   Presenter

Presenters' main role was to communicate to the whole class the representation of the task that was analyzed into the group. The central aim of the
presenter is to communicate the final learning product arisen by the group
investigation. Through this process, presenter had to utilize a range of skills
related to historical thinking like explaining and evaluating historical arguments and mentioning to the limits of historical knowledge.

5   Discussion

The analysis of the aspects that emerged from the data revealed a dialectical
interaction between historical thinking and inquiry skills to the extent that provides a meaningful framework about how IBL is perceived from the learners
and thus how this model can be enriched and extended to support ultimately
student learning and specific skills acquisition. As concerns to the advantages
of the IBL approach to promoting historical thinking were also well-documented in many previous studies (Nilsen, 2016; Hartzler-Miller, 2001; Wiley &
Voss, 1999). Although the IBL literature provided us a clear framework for esti-
mating the importance of implementing investigation techniques within the
History lesson as an entrepreneurial approach that fosters historical thinking,
it did not tell us what learners think about and how do they engage themselves
into the IBL process. In line with this observation, we attempted to reveal a
meaningful understanding of students' perspective about IBL implementation
in History classes and this was the basis of our analysis. Hence apart from their
preference to the IBL, we conclude to valuable results concerning the impact
of roles' implementation into students' involvement in the History content.
Moreover concerning the roles' shaping the results highlight the importance of
a question maker into the community of inquiry. This learner who poses critical
questions is the one that activates the inquiry group even in crucial and difficult
times. This result corresponds with previous literature that reports question
generation as an essential competency for historical thinking within the IBL
framework. The basis of this construct is that collaborative question making

enforces students to formulate their own conclusions about the past, based on an analysis of sources (Levy, Thomas, Drago, & Rex, 2013; Maggioni, 2010).

Moreover, in the current study students' inquiry skills were developed through their attempt to co-create decorative elements inspired by the classical period and accomplishing challenging tasks. As mentioned previously, IBL is a process of collaborative knowledge construction directly based on investigating a genuine problem (Evenson & Hmelo, 2000). Thus a crucial theme that arose was that learning tasks in the group investigations are not only considered as genuine problems that foster the inquiry prosses but also as facilitators for "doing history" and foster historical thinking skills in a multidimensional way.

References

Alfieri, L., Brooks, P. J., Aldrich, N. J., & Tenebaum, H. R. (2011). Does discovery-based instruction enhance learning? *Journal of Educational Psychology, 103*, 1–18.

Barron, B., & Darling-Hammond, L. (2008). Teaching for meaningful learning: A review of research on inquiry-based and cooperative learning. In L. Darling-Hammond, B. Barron, P. D. Pearson, A. H. Schoenfeld, E. K. Stage, T. D. Zimmerman, G. N. Cervetti, J. L. Tilson, & M. Chen (Ed.), *Powerful learning: What we know about teaching for understanding*. San Francisco, CA: Jossey-Bass.

Barton, K. C., & Levstik, L. S. (2011). *Doing history: Investigating with children in elementary and middle schools* (4th ed.). New York, NY: Routledge.

Bell, T., Urhahne, D., Schanze, S., & Ploetzner, R. (2010). Collaborative inquiry learning: Models, tools, and challenges. *International Journal of Science Education, 3*(1) 349–377.

Bruce, B. C., & Davidson, J. (1996). An inquiry model for literacy across the curriculum. *Journal of Curriculum Studies, 28*(3), 281–300.

Buck Institute for Education. (2017). *What is Project Based Learning (PBL)?* Retrieved June 1, 2017, from https://www.bie.org/about/what_pbl

Colapietro, V., Midtgarden, T., & Strandt, T. (2005). Introduction: Peirce and education: The conflicting processes of learning and discovery. *Studies in Philosophy and Education, 24*, 167–177.

Condliffe, B., Visher, M., Bangser, M., Drohojowska, S., & Saco, L. (2016). *Project-based learning: A literature review*. New York, NY: Manpower Demonstration Research Corporation (MDRC).

Deci, E. L., & Ryan, R. M. (2016). Optimizing students' motivation in the era of testing and pressure: A self-determination theory perspective. In J. Wang, C. W. Liu, & R. M. Ryan (Eds.), *Building autonomous learners: Research and practical perspectives using self-determination theory* (pp. 9–29). Singapore: Springer.

Donovan, M. S., & Bransford, J. D. (2005). *How students learn: History, mathematics and science in the classroom*. Washington, DC: The National Academies Press.

Evenson, D. H., & Hmelo, C. E. (2000). *Problem-based learning: A research perspective on learning interactions*. Mahwah, NJ: Lawrence Erlbaum.

Felton, M. (2009). Argumentation. In E. M. Anderman & L. H. Anderman (Eds.), *Psychology of classroom learning: An encyclopedia* (1st ed., pp. 51–56). Detroit, MI: Macmillan Reference USA.

Hartzler-Miller, C. (2001). Making sense of "best practice" in teaching history. *Theory and Research in Social Education, 29,* 672–695.

Johnson, D. W., & Johnson, R. T. (1999). *Learning together and alone*. Needham Heights, MA: Allyn and Bacon.

Johnson, D. W., Johnson, R. T., & Smith, K. A. (1998). Cooperative learning returns to college: What evidence is there that it works? *Change, 7*(8), 27–35.

King, D., & Ritchie, S. (2012). Learning science through real-world contexts. In *Second international handbook of science education*. Dordrecht, the Netherlands: Springer (Springer International Handbooks of Education, Vol. 24, pp. 69–79).

Kroll, B. M. (2005). Arguing differently. *Pedagogy, 5*(1), 37–60.

Kuhlthau, C. C., Maniotes, L. K., & Caspari, A. K. (2015). *Guided inquiry: learning in the 21st century* (2nd ed.). Santa Barbara, CA: Libraries Unlimited.

Lee, P. (2011). History education and historical literacy. In I. Davies (Ed.), *Debates in history teaching*. Abingdon: Routledge.

Lee, P., & Ashby, R. (2000). Progression in historical understanding among students age 7–14. *In Knowing, teaching, and learning history*. New York, NY: New York University Press.

Lee, P., & Shemilt, D. (2009). Is any explanation better than none? *Teaching History, 137,* 42–49.

Leijen, Ä., Valtna, K., Leijen, D. A. J., & Pedaste, M. (2012). How to determine the quality of students' reflections? *Studies in Higher Education, 37,* 203–217.

Levy, B. L. M., Thomas, E. E., Drago, K., & Rex, L. A. (2013). Examining studies of inquiry-based learning in three fields of education: Sparking generative conversation. *Journal of Teacher Education, 64*(5), 387–408.

Linn, M. C., & Eylon, B. S. (2011). *Science learning and instruction: Taking advantage of technology to promote knowledge integration*. New York, NY: Routledge.

Littleton, K., & Howe, C. (2010). *Educational dialogues: Understanding and promoting productive interaction*. London: Routledge.

Maggioni, L. (2010). *Studying epistemic cognition in the history classroom: Cases of teaching and learning to think historically* (Doctoral dissertation). University of Maryland.

Mercer, N. (2010). The analysis of classroom talk: Methods and methodologies. *British Journal of Educational Psychology, 80*(1), 1–14.

Morison, S. E. (1936). *Harvard College in the seventeenth century*. Cambridge, MA: Harvard University Press.

Nilsen, A. P. (2016). Navigating windows into past human minds: A framework of shifting selves in historical perspective taking. *Journal of the Learning Sciences, 25*, 372–410.

Noroozi, O., Biemans, H. J., Weinberger, A., Mulder, M., & Chizari, M. (2013). Scripting for construction of a transactive memory system in multidisciplinary CSCL environments. *Learning and Instruction, 25*, 1–12.

Nunex, J., & Leon, L. (2015). Autonomy support in the classroom. A review from self-determination theory. *European Psychologist, 20*(4), 275–283.

Pedaste, M., Maetos, M., Silman, L., De Jong, T., Van Reisen, S. A. N., Kamp, E. T., & Tsourlidaki, E. (2015). Phases of inquiry-based learning: Definitions and the inquiry cycle. *Educational Research Review, 14*, 47–61.

Pedaste, M., & Sarapuu, T. (2006). Developing an effective support system for inquiry learning in a web-based environment. *Journal of Computer Assisted Learning, 22*(1), 47–62.

Saunders-Stewart, K. S., Gyles, P. D. T., Shore, B. M., & Bracewell, R. J. (2015). Student outcomes in inquiry: Students' perspectives. *Learning Environments Research, 18*(2), 289–311.

Small, R. V., Laura, J., & Meredith, L. D. (2014). The motivational and information needs of young innovators: Stimulating student creativity and inventive thinking. *School Library Media Research, 17*, 1–36.

Van Joolingen, W. R., De Jong, T., & Dimitrakopoulou, A. (2007). Issues in computer supported inquiry learning in science. *Journal of Computer Assisted Learning, 23*(2), 111–119.

Vansledright, B. (1996). Closing the gap between school and disciplinary history. In J. Brophy (Ed.), *Advances in research on teaching: Teaching and learning history* (Vol. 6, pp. 257–289). Greenwich, CT: JAI Press.

VanSledright, B. (2002). *In search of America's past: Learning to read history in elementary school*. New York, NY: Teachers College Press.

Voet, M., & De Wever, B. (2018). Teachers' adoption of inquiry-based learning activities: The importance of beliefs about education, the self and the context. *Journal of Teacher Education*. doi:10.1177/0022487117751399

Walker, R. (1974). *The conduct of educational case study: ethics, theory and procedure in Innovation*. Evaluation Research and the Problem of Control SAFARI Interim papers. Norwich: Centre for Applied Research in Education University of East Arwlia.

Wiley, J., & Voss, J. F. (1999). Constructing arguments from multiple sources: Tasks that promote understanding and not just memory for text. *Journal of Educational Psychology, 91*(2), 301–311.

Wineburg, S. (2001c). Reading Abraham Lincoln: A case study in contextualized thinking. In S. Wineburg (Ed.), *Historical thinking and other unnatural acts: Charting the future of teaching the past* (pp. 89–112). Philadelphia, PA: Temple University Press.

Index

Printed in the United States
By Bookmasters